Better Homes and Gardens®

BIG BOOK OF HOME HOW-TO

WILEY

John Wiley & Sons, Inc.

D1361670

For general information about our other products and services, please contact our Customer Care Department within the United States at (877) 762-2974, outside the United States at (317) 572-3993 or fax (317) 572-4002.

Wiley also publishes its books in a variety of electronic formats and by print-on-demand. Some content that appears in standard print versions of this book may not be available in other formats. For more information about Wiley products, visit us at www.wiley.com.

ISBN 978-1-118-14128-1

Printed in the United States of America

10 9 8 7 6 5 4 3 2

Note to the Readers:
Due to differing conditions, tools, and individual skills, the publisher assumes no responsibility for any damages, injuries suffered, or losses incurred as a result of following the information published in this book. Before beginning any project, review the instructions carefully, and if any doubts or questions remain, consult local experts or authorities. Because codes and regulations vary greatly, you always should check with authorities to ensure that your project complies with all applicable local codes and regulations. Always read and observe all of the safety precautions provided by manufacturers of any tools, equipment, or supplies, and follow all accepted safety procedures.

TABLE OF CONTENTS

CHAPTER 1

WIRING BASICS **5**
Learn how your electrical system works, how to diagnose problems yourself,
and how easy it is to make basic wiring repairs and improvements.

CHAPTER 2

PLUMBING BASICS **36**
Learn how your home's plumbing works and how to keep it working well.
Here's the insight you need to fix the most common plumbing problems.

CHAPTER 3

CARPENTRY BASICS **70**
Construction tools and techniques finally make sense in this straightforward
introduction to home carpentry.

CHAPTER 4

INDOOR CARPENTRY PROJECTS **124**
Increase your home's beauty, value, and comfort with step-by-step projects
for upgrades all through the house.

CHAPTER 5

FLOORING **146**
Learn how to select, plan, and install or repair the most popular floorings,
from carpeting to hardwood.

CHAPTER 6

DOORS AND WINDOWS **161**
Fix those sticking window hinges or install a new sliding door.
All the ideas and instructions you need are here.

CHAPTER 7

ROOFING, SIDING, AND WEATHERIZATION **187**
From walls to rooftop, you can transform the exterior of your home
and cut your heating and cooling costs.

CHAPTER 8

TILING **207**
Step-by-step projects in this chapter will help you tile any surface in your home,
from bathroom floors to kitchen countertops.

CHAPTER 9

SURFACE FINISHING *252*
You can really save time and get better results when you work like a pro.
This chapter helps with all finishes, including paints, stains, and wallpaper.

INDEX *284*

WIRING BASICS

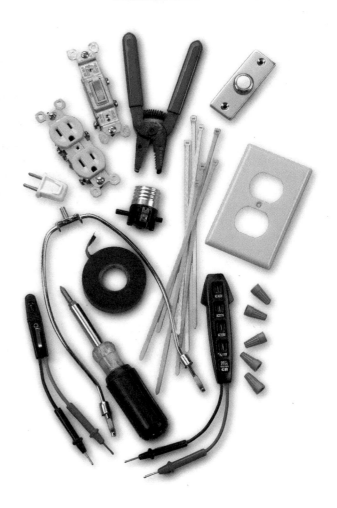

Chapter 1

Getting to Know Your Electrical System

How Circuits Work **6**
Service Panels **8**
Grounding and Polarization **10**
Household Circuits **11**
Mapping Your Circuits **12**

Wiring Tools and Materials

Essential Tools **13**
Specialized Tools **14**
Choosing Switches **15**
Choosing Receptacles **16**
Choosing Wire and Cable **17**
Choosing Boxes **18**
New Installation Switch/Receptacle Boxes **19**
New Installation Fixture/Junction Boxes **20**

Wiring Skills

Installing Boxes in Unfinished Space **21**
Overhead Light Placement **22**
Installing Boxes in Finished Space **23**
Stripping Wire **25**
Joining Wires **26**
Working with Wire **27**
Connecting Wires **28**

Electrical Troubleshooting and Repairs

Checking Incandescent Fixtures **29**
Troubleshooting Fluorescent Fixtures **30**
Testing and Replacing Switches **32**
Testing and Replacing Receptacles **34**

HOW CIRCUITS WORK

*E*lectricity is the flow of electrons through a conductor. In home electrical systems, wires, consisting of highly conductive copper wrapped in insulation for safety, are the conductors—the assigned pathway through which the electricity travels. A host of other items—a fork, a screwdriver, you—also can serve as conductors, sometimes with disastrous results. It's the goal of a safe electrical system to prevent this from happening.

Electricity always flows in a loop, known as a circuit. When a circuit is interrupted at any point, the electricity shuts off. As soon as the circuit is reconnected, the flow begins again.

Electricity is generated by your local electric company. Overhead and underground wires bring power from the utility company lines to a home's service head, also called a weatherhead because it can withstand wind, heat, and ice. Although the utility company sends high-voltage electricity along some of its power lines, by the time it reaches your house, it is 120 volts per wire.

The electricity passes through an electric meter, which measures how much enters the house. It proceeds to a service panel (also called the breaker box or fuse box), which distributes electricity throughout the house along individual circuits. Each circuit flows out of the service panel, through a number of fixtures and receptacles, and back to the service panel. (For more on service panels, see pages 8–9.)

To make a circuit, electricity is carried out of the service panel on "hot" wires that usually have black insulation, although they sometimes may be red, and is returned to the panel on neutral wires that have white insulation.

The service panel contains

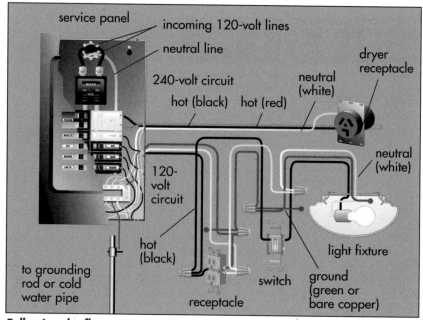

Following the flow

The flow of electricity in typical household circuits starts with the two 120-volt lines and single neutral line that enter the top of the service panel. Both 120-volt lines are used to make the 240-volt circuit, though only one neutral line is needed for the electricity to complete its loop. The 120-volt circuit has one hot wire (black) and one neutral wire (white), plus a copper ground wire (green). In case of a short, the ground wire carries the current safely into the ground.

circuit breakers or fuses—both are safety devices that shut off the power in case of a short circuit or other fault in the circuit (see pages 8–9).

Each circuit has a number of outlets that lead to smaller circuits through which the electricity flows. These outlets might include receptacles, fixtures, and switches. For example, a wall switch interrupts (off) or completes (on) the circuit to one or more light fixtures. A heavy-use appliance—such as a dishwasher, garbage disposal, or microwave oven—may need a circuit to itself.

Most circuits carry current of 120 volts which will give most people quite a jolt but will not seriously harm them if they should accidentally come into contact

with it. Most homes also have one or two 240-volt lines, which double the power by using two hot wires with one neutral wire. Because of the higher power, take special care when dealing with these.

Every electrical system must be grounded for safety. Grounding allows excess current to travel harmlessly into the earth in case of overload or a short circuit. Usually this is done by connecting a wire to a cold water pipe, to a grounding rod sunk deep into the ground, or sometimes to both.

Circuits in your home may be grounded with a grounding wire that is bare copper or green, or they may be grounded by means of the metal receptacle boxes and the metal sheathing that contains the wires (see pages 18–20).

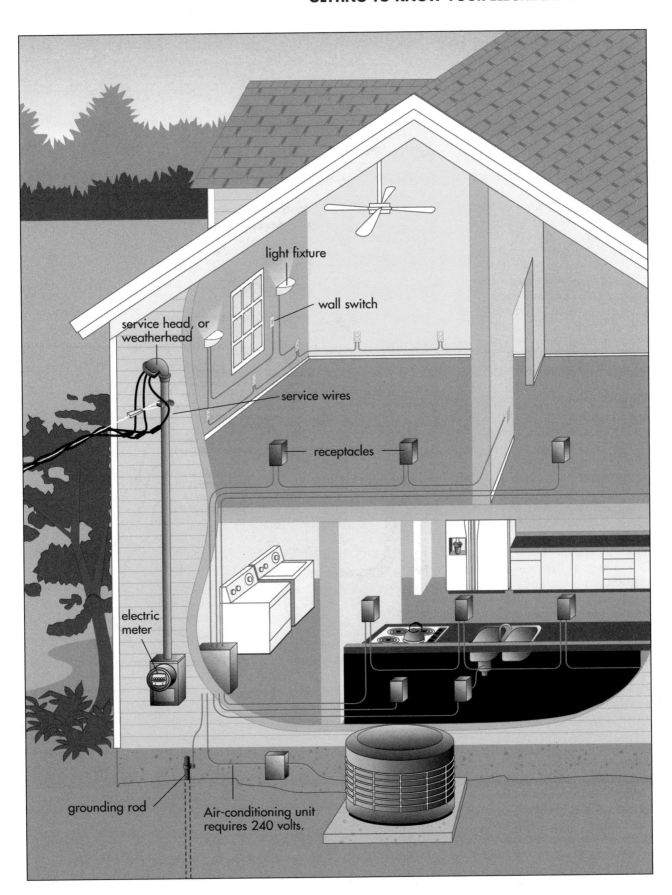

light fixture

wall switch

service head, or weatherhead

service wires

receptacles

electric meter

grounding rod

Air-conditioning unit requires 240 volts.

SERVICE PANELS

*E*lectrical projects always begin at the service panel, which is either a breaker box or a fuse box. When a short or an overload shuts down power to a circuit, this is where you go to restore the flow. It's also where you cut off power to a circuit before starting a project.

Power arrives from the meter through two main power wires, each of which carry 120 volts of electricity into the house. Usually these are black and/or red. In addition there is a white main neutral wire that carries electricity back to the utility. The main hot wires are connected to a main power shutoff. When you turn this off, you don't de-energize the hot wires, but you cut power to everything else in the box.

Breaker boxes

Emerging from a breaker box's main shutoff are two hot bus bars. The 120-volt breakers are each attached to one of these bars. (This means that if one of the main hot wires gets damaged outside your house, you will lose power to about half of the circuits in your house.) Each 240-volt breaker gets twice the power by being attached to both bus bars. When a circuit is overloaded or a short occurs, its breaker trips and shuts off power before the wires heat up and become a danger.

The main neutral wire is connected to the neutral bus bar. This bar is connected to a system ground wire, which leads to a grounding rod (see art on page 6). White wires for every circuit, and possibly bare or green ground wires, also connect to the neutral bus bar. As a result, each 120-volt circuit has a black or colored wire leading from a circuit breaker, a white wire leading to the neutral bus bar, and possibly a bare copper or green-covered ground wire also connected to the neutral bar. Each 240-volt circuit has two

wires leading to a circuit breaker. In addition, the 240-volt circuit has a neutral and, possibly, a ground wire connected to the neutral bus bar. Systems with conduit or armored cable do not need separate ground wires—the conduit or metal sheathing act as ground conductors.

For how to troubleshoot the several types of circuit breakers and how to check for the cause of shorts.

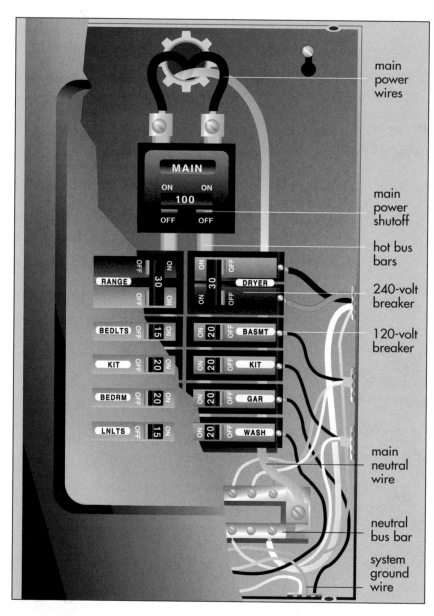

main power wires

main power shutoff

hot bus bars

240-volt breaker

120-volt breaker

main neutral wire

neutral bus bar

system ground wire

CAUTION!
LEAVE INCOMING WIRES FOR THE UTILITY COMPANY
If you suspect that the wires entering your house may be damaged in any way, do not attempt to work on them yourself. Have the utility company inspect them. Usually it will inspect and repair them for free.

Fuse boxes

If you have an older home that has not been rewired in the last 25 or 30 years, chances are that its electrical heart is a fuse box rather than a breaker box.

Fuse boxes are wired and work the same way as breaker boxes (see page 8), but instead of tripping as a breaker does, a fuse "blows" when there's too much current in its circuit. When this happens, you must eliminate the short or the overload, remove the blown fuse, and screw in or plug in a new one.

Power comes into a fuse box through two main power wires. (In a house with no 240-volt equipment, there may be only one of these.) Current flows through a main disconnect, in this case a pullout block that holds a pair of cartridge fuses.

Next in line are a series of plug fuses that protect the black hot wires of the individual circuits, often called branch circuits. Unscrewing a fuse disconnects its circuit. A neutral bus bar receives the main neutral wire and a neutral wire for each of the branch circuits. A system ground wire leads from the neutral bus bar to a grounding rod outside the house.

For tips on troubleshooting a fuse box.

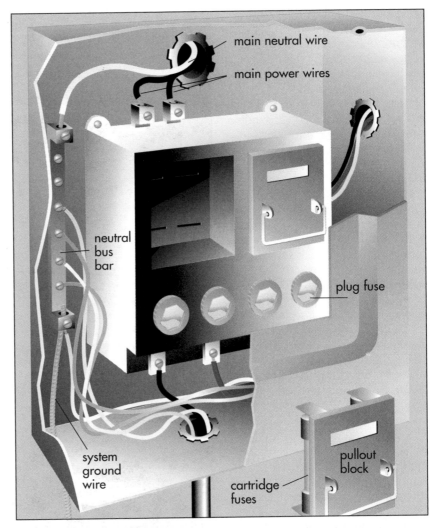

Typical plug fuse
A plug fuse is threaded and screws into the fuse box. Handle only the rim. Do not touch the threads while removing or replacing the fuse. For information on identifying and replacing a blown fuse.

Handling pullout blocks
Larger 240-volt circuits, as well as main shutoff fuses, often are protected by pullout blocks that contain cartridge fuses. If you need to pull out a cartridge fuse that is not in a pullout block, do not use your fingers. Get a fuse puller (see page 14).

GROUNDING AND POLARIZATION

Older homes often have receptacles and fixtures that are ungrounded, and many local codes do not require that they be rewired so they're grounded. Still, grounding is worth adding to your system because it adds protection against electrical shock. Grounding provides a third path for electricity to travel along, so if there is a leak of any sort, it will flow into the earth rather than into the body of a person who touches a defective fixture, appliance, or tool.

An electrical system is grounded with a grounding rod driven at least 8 feet into the ground outside the house or by connecting to a cold water pipe. Each individual branch circuit must be grounded as well, either with a separate wire that leads to the neutral bar of the service panel or with metal sheathing that runs without a break from each outlet to the panel. (In theory, electrical outlets can be grounded individually, but this is impractical.)

Some locations in your house—especially where the outlet and/or appliances may become wet—require ground-fault circuit-interrupter (GFCI) receptacles. Older, ungrounded circuits usually are protected by polarization, which is less effective than grounding but better than nothing. Grounded and polarized receptacles work only if they are wired correctly. See pages 34–35 to test for this.

See pages 34–35 to test for this.

CAUTION!
DON'T ALTER PRONGS ON PLUGS
Never clip or file down the prongs on a grounded or polarized plug. Go to the heart of the problem: Test and upgrade your circuit and receptacle.

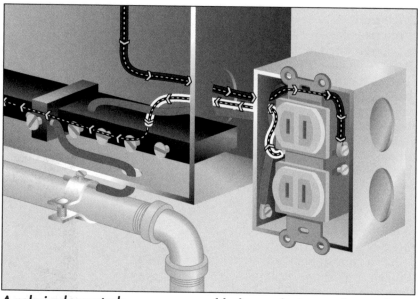

A polarized receptacle
A polarized outlet has one slot that is longer than the other. This is to ensure that the plug is inserted so that its hot current flows through black or red wires, and neutral current flows through white wires. Although not as safe as a grounded system, polarization is the next best thing.

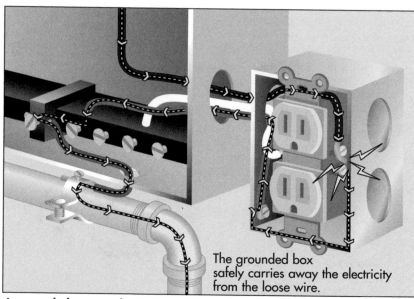

The grounded box safely carries away the electricity from the loose wire.

A grounded receptacle
The grounding circuit must follow an unbroken path to the earth. A third, rounded prong on a modern plug fits into the round slot in the receptacle. This slot connects to a wire—or to metal conduit or sheathing—that leads without interruption to the neutral bus bar of the breaker box. The system ground wire then leads from the bus bar to the earth. Instead of a grounding rod, a cold water pipe often is used for grounding because it is connected to water supply pipes that go deep under the ground.

HOUSEHOLD CIRCUITS

The electrical service in your house is divided into branch circuits, each of which supplies power to a defined area of your home. It is important to make sure that no branch circuit is carrying too great a load, or you will be constantly resetting breakers or replacing fuses. Some appliances need to have a circuit for themselves. An electric stove or dryer will have its own 240-volt circuit; other heavy-use appliances may require their own 120-volt circuits. More often a circuit supplies a number of outlets using a range of power.

To find out if a circuit is overloaded, add up the total power drawn by the circuit as outlined below. Check the breaker or fuse to see how many amps the circuit can deliver. If your total use exceeds the amperage the circuit can supply, change your usage. The solution may be as simple as plugging an appliance into a different receptacle—or you may have to add another circuit to your electrical system.

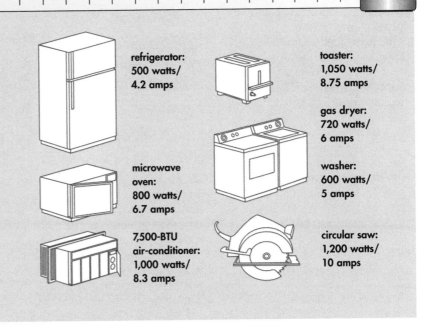

microwave oven circuit

240-volt circuit for electric stove

disposal circuit

dishwasher circuit

service panel

kitchen receptacle circuit

overhead lighting circuits

dining/living area, receptacle circuit

O lights
◍ receptacle

Typical circuit plan
A well-planned electrical system will have branch circuits that serve easily defined areas or purposes. Unfortunately, many homes—especially if they have been remodeled by do-it-yourselfers—have circuits that roam all over the house. Note that some appliances, such as the microwave oven, dishwasher, and disposal, need their own circuits. The electric stove needs its own 240-volt circuit. Otherwise, circuits are roughly organized by the rooms they serve and by their anticipated demand.

MEASUREMENTS

To figure your circuit loads, total the watts being used. Check the specification label on each appliance. Also note the wattage of the lightbulbs in fixtures on the circuit. Divide the total by 120 (the number of volts). The resulting number will tell you how many amperes ("amps") the circuit draws when all appliances and lights are on and whether or not you are placing too great a demand on it. Here are some typical watt and amperage figures for common household appliances.

refrigerator:
500 watts/
4.2 amps

toaster:
1,050 watts/
8.75 amps

gas dryer:
720 watts/
6 amps

microwave oven:
800 watts/
6.7 amps

washer:
600 watts/
5 amps

7,500-BTU air-conditioner:
1,000 watts/
8.3 amps

circular saw:
1,200 watts/
10 amps

MAPPING YOUR CIRCUITS

When you look inside the door of your service panel, do you see a detailed description of what each branch circuit controls? If not, make a chart yourself. You'll be glad you mapped the circuits the next time you have to turn off a circuit for repairs or improvements.

Begin by making a map of each floor in the house. Take care to include all receptacles, switches, appliances, and fixtures. Be aware that 240-volt receptacles will have their own circuits. With a large house, you may have to make more than one drawing per floor.

Mapping is best done with a helper to flip switches and test outlets while you stay at the box and write down findings. If you must work alone, plug in a radio turned to peak volume to find the general area covered by the circuit. The radio will go silent when you switch off the current. Test outlets to find the extent of the circuit.

1. Test each outlet.
Mark each circuit breaker or fuse with a number. Turn on all the appliances and lights on one floor. Plug a lamp into every receptacle and turn on. Turn off one circuit and have your helper write the circuit number next to each outlet that went dead.

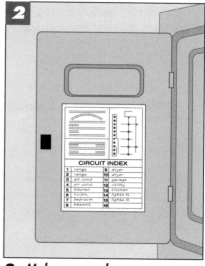

2. Make a record.
Continue the test with every circuit for every floor. Transfer the findings onto a sheet of paper you will affix to the inside of the circuit box door.

THE NEC

Electrical codes are based on the National Electrical Code (NEC), which is published by a non-profit organization and is upgraded periodically. The NEC takes up a huge book that covers every conceivable electrical situation. It provides the model on which virtually all local codes are based.

Some communities simply adopt the code as their own; others modify it. Any time you want to make a change in your electrical service, check the NEC and local codes before you begin.

3

LOAD WORKSHEET		
circuit #5		
voltage 120		
circuit breaker amperage 20		
(20x.80=16 amps)		
CUSTOMER	WATTS ÷ VOLTAGE	= AMPERAGE
coffee pot	650 ÷ 120	= 5.42
fluorescent work lites		
ballast amperage	=	.66
toaster	1050 ÷ 120	= 8.75
total exist. load		14.80
new exhaust fan		
	100 ÷ 120	= .83
new total load		15.63

3. Make a circuit load sheet.
To really get a fix on how your house uses electricity, combine the information you have just gathered with the power-use information printed on appliances. Write up a load sheet, as shown. It will help you assess capacity for future additions to your electrical system.

CAUTION!
HANDLE YOUR SERVICE PANEL WITH RESPECT
Take special care when working around a service panel. Remove cover plates only when you absolutely have to and replace them as soon as you can. Keep the door shut whenever you are not inspecting the panel. Lock it, if you think your kids may get at it. Remember that even if you have shut off the main power breaker or switch, there is still power entering the box.

ESSENTIAL TOOLS

You don't need to purchase an arsenal of specialized tools to do the electrical projects in this book. For most repairs, a minor outlay will be enough to equip you adequately.

Needle-nose and **lineman's pliers** are musts. You need the first to bend wires into the loops required for many electrical connections. Lineman's pliers make it possible to neatly twist wires together. Both also are used to cut wires. **Side-cutting pliers** make it easy to snip wires in tight places and are ideal for cutting sheathing off cable.

To strip wires use an **adjustable wire stripper** or a **combination tool** (which also crimps and cuts wire). If you're working with nonmetallic cable, use a **cable ripper** to remove the sheathing easily without nicking the wires. A simple **neon tester** will tell you if an outlet or fixture is live. A

beaded chain simplifies fishing thin, low-voltage wires or phone wires through walls.

General carpentry tools that come in handy when doing electrical work include an **electric drill** with a **spade bit** to make holes for cable to pass through; a **utility knife, screwdrivers**, a **keyhole saw** for cutting drywall, a **level**, a **hacksaw** for cutting conduit and metal-sheathed cable, and a **tape measure**.

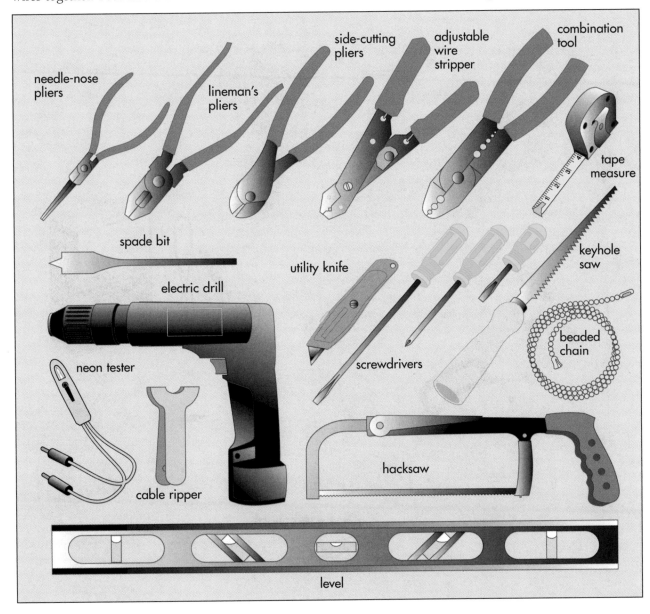

needle-nose pliers

lineman's pliers

side-cutting pliers

adjustable wire stripper

combination tool

tape measure

spade bit

utility knife

keyhole saw

electric drill

screwdrivers

beaded chain

neon tester

cable ripper

hacksaw

level

SPECIALIZED TOOLS

As you take on more complicated electrical projects, you will find that other tools are invaluable. Some of these tools are essential to such projects; others simply help you do a better, faster job.

If you need to drill holes deeper than the length of your spade bit, get a **bit extension.** A **soldering gun** with a spool of **lead-free, rosin-core solder** will be necessary if local codes require soldering.

Always use a **fuse puller** to remove a cartridge-type fuse; don't pull it by hand. A **BX cutter** (this tool can be rented) makes easy and safe work of cutting metal-sheathed cable. A **tubing cutter** quickly makes clean cuts in conduit. When working with conduit, use a **conduit bender** to shape the material without crimping it and **tongue-and-groove pliers** for tightening connectors. For running cable through finished walls and

ceilings or wire through conduit, a **fish tape** makes the job easier.

A **continuity tester** has a small bulb and battery for testing fuses, switches, and sockets with the power off. A **voltmeter** works with the power on or off and indicates the amount of voltage at an outlet. A **receptacle analyzer** runs a number of tests, telling you if your receptacle has a good connection and if it is properly grounded and polarized.

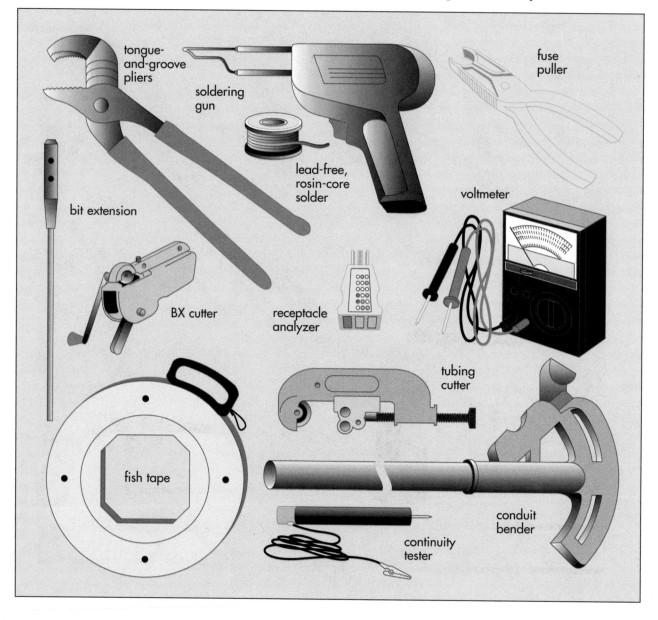

CHOOSING SWITCHES

Manufacturers offer a sometimes bewildering array of switches. To begin with you have a choice of colors—brown, ivory, and white are the most readily available. But the differences extend far beyond appearance.

For most of your needs you'll probably choose a **single-pole toggle,** which is available for a low price. "Toggle" simply refers to a switch that flips up and down.

Three-way and **four-way** switches are needed if you want to control a light from two or more separate switches. To learn about wiring them.

If you want to add a switch without putting in a larger box, a **double** switch may be the solution. It takes up the same amount of space as a single switch.

A **rocker** switch functions the same way as a standard toggle switch but is slightly easier to use.

A **dimmer** switch allows you to adjust lighting levels to suit your needs. A sliding dimmer brightens the light as you slide it upward. The rotary type comes in two versions. One version turns lights on or off with a push; the light level is altered by turning the knob. The other type dims the light as the knob is rotated counterclockwise until it turns off.

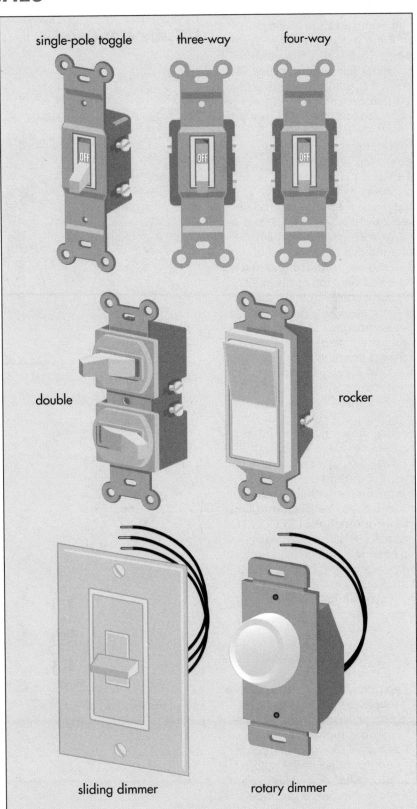

single-pole toggle   three-way   four-way

double   rocker

sliding dimmer   rotary dimmer

CHOOSING RECEPTACLES

A standard duplex receptacle has two outlets for receiving plugs. Each outlet has a long (neutral) slot, a shorter (hot) slot, and a half-round grounding hole. This ensures that the plug will be polarized and grounded (see page 10). Receptacles are rated for maximum amps. A **20-amp grounded receptacle** has a T-shaped neutral slot; use it only on 20-amp circuits. For most purposes, a **15-amp grounded receptacle** is sufficient. When replacing a receptacle in an ungrounded outlet box, use a **15-amp ungrounded receptacle**, intended only for use in older homes without ground wires in the circuits. Use a three-pronged plug adapter on an ungrounded receptacle only if the wall-plate screw is grounded (see page 35 to test this). The switch in a combination **switch/receptacle** can be hooked up to control the receptacle it's paired with.

A **20-amp single grounded receptacle** makes it nearly impossible to overload a critical circuit. For outdoors, in basements, or within 6 feet of a water fixture, install **ground-fault circuit-interrupter (GFCI)** receptacles. Select a **240-volt receptacle** based on the appliance amperage rating. Plugs required for appliances of 15, 20, 30, and 50 amps will have different prong configurations.

> ### CAUTION!
> REPLACE, DON'T CHANGE
> *Replace a receptacle with one that is just like the old one. Change types only if you are certain that the wiring is suitable. Do not replace an ungrounded outlet with a grounded one unless you know the box is grounded.*

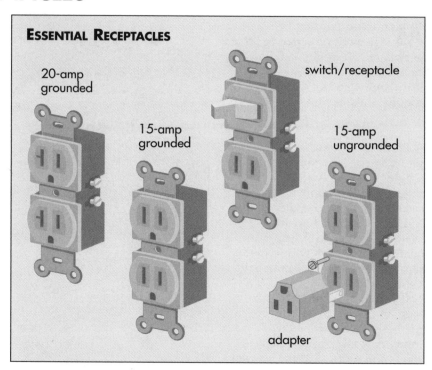

ESSENTIAL RECEPTACLES

20-amp grounded

15-amp grounded

switch/receptacle

15-amp ungrounded

adapter

SPECIALIZED RECEPTACLES

20-amp single grounded

50-amp 120/240-volt wall-mounted

GFCI receptacle

30-amp 120/240-volt floor-mounted

CHOOSING WIRE AND CABLE

Wire, cord, and cable (generically referred to as "conductors") are the pathways along which electricity travels. Wire is a solid strand of metal encased in insulation. Cord is a group of small strands encased in insulation. Cable is made of two or more wires wrapped in protective sheathing of metal or plastic.

Most local codes allow you to use nonmetallic sheathed cable (NM cable) inside walls, floors, and other places where it can't be damaged and won't get wet. Information printed on the sheathing tells you what is inside. The top example at right has two 14-gauge wires plus a bare ground wire, and is thus referred to as "14-2 G" cable ("G" for ground). Cable marked "14-3 G" has three wires plus a ground wire. Flexible armored cable (BX) contains wires wrapped in a flexible metal sheathing. It can be used for short runs in exposed areas such as attics or basements. BX needs no separate ground wire because the metal sheathing itself conducts the ground. Underground feed (UF) cable is watertight with the sheathing molded around the wire. Many municipalities permit this for underground lines.

Different gauge wires carry different amounts of electricity— 14-gauge carries a maximum of 15 amps, 12-gauge carries up to 20 amps, and 10-gauge wire up to 30 amps. Doorbells and other low-voltage circuits typically use 18-gauge wire. Unsheathed wires are pulled through flexible or rigid conduit. Flexible metal conduit, or Greenfield, looks like armored cable but doesn't contain wires. It is cut to length, wires are pulled through it, and the completed pieces installed. With conduit, you pull wires through it after it's installed.

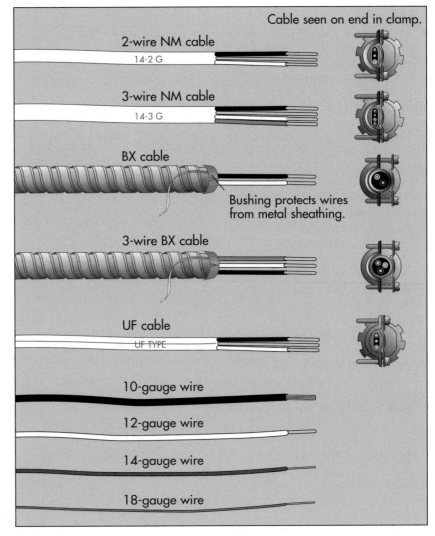

Cable seen on end in clamp.

2-wire NM cable
14-2 G

3-wire NM cable
14-3 G

BX cable
Bushing protects wires from metal sheathing.

3-wire BX cable

UF cable
UF TYPE

10-gauge wire

12-gauge wire

14-gauge wire

18-gauge wire

WHAT THE COLORS MEAN

Color	Function
white	neutral, carrying power back to the service panel
black	hot, carrying power from the service panel
red and other colors	also hot, color-coded to help identify which circuit they are on
white with black tape	a white wire that is being used as a hot wire
bare or green	a ground wire

CHOOSING BOXES

An electrical box has one primary function—to house electrical connections. Those connections might be to a switch, a receptacle, the leads of a light fixture, or other sets of wires.

Electrical codes require that all wire connections or cable splices be inside an approved metal or plastic box. You cannot bury a box inside a wall; they all must be accessible. This protects your home from the danger of fire and makes it easier to inspect and upgrade your wiring in the future.

Codes govern how many connections you're allowed to make within a box, depending on its size. If you must make more connections, you have to use a larger box (see chart at right).

There are boxes to suit most any depth of wall or ceiling, boxes to support heavy fixtures such as ceiling fans, and boxes for remodeling work and new construction. If, for instance, you'll be pulling cables through a finished wall, you can choose from a number of retrofit boxes that can be mounted with a minimum of damage to the wall.

Boxes for switches and receptacles serve as the workhorses in any electrical installation. Some of the metal ones can be "ganged" into double, triple, or larger multiples by removing one side and linking them together. Switch/receptacle boxes made of plastic are accepted by most codes, but they can't be ganged. If you are using conduit, Greenfield, or BX, you must use metal boxes to ground the system.

Utility boxes are surface-mounted in basements and garages to hold switches or receptacles. Boxes for fixtures or junctions may support lighting fixtures or split circuits into separate branches.

MEASUREMENTS
CHOOSING THE CORRECT BOX SIZE

Type of Box	Size in Inches (Height × Width × Depth)	Maximum Number of Wires Allowed in a Box		
		14-gauge	12-gauge	10-gauge
switch/ receptacle	3×2×1½	3	3	3
	3×2×2	5	4	4
	3×2×2¼	5	4	4
	3×2×2½	6	5	5
	3×2×2¾	7	6	5
	3×2×3½	9	8	7
utility	4×2⅛×1½	5	4	4
	4×2⅛×1⅞	6	5	5
	4×2⅛×2⅛	7	6	5
fixture/ junction	4×1¼ round or octagonal	6	5	5
	4×1½ round or octagonal	7	6	6
	4×2⅛ round or octagonal	10	9	8
	4×1¼ square	9	8	7
	4×1½ square	10	9	8
	4×2⅛ square	15	13	12
	4¹¹⁄₁₆×1½ square	14	13	11
	4¹¹⁄₁₆×2⅛ square	21	18	16

EXPERTS' INSIGHT

BOX CAPACITY

Overcrowd a box and you risk damaging wire connectors, piercing insulation, and cracking a switch or receptacle, any of which could cause a short. That is why codes spell out how many wires you can install in a box.

The chart above gives standard requirements. Other items may add to the total number of wires a box can hold. As you count wires, keep in mind these rules:

■ Don't count fixture leads (the wires that are connected to the fixture).

■ Count a wire that enters and leaves without a splice as one.

■ Count each cable clamp, stud, or hickey inside the box as one wire.

■ Count each receptacle or switch as one.

■ Count grounding wires entering a box as one, but do not count grounding wires that begin and end in the box.

NEW INSTALLATION SWITCH/RECEPTACLE BOXES

These boxes are designed for quick installation when the framing is exposed. They all have built-in gauges to make it easy for you to install them flush with the surface of the finished wall.

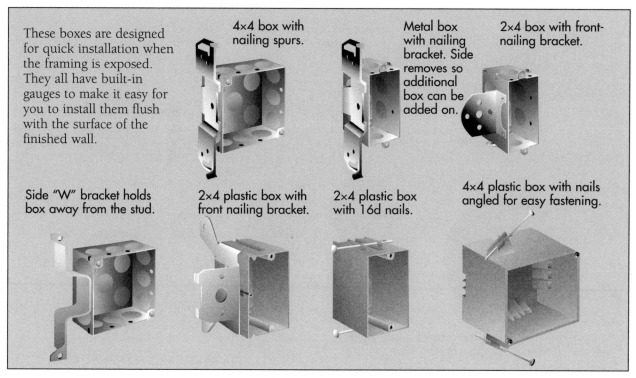

4×4 box with nailing spurs.

Metal box with nailing bracket. Side removes so additional box can be added on.

2×4 box with front-nailing bracket.

Side "W" bracket holds box away from the stud.

2×4 plastic box with front nailing bracket.

2×4 plastic box with 16d nails.

4×4 plastic box with nails angled for easy fastening.

RETROFIT SWITCH/RECEPTACLE BOXES

When installing new electrical service where the walls are finished, use boxes designed to minimize damage to the wall. If the special clips do not work, you may be able to attach the boxes to framing pieces with screws driven through holes inside the boxes.

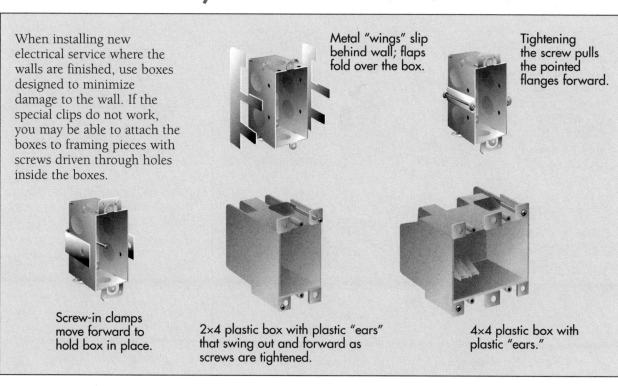

Metal "wings" slip behind wall; flaps fold over the box.

Tightening the screw pulls the pointed flanges forward.

Screw-in clamps move forward to hold box in place.

2×4 plastic box with plastic "ears" that swing out and forward as screws are tightened.

4×4 plastic box with plastic "ears."

NEW INSTALLATION FIXTURE/JUNCTION BOXES

"New installation" wiring refers to work done on a freshly framed wall. With no drywall or plaster in the way, it is easy to install ceiling fixture boxes that are solid enough to hold a heavy chandelier or a fan. Remember that all junction boxes must remain accessible— never cover them with drywall.

Telescoping brackets allow you to position these boxes anywhere between joists.

Metal octagonal box requires framing behind it if it is to support a heavy fixture.

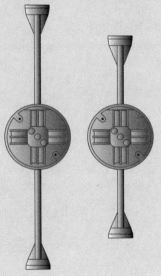

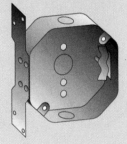

Round plastic fixture box has a bracket with sharp points so you can quickly tap it in place, then secure it with screws.

Octagonal junction box with side bracket is nailed to framing.

RETROFIT FIXTURE/JUNCTION BOXES

The retrofitting of adding new wiring to old walls is challenging. Often it's not easy to secure a fixture box when there's drywall or plaster in the way. For heavy ceiling fixtures, use a brace bar that can be slipped into the hole and expanded from joist to joist.

A shallow box like this is sometimes needed in older homes with plaster walls.

"Wings" come forward as you tighten their screws, clasping the box to the plaster or drywall.

Most retrofitting starts with standard junction boxes located in accessible areas.

INSTALLING BOXES IN UNFINISHED SPACE

To wire a room with unfinished walls, such as a basement remodeling or a room addition, you'll need boxes fastened to the framing. When attaching the boxes, be sure they protrude from the framing the same thickness as your drywall or paneling—usually ½ inch. Run cable from box to box and to the service panel.

After you've roughed in the wiring, but before you install the switches and receptacles, put up the drywall on the walls and ceiling. Finish and prime the surfaces, and install the devices in the boxes.

YOU'LL NEED...

TIME: About 3 hours for installing 10 boxes.
SKILLS: Basic carpentry skills.
TOOLS: Tape measure, hammer or drill with screwdriver bit.

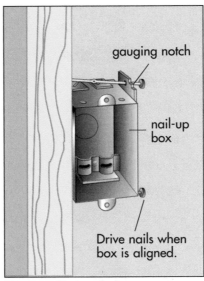

Nonmetallic handy box
Many boxes have a series of gauging notches on their sides. Determine the thickness of the drywall and/or paneling you will be installing, and align the box to the appropriate notch as you attach it. A nail-up box like this one is the easiest to install.

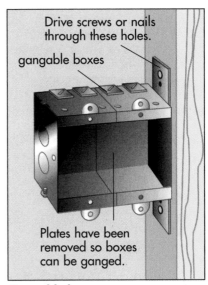

Gangable boxes
These have detachable sides, so you can attach them together to form double- or triple-size boxes. To attach such boxes without special mounting hardware, simply drive screws or nails through the holes and into the framing.

MEASUREMENTS

PLACING BOXES

In a typical room, place switch boxes 48–50 inches above the floor and receptacles 12–16 inches above floor level. Check with local codes to see how many receptacles you will need. In most cases they must be placed so that no point along any wall is more than 6 feet from a receptacle. This means that you'll have to install at least one receptacle every 12 feet along the wall. For kitchens and bathrooms, special requirements apply.

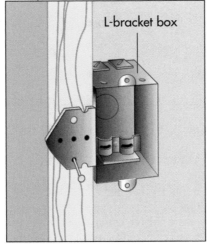

L-bracket box
Some L-bracket boxes adjust to suit the thickness of your wall material. Others accommodate only one thickness. Hold the box in position against the framing, and drive two nails or screws through the holes in the bracket.

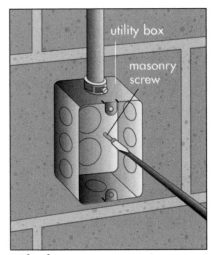

Utility box
Use a utility box and conduit or armored cable in an area where you don't need a finished appearance. If you're attaching boxes to masonry, use anchors or masonry screws.

*F*ixture and junction boxes are easy to install in unfinished space. Install boxes so they will be flush with the finished surface of the ceiling or wall. Do not place any electrical box where it will be covered by drywall or paneling.

If there is a joist at the spot where you want the box, use a box with a **hanger bracket** or an **L-bracket.** This page shows various types available—some designed for installing from below, some for installing from above. These fasten to the joist with screws or nails. When attaching, allow for the thickness of the ceiling material.

If you need to install a fixture box between joists, use a box with a **bar hanger.** Attach the ends of the brackets to the joists, and slide the box into the desired position.

Junction boxes protect wire connections or cable splices. Some junction boxes come with brackets. Others just nail or screw to a joist, stud, or rafter.

Regardless of the type of box you're installing, always secure it with two fasteners. If the box will be supporting a ceiling fan or other heavy fixture, make sure it's anchored securely enough to carry the weight. If a box has been correctly mounted but still doesn't feel firm enough, add a framing piece and secure it to that as well.

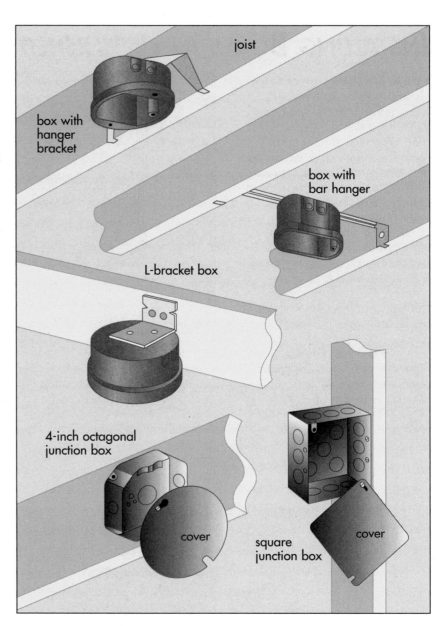

joist

box with hanger bracket

box with bar hanger

L-bracket box

4-inch octagonal junction box

cover

square junction box

cover

OVERHEAD LIGHT PLACEMENT

■ One pleasing way to light a room is with recessed can lights or small fixtures. To plan for a group of symmetrically placed lights, make a map of your ceiling and experiment by drawing circles, each of which represents the area lit up by a recessed fixture.

■ When you experiment with your design, try to arrange the lights so they are half as far from the walls as they are from each other. A pleasingly symmetrical pattern usually results. Start by arranging lights 6 feet apart and 3 feet from walls. Position them at least 4 feet apart. Add to your plan any suspended or track lighting you need for task illumination or to accent an attractive area of the room.

■ Don't expect to achieve an arrangement that's perfectly symmetrical; few ceilings will allow for that. Also keep in mind that with recessed lighting, you may not be able to put all the lights exactly where you want them because there will be joists in the way. In most cases, a less-than-perfect arrangement will not be noticeable.

INSTALLING BOXES IN FINISHED SPACE

Installing electrical work is a greater challenge when the walls and ceilings are finished. Often patching and painting can take far more time than the electrical work itself! Plan the placement so you avoid making unnecessary holes.

Wherever possible, avoid making contact with the framing. Using special boxes designed for installation in finished space, you often can simply make a hole the size of the box and secure the box to the wall or ceiling surface.

Before you begin, plan how you're going to get cable to the new location.

YOU'LL NEED...
TIME: About 30 minutes a box, not including running new wire.
SKILLS: Simple skills are required.
TOOLS: Keyhole saw, screwdriver, needle-nose pliers, utility knife, and neon tester.

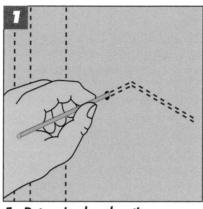

1. Determine box location.
Drill a small hole in the wall. Insert a bent wire and rotate it. If you hit something, you've probably found a stud. Try 6 inches to one side. If you strike wood again, you may have hit a fire block. Drill another hole 3 inches higher or lower. Keep trying until you can rotate the bent wire freely.

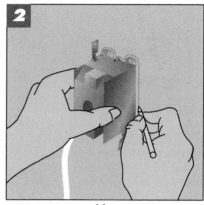

2. Trace around box.
Some boxes come with a template that can be held against the surface and traced around. Otherwise, use the box itself and center it on the hole you could rotate the wire in. Make sure the template or box is plumb before you mark the outline.

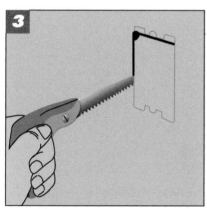

3. Cut the opening.
Carefully cut around the traced outline. If the surface is drywall, use a utility knife. If you are cutting into plaster walls, use a keyhole saw. If the plaster is crumbly, mask the outline with tape. For a wood-surfaced wall, drill a ¼-inch access hole in each corner and use a saber saw. Run cable.

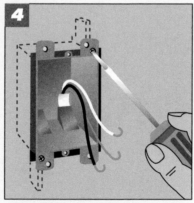

4. Fasten with side clamps...
Side-clamp boxes grip the wall from behind when you tighten the screws. Pull 8 inches of cable through the box and insert the box. Hold the box plumb as you tighten the clamps. Alternate from side to side as you work so the box seats evenly. Avoid overtightening the clamps.

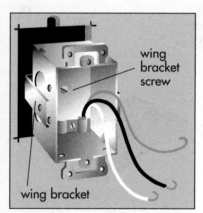

wing bracket screw

wing bracket

...or tighten wing bracket screws.
Loosen the screw centered in the receptacle box until the wing bracket is at maximum extension from the back. Hold the wings against the body of the box and push the box into the hole. Tighten the screw until the box is held firmly in place.

box attached to framing

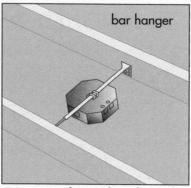

bar hanger

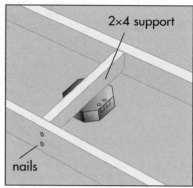

2×4 support

nails

With access from above
A ceiling box must support a fixture, so it must be securely attached to the framing. If you are fortunate enough to have

attic space above, the job can be done without damaging your ceiling. Mark the location of each box on the ceiling, and drive nails as reference points.

Cut the hole for the box. If there is a nearby joist, attach an L-bracket box directly to it. If not, either use a bar hanger or frame in a 2×4 support.

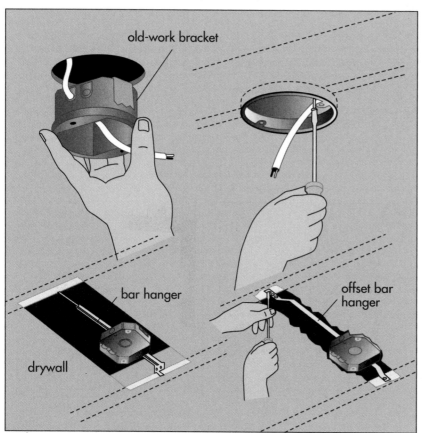

old-work bracket

bar hanger

drywall

offset bar hanger

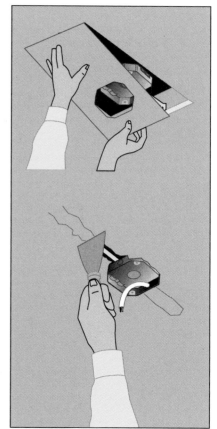

With no access from above
If you cannot work from above, use one of these methods. For light fixtures that weigh less than 5 pounds, use an old-work bracket. Cut the hole the size of the box, slip the bracket in, telescope it to fit between two joists, and attach the box to it.

For heavier fixtures, such as chandeliers and ceiling fans, make an opening in the ceiling and install hanging hardware. With a drywall ceiling, cut out a large rectangle and install a bar hanger. With plaster, chip out a path and use an offset bar hanger.

Repair the ceiling.
After checking the electrical installation, patch the ceiling. With drywall, you may be able to use the same piece you cut out. Nail the panel to the joists, and tape the seam with joint compound. For a plaster ceiling, fill with patching compound.

STRIPPING WIRE

Before making electrical connections, you'll need to remove some of the sheathing that encases the three or four wires of the cable and strip some of the insulation that coats the individual wires. Stripping techniques are simple, but exercise care when removing sheathing in order to avoid damaging any of the underlying insulation. Also be careful to strip the insulation without nicking the copper wire—this would weaken it.

Strip wires before inserting them into the box. That way, if you make a mistake, you can cut off the damaged portion and try again.

YOU'LL NEED...

TIME: About 5 minutes or less.
SKILLS: Simple stripping.
TOOLS: Cable ripper, utility knife, side cutters and combination tool or adjustable wire stripper.

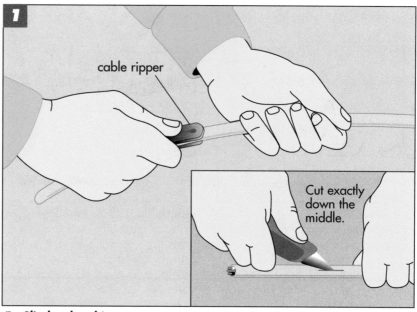

1. Slit the sheathing.
The easiest way to remove plastic sheathing from nonmetallic sheathed cable is to use an inexpensive cable ripper. Slip 6 to 8 inches of cable into the ripper's jaws, squeeze, and pull. This slits open the sheathing without damaging the insulation of internal wires. The same job can be done with a knife, but you must be careful: Run the blade right down the middle so it doesn't strip insulation from the wires.

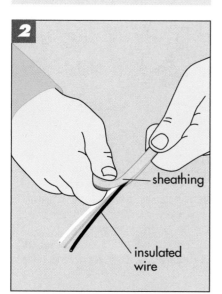

2. Peel back the sheathing.
Pull back the sheathing you have just slit, as well as the paper wrapping or strips of thin plastic, if any. You'll find two or three separately insulated wires, as well as a bare ground wire.

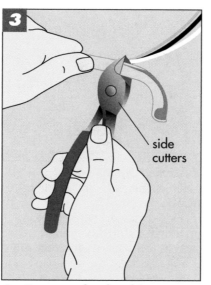

3. Cut away the sheathing.
Cut off the sheathing and paper. Remove the slit sheathing with a pair of side cutters. Or use a utility knife, taking care to point the blade away from the wires.

CAUTION!
This job is simple but it must be done with great care or you could end up with dangerous electrical shorts. If you think you may have accidentally damaged some insulation, cut the cable back to a place behind the potentially dangerous spot and start again.
Another possible problem: If you cut into the copper wire while stripping the insulation, you can weaken the wire so that it is liable to break while you are making a connection later.

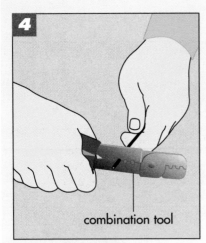

combination tool

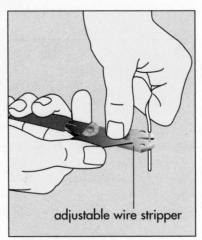

adjustable wire stripper

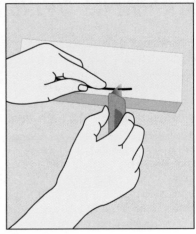

4. Strip the wire.

To strip insulation from wires, use a combination tool, which has separate holes for the different sizes of wires. Locate the wire in the correct hole, clamp down, give it a twist, and

pull the tool away from you. With an adjustable stripper, set it for the wire size, twist, then pull the tool away from you. Stripping also can be done with a utility knife, but be careful not to dig into the copper wire.

Place the wire on a scrap piece of wood, hold the blade at a slight angle, and strip the insulation by slicing off thin strips until you reach wire.

JOINING WIRES

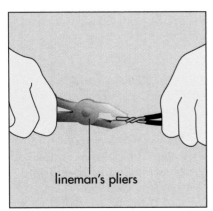

lineman's pliers

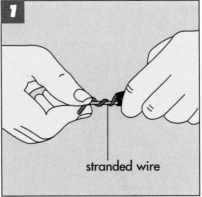

stranded wire

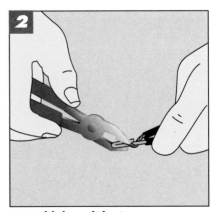

Joining solid wires

Join solid wires by using a pair of lineman's pliers. Cross the two wires, grab both wires with the pliers, and twist clockwise. Both wires should twist—do not just twist one wire around the other. Twist for several revolutions, but don't twist so tightly that the wires are in danger of breaking. Screw a wire connector onto the two wires (see page 27).

1. Joining stranded to solid wires

Often a stranded wire (made of many thin wires) has to be spliced to a solid wire, as when hooking up a light fixture or dimmer switch. Because the stranded wire is more flexible, the two won't twist together. Wrap the stranded wire around the solid wire.

2. Fold the solid wire over.

Bend the solid wire so it clamps down on the stranded wire. Screw a wire connector onto the two wires (see page 27), and wrap the connection with electrician's tape.

WORKING WITH WIRE

The final—and most gratifying—phase of an electrical installation comes when you tie all those wires together and attach them to the switches, light fixtures, and receptacles. Don't take shortcuts with wire connections and splices. Cap splices with wire connectors rather than only tape, and wrap tape around each connector. Make pigtails (see page 28) wherever they are needed instead of trying to connect two or more wires to a terminal. Finally, don't overcrowd a box with too many wires (for limits, see chart on page 18).

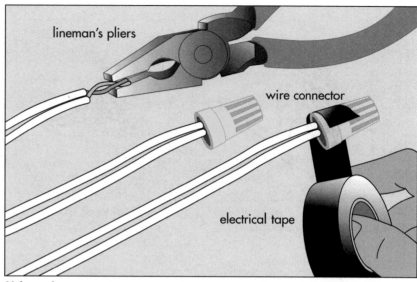

HOW MANY WIRES IN A CONNECTOR?

Wire connector	12-gauge wires	14-gauge wires
red	2–4	2–5
yellow	2–3	2–4
orange	2	2–4

Using wire connectors

To complete a splice of two or more wires, use wire connectors. These come in a variety of sizes. Select the size you need depending on how many wires you will connect as well as the thickness of the wires (see chart, left). Wire connectors firm up the splice and protect bare wires better than tape. First twist the wires firmly together. Do not depend on the connector to do the joining. Twist the wire connector on, turning it by hand until it tightens firmly. As a final precaution, wrap the connector clockwise with electrical tape, overlapping the wires.

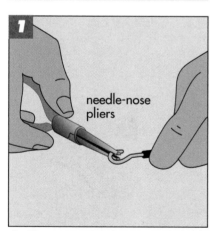

1. To connect a wire to a terminal, form a loop.
Strip just enough wire to wrap around the terminal—about ¾ inch. Then form it into a loop using needle-nose or lineman's pliers. It takes practice to make loops that lie flat and are neither too big nor too small.

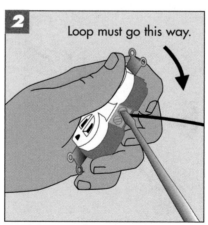

2. Fasten to the terminal.
Hook the wire clockwise around the terminal so that tightening the screw will close the loop. With receptacles, the black wires go to the brass side, white to silver. Tighten firmly, but avoid overtightening, which can damage the device. If you do crack a device in any way, throw it out.

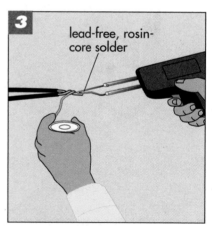

3. Solder a splice.
A few codes require that splices be soldered. More often, soldering house wiring is prohibited. If you need to solder a splice, start by twisting the wires together. Heat the wires with a soldering iron, then touch lead-free, rosin-core solder to the splice. The solder should melt into the splice.

CONNECTING WIRES

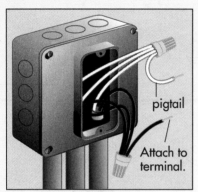

Add a pigtail where two or more wires attach to a terminal...
Never attach more than one wire to a terminal. Codes prohibit it, and it's unsafe because terminal screws are made to hold only one wire. An easier way to join many wires to a terminal is to cut a short piece of wire (about 4 inches), strip both ends, and splice it to the other wires as shown to form a pigtail.

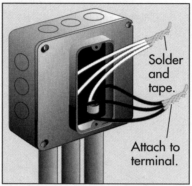

...or make a soldered splice.
Twist wires together so that one extends 1 inch beyond the splice. Solder the twist and loop the extended wire. Tape the soldered splice before screwing the wire to the terminal.

> **CAUTION!**
> Make sure local codes permit soldering.

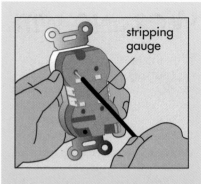

> **CAUTION!**
> Most receptacles and switches have connection holes in the back. To make a connection, strip the wire (a stripping gauge often is provided, showing you how much insulation to remove) and poke it into the correct hole. On a receptacle the holes are marked for white and black wires. However most professionals do not use these holes. Wires inserted this way are simply not as secure as those screwed to a terminal.

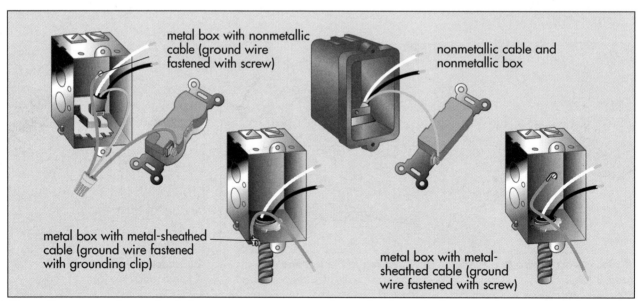

Grounding receptacles and switches
How you ground devices like receptacles and switches depends on the type of wiring you're using as well as the type of box. With flexible armored cable (BX), Greenfield, or rigid conduit, the metal of the wiring casing and the metal of the box substitutes for the grounding wire. Simply by attaching the device firmly to the box, you have grounded it. Some local codes require that you also attach a short grounding wire, as shown. If you're working with nonmetallic sheathed cable (Romex) and metal boxes, connect short grounding wires to the box and to the device. With nonmetallic boxes, the cable's grounding wire connects directly to the device.

CHECKING INCANDESCENT FIXTURES

*T*hough they vary widely in style, most incandescent fixtures have the same arrangement of components (see illustration, below right).

Mounting screws hold a canopy plate against the ceiling. The canopy has one or more sockets for bulbs. A translucent diffuser or globe cuts down on the glare of bare lightbulbs. In newer fixtures, a ring of fiber insulation provides added protection from heat damage to the wires and ceiling.

If a fixture shorts out, causing a circuit to blow and/or creating sparks, the problem is probably in the fixture. If it simply refuses to light, the wall switch may be faulty (see pages 32–33).

> **CAUTION!**
> USE THE RIGHT BULBS
> *A label on the fixture will tell you the maximum bulb wattage allowed. Don't install higher-wattage bulbs or your fixture will overheat, burn up bulbs quickly, and become dangerous.*

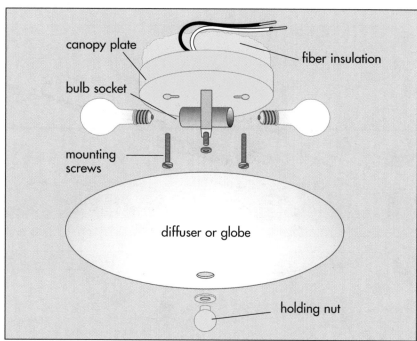

Labels: canopy plate, fiber insulation, bulb socket, mounting screws, diffuser or globe, holding nut

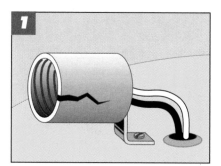

1. Inspect the socket.
Shut off the circuit that supplies power to the fixture. Inspect the socket. If it is cracked, or if its wires are scorched or melted, replace it or the entire fixture. If it's OK, remove the bulb and check the contact at the socket's base. If there's corrosion, scrape the contact with a flat screwdriver or steel wool, and pry up on it. Turn on circuit and retry.

2. Check the wiring.
If the problem remains, shut off the circuit again, loosen or remove the mounting screws, and drop the fixture from its outlet box. Check for loose connections and for nicked insulation. If you see drywall paper that is slightly

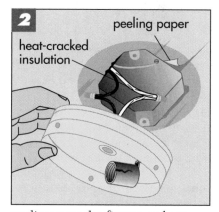

Labels: heat-cracked insulation, peeling paper

peeling near the fixture or heat-cracked wire insulation, your fixture is overheating. This means either that it is faulty or you need to reduce the wattage of the bulbs. Wrap any bare wires with electrical tape.

> **SAFETY**
>
> **KEEP THE FIBER INSULATION**
> Although it makes installation a bit more difficult, don't remove the fiber insulation in the canopy plate. It provides extra protection against shorts.

TROUBLESHOOTING FLUORESCENT FIXTURES

The heart of a fluorescent fixture is its ballast, an electrical transformer that steps up voltage and sends it to a pair of lamp holders. The current passes through the lamp holders and excites a gas inside the fluorescent tube, causing its phosphorus-coated inner surface to glow with cool, diffused light.

Because they produce far less heat, fluorescent tubes last much longer than incandescent bulbs and consume considerably less electrical energy. However, problems with the fixtures sometimes arise. The ballasts burn out after years of steady use, and the lamp holders are easily cracked if they get bumped.

Older units have starters that must be replaced periodically.

YOU'LL NEED...

TIME: To inspect a fixture and replace a ballast (for example), about an hour.
SKILLS: No special skills needed.
TOOLS: Screwdriver.

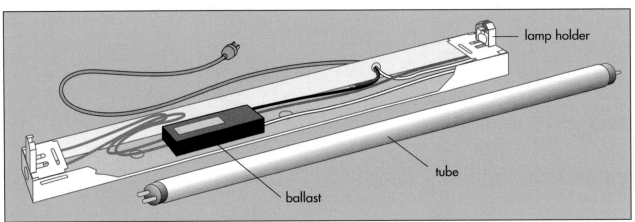

lamp holder

tube

ballast

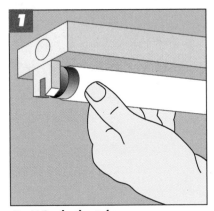

1. Wiggle the tube.

Fluorescent tubes rarely burn out abruptly; they flicker or dim. If a tube suddenly stops lighting, try wiggling and rotating its ends to make sure it's properly seated.

CAUTION!
Never get rid of burned out tubes by breaking them. They contain mercury. Dispose of them whole or request disposal guidelines.

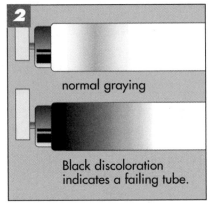

normal graying

Black discoloration indicates a failing tube.

2. Replace a worn-out tube.

A working tube usually has a grayish tinge near its ends. If the tube is uniformly dim, it may simply need washing. To wash a tube, remove it from the fixture, wipe it with a damp cloth, and then replace the tube. If the tube ends turn dark gray or black, the tube is failing and needs to be replaced. Purchase a tube that is the same length and wattage as the old one.

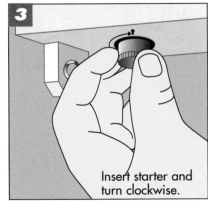

Insert starter and turn clockwise.

3. Replace the starter.

Older, delayed-start fluorescent lights flicker momentarily as they light up. If the flickering continues for more than a few seconds, make sure the starter is seated properly. Push it in and turn clockwise. When the ends of a tube light up but its center does not, the starter is defective. Press in and turn counterclockwise to remove it. Insert a new starter and turn clockwise.

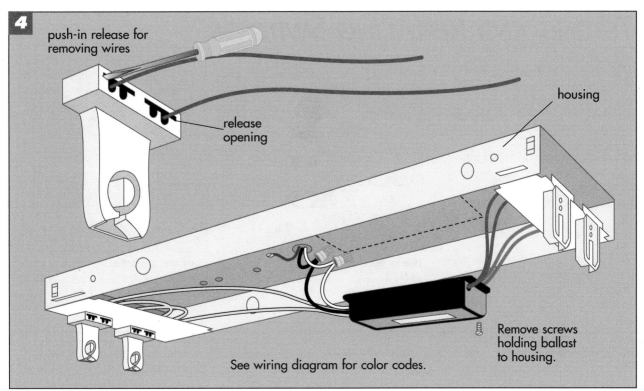

4

push-in release for removing wires

release opening

housing

Remove screws holding ballast to housing.

See wiring diagram for color codes.

4. Replace the ballast.

If the fixture hums or oozes a tarlike goop, the ballast needs replacing. (You may be better off replacing the entire unit. Compare prices.) **NOTE:** *Shut off the power.* To remove the ballast, release the wires at the sockets by pushing a screwdriver into the release openings. Unscrew the ballast and disconnect wires to power source. Reassemble with the new ballast.

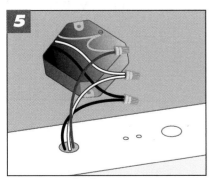

5

5. Inspect the box.

If none of these steps locates the problem, you may not have power going into the fixture. Remove the fixture, and look for loose connections and broken or bare wires in the outlet box.

TESTING AND REPLACING SWITCHES

After getting flipped thousands of times, a switch can wear out. Unless the problem is a loose wire connection, there is usually no way to repair a faulty switch; you'll need to replace it.

It is easy to test switches and easy to replace them. If you want to replace your old switch with something more sophisticated—for example, a dimmer—check out the switch options presented on page 15.

YOU'LL NEED...

TIME: About 30 minutes to test and replace a switch.

SKILLS: Using testers (we'll show you how) and connecting wires to screw terminals.

TOOLS: Neon tester, continuity tester, and screwdriver.

CAUTION!

Hold only the metal flanges of the switch when pulling it out of a box. Be very careful not to touch the terminal screws or to allow the screws to touch the edge of the box.

TOOL TIP

SAFE USE OF A CONTINUITY TESTER

Never use a continuity tester on wires that might be live. Always shut off power and disconnect wires before testing. The continuity tester uses a battery that generates a small current to test for the flow of electricity from one point to another. It is not made to carry household current.

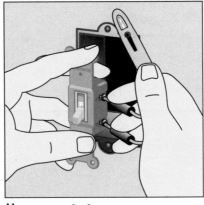

Use a neon tester...
NOTE: *Shut off power.* Remove the cover plate and the screws holding the switch. Pull the switch out from the box. Turn the switch to OFF and restore power to the circuit. Touch the probes of a neon tester to the switch's screw terminals. If the tester glows, the box has power. Turn the switch on. Touch the probes to the terminals again. If the tester glows this time, the switch is blown and must be replaced.

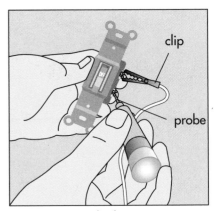

...or use a continuity tester.
An easy way to test a switch is to use a continuity tester. Shut down the circuit leading to the switch and remove the switch from the box. Disconnect all wires. Attach the tester clip to one of the terminals and touch the probe to the other. If the switch is working, the tester will glow when the switch is on and not glow when the switch is off.

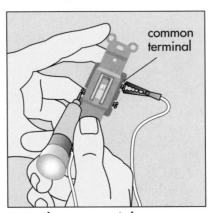

Test a three-way switch.
To check out a three-way switch, shut off the circuit and attach the clip to the common terminal (it's usually labeled on the switch body). Touch the probe to one of the other screw terminals and flip the switch. If it's OK, the tester will light when touching one of the two terminals. Flip the switch. The tester should light when the other terminal is touched.

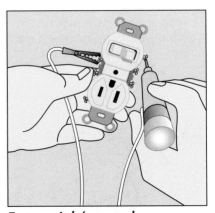

Test a switch/receptacle.
To test a device that has both a switch and a receptacle, attach the continuity tester clip to one of the top (switch) terminals and touch the probe to the top terminal on the other side. If the switch is working, the tester will glow when the switch is on, and not glow when it is off.

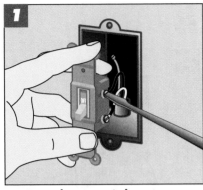

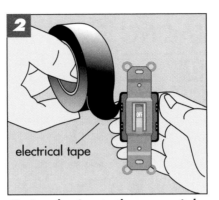

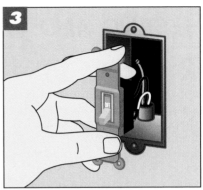

1. To replace a switch, remove the old switch.
NOTE: *Shut off power.* If a switch is damaged, remove the screws holding the switch to the box and gently pull out the device. Loosen the screw terminals and disconnect the wires.

2. Attach wires to the new switch.
Inspect the wires in the box and wrap any damaged insulation with electrical tape. Attach the wires to the terminals of the new switch and wrap electrical tape around the body of the switch so the terminals are covered.

3. Reinstall the switch.
Carefully tuck the wires and switch back into the box and connect the switch to the box by tightening the mounting screws. Don't force anything; switches crack easily.

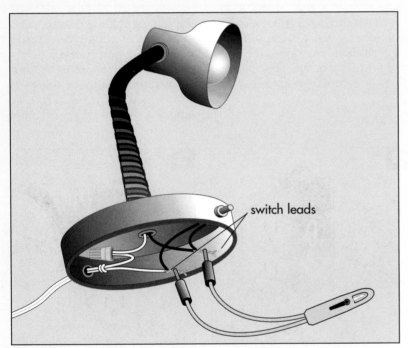

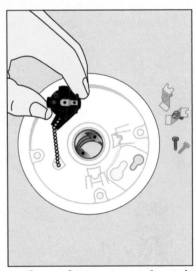

Test a fixture-mounted switch.
Small switches that mount on fixtures work by pull chain, flipping up and down, or twisting. These switches are not long-lived, so if the light does not work and the bulb is not blown, there is a good chance that the problem is with the switch. To test, shut off power to the fixture (or unplug it).

Remove the connectors holding the switch's leads. Leave the bare wires twisted together, and arrange them so the connections are not in danger of touching each other or anything else. Restore power to the fixture and carefully touch a neon tester to the connections. If the switch is turned on and the tester lights, the switch is bad.

Replace a fixture-mounted switch.
NOTE: *Shut off power.* Remove the fixture and disconnect the wires. Release the pull-chain switch by loosening the terminal screws and two screws in the base of the socket. Install a replacement switch and remount the fixture.

Other porcelain fixtures have an integrated switch. In such cases, replace the entire fixture. Lamp pull chains cannot be repaired. Buy a new pull-chain socket and replace the old one.

TESTING AND REPLACING RECEPTACLES

Receptacles can be damaged in ways that are not readily apparent. Small cracks can lead to a short. As receptacles grow old, they may hold plugs in place less firmly. The good news is that receptacles are inexpensive and easy to replace. Don't hesitate to replace one for any reason, such as because it is paint-glopped or the wrong color. However, if you want to replace your receptacle with one of a different type—for example, replace an ungrounded receptacle with a grounded one—read pages 10 and 16 first.

YOU'LL NEED...

TIME: About 5 minutes to test and 15 minutes to replace a receptacle.
SKILLS: Using a tester (we'll show you how) and connecting wires to terminals.
TOOLS: Neon tester, receptacle analyzer, and screwdriver.

1. To test for a faulty receptacle, see if receptacle is live.
With the power to the circuit on, insert one probe of a neon tester into each slot of the receptacle. Do not touch the metal probes; only touch the insulated wires of the tester. If the tester glows, the receptacle is working. Test both plugs of a duplex receptacle.

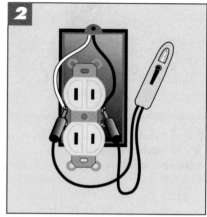

2. Test for power to the box.
If the receptacle is not live, check its power source. Shut off power to the outlet at the service panel, remove the cover plate, disconnect the screws holding the receptacle to the box, and pull the receptacle out. Restore power, and touch one probe of the neon tester to a brass screw terminal and the other to a silver-colored terminal. The tester light will glow if power is coming to the receptacle.

1. To replace a receptacle, remove the old receptacle.
NOTE: *Shut off power.* Note which wires are attached to which terminals. If necessary, make notations on pieces of tape and wrap them on the wires. Loosen the terminal screws and disconnect the wires.

2. Wire the new receptacle.
Inspect the wires in the box, and wrap electrical tape around any damaged insulation. Attach the wires to the receptacle, positioning each wire so it hooks clockwise on the terminal screw. Firmly tighten the terminal screws.

3. Wrap with tape and install.
Wrap the body of the receptacle with electrical tape, so that all the terminals are covered. Carefully tuck the wires and the receptacle into the box and connect the receptacle to the box by tightening the mounting screws. Don't force the receptacle into place—it may crack.

Test for grounding and polarization.

Do not turn off the power. Insert one prong of a neon tester into the short (hot) slot and the other into the grounding hole. If the tester glows, the receptacle is grounded and the slots are polarized. If the tester doesn't glow, put one probe in the grounding hole, the other in the long slot. If the tester glows, hot and neutral wires are reversed. If the tester doesn't glow in either place, the device isn't grounded.

Test a two-slot receptacle.

With the power on, insert one probe of a neon tester into the short (hot) slot, and touch the other probe to the cover plate screw (above). The screw head must be clean and paint-free. Or, remove the cover plate and insert one probe in the short slot and touch the other to the metal box (above right). If the neon tester glows, the box is grounded, and you can install a grounded three-hole receptacle.

If the tester doesn't glow, insert one prong into the long (neutral) slot and touch the other to the cover-plate screw or the box. If the tester glows, the box is grounded, but the receptacle is not correctly polarized; the hot and neutral wires are reversed. If the tester doesn't glow in either position, the box is not grounded. Do not install a three-hole receptacle.

TOOL TIP

USING A RECEPTACLE ANALYZER

With this handy device, you can perform a series of tests almost instantly without having to dismantle anything.

Leave the power on, but unplug all equipment and flip all switches to off on the circuit of the receptacle you will be testing. Plug the analyzer in. A combination of glowing lights will tell you what is happening with your receptacle (far right).

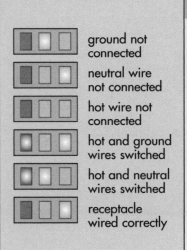

ground not connected

neutral wire not connected

hot wire not connected

hot and ground wires switched

hot and neutral wires switched

receptacle wired correctly

PLUMBING BASICS

Chapter 2

Plumbing Tools
Essential Tools **37**
Specialized Tools **38**

Minor Plumbing Improvements and Repairs
Preventing Freeze-Ups **39**
Fixing Leaks and Frozen Pipes **40**
Identifying Stem Faucets **41**
Pulling Out Handles and Stems **42**
Repairing Diaphragm and Cartridge Stems **43**
Repairing Leaks from Handles **44**
Replacing and Grinding Seats **45**
Repairing Cartridge Faucets **46**
Repairing Rotating Ball Faucets **48**
Repairing Ceramic Disk Faucets **50**
Repairing Gasketed Cartridge Faucets **52**
Sealing Leaky Base Plates **53**
Fixing Sprayers, Diverters, and Aerators **54**
Stopping Leaks in Flexible Supply Lines **55**
Repairing Toilets **56**
Fixing Tank Run-On **57**
Fixing Leaky Tanks and Bowls **59**
Repairing Tub and Shower Controls **60**
Opening Clogged Drains **62**
Using Simple Unclogging Methods **63**
Dismantling Fixture Traps **64**
Replacing Sink Strainers **65**
Augering Techniques **66**
Unclogging Showers **66**
Unclogging Tubs **67**
Cleaning Drum Traps **67**
Unclogging Toilets **68**
Cleaning Showerheads **69**

ESSENTIAL TOOLS

Plumbing does not require a lot of expensive tools, and even those that you may use for only one job are well worth the cost. The money you save by doing your own work will pay for them many times over. Using the tools shown on this page, you can tackle most plumbing projects.

To clear drain lines, get a **plunger.** The type shown here, with the extra flange extending downward, is ideal for toilets and also works well on bathtubs and sinks. Use a hand-cranked **drain auger** to clear away clogs that won't plunge away. For toilets, use a **closet auger**.

To disassemble and connect pipes and to make many other plumbing repairs, purchase a pair of high-quality **tongue-and-groove pliers** that adjust to grab almost any size pipe. A standard **adjustable pipe wrench** is essential for working with threaded iron pipe. An **adjustable Crescent wrench** will fit the nuts on faucets and other fixtures.

To cut pipe, use a **hacksaw**. Hacksaw blades dull quickly so have extra blades on hand.

For running new pipes through walls, you will need a **drill** with plenty of **spade bits**. To cut away drywall or plaster to make room for the plumbing, use a **keyhole saw**. A **flashlight** comes in handy when you need to peer into wall cavities and under sinks.

For delicate chores such as removing faucet O-rings and clips, have a pair of **needle-nose pliers** on hand. And have a ready supply of general-purpose tools, including **screwdrivers**, a **putty knife**, a **utility knife**, and a **tape measure.**

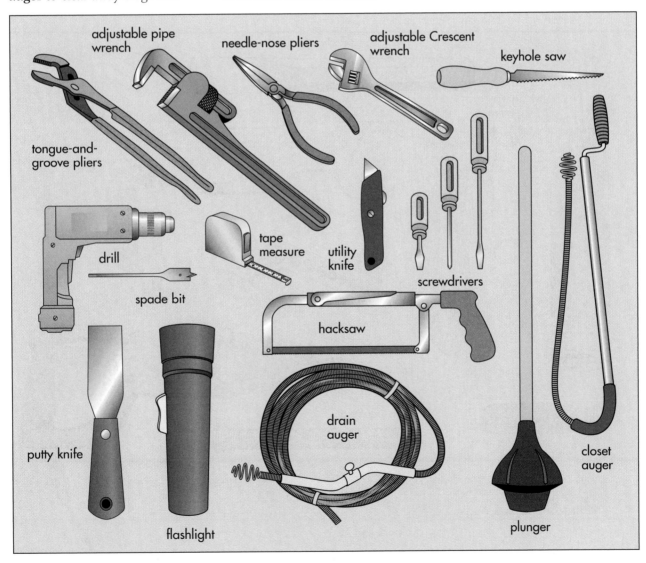

adjustable pipe wrench

needle-nose pliers

adjustable Crescent wrench

keyhole saw

tongue-and-groove pliers

drill

spade bit

tape measure

utility knife

screwdrivers

putty knife

flashlight

hacksaw

drain auger

plunger

closet auger

SPECIALIZED TOOLS

Some tools are designed for specialized plumbing tasks. Choose the ones that will help you work with your materials and fixtures.

If you will be soldering copper pipe, you must have a **propane torch.** If you have a lot to do, pay the extra money for a self-igniting model. Otherwise, get an inexpensive **spark lighter.**

To bend flexible copper tubing without kinking it, use a **tubing bender.** A two-part **flaring tool** is necessary if you want to make flare joints in copper tubing. If you plan on cutting copper pipe or tubing, buy a **tubing cutter.** It makes easier and cleaner cuts than a **hacksaw** and will not squeeze tubing out of shape. For cutting plastic supply pipes, a **plastic tubing cutter** makes the job easier. To set the proper incline for drain pipes, you'll need a **level.**

When working on faucets and sinks, you will sometimes need a **basin wrench** to get at nuts you cannot reach with pliers. If you have a damaged faucet seat that needs replacing, don't take a chance with a screwdriver—use a **seat wrench.** For those big nuts that hold on the basket strainers of kitchen sinks, you may need a **spud wrench.**

When plunging and augering don't clear out a clog, a **blow bag** will often do the trick: hook up a garden hose to it, insert it into the drain pipe, and turn on the water.

For large-scale demolition, notching studs and joists, and quickly cutting galvanized pipe, a **reciprocating saw** makes the job much easier. If you need to chip away tiles to get at plumbing, use a **cold chisel.**

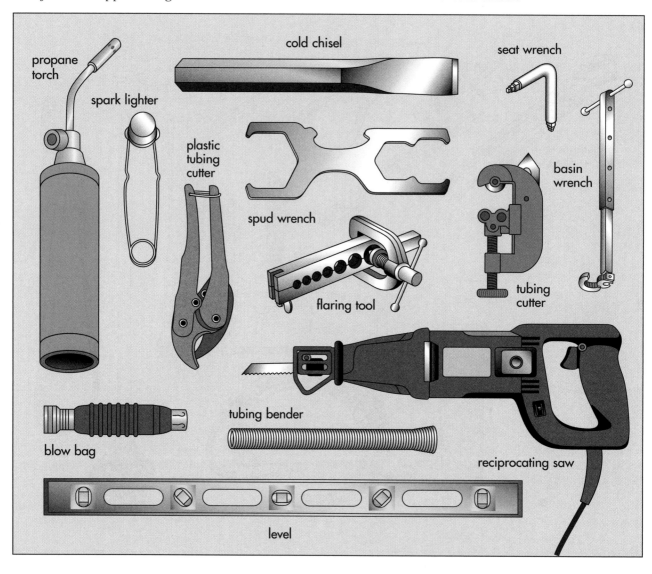

PREVENTING FREEZE-UPS

Ice-cold tap water may taste refreshing, but it also can be a chilling sign that your plumbing is in trouble. Burst pipes from freezing are difficult and expensive to fix, so take precautions if there is reason to believe that your system will not survive the coldest days of the year. New homes with pipes placed near an exterior wall can be as prone to having frozen pipes as poorly insulated older homes. Often the best solution is insulating the wall or ceiling that contains the pipes. This helps keep your home warm and protects your pipes. This page shows some additional ways to prevent plumbing freeze-ups.

YOU'LL NEED...

TIME: About three hours to prepare the average home.
SKILLS: Beginner carpentry and plumbing skills.
TOOLS: Knife and flashlight.

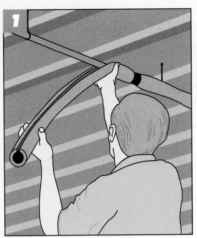

1. Insulate the pipes.
Insulation goes a long way toward preventing freeze-ups, as long as every square inch of pipe—including connections—is protected. Pipe jacketing comes in standard lengths that can be cut with a knife and secured with electrical tape. Ordinary insulation, cut in strips and bundled around pipes, works equally well for less cost but more labor. In an extremely cold wall or floor, pack the entire cavity with insulation. Also consider insulating long hot water runs, especially those that pass through unheated spaces. The added insulation will conserve water-heating energy.

2. Wrap pipes with heat tape.
Electric heat tape draws only modest amounts of current, so it is safe and inexpensive to use. Wrap tape around the pipe, and plug the tape into a receptacle. A thermostat turns the tape on and off as needed. However tape will not work during a power outage—the very time when the protection may be most needed.

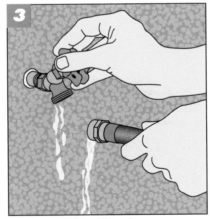

3. Protect the sill cock.
Before winter, remove and drain garden hoses to prevent them from splitting. Shut off the water leading to the sill cock, allow it to drain, and leave it open. If there is no indoor shutoff, install one, or install a freeze-proof sill cock—an improvement that may be required by local codes.

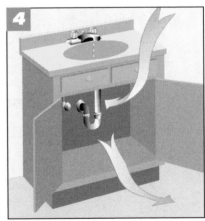

4. Precautions for very cold days
As a preventive measure on extremely cold days, turn on the faucets that have vulnerable parts and let water trickle continuously. If there is a cabinet underneath, open its doors to let room heat warm the pipes. Use a small lamp to warm pipes that run through cold areas.

FIXING LEAKS AND FROZEN PIPES

Water escaping from a pipe can wreak havoc in your house. Even a tiny leak that is left to drip day and night will soon rot away everything in its vicinity. A pipe that freezes and bursts can produce a major flood.

As soon as you spot a leak, shut off the water to take pressure off the line. Then locate exactly where the problem is. If the pipe is not visible, this may be difficult: Water can run quite a ways along the outside of the pipe, a floor joist, or a subfloor before becoming visible. Eventually, any leaking pipe must be replaced. Here are emergency measures to temporarily stop the flow.

YOU'LL NEED...

TIME: An hour or so to clamp or apply epoxy to a leak.
SKILLS: No special skills needed.
TOOLS: Screwdriver and putty knife.

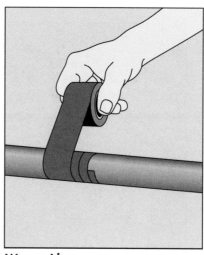

Wrap with tape.
For a pinhole leak, dry off the pipe, and wrap it tightly with several layers of duct tape. Wrap it about 6 inches on either side of the hole. This is extremely temporary, but the tape should hold while you make a trip to the hardware store for a pipe clamp and rubber gasket.

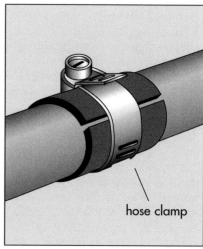

hose clamp

Apply a clamp.
An automotive hose clamp with a piece of rubber—both available at any hardware store—makes a somewhat better leak-stopper. Again, it works only for pinhole leaks. Wrap the rubber around the pipe, and tighten up the clamp. Be sure that the clamp itself is placed directly over the hole.

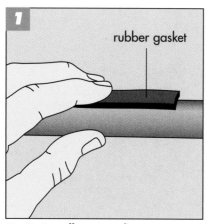

rubber gasket

1. To install a pipe clamp, position the gasket.
The best temporary solution to a leaking pipe is a pipe clamp specially made for this purpose. It will seal small gashes, cracks, and pinhole leaks. It also is semipermanent—expect it to last several years. Position the rubber gasket so the hole is centered under it.

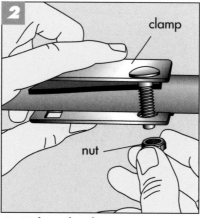

clamp

nut

2. Tighten the clamp.
Assemble the clamp pieces around the gasket and tighten. Take care that the gasket does not move as you work. Tighten all four nuts evenly, working from nut to nut until all are tight.

EXPERTS' INSIGHT

IT MAY NOT BE A LEAK...
If a pipe shows drips all along its length, it may be condensing water from humid air rather than leaking. Wrap it with insulation to stop the condensation (see page 39).

...OR IT MAY BE MORE
An isolated leak may be a sign that pipes are aging. The galvanized pipe common to older homes tends to rust from the inside out. Once a leak appears, expect others to follow. If the pipes in your house have begun to deteriorate, buy a supply of pipe clamps to fit your lines.

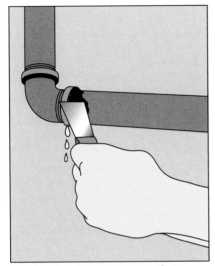

Apply plumber's epoxy at fittings.

If the leak is coming from a fitting, don't try to clamp it. Your best bet is plumber's epoxy. Unless the leak is a real gusher, don't shut off the water. The epoxy comes in two parts. Cut a piece of each and knead them together until the color is uniform. Pack the epoxy into the connection by pushing it in with your thumb or a putty knife. Pack it until the leak stops.

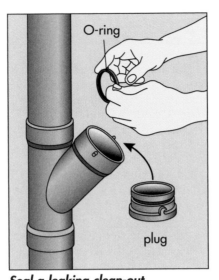

Seal a leaking clean-out.

Drain lines are less leak-prone than supply lines. Once in a while, however, a clean-out plug may seep waste water. Warn everyone in the household not to use any fixtures. Remove the plug (it may screw out or pull out). Reseal screw-in plugs by applying Teflon tape to the male threads. If it has an O-ring, replace it.

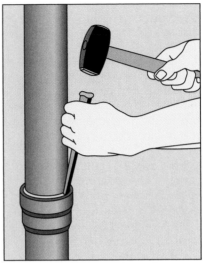

Tighten joints in cast-iron pipe.

If you have a leak at the joint of cast-iron pipes, it is usually easy to deal with. For the hub-and-spigot type shown here, use a hammer and chisel to tamp down the soft lead that fills the joint. Don't whack the pipe hard—you could crack it. If you have the no-hub system, tightening the clamp will likely stop the leak.

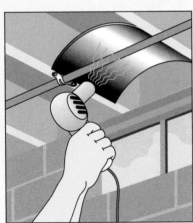

To thaw exposed frozen pipes, heat with a blow dryer...

Open the faucet the pipe supplies so any steam can escape. If it is exposed, apply heat directly with a hair dryer or a heat gun turned to its lowest setting. Move the dryer or gun back and forth—don't hold it in one spot.

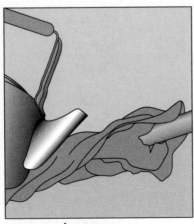

...or pour hot water.

Another solution for an exposed frozen pipe is to wrap a cloth around it, then pour boiling water over the cloth. Allow the water to cool, pour again, and repeat until the pipe is thawed. Be sure a faucet is open while you do this so steam can escape.

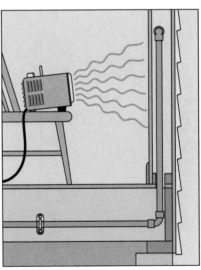

Thaw concealed pipes.

If the pipes are concealed, thawing will take more time. Open a faucet. Beam a heat lamp or electric space heater at the wall containing the pipe. Monitor closely to make sure the heat doesn't damage the wall surface.

IDENTIFYING STEM FAUCETS

When a faucet develops a leak—most often, a drip from the spout or a leak around the base—the problem is usually easy to fix. Very likely, you'll be able to purchase a repair kit for your type of faucet. Repair techniques vary from faucet to faucet, but in most cases you can easily do it yourself. When buying replacement parts, take the old unit to the store. If the faucet cannot be repaired, it is not difficult to replace it with a new one.

The first step is to identify the type of faucet you have. The anatomy drawings here and on pages 46, 48, 50, and 52 show you the various types.

The most common type is the seat-and-washer faucet, often called a compression faucet. All stem faucets have separate hot and cold controls. In its off position, the stem compresses a flexible washer on the stem into a beveled seat located in the faucet base, stopping the flow of water. As the washer wears, you have to apply more and more pressure to turn off the unit. That's when dripping usually begins.

Two newer versions are types of washerless stem faucets—cartridge and diaphragm. The cartridge type rotates rather than raising and lowering to control flow. It uses a rubber seal and O-rings. The diaphragm type uses a durable diaphragm instead of the seat washer.

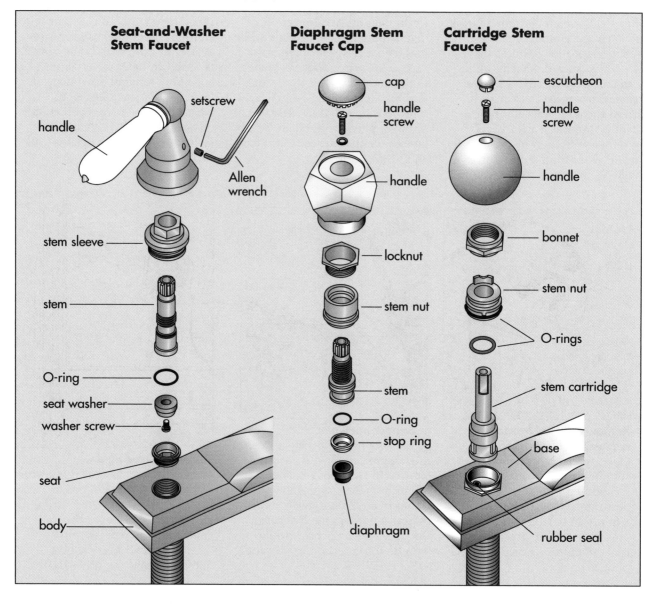

Seat-and-Washer Stem Faucet

handle — setscrew — Allen wrench — stem sleeve — stem — O-ring — seat washer — washer screw — seat — body

Diaphragm Stem Faucet Cap

cap — handle screw — handle — locknut — stem nut — stem — O-ring — stop ring — diaphragm

Cartridge Stem Faucet

escutcheon — handle screw — handle — bonnet — stem nut — O-rings — stem cartridge — base — rubber seal

PULLING OUT HANDLES AND STEMS

The first step in replacing the inner workings of a stem faucet is to pull out the handles and stems and take them to the store so you can buy proper replacement parts. If you can identify the faucet by brand name, it will be easier to find the right part. Often no brand name is visible, so you'll have to take out the stem and compare it with the drawings on pages 42, 46, 48, 50, and 52.

Note: When working on faucets, shut off the water.

YOU'LL NEED...

TIME: About 15 minutes, unless the parts are stuck.
SKILLS: No special skills needed.
TOOLS: Screwdriver, tongue-and-groove pliers, and possibly a handle puller.

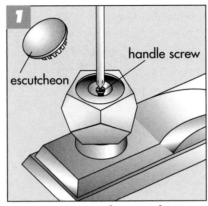

1. Remove escutcheon and screw.
If your handle is round, it is probably connected to the stem with a screw from the top. You may have to pry off an escutcheon (usually marked "H" or "C") to get to it. Some handles are attached with setscrews—see the handle on the seat-and-washer stem faucet on page 42. Remove the setscrew with an Allen wrench and pull the handle off.

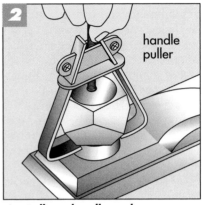

2. Pull out handle and stem.
Usually, the handle will come out if you pull it up firmly or pry it up with a screwdriver. Take care not to mar the finish on the handle. If it is really stuck, use a handle puller that grips the handle from underneath and draws the handle off the stem. Once the handle is off, unscrew the stem with pliers.

REPLACING SEAT WASHERS

Perhaps the most common plumbing repair of all is replacing a seat washer. If yours is a seat-and-washer stem faucet, the washer often becomes worn. Most commonly, there is a depression running in a ring around the washer, or the washer has begun to crumble from old age.

If a washer wears out quickly, the seat is damaged and nicks the washer every time you shut the water off, making the faucet drip (see page 53 to replace a seat).

YOU'LL NEED...

TIME: About 30 minutes, plus a trip to your supplier if you don't have the right washer.
SKILLS: No special skills needed.
TOOLS: Screwdriver.

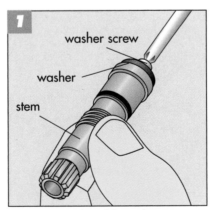

1. Remove the old washer.
Examine your washer. If it is damaged in any way, remove the washer screw and pull the old washer off. Clean away any debris or deposits from the bottom of the stem. Take your stem and old washer to your supplier if you are not sure how to select a new washer that will fit.

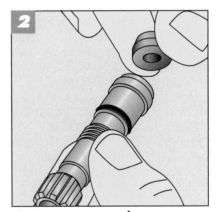

2. Insert a new washer.
Find a washer the exact same size and shape as the old one. If the old washer has been squashed out of shape, this may be difficult to determine, so double-check by slipping the new washer onto the bottom of the stem. It should fit snugly. Replace and tighten the screw, and reinstall the stem.

REPAIRING DIAPHRAGM AND CARTRIDGE STEMS

Diaphragm and cartridge stem faucets are just as easy to repair as seat-and-washer stem faucets. Often the most difficult part of the job is finding the right parts. There are hundreds of O-ring sizes. The safest way to choose is to remove the stem, take it to your supplier, and show it to a salesperson. That way, the O-rings fit the stem exactly.
NOTE: *Be sure to shut off the water before removing stems.*

YOU'LL NEED...
TIME: Just a few minutes, once you've got the right parts, the faucet handle is removed, and the stem unscrewed.
SKILLS: No special skills needed.
TOOLS: Small screwdriver or a sharp-pointed tool.

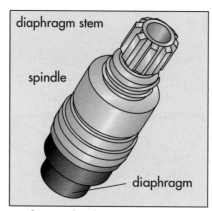

Replace a diaphragm.
Sometimes called a top hat stem, a diaphragm stem has a diaphragm that functions much like a seat washer. To replace it, simply pull off the worn diaphragm, and snap a new one on.

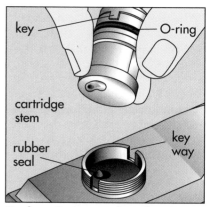

Replace O-ring, seal, and spring.
For a cartridge stem, fix leaks by replacing the seal and O-ring. Remove the rubber seal from the base of the faucet with the sharpened end of a pencil; a small spring will come out as well. Remove the O-ring by hand, or carefully pry it off with a sharp tool. Lubricate the new parts lightly with heatproof grease after you install them.

REPAIRING LEAKS FROM HANDLES

If the faucet leaks around the handle, you'll need to remove the stem to get at the source of the problem. Older faucets have packing wound around the top of the stem to keep water from seeping out the top. Don't be put off by this old-fashioned material; it is easy to replace, and new packing will last for years. Newer stems have O-rings. Once you have the stem out, inspect the rest of the faucet and replace any parts that look as if they're starting to wear out. **NOTE:** *Be sure to shut off the water.*

YOU'LL NEED...
TIME: Fifteen minutes to repack a spindle and replace an O-ring.
SKILLS: No special skills needed.
TOOLS: None.

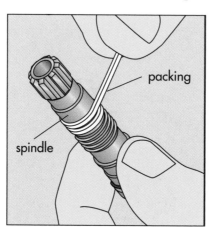

Wrap on new packing string.
If your faucet has packing wound around the spindle just under the packing nut, remove all of it and clean the spindle. Use either Teflon tape or strand packing, and wind it fairly tight. Leave just enough room so the packing nut can be screwed on when the stem is replaced.

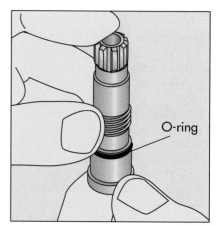

Replace the O-ring.
Newer stems have an O-ring instead of packing. Simply remove the old O-ring, and replace it with one that fits exactly. Lightly lubricate the O-ring with heatproof grease after you install it and before you reinstall the stem.

REPLACING AND GRINDING SEATS

When the spout of a stem faucet (either a seat-and-washer or a diaphragm type) leaks, be sure to inspect the seat as well as the washer or diaphragm. If the seat is pitted or scored, it is scraping the washer or diaphragm every time you turn the faucet off. It will quickly damage a seat washer, and your faucet will leak again even after you've fixed it.

If the seat is damaged, it is best to replace it. Sometimes, however, it is hard to extract the old one. In those cases, try grinding it smooth with a special tool.

You'll Need...

TIME: About 20 minutes to replace or grind a seat, once you have the part or tool.
SKILLS: No special skills needed, but you must work carefully.
TOOLS: Flashlight and seat wrench or seat cutter.

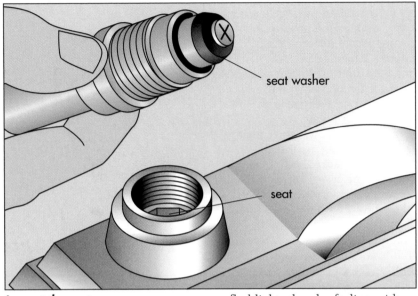

Inspect the seat.
Remove the stem (see page 42), and inspect the washer or diaphragm. If it looks cut up, the likely cause is a damaged seat. Whether the washer or diaphragm looks damaged or not, examine the seat, first by looking at it with a flashlight, then by feeling with your finger. If it appears or feels less than smooth, your washer or diaphragm will have a hard time sealing water off when you crank down on the handle. The seat needs to be replaced or ground smooth with a seat grinder.

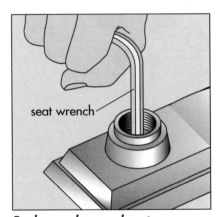

Replace a damaged seat.
Though it is sometimes possible to remove a seat with a screwdriver, this is risky—you may damage the seat so that it cannot be removed. Purchase a seat wrench, which is designed to remove seats of various sizes. Insert it into the seat, push down firmly, and turn counterclockwise. Install the new seat with the same tool.

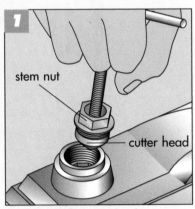

1. Use a seat grinder for a seat that cannot be removed.
Purchase a seat grinder. Slip the stem nut over the shaft of the seat grinder—it helps stabilize the grinder. Select a cutter head that fits easily inside the body and is as wide as the seat.

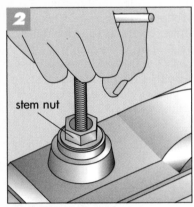

2. Rotate the grinder.
Screw the stem nut into the faucet body to hold the shaft securely without wobbling. Push down gently, and turn the handle clockwise three full rotations. Remove the grinder and inspect the seat with a flashlight. If it is not smooth, try again.

REPAIRING CARTRIDGE FAUCETS

Most washerless faucets use a combination of seals and O-rings to control and direct water. A cartridge faucet (manufactured by Kohler, Moen, Price-Pfister, and others) uses a series of strategically placed O-rings and/or seals.

In the type shown, the cartridge O-rings fit snugly against the inside of the faucet body. One O-ring forms a seal between the hot and cold supply lines. The others protect against leaks from the spout and from under the handle. On swivel-spout models, another ring protects against leaks from under the spout. Raising the handle lifts the stem so it slides upward inside the cartridge. Holes in the stem align with the openings in the cartridge in various combinations.

Other types have fewer O-rings and use other types of seals. Repair kits are available for each manufacturer and model.

When this type of faucet leaks, you can replace either the O-rings or the cartridge itself if it has corroded. Because the design is simple, repairs usually don't take long. In fact, disassembly is usually the bulk of the work, and your only problem may be finding the retainer clip that holds the cartridge in the faucet.

YOU'LL NEED...

TIME: About an hour, once you have the replacement parts.
SKILLS: No special skills needed.
TOOLS: Screwdriver, needle-nose pliers, and tongue-and-groove pliers.

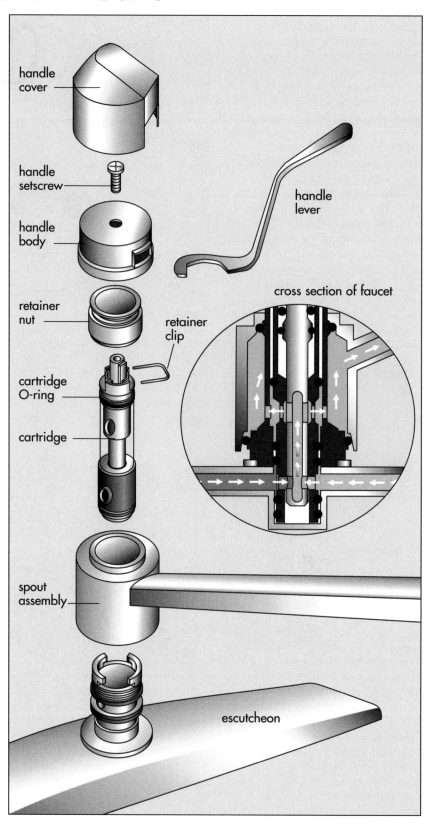

handle cover

handle setscrew

handle body

handle lever

retainer nut

retainer clip

cross section of faucet

cartridge O-ring

cartridge

spout assembly

escutcheon

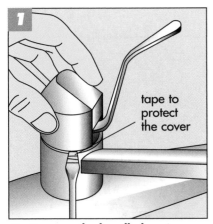

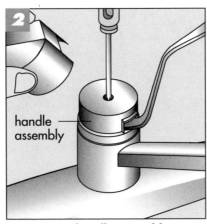

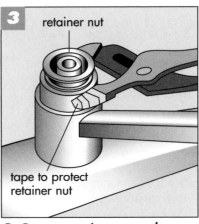

1. Remove the handle housing.
NOTE: *Shut off the water and drain the line.* Cartridge faucets vary in design from model to model, but you disassemble most of them as follows: Pry off the decorative cover that conceals the handle screw. Be careful not to crack the cover in doing so; most are made of plastic. You may need to remove an external retaining clip to get the cover off.

2. Remove handle assembly.
Cover the drain with a rag to avoid losing any small parts. Beneath the handle housing is a setscrew that holds the handle in place. Remove the handle screw, and lift off the handle body and lever. If there is no retainer nut (next step), lift out the spout.

3. Remove retainer nut and spout.
Swivel-spout models will have a retainer nut. Unscrew it, then lift off the spout.

You'll need to disassemble some models differently. Pry off the cap on top of the faucet, remove the screw, and remove the handle by tilting it back and pulling up. Then remove the plastic threaded retaining ring.

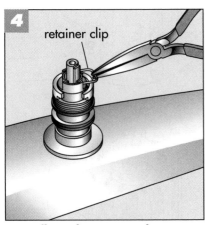

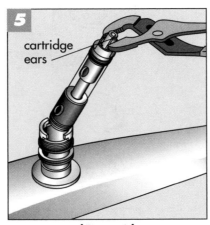

4. Pull out the retainer clip.
Depending on the model you have, you may need to lift off a cylindrical sleeve to get at the cartridge. You should now be able to see the retainer clip, a metal piece that holds the cartridge in place. Use needle-nose pliers to remove the clip from its slot. Be careful not to misplace it.

5. Remove the cartridge.
With tongue-and-groove pliers, lift the cartridge from the faucet body. Take note of the position of the cartridge ears, and be sure that when you put the cartridge back in, its ears are facing in the same direction. Otherwise, hot and cold will be reversed. If you are replacing O-rings, give them a light coating of heatproof lubricant. When reassembling the faucet, tighten firmly, but don't crank down hard—there are many plastic parts that can crack.

EXPERTS' INSIGHT

BUY QUALITY REPLACEMENT PARTS
Your local hardware store or building supply center may have replacement parts that are inexpensive but a bit flimsy. As long as you are investing a fair amount of your time in making the repair, pay the relatively small extra cost to install long-lasting parts. It usually is best to buy replacement parts made by the faucet manufacturer, rather than by a general supplier that only makes replacement parts.

If you cannot find the manufacturer's name on the faucet, remove the parts and take them to your supplier to ensure the right match.

REPAIRING ROTATING BALL FAUCETS

Inside a rotating ball faucet a slotted ball sits atop a pair of spring-loaded seals. When the handle is lowered to the "off" position, this ball, held tight against the seals by the faucet's cap, closes off the water supply. This type of faucet is often called a Delta faucet, after its primary manufacturer.

As the handle is raised, the ball rotates in such a way that the openings align with the supply line ports. This allows water to pass through the ball and out the spout. Moving the handle to the left allows more hot water to flow out; moving it to the right adds cold water.

Most leaks can be fixed by replacing the ball and gaskets in the faucet (see page 49). In addition, seals and springs can give out and need replacement.

These faucets also can spring leaks from around the handle and, with swivel-spout models, from under the base of the spout. Handle leaks indicate that the adjusting ring has loosened or the seal above the ball is worn.

Leaks from under the spout result from O-ring failure. Inspect the rings encircling the body and—on units with diverter valves for a sprayer—the valve O-ring. Replace the O-rings if they look worn.

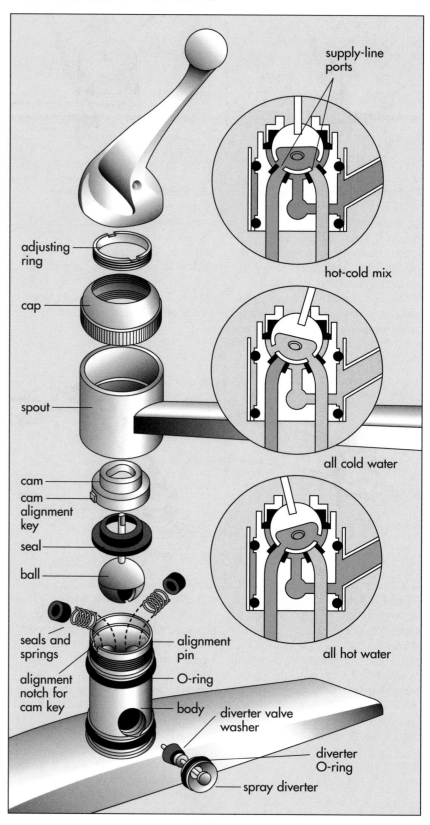

adjusting ring

cap

spout

cam

cam alignment key

seal

ball

seals and springs

alignment notch for cam key

alignment pin

O-ring

body

supply-line ports

hot-cold mix

all cold water

all hot water

diverter valve washer

diverter O-ring

spray diverter

> **CAUTION!**
> To avoid damage to flooring and walls, turn off supply lines or the main water valve.

YOU'LL NEED...
TIME: About two hours to rebuild and reassemble a faucet.
SKILLS: Patience and an eye for detail.
TOOLS: Allen wrench, adjustable pliers, wrench that comes with the rebuild kit, and awl or other sharp-pointed tool.

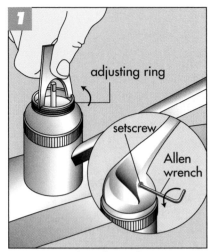

1. Remove handle and cap.
Shut off the water supply and drain the lines by lifting straight up on the handle. Using an Allen wrench, loosen the setscrew that holds the handle in place (see inset above). Loosen the adjusting ring using the wrench that comes packed with your purchased repair kit.

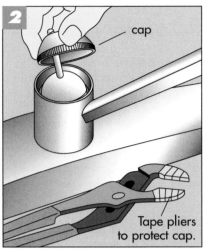

2. Disassemble cam, ball, spout.
Unscrew the cap with cloth- or tape-covered adjustable pliers. Lift out the cam assembly, the ball, and, in the case of a swivel-spout faucet, the spout. The spout fits tightly against the O-rings of the body, so it may prove stubborn. Be careful not to scratch the spout as you remove it.

3. Remove seals and springs.
To remove worn seals and springs from the body, insert a pencil into each seal to pull it out. Check for blockage at the supply inlet ports and scrape away any buildup. Then insert new springs and seals.

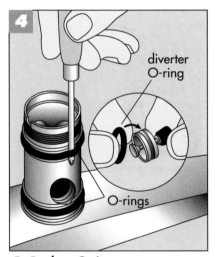

4. Replace O-rings.
If the faucet has a swivel spout, remove the O-rings by prying them away from the body using an awl or other sharp-pointed tool. Roll the new ones down over the body until they rest in the appropriate grooves. Replace the diverter O-ring in the same way. Lightly coat the O-rings and the inside of the spout with heatproof grease.

5. Reassemble.
Be sure to align the slot in the side of the ball with the pin inside the body. Also, the key on the cam assembly fits into a corresponding notch in the body. Hand-tighten the cap and tighten the adjusting ring for a good seal between the ball and the cam. If the faucet leaks, tighten further.

EXPERTS' INSIGHT

Select quality parts
Repair kits of lesser or greater quality are available for this type of faucet. Some include plastic balls; others include longer-lasting metal parts. If your hardware store only has the cheaper kit, try a plumbing supply store for a kit with longer-lasting, though more expensive, parts.

Consider a complete rebuild
When a faucet is old enough to have one part wear out, other parts will soon wear out as well. As long as you are fixing one part of the faucet, do a complete rebuild.

REPAIRING CERAMIC DISK FAUCETS

When you raise the faucet lever of a disk faucet, the upper disk in the cartridge slides across the lower disk, allowing water to enter the mixing chamber. The higher you raise the lever, the more water enters through the inlet ports of the faucet body. Moving the lever from side to side determines whether hot or cold water or a mixture of the two comes out of the spout.

The disk assembly itself, generally made of a long-lasting ceramic material, rarely needs replacing. However, the inlet ports can become clogged with mineral deposits. If this happens, simply disassemble the faucet and scrape away the crusty buildup.

If the faucet leaks at the base of the lever, one or more of the inlet seals on the cartridge may need replacing. See page 51 for how to replace the seals and the cartridge. While the faucet is dismantled, replace all of the seals. If one is worn, the others don't have long to live. Before you go to your supplier, get the brand name of your faucet from the faucet body—or take the disk assembly along. You probably can buy a repair kit with the parts you need.

> ### YOU'LL NEED...
> **TIME:** About an hour for repairs.
> **SKILLS:** No special skills needed.
> **TOOLS:** Small screwdriver and tongue-and-groove pliers.

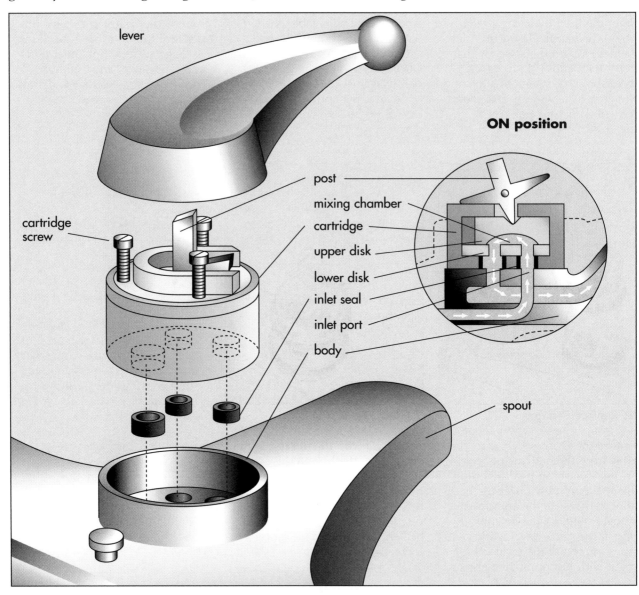

lever

ON position

post
mixing chamber
cartridge
upper disk
lower disk
inlet seal
inlet port
body

cartridge screw

spout

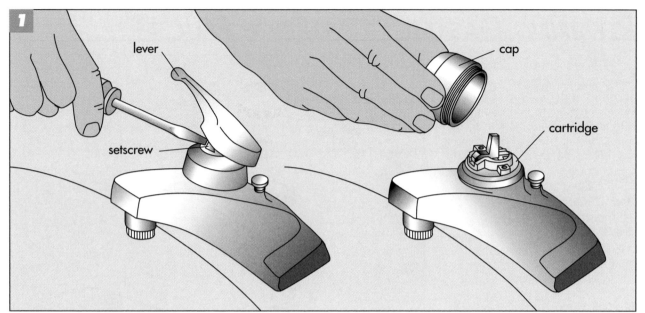

1. Remove the lever and cap.
Note: *Shut off the water.*
Under the lever you'll see a setscrew that holds the lever to the lever post. Use an appropriately sized screwdriver to unscrew the setscrew—don't try to unscrew it with a knife or you may damage it. Loosen the screw until you can raise the lever off the post. You may have to gently pry it off with a large screwdriver.

Lift off or unscrew the decorative cap that covers the cartridge. Then loosen the screws holding the cartridge to the faucet body and lift out the cartridge.

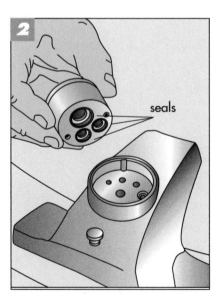

2. Remove the seals.
On the underside of the cartridge you'll find a set of seals. Pull them out with your fingers or carefully use a sharp-pointed tool, being careful not to scratch the cartridge.

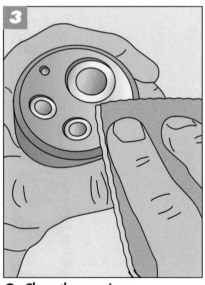

3. Clean the openings.
Check the openings for sediment buildup and clean it. Use a nonmetallic scrubber or a sponge.

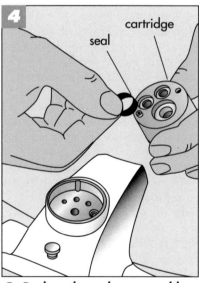

4. Replace the seals; reassemble.
Put the seals back or install replacement seals. Reassemble the faucet. Turn the water back on and test. If the faucet continues to leak after you have cleaned the cartridge and replaced the seals, install a new cartridge.

REPAIRING GASKETED CARTRIDGE FAUCETS

Gasketed cartridge faucets use a gasket with a group of openings at the bottom of the faucet cartridge to mix hot and cold water and direct water to the spout. Newer models have ceramic cartridges; older ones have plastic.

YOU'LL NEED...

TIME: About an hour, plus shopping time.
SKILLS: Basic plumbing skills.
TOOLS: Screwdriver, and tongue-and-groove pliers.

Note: *Shut off the water before disassembling.*

If you're trying to fix a leak from the body of the faucet, first try tightening the cap by hand—do not crank down on it with a wrench. If that doesn't work, disassemble the faucet and replace the two O-rings. Coat them lightly with heatproof grease.

To disassemble, pry off the escutcheon and remove the lever screw. Lift off the lever and unscrew the cap and the retainer nut. The other parts will pull out.

If you're trying to fix a drip from the spout, the cartridge probably needs to be replaced. Check the retainer nut as well. If its threads are stripped, replace it.

These parts are specific to the faucet manufacturer, so take the old parts with you when you go to the store to make sure you buy the right replacement parts.

If the faucet operates stiffly, debris may have built up in the cartridge. In most cases, it will be more trouble to clean the cartridge than it is to buy a new one and replace it.

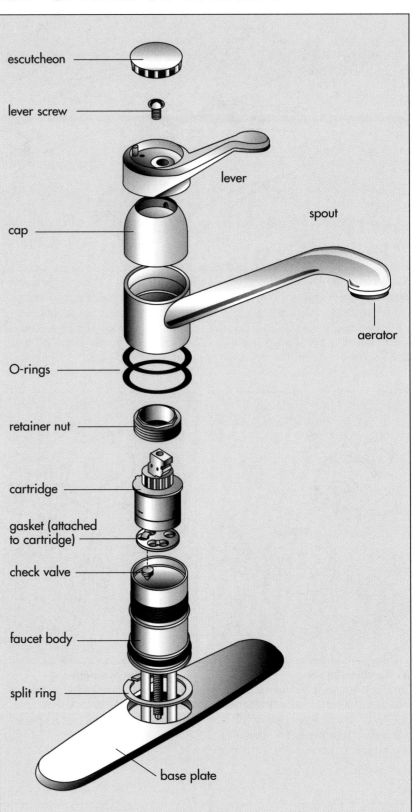

SEALING LEAKY BASE PLATES

If you find water in the cabinet below the sink, it could be from three places—the supply lines, the drain, or water leaking into the cabinet from under the faucet base plate. The problem may be solved by simply tightening the supply lines (see page 55). If the leak comes from the drain, see page 65. If neither of those is the cause, you may have a leaky base plate that allows splashed water to seep through mounting holes. Follow the steps on this page to solve this last problem.

YOU'LL NEED...

TIME: Two hours to remove, seal, and replace the faucet.
SKILLS: Basic plumbing skills.
TOOLS: Putty knife, and tongue-and-groove pliers or basin wrench.

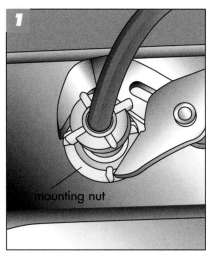

mounting nut

1. Tighten the mounting nuts.
It may be that your faucet is not held tight against the sink. Get under your sink in as comfortable a position as possible and tighten the mounting nuts. If you can't turn them with pliers, use a basin wrench. If this does not solve the problem, try Step 2.

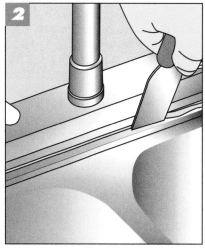

2. Loosen, stuff with putty.
First try to fix the leak without removing the faucet. Loosen the mounting nuts enough to raise the faucet base about a half inch above the sink. Scrape out any hardened gunk. Holding the base plate just above the sink, stuff plumber's putty under it evenly. Retighten the mounting nuts. If it continues to leak, proceed to Step 3.

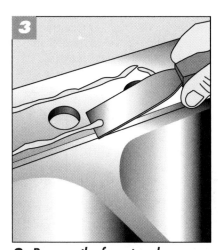

3. Remove the faucet and scrape.
NOTE: *Shut off the water and drain the line.* To entirely reseat the base plate, remove the faucet. Disconnect the supply lines, remove the mounting nuts, and pull the faucet out. Scrape any old putty away and clean the area thoroughly. Take care not to scratch the sink.

gasket

4. Replace the gasket...
If the faucet has a gasket, throw it out, and replace it with a new one. If you have trouble finding a replacement, a new gasket can be made by purchasing a piece of rubber of a similar thickness. You can use the old gasket as a pattern and cut out a new one.

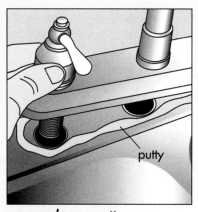

putty

...or apply new putty.
Many plumbers believe putty lasts longer than gaskets, so even if your faucet has a gasket, you may want to discard it and apply putty instead. Roll a rope of putty, about ¼ inch in diameter, and apply it to the sink or to the underside of the faucet. Reinstall the faucet, and check for leaks.

FIXING SPRAYERS, DIVERTERS, AND AERATORS

Sink sprayers can be obstructed at the connections, gaskets, and the nozzle. If your faucet has low water pressure, check the aerator. Aerators may develop leaks if their seals are worn, or they can get clogged up. See below to unclog. If water doesn't come out of the sprayer, the problem is most likely a faulty diverter valve: You can replace either the rubber seal or the diverter. Remove the diverter and take it to your supplier to be sure you get the correct replacement.

Diverters vary in shape and location, but all work in much the same way. When water isn't flowing toward the spray outlet, the valve remains open and directs the water flow toward the spout. When you press the sprayer lever, the flow of water shifts toward the sprayer head.

YOU'LL NEED...

TIME: One to two hours.
SKILLS: Basic plumbing skills and attention to detail.
TOOLS: Tongue-and-groove pliers, old toothbrush, and awl or nail.

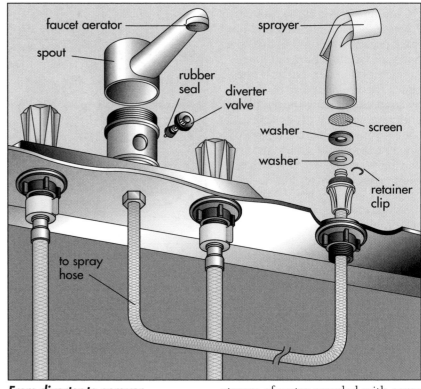

From diverter to sprayer
In a typical one-handle faucet, remove the spout to find the diverter; it's usually located in front.

If you get low or no water pressure from the sprayer, first check the hose for kinks. A slow stream of water coupled with some water coming from the spout may signal a stuck valve or a worn washer or O-ring. Replace the rubber parts or the diverter valve. Or the sprayer screen may be clogged (see below).

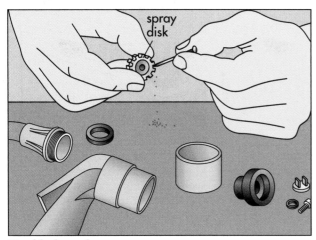

Troubleshoot the sprayer.
Minerals may be restricting the flow of water through the sprayer. Clean the spray disk with an awl or a nail as shown. Replace any worn parts and tighten all the connections.

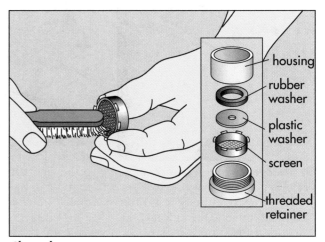

Clean the aerator.
To clean out the aerator, unscrew it from the faucet spout and disassemble it. Brush all the parts clean and soak the pieces in vinegar overnight. If it is heavily clogged, just buy a new one.

STOPPING LEAKS IN FLEXIBLE SUPPLY LINES

There are three basic types of flexible supply lines. Plain or chrome-plated copper tubing uses ferrules and nuts for connections. Flexible plastic lines use knobby ends that take the place of ferrules. Flexible supply lines—either plastic or stainless-steel-braided—use nuts preattached at each end. The last type is the easiest to use. Be sure you buy lines that are long enough.

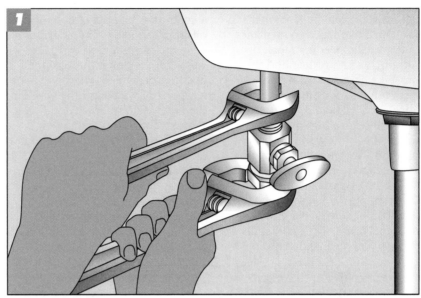

1. Tighten the nuts.
Often fixing a leak is simple—just tighten the nut at the point where you see a leak. Take care not to crank down too hard; you can crack the nut or strip the threads.

Use only adjustable wrenches, not pipe wrenches. If the leak persists, loosen the nuts and recoat the threads or ferrules with Teflon tape or pipe joint compound as shown in Step 2.

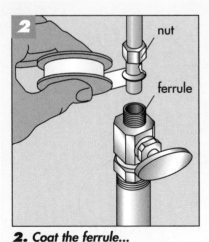

2. Coat the ferrule...
Note: *Be sure to shut off the water, and drain the line.*
If you have a tubing-and-ferrule arrangement, remove the nut and pull the line at least partway out. Take care not to kink it. Coat the ferrule with joint compound or wrap it with Teflon tape. Hook it back up, tighten, and test.

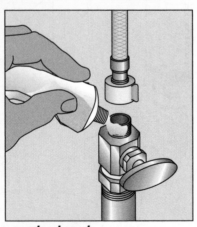

...or the threads.
If you have a plastic or braided flexible line, shut off the water, unscrew the nut, and apply joint compound or Teflon tape to the male threads of the shutoff valve or the faucet. Reconnect, tighten, and test.

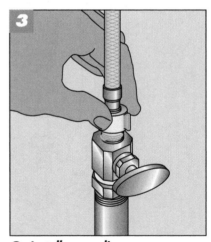

3. Install a new line.
If these measures do not solve your problem quickly, don't keep fussing with the old line. Shut off the water and remove the old supply line. Buy a new flexible line, apply Teflon tape or joint compound to the male threads, and screw the new flexible line on. Tighten both ends and test.

REPAIRING TOILETS

Because it gets used so often, your toilet has a good chance of eventually needing repair. Although some people find the prospect of working on a toilet distasteful, as long as you flush it once or twice before beginning, you will be dealing with clean water only. (If it won't flush, see page 68.) You may find some rust and sediment in the tank.

The inner parts of a toilet are fairly simple. When someone flips the flush handle, a chain reaction of events starts. The handle lifts the trip lever, which in turn pulls a chain that lifts the tank flapper off the flush valve. (In older units, a lift rod raises a tank ball.) As water rushes down through the opening into the bowl, the reservoir of water and the waste in the bowl yield to gravity and pass through the toilet's trap, down through the closet bend, and out a drain line.

Inside the tank, the float (or in older systems the float ball) descends along with the outrushing water until, at a predetermined level, the shutoff rod is attached to trips the ballcock, which is a water supply valve. At the same time, the tank flapper settles back into the flush valve, stopping water from leaving the tank. The ballcock opens to shoot a new supply of water into the tank through a refill tube and into the bowl through the overflow tube. When the float rises to its filled position, the ballcock shuts the water off.

A wax ring seals the toilet bowl to a flange on the closet bend and keeps water from leaking out onto the floor. A spud gasket seals the tank to the bowl.

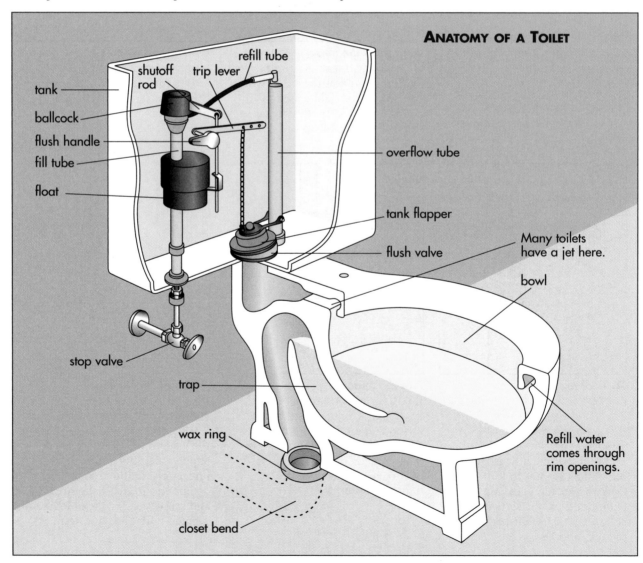

ANATOMY OF A TOILET

- refill tube
- shutoff rod
- trip lever
- tank
- ballcock
- flush handle
- fill tube
- float
- overflow tube
- tank flapper
- flush valve
- Many toilets have a jet here.
- bowl
- stop valve
- trap
- wax ring
- Refill water comes through rim openings.
- closet bend

TOILET REPAIR CHART

Symptom	Cause	Repair
Water continuously trickles or runs into tank and/or bowl (tank run-on).	Water level is too high. Flapper or tank ball isn't sealing properly. Ballcock is faulty.	Adjust trip lever chain, adjust water level in tank, or replace leaky float (see below). Clean the flush valve under the flapper, or replace worn flapper. Repair or replace ballcock.
Bowl overflows when flushed. Toilet flushes incompletely.	Trap or drain is partially clogged. Trap or bowl is clogged.	Run a toilet auger through the toilet (see page 68), or clear drain (see page 69).
Tank leaks.	Water is spraying up against the lid. Gasket between tank and bowl is faulty. Tank is cracked.	Anchor the refill tube so it sprays into the overflow tube. Replace the spud gasket. Replace the tank.
Bowl leaks. Leak appears as a wet spot on the floor.	Wax ring is not sealing. Bowl is cracked.	Pull up the toilet and replace the wax ring (see page 59). Replace the bowl.
Tank "sweats"—drops of water appear on the outside.	Condensation occurs due to difference in temperature between air and tank water.	Buy an insulation kit and install in the inside of the tank.

FIXING TANK RUN-ON

Most of a toilet's mechanical action goes on inside the flush tank, and that's where most common toilet problems develop. If water continually trickles or flows into the tank and/or bowl, start with the simplest diagnosis: The float may be rising too high, causing water to trickle down the overflow tube. If fixing that doesn't solve the problem, see if the chain is tangled or has fallen off. Check flapper and ballcock (see page 56).

YOU'LL NEED...

TIME: Five minutes to adjust the float; a half hour to adjust and clean the flush valve; one hour to replace a ballcock.
SKILLS: General mechanical aptitude.
TOOLS: Screwdriver and tongue-and-groove pliers.

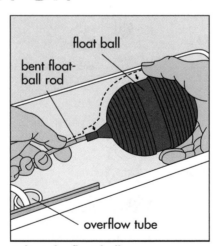

float ball

bent float-ball rod

overflow tube

Adjust the float ball.
Remove the tank lid, and look to see if the water level is too high—it should not be above the overflow tube. If it is, the water will shut off when you pull up on the float ball. Bend the rod slightly downward so the float ball sits a bit lower. With a float like the one shown on page 56, adjust the clip.

Check the float for damage.
A cracked float takes on water. When this happens, the ball won't rise enough to trip the ballcock. To check out this possibility, agitate the ball. A faulty ball will make a swishing sound. Unscrew a faulty float ball, and replace it with a new one.

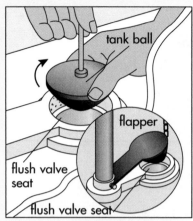

Fix a leaky flush valve seat.
If water continually trickles into the bowl, and perhaps even causes the toilet to weakly flush occasionally, the problem is probably in the flush valve. It has two parts: a flapper or a tank ball, and the flush valve seat into which the flapper or ball drops to seal the bottom of the tank while it fills. Often the seat simply needs cleaning.

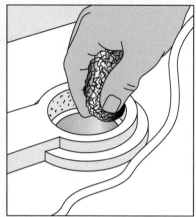

NOTE: Shut off the water to the tank, and flush the toilet to get the water out. Check the tank ball or flapper. If it has gunk on it, wipe it clean and smooth it using an abrasive pad. Once it's cleaned, feel the valve seat to see if it is pitted or corroded if it's metal. Flexible seats can be pried out and replaced. If you have a damaged metal seat, replace the entire flush valve.

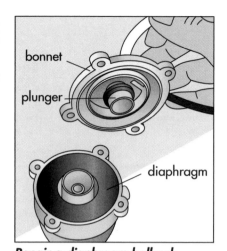

Repair a diaphragm ballcock.
NOTE: Shut off the water and flush the toilet. Remove the four screws on top of the ballcock, and lift off the bonnet. Clean out any deposits. Replace any worn parts, including the plunger. If a number of parts look worn, replace the entire ballcock.

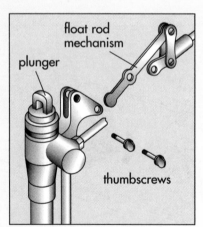

Repair a plunger ballcock.
NOTE: Shut off the water and flush the toilet. This is the oldest type of ballcock, and there are a number of parts that can go bad. You may need to replace it with either a diaphragm or float-cup ballcock. But first try cleaning and replacing the washers.

Remove the thumbscrews holding the float rod mechanism

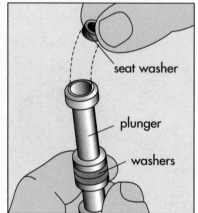

in place, then lift it out and set it aside. Remove the plunger by pulling up on it. Typically you'll find a seat washer as well as a couple of other washers. (In very old models, you may even find leather washers.) Remove and replace all of the washers, reassemble the mechanism, and turn the water back on.

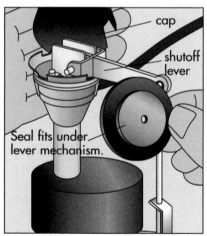

Repair a float-cup ballcock.
NOTE: Shut off the water and flush the toilet. This is the newest and the simplest design, and it rarely acts up. Pry off the cap, then remove the bonnet by lifting the shutoff lever on the float rod mechanism, pushing the mechanism down, and twisting counterclockwise firmly. Clean out any gunk, and replace the seal if it looks worn.

FIXING LEAKY TANKS AND BOWLS

Puddling of water on the floor near the toilet can be fixed in several ways. On a hot, humid day, condensation dripping from the cool outside of the tank or bowl could be substantial enough to make a puddle. You can simply live with it or install rigid-foam tank insulation.

A chronic leak probably means a faulty water supply connection, spud gasket, or wax ring. Often you simply need to tighten the hold-down bolts to solve the problem. A crack in a tank can sometimes be patched from the inside with silicone sealant. A cracked bowl should be replaced.

YOU'LL NEED...

TIME: About two hours to replace a spud gasket or a wax ring.
SKILLS: No special skills, but be careful not to crack the toilet.
TOOLS: Wrenches, screwdriver, and putty knife.

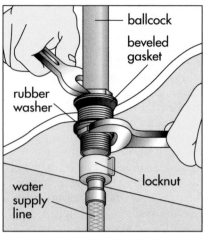

A leak at the water supply line
If the leak comes from where the water supply enters the tank, first tighten the locknut. If that doesn't work, shut off the water, flush the toilet, and sponge out the water that remains in the tank. Disconnect the water supply line, remove the locknut, and replace the old beveled gasket and rubber washer with new ones.

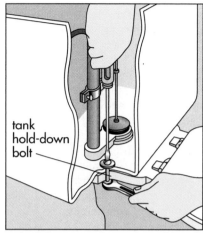

A leak between the tank and bowl
Extended use can cause the tank hold-down bolts to loosen enough to produce a leak at the spud gasket. Use a screwdriver and a wrench to tighten the bolts to squeeze the tank against the spud gasket. If the leak persists, shut off the water, flush, and sponge out any water. Detach the supply line, remove the hold-down bolts, lift out the tank, and replace the spud gasket. Reassemble.

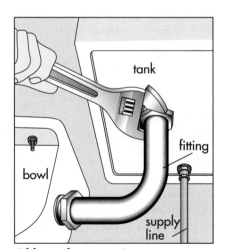

Older-style connections
With some old toilets, the tank connects to the bowl with a fitting. If leaks develop at either end of the fitting, tightening the nuts may stop the leak. If not, take the toilet apart and replace any worn parts from a plumbing supply source.

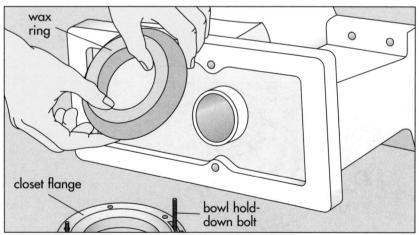

A leak at the base of the bowl
If the bowl is cracked, you'll have to replace it. If the bowl is sound, try gently tightening the hold-down nuts. If that doesn't stop the leak, replace the wax ring. Begin by shutting off the water, flushing the toilet, and sponging out any remaining water. Disconnect the water supply line, and remove the nuts on the hold-down bolts. Lift out the toilet. Scrape away the old wax ring and any old putty on the bottom of the bowl. Press a new wax ring in place according to the manufacturer's directions. Reinstall the toilet.

REPAIRING TUB AND SHOWER CONTROLS

Tub and shower controls work much the same way as sink faucets, so repairing them involves many of the same operations, except you are working horizontally rather than vertically. Also tub and shower controls are a bit more complicated because in addition to mixing hot and cold water, they must divert water either to the tub spout or to the showerhead. The drawings on these pages show the inner workings of common types.

Sometimes the parts are hard to get at. You may have to chip away at tiles in order to get your tools to the shower control parts.

If a shower control body is damaged and needs to be replaced, look at the other side of the wall to see if you have an access panel. If so you may be able to work from behind and minimize damage to your shower wall. Usually replacing a shower control body means tearing up a shower wall and retiling.

Note: Be sure to shut off the supply stop valves, built-in shutoff valves, or the main water valve before making these repairs.

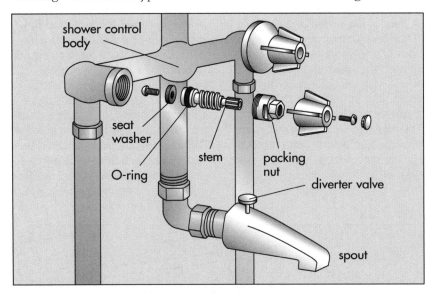

Two-handle control
The handles on these usually contain stems with washers. Each washer presses against a seat in order to shut the water off (see pages 43–52). To stop a drip, shut off the water, and remove the stem—you may have to use a special stem wrench or a deep socket, or chip away at the tiles to get at the packing nut. Replace the washer and the seat, if necessary, just as you would on a sink faucet (see page 54). If the diverter valve on the spout is not working properly, replace the spout.

Three-handle control
This type is much like a two-handle control but it has a central handle that controls a diverter valve. The valve directs water either up or down—out the showerhead or out the spout. If the diverter valve sticks or if it does not completely divert water to either the showerhead or to the spout, shut off the water and remove the valve just as you would a regular stem (see page 54). Take it apart, clean it, and replace any washers or O-rings. Or, replace the whole stem with a new one.

One-handle ball control

This type has seals and springs like ball-type sink faucets, so repairs are similar to those shown on pages 48–49. As the handle is raised, the ball rotates in such a way that its openings begin to align with the supply line ports, allowing water to pass through the ball and out the spout.

Impeded flow is usually the result of clogged orifices or worn seals. Shut the water off and remove the ball—a few ball controls have setscrews that you may have to remove to do this. Clean out the orifices, replace any worn rubber parts, and lubricate the new seals with heatproof grease.

While you have the faucet apart, check the ball for wear and corrosion; if you find either, replace the ball.

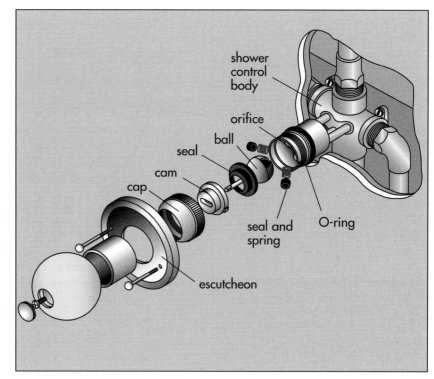

One-handle cartridge control

There are other configurations of one-handled cartridge controls besides the one shown here, so you may have to search out the location of your parts, such as the retaining clip. Parts are usually made of plastic; be careful not to crack them.

To repair a leak or limited flow, remove the handle, unscrew the retainer nut, and pull out the cartridge. Clean away any deposits and replace worn rubber or plastic parts. Lubricate all rubber parts with heatproof grease. Or simply replace the cartridge itself. When you remove the cartridge, be sure to note its original position and insert the new one the same way. If you don't, your hot and cold water will be reversed.

See pages 46–47 for more on repairing cartridge faucets.

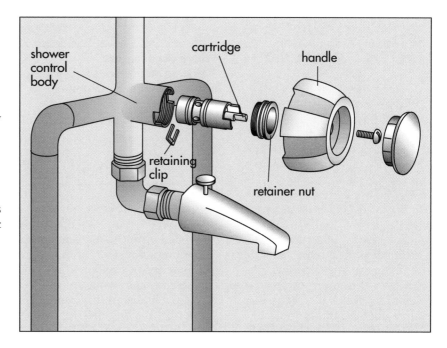

OPENING CLOGGED DRAINS

Sooner or later every homeowner encounters a clogged drain. If you hire a professional to clear it out, you will usually get a better price if you call someone who specializes in clearing drains rather than a general plumber. But it will still cost you plenty; a professional's time costs the same whether the job requires something highly specialized or something you could have done yourself.

Most clogs are not due to faulty plumbing but to the slow buildup of solids that sink drains aren't intended to cope with. Only toilets are plumbed to handle solid waste; sinks, tubs, and showers have drains designed to carry away water only. Hair, grease, soap, food scraps, and gunk will clog up a drain. With a few basic tools, you can clear most clogs and get the system flowing again.

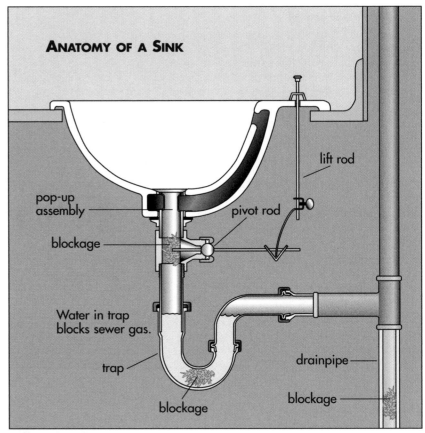

ANATOMY OF A SINK

lift rod

pop-up assembly

pivot rod

blockage

Water in trap blocks sewer gas.

trap

drainpipe

blockage

blockage

Where clogs happen
The slow buildup of soapy slime inside a drainpipe, a point of resistance such as a drain assembly, or a sharp bend in the drain can cause a clog. If a fixture is often clogged, install a strainer to keep solids from going down the drain. It will be well worth cleaning the strainer occasionally.

TOOLS TO USE

POWER AUGERS
■ For extra augering power, rent or buy a power auger or an augering attachment for a drill. The drill attachment is less expensive but not as sturdy as a power auger.
■ A high-quality tool will have a second cable that runs through the middle of the wound-wire augering cable. This keeps the auger cable from kinking, and it allows you to retrieve the auger cable if it should break. If your auger does not have this second cable and it breaks—a real possibility, especially if you are doing heavy-duty augering—you'll have a length of auger cable stuck in your pipe.

EXPERTS' INSIGHT

USING DRAIN CLEANERS
■ If your drain is completely stopped up and water is not moving through it at all, do not use a drain cleaner. It will not help the problem, and some types will actually harden if they cannot get through, making the clog worse. Drain cleaner can damage pipes, and it might splash you when you plunge or auger the drain.
■ If your drain is sluggish, use only nonacid drain cleaners (sodium hydroxide and copper sulfide are safe). Pour them in when the drain is sluggish, not when it is completely stopped. Regular use of a drain cleaner can keep the pipes clear of hair, soap, grease, and so on.
■ To maintain a smooth-flowing drain, every week or so run very hot water into the drain for a minute or two. This will clear away small amounts of grease and soap and keep them from building up.

USING SIMPLE UNCLOGGING METHODS

When a sink clogs up, first figure out where the blockage might be. It could be anywhere along the three main sections of a household drain system: in the fixture drain, in the drain stack that serves multiple fixtures, or in the main sewer line that carries waste out of the house. Usually the problem will be close to a fixture because the drain pipe and trap near a fixture are narrower than the stack and main sewer lines they tie into. To verify that the clog is near the fixture, check other drains in your home. If more than one won't clear, something is stuck in a drain stack. If no drains work, the problem is farther down the line, probably in the main sewer line.

YOU'LL NEED...

TIME: An hour or two to perform the operations shown.
SKILLS: No special skills needed.
TOOLS: Screwdriver, auger, and plunger.

EXPERTS' INSIGHT

PLUNGING SINKS WITH MORE THAN ONE DRAIN

■ When plunging a double sink, it's best to have a helper block up one of the drain holes by pressing a wet rag firmly into it, while you plunge the other drain hole.

■ A dishwasher drains through a hose into the disposal or the sink plumbing. Before plunging, use a C-clamp and two wood blocks to seal the drain hose and keep water from backing into the dishwasher.

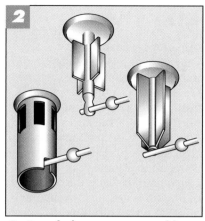

1. Clean the strainer.
Clearing a sink may involve nothing more than removing the strainer or stopper from the drain opening. Push the stopper up and pull away any soap, hair, food matter, or other debris that may clog the opening or be dangling down into the drain.

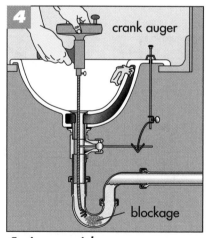

2. Detach the pop-up assembly.
The strainers in kitchen sinks and many bathroom sinks simply lift out. Others require a slight turn before they will come out. With some, you must pull out the pivot rod before the stopper will come out. If you want to auger the sink, you will have to remove the pivot rod (see below).

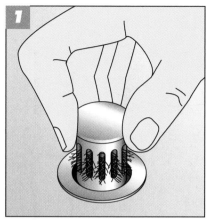

rags stuffed in overflow outlet

blockage

3. Plunge a sink.
A plunger uses water pressure to blast out obstructions and suction to bring stuff up. The plunger's rubber cup must seal tightly around the drain opening. Water in the sink helps create a seal; rubbing petroleum jelly on the plunger rim also helps. Stuff a rag into any openings, such as an overflow outlet. Push and pull rapidly with the plunger.

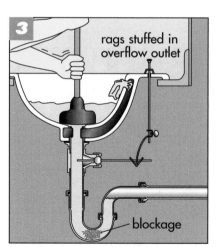

crank auger

blockage

4. Auger a sink.
If plunging doesn't work, fit an auger down the drain. Cranking the auger handle rotates a stiff spring that bores through a stubborn blockage. Augering may push blockage through, or it may snag something so you can pull it up and out. If none of these techniques works, see page 66.

DISMANTLING FIXTURE TRAPS

When plunging doesn't clear a clog, or if you've dropped something valuable into a drain, your next step is to dismantle the trap. Before dismantling the trap, see if it has a nutlike clean-out fitting at its lowest point. If so, open it, and fit the auger into the hole. If there is no clean-out, don't be discouraged. Dismantling a trap is not all that difficult or time-consuming. Usually, the worst part of the job is getting a wrench into position if the trap is in an awkward place.

YOU'LL NEED...

TIME: About an hour to dismantle and reassemble a trap.
SKILLS: Beginner plumbing skills.
TOOLS: Tongue-and-groove pliers, Teflon tape or pipe joint compound, some extra washers, and a dishpan or bucket.

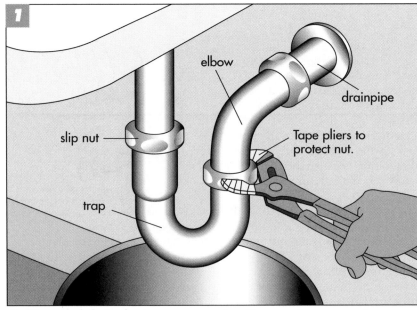

1. Open and drain the trap.
Turn off the faucet firmly. As an extra precaution, turn off the supply valves. Position a bucket to catch the water that will spill out when you remove the trap. Loosen the slip nuts that secure the trap. Protect the nuts from scratches by wrapping electrical tape around the jaws of your wrench or pliers. After a half-turn or so, the nuts can be unscrewed by hand.

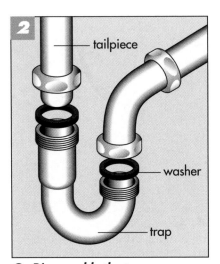

2. Disassemble the trap.
The joints of the trap have a nut and a flexible washer. Keep track of these by pushing them up the tailpiece and elbow. Dump out the water that sits in the trap.

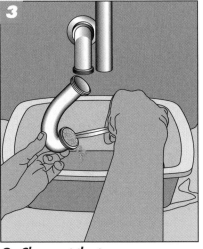

3. Clean out the trap.
Remove any gunk that has collected. Clean the inside of the trap with a small wire brush, or run a piece of cloth through it. Replace any washers that show signs of wear and slide the trap back into position.

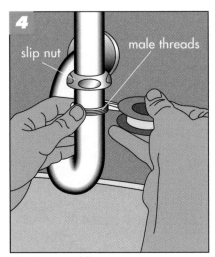

4. Reassemble.
Wrap the male threads with Teflon tape or brush on joint compound. Position trap, slide washers into place, and hand-tighten the slip nuts. Use an adjustable wrench for final tightening. Test for leaks by filling the bowl then removing the plug. Tighten slip nut if necessary.

REPLACING SINK STRAINERS

A slight leak under the sink at the tailpiece is likely the result of a poor seal between the strainer body and the sink. To check for this, plug the sink, fill the bowl, and look for drips. If water drips from where the strainer body joins the sink, disassemble the strainer and apply new putty. Leaks may also occur where the tailpiece joins the strainer body. If so, tighten the slip nut. If that does not solve the problem, replace the washer.

YOU'LL NEED...

TIME: About two hours to disassemble and reassemble a strainer.

SKILLS: Intermediate plumbing techniques.

TOOLS: Adjustable wrench (and possibly a spud wrench), putty knife, plumber's putty, and pipe joint compound or Teflon tape. You may need replacement parts.

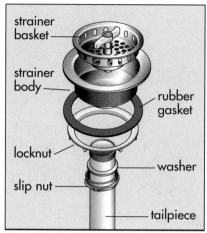

Sink strainer parts

Waste that would clog the drain is captured by the sink strainer. Its wide bowl is held snug against the sink bottom by the locknut. Putty and a rubber gasket sandwich the sink for a tight seal. The next important joint is where the strainer body meets the tailpiece. Here the seal is made watertight with a washer and a slip nut.

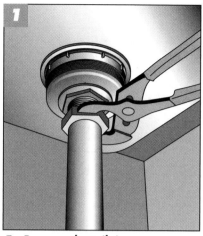

1. Remove the tailpiece.

Loosen the slip nut beneath the strainer body and the slip nut above the trap bend using an adjustable wrench. Finish unscrewing it by hand and remove the tailpiece.

2. Remove the locknut.

Removing the locknut can be difficult, especially if it is hard to get to. Consider purchasing a spud wrench, which is specially designed to fit on locknuts. Otherwise, place a screwdriver against a rib and tap gently with a hammer to loosen the nut.

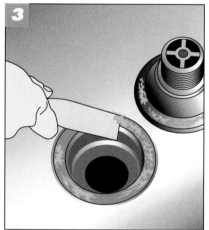

3. Remove old putty.

Use a putty knife to scrape the old putty from the drain opening. Clean the opening thoroughly with a scouring pad soaked with paint thinner. If you will be reusing the strainer, clean off the flange of the strainer as well.

4. Apply putty and reinstall.

Make a rope of putty, and place it on the lip of the drain opening. Press the strainer into the opening. From under the sink, slip on the rubber gasket and the friction ring; screw on the locknut. Tighten the locknut until the strainer nests completely into the sink. Reinstall the tailpiece.

AUGERING TECHNIQUES

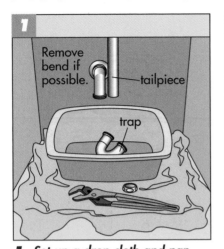

1. Set up a drop cloth and pan.
Be prepared for a mess. Place a drop cloth and a dishpan below the drain opening. Wearing gloves, remove the trap and elbow (see page 64) as well as the pipe leading to the wall. Loosen the setscrew of the auger, and push the auger cable in until you feel it meet resistance.

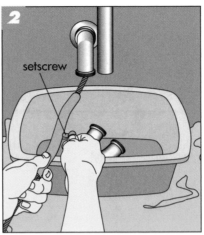

2. Set the screw and crank.
Give yourself 6 to 8 inches of cable to work with, and tighten the setscrew. Crank the auger handle clockwise, and push in until the auger moves forward. Once it is past an obstruction, like a bend in the pipe, you may be able to push the cable in without cranking.

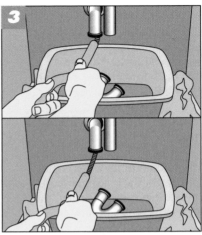

3. Push and pull.
Augers can pass through soft obstructions such as soap clogs. Use a push-and-pull motion to ream out such clogs. If the auger comes to a place where it will not crank easily, pull it out; often the blockage will come out with it. Sometimes you can use the auger to clear the line by pushing the blockage through to a larger pipe.

UNCLOGGING SHOWERS

If a shower stall drains sluggishly, try filling the base with an inch of water and plunging. If the clogged shower drain does not respond to plunging, remove the strainer and attempt to clear the blockage with the two methods shown here. Begin by prying up the strainer with a screwdriver. (Some strainers may have a center screw. Remove it, then pry up.)

YOU'LL NEED...
TIME: Allow yourself two hours to try both methods.
SKILLS: Beginner plumbing skills.
TOOLS: Auger, garden hose attached to a spout, and rags.

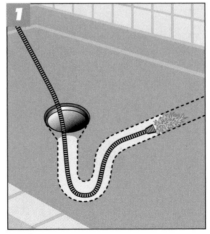

1. Run an auger.
Push an auger down the drain and through the trap. Push and pull to remove a soap clog. If the auger hits a blockage, pull out the auger. The blockage may come with it. If it doesn't, push the auger to try to force the clog into a larger pipe.

2. Push in a hose.
If all else fails, try forcing out the blockage with a hose. Stick it in as far as it will easily go and pack rags tightly around the hose at the drain opening. Hold everything in place and have a helper turn the water fully on and off a few times.

UNCLOGGING TUBS

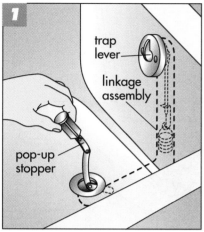

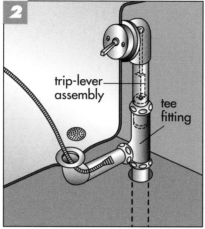

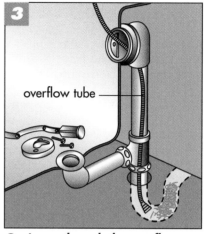

1. Plunge.
Try plunging first. If your tub has a pop-up stopper, remove it before plunging. Wiggle it to free the linkage assembly—the mechanism that connects the trap lever with the stopper mechanism. Before plunging, plug the overflow and run an inch or so of water in the tub to help the plunger seal.

2. Auger through the strainer.
If plunging doesn't work, thread in an auger. The tub will have a stopper or a trip-lever assembly like the one above. Pry up or unscrew the strainer to insert the auger. This method will reach only to the tee fitting. If the clog is farther down, you'll have to go through the overflow tube.

3. Auger through the overflow.
Remove the pop-up or trip-lever assembly by unscrewing the overflow plate and pulling out the parts. Feed the auger down through the overflow tube and into the trap and beyond. If the auger goes in a long way and the stoppage remains, find a clean-out point on the main drain and auger there.

CLEANING DRUM TRAPS

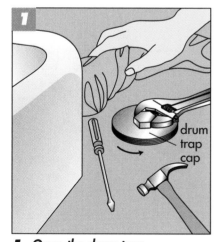

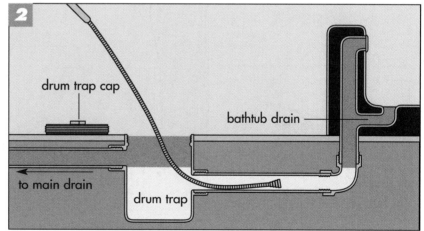

1. Open the drum trap.
Many older bathrooms have a removable metal cap on the floor, usually near the tub. This covers a drum trap. Before opening it, bail out the tub and remove standing water with rags or a large sponge.

2. Auger through the drum trap.
Removing the cap may be difficult. If a wrench does not do the trick, use a hammer and cold chisel or screwdriver. Damage the trap cap if necessary (it can be replaced easily), but don't hurt the threads on the trap. Open the trap slowly, watching for water to well up

around the threads. If the trap is full, work the auger away from the tub toward the main drain. If the trap is only partially full (as shown), the obstruction is between the tub and the trap, so auger back and forth. Drum traps are no longer to code and should be replaced with a P-trap as shown on page 66.

UNCLOGGING TOILETS

When a toilet clogs, do not continue to flush it. Additional flushing will not push objects through and may flood the bathroom floor. Instead bail out the toilet until the bowl is about half full. More water than this can lead to a sloshy mess while plunging, but too little water will prevent the plunger from making a tight seal around the bowl's outlet. Add water to the toilet if necessary. Most toilet clogs occur because the toilet trap is blocked. If plunging and using a toilet auger do not clear things up, the waste-vent stack may be blocked.

CAUTION!

Never attempt to unclog a toilet with a chemical drain cleaner. Chances are, it won't do the job, and you'll be forced to plunge or auger through a strong solution that could burn your skin or eyes.

EXPERTS' INSIGHT

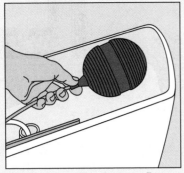

How to stop a toilet overflow

If the toilet begins to overflow, act fast. Remove everything atop the tank, and take off the lid. Pull the float up, and push down on the flapper at the tank bottom. The flush will stop.

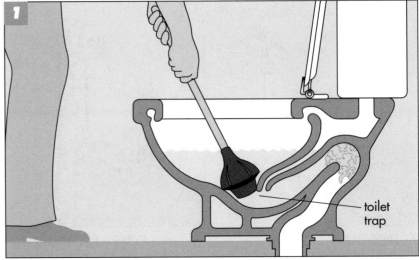

toilet trap

1. Plunge.

An ordinary plunger can clear a toilet, but the molded-cup type shown here generates stronger suction. Work up and down vigorously for about a dozen strokes, then quickly yank away the plunger.

If the water disappears with a glug, it's likely the plunging has succeeded. But don't flush yet. First pour in more water, until the bowl empties several times. If plunging doesn't work, the toilet will have to be augered.

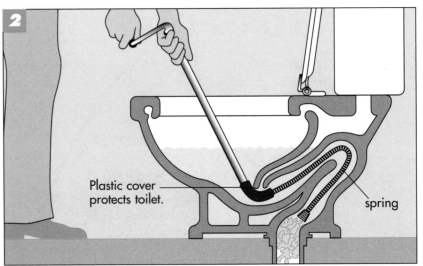

Plastic cover protects toilet.

spring

2. Use a closet auger.

A closet auger makes short work of most toilet stoppages. This specialized tool has a long handle with a plastic cover at the bend to protect your toilet from scratches. To operate the auger, pull the spring all the way up into the handle so the spring barely protrudes from the plastic

protective cover. Insert the bit into the bowl outlet and crank. If you meet resistance, pull back slightly, wiggle the handle, and try again. A closet auger can grab and pull many blockages, but not solid objects such as toys. If you hear something other than the auger rattling around, remove the toilet to get at the item.

CLEANING SHOWERHEADS

If your showerhead sprays unevenly, take it apart and clean it or replace it. If it leaks at the arm, or if it doesn't stay in position, tighten the retainer or collar nut. If that doesn't work, replace the O-ring—or replace the showerhead.

If you want to replace your showerhead, take the old one with you to your supplier to make sure you get one that will fit your pipe. You'll find a wide range of styles and features.

YOU'LL NEED...

TIME: About an hour for removal and scrubbing; overnight soaking for a thorough cleaning.
SKILLS: Basic plumbing skills.
TOOLS: Wrench, screwdriver, sharp-pointed tool or thin wire, and old toothbrush.

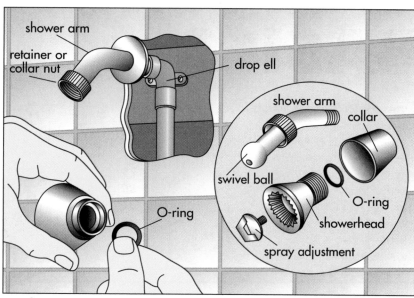

Two basic types
Newer showerheads simply screw onto the shower arm, the chromed pipe that extends from the wall. Older models require a shower arm with a ball-shaped end that acts as a swivel (see inset). In most cases you can switch to a newer style by replacing the shower arm. If you wish to replace the shower arm, remove it from the drop ell. Wrap Teflon tape around the male threads of the new shower arm before screwing it into place.

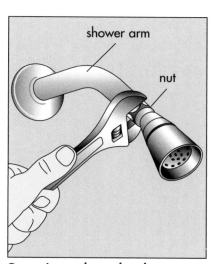

Removing a showerhead
This is a simple matter of unscrewing the nut at the shower arm. Take care not to mar the finish of the shower head or arm: Use a wrench rather than pliers. For an added precaution, cushion your wrench with a rag as you work.

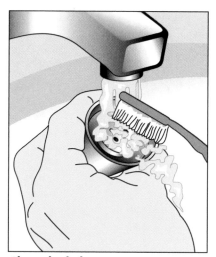

Clean the holes.
Shower heads often spray unevenly because the tiny holes have gotten clogged with mineral deposits. Use an old toothbrush to clean the head. Then run a sharp blast of water backward through the showerhead.

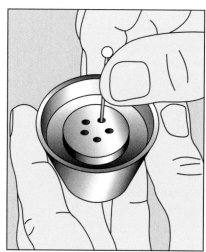

Dismantle and clean.
For a thorough cleaning, take the head apart, use a pin to poke out any mineral buildup or debris, and brush away all deposits. Then soak the parts in vinegar overnight to dissolve remaining mineral deposits. Reassemble and reinstall the showerhead.

CARPENTRY BASICS

Chapter 3

Carpentry Tools and Materials
Selecting Hand Tools *71*
Selecting Specialized Power Tools *75*
Selecting and Buying Lumber *77*
Selecting Softwoods *79*
Selecting Hardwoods *80*
Selecting Sheet Goods *81*
Selecting and Ordering Molding *83*
Selecting Nails *84*
Selecting Screws and Bolts *85*
Selecting Hardware *86*

Carpentry Techniques
Measuring and Marking *88*
Holding and Measuring in Place *90*
Squaring, Plumbing, and Leveling *91*
Cutting with a Circular Saw *94*
Using a Miter Box *96*
Making Inside and Contour Cuts *97*
Drilling *99*
Nailing *103*
Fastening with Screws *105*
Fastening with Bolts *107*
Removing Nails and Screws *108*
Gluing and Clamping *110*
Caulking and Applying Mastic *111*
Making Simple, Strong Joints *112*
Shaping and Planing *114*
Sanding *116*
Filling and Finishing *118*

Carpentry Projects
Installing Molding *120*
Installing Base Molding *121*
Installing Crown Molding *122*

SELECTING HAND TOOLS

Often, the right hand tool makes your job easier and yields better results. Hand tools are relatively inexpensive so it's easy to gather quite a collection. To avoid becoming a tool junkie who fills the basement with tools that will never be used, assemble a basic tool kit and add to your collection only when the job at hand requires a new tool.

Typically, the top-of-the-line contractor-type tool model will be of higher quality than an average homeowner needs, but inexpensive tools will not perform well. Your best choice is a mid-priced model. If you need a tool to complete an unusual task and probably won't need it very often, go with the cheaper version.

Few tools see more action than the flexible **tape measure.** Buy a 25-foot one with a 1-inch-wide blade; this will extend farther and last longer than a ¾-inch one. Some carpenters prefer a folding ruler for smaller jobs. Purchase one with a metal pull-out extension for making precise inside-to-inside measurements (see page 88).

A **framing square** (also called a carpenter's square) is used to check corners for square and to mark for rafters and stringers. More often, you'll need a smaller square. A triangular **speed square** is easy to use, allows you to quickly figure 45-degree-angle cuts, and holds its shape after getting banged around. It slips into your back pocket and is handy for quickly marking cut lines on planks and framing material. A **combination square** is helpful for scribing lines (see page 91). A **T-bevel** can be set to duplicate an angle.

Plumb and level large and small projects with a **carpenter's level.** A 2- or 4-foot model works well for most projects. A **plumb bob**

establishes true vertical lines. Snap long, straight lines with a **chalk line.** A chalk line also can double as a plumb bob.

Although you will do most of your cutting with power tools, a **handsaw** still comes in handy. You may want to choose a smaller saw that fits into a tool box. For accurate miter cuts, use a **backsaw** and **miter box.** Use a **drywall saw** to cut curves in drywall. To make rough curved cuts in wood, choose a **keyhole saw.** Cut intricate and precise curves in thin materials with a **coping saw.**

Wood chisels enable you to shape mortises and make rough notches in places where a saw will not reach. Choose chisels with metal-capped handles. Have a **utility knife** close at hand for razor-sharp cuts. Most people prefer one with a retractable blade. To shave wood along the length of a board, use a **plane** for the smoothest cut. For final shaping, use a **rasp** or a **wood file.**

Buy a **hammer** that is comfortable and solidly built. The most popular model weighs 16 ounces and has curved claws. You'll find a baffling array of specialty hammers, including framing and wallboard hammers. Stick to the basic curved-claw hammer. To sink the heads of finishing nails below the surface of the work, use a **nail set.**

Have plenty of **screwdrivers** on hand; get various sizes of both Phillips-tipped and slot-tipped types, or buy a combination screwdriver that has four tips in one tool. Make pilot holes for small screws with an **awl.**

To fasten nuts, bolts, and lag screws, use an **adjustable wrench.** For holding pieces of wood firmly, have **C-clamps** of various sizes handy. A pair of **locking pliers** helps to hold fasteners or pieces of wood tight while you work.

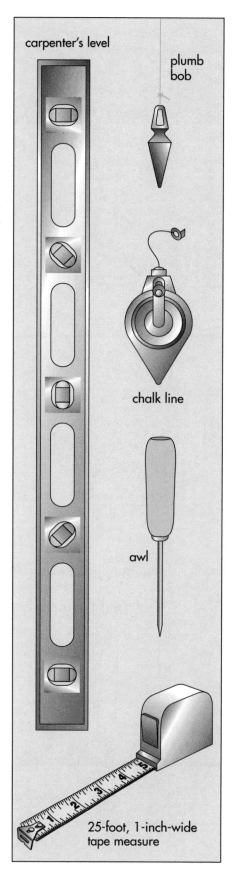

carpenter's level

plumb bob

chalk line

awl

25-foot, 1-inch-wide tape measure

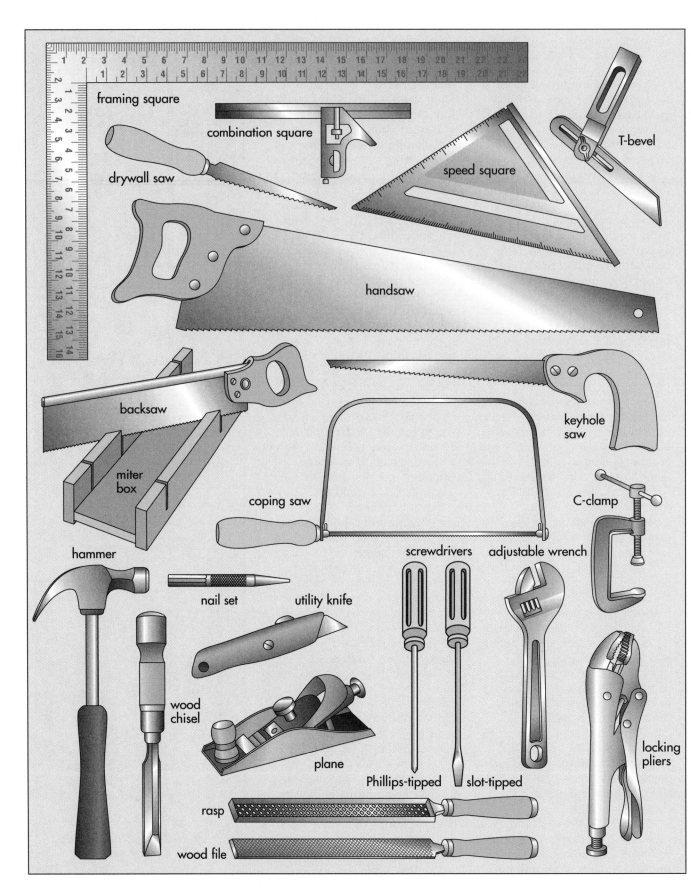

framing square

combination square

drywall saw

speed square

T-bevel

handsaw

backsaw

miter box

coping saw

keyhole saw

C-clamp

hammer

nail set

utility knife

screwdrivers

adjustable wrench

wood chisel

plane

Phillips-tipped

slot-tipped

locking pliers

rasp

wood file

Tongue-and-groove pliers are one of the most useful tools you can buy so it makes sense to pay extra for a high-quality pair. They grab most anything firmly and work well for pulling nails. **Lineman's pliers** enable you to grab things tightly from the front rather than the side of the tool and also will cut nails or screws. **Side-cutting pliers** enable you to cut nails nearly flush to the surface. They also are useful for grabbing the pointed ends of finishing nails to pull them out of the back of molding without marring the face.

A **flat pry bar** is indispensable. With it, you can pry apart fastened lumber pieces with minimal damage to the wood. It also is handy for levering heavy objects into place; for example, reattaching a door on its hinges.

A **cat's paw** (also called a nail puller) makes it easy to pull nails, although it will damage the wood (see page 108). It's indispensable if you are planning any demolition.

For patching damaged walls and for taping drywall, have a variety of sizes of **taping knives** to apply wallboard compound (see pages 144–145). If you have 6-, 8-, and 12-inch blades you will be prepared to tape or patch most any surface. If you have a lot of drywall to cut, you'll thank yourself for buying a **drywall square.** You'll find it is also very useful for marking cut lines on pieces of plywood.

Sanding large wall and ceiling areas is much easier if you have a **pole sander.** Buy a smaller sanding block for detail work (see pages 116–117).

Use a **caulking gun** to fill cracks with caulk or to apply construction adhesive. Purchase a **staple gun** to attach sheets of plastic or felt or to install fiberglass insulation batts.

A **forming tool** is easier to use than a plane for working wood, but it will not cut as straight or as smooth. It is more versatile, however, and comes in handy for fine-tuning anything from foam board to wallboard.

When you need to stabilize something that is too thick to handle with a C-clamp, use a quick-fitting **adjustable clamp.** To clamp a straightedge in place or hold thin materials that might be marred by a C-clamp (see page 72) or adjustable clamp, use a **squeeze clamp** (see page 110 for other specialized clamps).

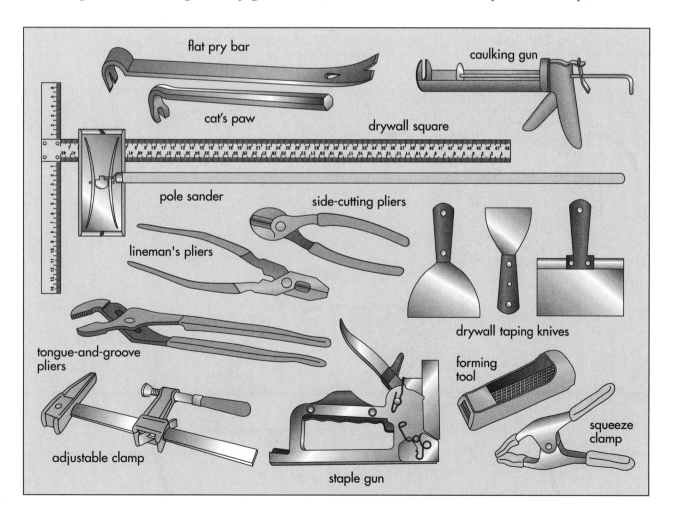

flat pry bar

caulking gun

cat's paw

drywall square

pole sander

side-cutting pliers

lineman's pliers

tongue-and-groove pliers

drywall taping knives

forming tool

adjustable clamp

squeeze clamp

staple gun

SELECTING BASIC POWER TOOLS

A circular saw, a power drill, and a sabersaw are musts for your basic tool kit. With the two saws you can make straight and curved cuts quickly in almost any material. The drill lets you make holes of almost any size and drive screws quickly and easily. With these three tools, you can handle most any household carpentry job.

A **circular saw** crosscuts, angle-cuts, rips (cuts lengthwise), and even bevels lumber easily and cleanly. Don't worry if the saw has a plastic housing; many plastics are very strong. Do take a look at the metal baseplate. A baseplate made of thin, stamped metal can warp; look for a thicker base made of extruded or cast metal. A saw that takes 7¼-inch blades is the usual choice. It lets you cut to a depth of about 2½ inches at 90 degrees and to cut through a piece of 2× lumber even when the blade is set at 45 degrees.

Horsepower is not important when choosing a circular saw. Instead, look at the amperage and the type of bearings. A low-cost saw pulls only 9 or 10 amps and runs on rollers or sleeve bearings. This means less power, a shorter life because it heats up easily, and less precise cuts because the blade wobbles somewhat. Better saws are rated at 12 or 13 amps and run on ball bearings. This combination of extra power and smoother operation makes for long life and more precise cutting. Worm-drive saws, which are the most powerful saws and have the longest-lasting bearings, are heavy and hard to use. As is often the case, a mid-priced saw is your best choice.

Be sure to get a variable-speed, reversible **power drill**. Unless you will be doing heavy-duty work, you don't need one with a ½-inch chuck; a ⅜-inch one is fine. Buy a drill that pulls at least 3.5 amps. A keyless chuck makes changing bits quick and easy, but some people prefer a keyed chuck for a tighter grip on the bit.

A **cordless drill** frees you to work without the mess of electrical cords. Buy one that uses at least 9.6 volts, preferably more. If possible, get an extra battery pack so you won't have to wait for a battery to charge.

When buying a **sabersaw**, examine the baseplate and the mechanism for adjusting it. On cheaper saws, these are flimsy and eventually wobble, making it difficult to keep the blade aligned vertically. Variable speed is a useful option. A saw pulling 3 amps or more handles most difficult jobs.

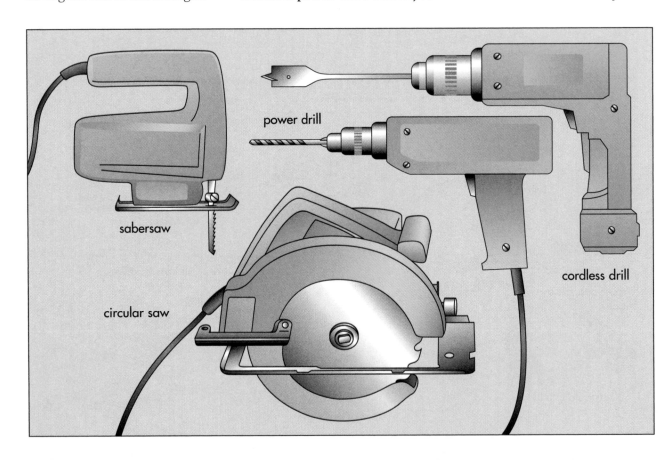

power drill

sabersaw

cordless drill

circular saw

SELECTING SPECIALIZED POWER TOOLS

The more carpentry jobs you take on, the more power tools you will need or want to own. Many of these are high-priced items, so do some careful research before making a purchase. If the tool is one you will turn to often, pay extra money to get a good-quality one that will last. If you will use it only rarely, settle for a lesser-quality tool.

To determine the quality of a tool, check the amperage rather than the horsepower. Compare models and avoid buying the one with the lowest amperage rating. A plastic housing is not necessarily a sign of poor quality. But do check any mechanisms and metal

attachments to see if they're solid. A tool with ball bearings runs smoother and lasts longer than one with other types of bearings.

For quick sanding of large areas, nothing beats a **belt sander.** Make sure it uses belts that are easily available—3×24 inches is the most common size. A good belt sander is fairly heavy and has a large dust collector. You can switch from rough to fine sanding belts; however, because a belt sander is difficult to handle for fine work, you probably will want to use another method for the final sanding—either a hand-sanding block or a smaller mechanized sander, such as a **random-orbit**

sander. It works by moving rapidly in small circles. Some people prefer the finish of an older-style vibrating sander, which simply moves back and forth. Some units switch from random-orbit to vibrating action.

With a **router,** you can mill lumber to a wide variety of shapes. If you choose a solid model with plenty of power and a base that won't warp with age, you can produce pieces that are just as straight and smooth as millwork from a factory.

If you plan a project that calls for joining two pieces of lumber side by side, a **biscuit joiner** produces professional-looking results with ease.

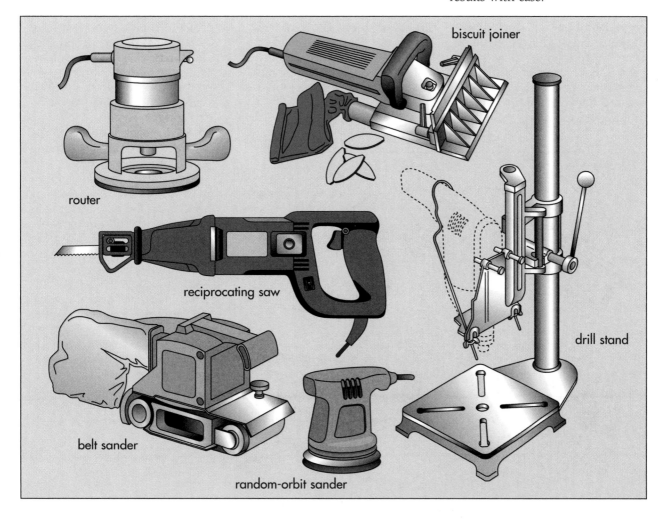

router

biscuit joiner

reciprocating saw

drill stand

belt sander

random-orbit sander

Need to drill holes that are precisely vertical? You can purchase a drill press or a **drill stand** that uses a regular power drill. A stand is less expensive than a drill press, but does take more time to set up and use.

For demolition work, nothing beats a **reciprocating saw.** It can make cuts in places where no other saw will reach. If you need to remove portions of walls or floors, this tool can save you a lot of time and frustration.

If you have to cut a lot of molding or exterior siding, consider a **power miter saw.** This tool (also called a chopsaw or cutoff saw) is simply a circular saw mounted on a pivot assembly. It makes quick, precise crosscuts and miter cuts. Make sure you get a saw large enough to cut all the way through the stock you want to cut; a 10-inch blade handles most projects. Unless you will be doing complicated framing, there is no need to buy a model that makes compound miter cuts.

Use a **bench grinder** to sharpen tools and shape wood and metal

objects. Clamp it to your work bench, and it will be ready to use at a moment's notice.

With a good **tablesaw** you can make perfectly straight, long cuts. Use it for dado cuts as well. It also works for crosscuts and miter cuts, but not as easily as a power miter saw. Choose a model that has a solid table that will not wiggle as you work on it, a fence that stays firmly in place, and a powerful motor. Keep in mind that you will need a good deal of room in your shop if you are going to use a tablesaw to cut sheets of plywood or long pieces of lumber.

A **radial-arm saw** is a general-purpose power saw. It makes long cuts like a tablesaw and crosscuts and miter cuts like a power miter saw. But like many multipurpose tools, it takes more time to do the job with it than with more specialized tools. Homeowners with limited space and funds, however, find this tool works quite well for a variety of cutting jobs; others prefer to buy the more specialized tools.

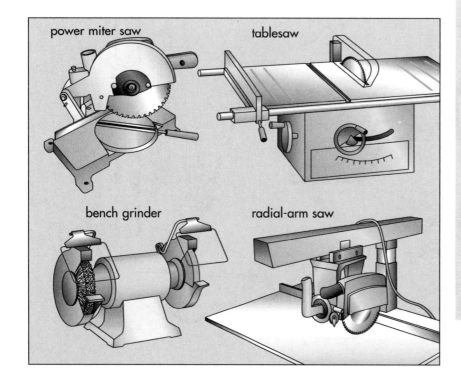

power miter saw

tablesaw

bench grinder

radial-arm saw

SELECTING AND BUYING LUMBER

As you learn carpentry techniques, it's important to become familiar with the characteristics and uses of various types of lumber and how to choose the wood that will work best for a particular project.

There are two basic types of lumber—softwoods, typically made from coniferous trees, and hardwoods, made from deciduous trees. Wood is graded according to how many knots it has and the quality of its surface (see the chart below for the most common grades). Some lumberyards have their own grading systems, but they usually simply rename these standard grades.

No matter what species of lumber you buy, be on the lookout for the types of wood problems shown at *right*. A board that is heavily **twisted, bowed, cupped,** or **crooked** usually is not usable, although some bows will lie down as you nail them in place. **Knots** are only a cosmetic problem unless they are loose and likely to pop out. **Checking,** which is a rift in the surface, also is only cosmetic. **Splits** cannot be repaired and will widen in time. Cut them off.

The nominal dimensions of wood are used when ordering lumber. Keep in mind that the actual dimensions of the lumber will be less (see the chart on page 78). Large quantities of lumber are sometimes figured by the board foot. A board foot is the wood equivalent of a piece 12 nominal inches square and 1 inch thick (see chart at *bottom*). Most lumberyards will not require you to figure board feet.

SOME COMMON GRADES OF WOOD

Grades	Characteristics
Clear	Has no knots.
Select or select structural	Very high-quality wood. Broken down into Nos. 1–3 or grades A–D; the lower grades will have more knots.
No. 2 common	Has tight knots, no major blemishes; good for shelving.
No. 3 common	Some knots may be loose, often blemished or damaged.
Construction or standard	Good strength; used for general framing.
Utility	Economy grade used for rough framing.

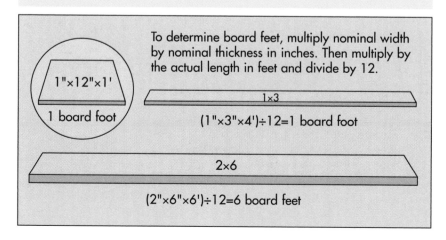

To determine board feet, multiply nominal width by nominal thickness in inches. Then multiply by the actual length in feet and divide by 12.

1"×12"×1'
1 board foot

1×3
(1"×3"×4')÷12=1 board foot

2×6
(2"×6"×6')÷12=6 board feet

LUMBER SELECTOR

Type	Description and Uses	Nominal Sizes	Actual Sizes
Furring	Rough wood of small dimensions. For furring drywall and paneling, interior and exterior trim, shimming, stakes, crates, light-duty frames, latticework, and edging.	1×2 1×3	$3/4 \times 1 1/2$ $3/4 \times 2 1/2$
Finish lumber	Smooth-finished lumber. For paneling, trim, shelving, light framing, structural finishing, forming, siding, decking, casing, valances, cabinets, built-ins, and furniture.	1×4 1×6 1×8 1×10 1×12	$3/4 \times 3 1/2$ $3/4 \times 5 1/2$ $3/4 \times 7 1/4$ $3/4 \times 9 1/4$ $3/4 \times 11 1/4$
Tongue-and-groove	Tongues and grooves fit into each other for a tight fit. For decorative interior wall treatments, exterior siding, flooring, and subflooring.	1×4 1×6 1×8	Actual sizes vary from mill to mill
Shiplap	One edge fits on top of the other. For decorative wall treatments, siding, decking, exterior sheathing, subflooring, and roof sheathing.	1×4 1×6 1×8	$3/4 \times 3 1/8$ $3/4 \times 5 1/8$ $3/4 \times 6 7/8$
Dimensional lumber	Studs are usually 2×4, sometimes 2×6. "Planks" are 6 or more inches wide. For structural framing (wall studs, ceiling and floor joists, rafters, headers, top and bottom plates), structural finishing, forming, exterior decking and fencing, and stair components (stringers, steps).	2×2 2×3 2×4 2×6 2×8 2×10 2×12 4×4 4×6 6×6	$1 1/2 \times 1 1/2$ $1 1/2 \times 2 1/2$ $1 1/2 \times 3 1/2$ $1 1/2 \times 5 1/2$ $1 1/2 \times 7 1/4$ $1 1/2 \times 9 1/4$ $1 1/2 \times 11 1/4$ $3 1/2 \times 3 1/2$ $3 1/2 \times 5 1/2$ $5 1/2 \times 5 1/2$
Glue-laminate	Layers of dimensional lumber laid flat on top of each other and laminated into one solid piece. Used for rafters, joists, and beams. Can be stained for exposed beams.	4×10 4×12 6×10 6×12	$3 1/2 \times 9$ $3 1/2 \times 12$ $5 1/2 \times 9$ $5 1/2 \times 12$
Micro-laminate	Veneers glued together with crossing grains like plywood, only thicker. For rafters, joists, and beams.	4×12	$3 1/2 \times 11 3/8$

SELECTING SOFTWOODS

Unless you're installing major structural components, such as floor or ceiling joists, that will bear significant weight, you can't make a serious mistake when buying softwoods. In most cases, you simply want to buy the wood that looks best or is the least-expensive alternative.

Softwood usually is less expensive than hardwood (see page 80) because it comes from trees that grow faster. In general, the disadvantage of softwood is evident in its name; it actually is soft. If you use softwood for furniture and other objects that will get handled and bumped against, plan on applying a hard finish or paint. Even then, it will

not be as durable as hardwood.

Most retail suppliers stock only a few species of softwood. The chart below summarizes the chief characteristics of each. In most cases, you won't be choosing between species, but between grades of lumber. Which grade you choose depends on the nature of your project.

Softwood grading is tricky because several grading systems exist. Most often, however, you'll find two general classifications: select and common.

Use select lumber, which comes in several subgrades, for trim or cabinetry where finished appearance counts. For all other projects, common lumber will do

nicely. Common lumber is graded as No. 1, No. 2, and No. 3.

With some suppliers, you can dispense with the grades and talk about more straightforward categories, such as "clear" (without knots) and "tight-knot" (having only small knots without cracks).

Of course, the better the grade—that is, the fewer the defects—the more you pay for the product. Often, however, a better grade is only slightly more expensive. Once you gain some experience, if you sort through the lumber rack carefully, you often can find pieces that are out of their class—for instance, a piece of No. 2 common that actually could have been classified as select.

SOFTWOOD SELECTOR

Species	Characteristics	Common Uses
Cedar, cypress	Similar to redwood—only the darker wood is rot-resistant. Weak, brittle; resists warping; pleasant aroma; easy to cut.	Siding, paneling, rough trim, roof shingles and shakes, decks.
Fir, larch	Heavy, very strong, hard; holds nails well; good resistance to warping and shrinkage; somewhat difficult to cut.	Framing studs, joists, posts, and beams; flooring; subflooring.
"Hem/fir"	A general classification that takes in a variety of species. Lightweight, soft, fairly strong; warps easily; may shrink; easy to cut.	Framing, exterior fascia, flooring, subflooring, trim.
Pine	From eastern, northern, and western trees. Very light, soft, fairly weak; good resistance to warping, but with a tendency to shrink; easy to cut.	Paneling, trim (molding), flooring, cabinets.
Redwood	Durable and resistant to rot and insects if you get the darker-colored heartwood. Light, soft, not as strong as fir or Southern pine; tendency to split; easy to cut.	Exterior posts and beams, siding, paneling, decks, fences.
Southern pine	Very hard, stiff, excellent strength; holds nails well; has a tendency to crack, splinter, warp; cuts with average ease.	Framing, subflooring.
Spruce	Lightweight, soft, fairly strong; resistant to splitting and warping; easy to work.	Framing, flooring, subflooring, trim (molding).
Treated lumber	Several species can be treated—most often, fir, "hem/fir," and Southern pine are used. Green or brown color will fade in time, leaving the wood a dirty gray; extremely resistant to rot and insects.	Bottom framing plates that rest on concrete; other framing that might come into contact with water, decks, fences.

SELECTING HARDWOODS

You can buy various types of plastic-laminated products made to look like hardwood, but there is no substitute for the real thing. Hardwood flooring and trim give a home an elegance unmatched by any other product. For furniture and cabinetry, nothing quite measures up in appearance and durability.

Unfortunately, hardwood trees grow slowly, so prices tend to be higher than for softwood. But prices fluctuate widely from year to year, and often the difference is surprisingly small. Oak flooring, for example, is sometimes cheaper than softwood flooring.

The more expensive hardwoods are milled to make use of virtually every splinter of wood. Instead of the standard sizes, some hardwoods are sold in pieces of varying lengths and widths. Sometimes the boards are smooth-surfaced only on two sides (S2S), leaving the edges rough. Hardwoods may be priced by the board foot (see page 77).

Hardwood grading differs from that of softwoods. It is based primarily on the amount of clear surface area on the board. The best grade is FAS (firsts and seconds), which is the most knot-free. Select boards have defects on one side only: No. 1 Common has tiny, tight knots; No. 2 Common has larger knots.

Most lumberyards and home centers can't afford to maintain an extensive inventory of hardwood lumber and generally stock only a limited assortment of a few species. For the best selection, find a store that specializes in hardwoods. They stock or can order a wide selection of species.

EXPERTS' INSIGHT

HARDWOOD FROM MANAGED FORESTS

Concerned that your lumber may come from irreplaceable forests? The Forest Certification Resource Center lists suppliers of wood products derived from sustainable forests. You can search the FCRC's on-line data on contact it on the Internet at: http://www.certifiedwood.org/

HARDWOOD SELECTOR

Species	Characteristics	Common Uses
Birch	Hard, strong; fine-grained; resists shrinking and warping. Similar in color to maple—sometimes used as a cheaper replacement. Finishes fairly well; hard to cut.	Paintable cabinets, paneling, furniture.
Mahogany	Durable; fine-grained; resistant to shrinking, warping, and swelling. Finishes well; easy to cut. (Not to be confused with lauan mahogany, a much cheaper material that is used for veneers and plywoods.)	Fine furniture, cabinets, millwork, veneers.
Maple	Extremely hard, strong; pieces with bird's-eye or wavy grains are highly prized. Color ranges from reddish to nearly white in color. Finishes well; difficult to cut.	Flooring (basketball and bowling alley floors are made of maple), butcher blocks, veneers, millwork, and molding.
Poplar	Lightweight, soft for a hardwood; fine-grained. White to yellow-brown in color. Paints well; easy to cut.	Paintable furniture, cabinets, trim, places where a less-expensive hardwood will do.
Red oak	Hard, strong, rigid; pronounced open grain; resists warping, but may shrink if not well dried. Reddish color. Finishes well; moderately hard to cut.	Flooring, furniture, cabinets, molding, stair rails.
Walnut	Hard, heavy, extra strong; fairly pronounced, straight grain; resists warping and shrinking. Light to dark brown in color. Finishes well; cuts fairly easily.	Fine furniture and cabinets, millwork, paneling, inlays, veneers.
White oak	Hard, strong; open-grained, but not as pronounced as red oak; resists shrinking and warping. Golden color. Finishes well; moderately hard to cut.	Better than red oak for flooring—less variation in color. Millwork, molding, furniture, cabinets, stair rails, balusters.

SELECTING SHEET GOODS

Sheet goods are easy to work with and an inexpensive way to neatly cover large surface areas. For many applications, they provide the strength and appearance you need at a fraction of the cost of dimensional lumber.

Plywood is made by laminating thin layers (or plies) of wood to each other using water-resistant glue. The plies are sandwiched with the grain of each successive ply running at 90 degrees to the grain of the previous layer. This gives plywood its tremendous strength, as you will find if you try to break a piece in two. The front and back surface plies may be made of softwood, usually fir, or hardwood. A plywood face surface rated "A" is smooth and free of defects; "B," "C," and "D" faces are progressively rougher. Both faces need not be graded the same, for example, "A-C." T–111 plywood siding is made with exterior adhesive and a rough veneer.

Wood particles, sawdust, and glue are compressed and bonded together by heat to form **particleboard** and **hardboard.** This process produces a material that is hard, but easy to break. Hardboard comes in tempered (very hard) and untempered (softer) composition and is available in a variety of textures. Particleboard also comes in a variety of densities. Particleboard laminated with a plastic surface is handy for cabinet construction. **Waferboard** is made by a similar process, but with scraps of thin wood rather than sawdust, making it similar to plywood.

Drywall, sometimes called wallboard, is made of gypsum powder sandwiched between layers of heavy paper. **Cement board** is made with crushed rock and a nylon mesh.

SHEET GOODS SELECTOR

Material	Grades and Common Types	Thickness (in inches)	Common Panel Sizes (in feet)	Typical Uses
Plywood sheathing	C-D, C-D Exterior	$\frac{3}{8}$, $\frac{1}{2}$, $\frac{5}{8}$, $\frac{3}{4}$	4×8	Sheathing, subflooring, underlayment, structural supports. Tongue-and-groove and shiplap versions are available.
Finish plywood	A-B, A-C, B-C	$\frac{1}{4}$, $\frac{3}{8}$, $\frac{1}{2}$, $\frac{5}{8}$, $\frac{3}{4}$	4×8, 2×4	Cabinets, cabinet doors, shelves, soffits.
Hardwood plywood	A-A (or A-2), G1S (good one side); hardwood side sometimes labeled N	$\frac{1}{4}$, $\frac{3}{4}$	4×8, 2×4	Cabinets, cabinet doors, shelves, wall panels.
Lauan subflooring	Only one type	$\frac{1}{4}$	4×8, 2×4	Underlayment for vinyl tiles or sheet goods, backing for cabinets.
T-111 siding	Rough, with grooves variously spaced	$\frac{3}{8}$, $\frac{1}{2}$, $\frac{5}{8}$	4×8, 4×9	Exterior siding.
Waferboard	Only one type	$\frac{1}{4}$, $\frac{7}{16}$, $\frac{1}{2}$, $\frac{3}{4}$	4×8	Roof sheathing, underlayment.
Particleboard	Density of material varies	$\frac{1}{4}$, $\frac{3}{8}$, $\frac{1}{2}$, $\frac{5}{8}$, $\frac{3}{4}$	4×8, 2×4	Underlayment, core material for laminated furniture and countertops.
Hardboard	Standard, tempered, perforated	$\frac{1}{8}$, $\frac{1}{4}$	4×8, 2×4	Underlayment, drawer bottoms and partitions, cabinet backs, perforated tool organizers.
Drywall	Standard, greenboard (water-resistant)	$\frac{3}{8}$, $\frac{1}{2}$, $\frac{5}{8}$	4×8, 4×10, 4×12	Interior walls.
Cement board	Only one type	$\frac{5}{16}$, $\frac{1}{2}$	32"×60"	Backing for wall tiles, underlayment for ceramic floors.

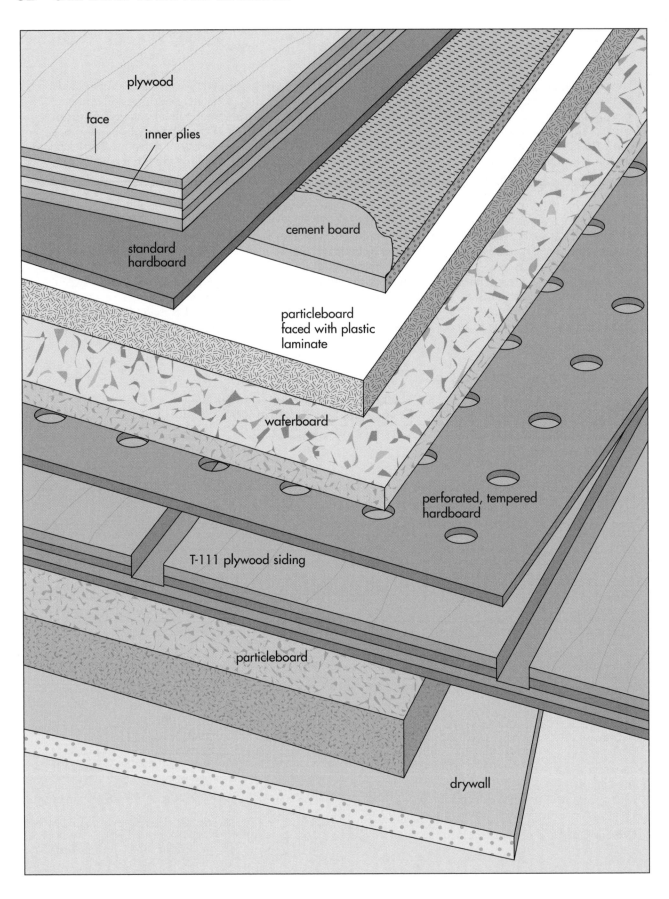

plywood

face

inner plies

standard
hardboard

cement board

particleboard
faced with plastic
laminate

waferboard

perforated, tempered
hardboard

T-111 plywood siding

particleboard

drywall

SELECTING AND ORDERING MOLDING

All rooms use at least some molding, usually along the base of walls and around windows and doors. In those places, molding covers up gaps. Other molding protects corners from dents or protects walls from damage by chair backs. In other places, such as around mantels, along the ceiling, and where paint and wall coverings meet in the middle of a wall, molding serves a decorative function. The molding you choose goes a long way toward defining the look of a room, whether it's minimalist or lushly decorative.

Molding is available in random lengths from 6 to 16 feet. Most is made of softwood, usually pine. Some popular types are available in hardwood, usually oak. These are a little more expensive.

The cost of molding does add up, so make a list of each piece you need, rounding the length up to the nearest foot, then add 5 percent to allow for trimming and fitting. See pages 120–123 for molding installation tips.

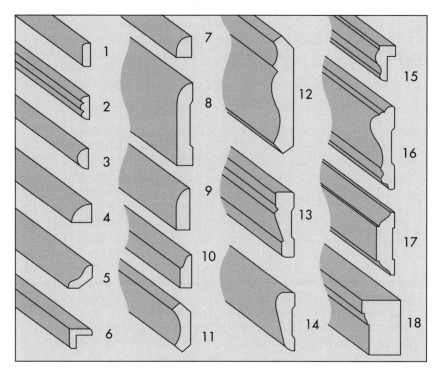

Money $ Saver

ALTERNATIVE MATERIALS

■ Finger-jointed molding is made of short pieces joined end to end. It costs less than regular molding, but you may need to sand the joints smooth.
■ Plastic molding is inexpensive, but has wood-grain finishes that may not suit your style. (Some can be painted.)
■ If you plan to paint molding rather than stain it, you may be able to save time and money with a preprimed molding.
■ Paper-covered hardboard molding also costs less, but can be difficult to cut neatly and the paper may tear later.

MOLDING SELECTOR

Common Types	Typical Uses
Screen bead; regular (1) and fluted (2)	Both cover seams where screening fastens to frames; finish edges of shelves.
Half round (3)	Serves as screen bead, shelf edging, and lattice.
Quarter round (4)	Serves as base shoe and inside corner guard.
Inside corner (5) and outside corner (6)	Both conceal seams and protect areas where walls meet at corners.
Base shoe (7) and baseboard (8)	Both trim and protect walls at their base.
Stop; ranch (9) and colonial (10)	Both attach to door jambs to limit door swing; hold inside sash of windows in place.
Cove (11) and crown (12)	Both trim and conceal joint between walls and ceilings.
Casing; colonial (13) and ranch (14)	Both trim around interior windows and doors.
Plycap (15)	Conceals plywood edge; tops off wainscoting.
Chair rail (16)	Protects walls from chair backs; hides seams where wall materials meet.
Batten (17)	Conceals vertical and horizontal panel seams.
Brick mold (18)	Used with all types of exterior cladding (not just brick) to trim around doors and windows.

Selecting Nails

Many types and sizes of nails are available, each one engineered for a specific use. The differences may seem small, but they can have a significant effect on the soundness and appearance of your job. Here's a guide to choosing among the standard types of nails:

Use **common** nails and **box** nails for framing jobs. Box nails are a bit thinner for lighter work. **Cement-coated** nails drive in more easily and hold more firmly. Use **roofing** nails for roof shingles and wherever a wide head is needed to hold material that might tear if a smaller head is used. Choose hot-dipped over electroplated **galvanized** nails; they'll last much longer.

Casing and **finishing** nails handle medium- and heavy-duty finishing work. For very fine work, use **wire brads. Ring-shank** and **spiral** nails grab wood more tightly than conventional nails. Specially hardened **masonry** nails penetrate mortar joints, brick, and even concrete. **Corrugated fasteners** are used mainly for strengthening wood joints; they do not hold well by themselves.

You can save money by buying nails in bulk, rather than in the box. However, it is handy to have boxes marked with the nail size.

MEASUREMENTS

PENNIES AND INCHES
In Great Britain in the 1400s, you could buy 100 medium-size nails for 8 pennies. It didn't take long for inflation to destroy that designation, but we use the term penny to this day to size nails. The abbreviation "d" for penny is derived from *denarius,* a small, silver Roman coin used in Britain that, from early times, equated with a penny.

Inch equivalent of nails sizes:
3d=1¼"	10d=3"
4d=1½"	12d=3¼"
6d=2"	16d=3½"
7d=2¼"	20d=4"
8d=2½"	

THE NAIL FOR THE JOB
Use nails three times as long as the thickness of the material you are fastening. For instance, to attach a 1×4 (¾ inch thick), a 6-penny nail (2 inches long) will be a bit short. An 8-penny nail (2½ inches long, a little more than three times the thickness of the 1×4) will do better. Make sure the nail will not poke through the material to which you are fastening.

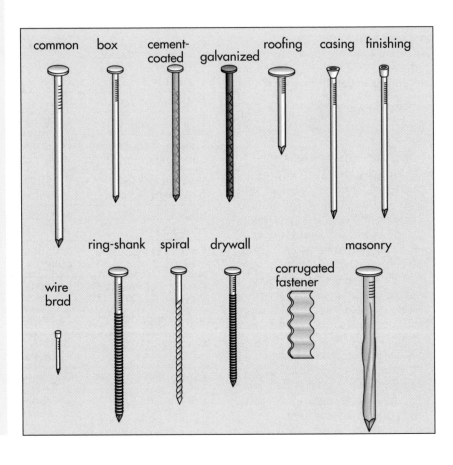

SELECTING SCREWS AND BOLTS

For the few seconds they take to drive in, nails do a remarkable holding job. Yet for the little extra time it takes to drive in a screw, you get a tighter-holding fastener, a neater appearance, and another plus—ease of disassembly. In fact, drywall screws teamed with cordless electric drills have created a mini-revolution in fasteners, including everything from deck screws to general-purpose wood screws.

The most common slot configurations for screws are the **slotted head** and the **Phillips head**, which has an X-shaped slot. **Square-drive** screws are more rare, but are growing in popularity.

There are three head shapes from which to choose. A **flathead** screw can be driven flush with or slightly below the surface of the wood. Use **ovalhead** screws with trim washers for a finished appearance. Install **roundhead** screws when you want the screw head to show.

General-purpose or **drywall** screws offer an inexpensive and easy way to fasten items together. You can buy them by the pound, and they drive easily using a drill with a screwdriver bit. **Trim head** screws use a smaller Phillips or square-drive bit. They hold better than finishing nails, but the countersink hole will be larger.

Use **masonry** screws (often referred to by the brand name Tap-Con) to fasten material to masonry or concrete surfaces. Simply drill the correct-size hole in the masonry surface and drive in the screw. Drive a **hanger** screw into a ceiling joist and fasten the object to be hung using the nut and thread on its lower half.

Use **lag** screws for heavy-duty fastening. Drill a pilot hole and drive in the screw with a wrench.

As with nails, screws should be three times as long as the thickness of the board being fastened. When buying screws, specify the gauge (diameter) you want. The thicker the gauge, the greater its holding power. Make sure you have the correct-size drill bit if drilling pilot holes (see the box at right). For more on driving in screws.

Machine bolts have a head that can be turned with a wrench. **Carriage bolts** have round heads for a finished appearance. When buying bolts, be sure to get the correct gauge and length; it must be longer than the materials you are fastening, so you can add the nut and washers. (For more on fastening with bolts, see page 107.) Thin metal can be joined with self-tapping **sheet-metal screws**.

EXPERTS' INSIGHT

DRILLING PILOT HOLES

To see if a drill bit is the correct size to make your pilot hole, grip both bit and screw together with your fingers. The bit should be slightly thinner than the width of the screw threads.

The thickness of a pilot hole can vary depending on the wood. With softwoods, you can use a smaller hole than you would with hardwoods. Always drill a test hole and make sure the screw will hold tight before you proceed to drill a number of holes in the finished material.

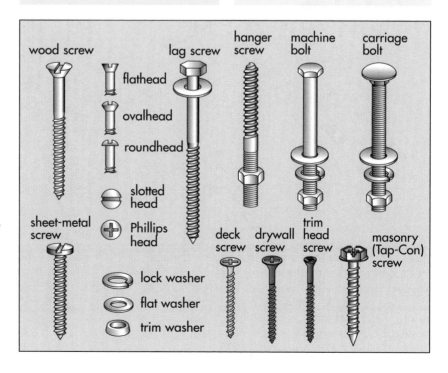

SELECTING HARDWARE

The items shown on these two pages represent just a few of the options available in specialized hardware. At your hardware store or home center, you'll find a product designed for almost every conceivable carpentry need.

When you want to strengthen a weak wood joint, reach for a metal plate or brace, as shown *below left.* **Mending plates** reinforce end-to-end joints; **T-plates** handle end-to-edge joints. **Flat corner irons** strengthen corner joints by attaching to the face of the material; **angle brackets** do the same thing, but attach to the inside or outside edges.

Shelf standards, as shown *below right,* come in a variety of configurations and finishes suitable for utility or more decorative uses. Most standards can be installed on the wall or into supports behind the shelves. Some standards can be installed on either side of the shelves. **Adjustable standards and brackets** come in a variety of colors, sizes, and finishes. Use **utility brackets** for nonadjustable shelving in places where appearance is not important. **Closet rod brackets** let you attach a shelf and a closet rod to the same piece of hardware.

There is a large choice of door and cabinet hardware, as shown on *page 87.* Most full-size doors hang on the classic **butt hinge,** *opposite.* **Piano hinges** mount flush on cabinets and chests, combining great strength with a slim, finished look. **Strap hinges** and **T-hinges** often are used on gates and trunk lids.

There are four basic types of cabinet hinges. **Decorative hinges** work only for doors that are flush with the frame. Use **front- or side-mount offset hinges** for doors that are either flush with the frame or that have lips that overlay the frame. If a door completely overlays the frame, use a **pivot hinge** or a self-closing **European-style hidden hinge.** To open your cabinet doors, fit them with **knobs** or **pulls,** available in many sizes and styles. **Friction, roller, bullet,** or **magnetic catches** keep cabinet doors closed. (If you are using self-closing hinges, these catches aren't necessary.)

For smooth-operating drawers, choose side-mounted **drawer slides** like the one shown on *page 87.* For extra household security, add a **chain lock** to your door.

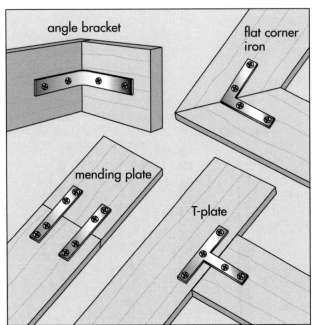

Select appropriate joint and reinforcing hardware.
For a quick and fairly permanent joint or repair, use inexpensive plates like these. For best results, clamp the material together before attaching the plates. Drill pilot holes as centered as possible; otherwise, screws may pull the joint apart as they are driven in.

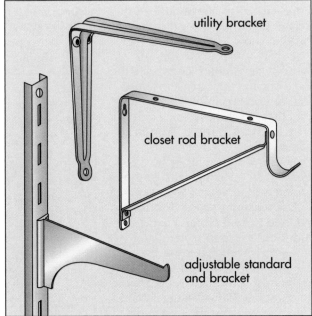

Choose from many types of shelf brackets.
If you've ever tried to make a shelf bracket out of lumber, you'll know how much time and effort is saved by these handy pieces of hardware.

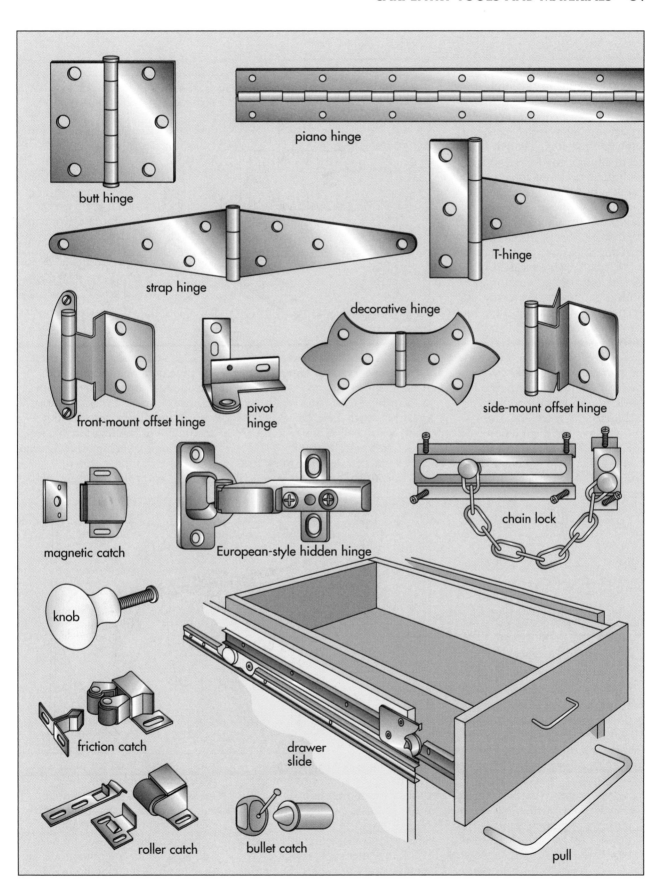

butt hinge

piano hinge

T-hinge

strap hinge

front-mount offset hinge

pivot hinge

decorative hinge

side-mount offset hinge

magnetic catch

European-style hidden hinge

chain lock

knob

friction catch

drawer slide

roller catch

bullet catch

pull

MEASURING AND MARKING

Accurate measuring and marking are the bases of successful carpentry. A mistake in measuring often means wasted time and material. Though it may seem simple, good measuring technique does not come naturally. It takes practice.

Don't rush your measuring. Take your time and double-check your work. Adopt the carpenters' maxim, "Measure twice, cut once."

No matter what measuring device you use, get comfortable with it and learn how to read it accurately. Many a board has met its ruin because someone couldn't distinguish a ¼-inch mark from a ⅛-inch mark. Once you've made a measurement, don't trust your memory. Jot down the figure on a piece of paper or a wood scrap.

Marking, not reading, the measurement is the difficulty. Make a clear mark (see page 89) using a sharp No. 2 pencil, the thin edge of a sharpened carpenter's pencil, a knife, or a scratch awl (especially if working with sheet metal).

Make a clear mark (see page 89)

EXPERTS' INSIGHT

COMPARE MEASURING DEVICES

Odd as it may seem, different measuring tapes or rulers can differ slightly—differences that will show up when dealing with long spans of lumber. This can lead to frustration if you are calling out measurements for someone else to cut. Before you accuse your partner of sloppy cutting, compare measuring devices to be sure they're calibrated the same.

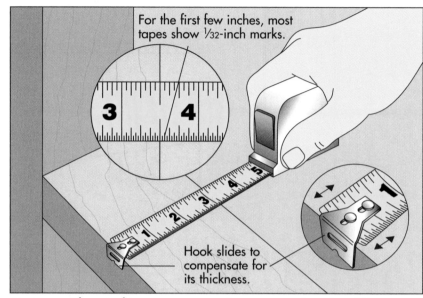

Measure with a steel tape.
A steel tape is the most popular measuring device because it does most jobs with ease. Note that the hook at the end of the tape slides back and forth slightly to compensate for its own thickness. This means that whether you hook the tape on a board end for an outside measurement or push it against a surface for an inside measurement, the result will be accurate. For the first few inches of most tapes, each inch is divided into ¹⁄₃₂-inch increments to facilitate extra-fine measurements.

For the first few inches, most tapes show ¹⁄₃₂-inch marks.

Hook slides to compensate for its thickness.

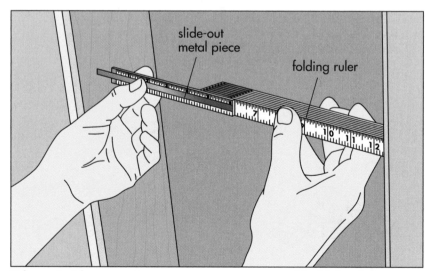

slide-out metal piece

folding ruler

Take an inside measurement.
Where outside measurement is difficult (here the drywall is in the way of measuring between the outside edges of the 2×4s) make an inside-to-inside measurement. A folding ruler with a slide-out metal piece works best. Extend it, measure, and hold the slide with your thumb until the measurement is transferred. You can use a tape measure for such measurements, but it is difficult to be accurate because you have to add an amount to compensate for the length of the tape body.

Make a V mark, not a line.

Marking with a simple line often leads to inaccuracies. By the time you're ready to saw, it's easy to forget which end of the line marks the spot—or where to cut on a thick line from a blunt pencil. For greater accuracy, mark your measurements with a V so you know precisely where to strike the cut line. To ensure pinpoint accuracy, place the point of your pencil at the V, slide the square to it, then make your line.

If you need to extend cut lines across several boards, use a framing square. For longer lines, use a drywall square.

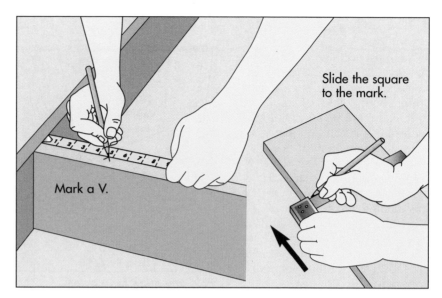

Mark a V.

Slide the square to the mark.

Mark for rip cuts.

Need to mark a cutoff line along the length of a board or a piece of plywood? If the line is parallel to the edge of the board and accuracy isn't critical, use your tape measure as a scribing device. Hold your tape so that a pencil laid against its end will make the correct line. Hold the tape and pencil firmly and pull evenly toward you, letting the tape body or your thumbnail slide along the board edge. For sheet goods, first mark the cutoff line at both ends, then snap a chalk line between the two marks, or clamp a straightedge in place and draw a mark.

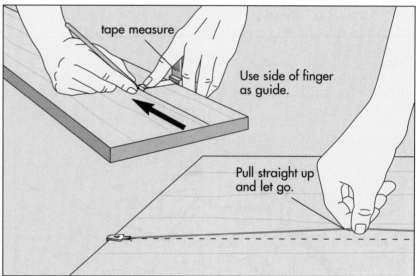

tape measure

Use side of finger as guide.

Pull straight up and let go.

Allow for the saw kerf.

When you cut material, the saw blade reduces some of it to sawdust. So, when measuring, you must allow for the narrow opening left in the blade's wake—called the kerf. Usually, a kerf is about ⅛ inch wide. If you're making just one cut, account for the kerf by marking the waste side of the cutoff line with an X. There's no confusion then as to the side of the line on which to cut.

If you are cutting multiple pieces out of the same piece of lumber, make double marks to allow for the kerf. Otherwise, you will cut each piece too short.

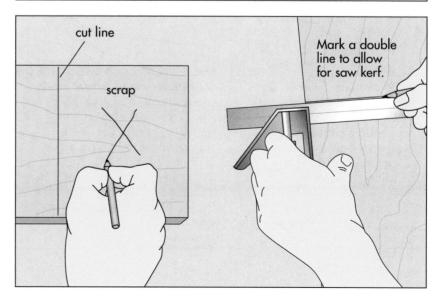

cut line

scrap

Mark a double line to allow for saw kerf.

HOLDING AND MEASURING IN PLACE

The most accurate and mistake-proof way of measuring is not to use a measuring device at all. Simply hold a piece where it needs to fit and mark it. You can do this for a simple cutoff. At other times, such as when you need to cut a board in two directions, use a combination of techniques: Hold and mark, then measure. Often this method isn't feasible, especially where access is limited or when the lumber being cut is too bulky to be held in place. But take advantage of this foolproof approach when you can.

YOU'LL NEED

TIME: Less than a minute for most measurements.
SKILLS: A steady hand and a good eye for accurate marking.
TOOLS: Pencil, speed square.

Hold this end as far out as possible— it should barely touch the board.

Hold and mark for a cutoff.
When you need to cut a board to length, begin by checking one end of the board for square. Press the square-cut end against one side of the opening, and mark the other end for cutting. To avoid distorting the measurement, don't push the square-cut end into the space any more than needed.

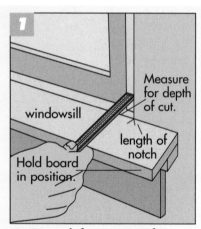

windowsill

Measure for depth of cut.

length of notch

Hold board in position.

1. To mark for a cutout, first measure the depth of the cut.
When you need to cut a board in two or three directions to make it fit around something, begin by holding the board in place. Make a small mark showing where the cutout is to be cut to length. Then measure how deep the cutout must be by measuring the distance between the leading edge of the board and the place where it must end up once it's cut.

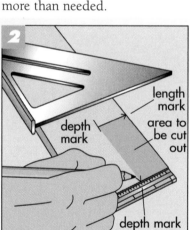
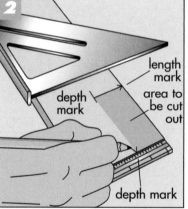

length mark

area to be cut out

depth mark

depth mark

2. Transfer measurement mark.
Use a square to extend the length mark. With a tape measure, transfer the depth measurement to two places on the board—at the length mark and at the end of the cutout. Use a square to draw a line from the length mark to the depth mark. With a straightedge, mark a line between the two depth marks.

16" mark at middle of stud location

Lay out a plate for a stud wall.
When building a wall, the studs (upright 2×4s) must be 16 inches on center; that is, you want 48- or 96-inch drywall or paneling sheets to end in the middle of a stud. To make marks for studs, mark every 16 inches, minus ¾ inch (15¼ inches, 31¼ inches, and so on). Measure over 1½ inches and make another mark. Draw lines at your marks and an X between to show stud location (see page 89).

SQUARING, PLUMBING, AND LEVELING

Most carpentry projects—from making simple shelves to building walls—require that you square the work. Check for square at every stage of your work: corners, uprights, and board ends.

Making sure that work is plumb and level is equally important. Walls, cabinets, doors—nearly every permanent installation—must be plumb (perpendicular to the earth) and level (parallel to the earth). Don't assume existing walls or floors are square, level, or plumb. Most often they are not because of imperfect construction or settling that has taken place over the years. Techniques shown in this section will help you keep your carpentry projects straight and true.

YOU'LL NEED

TIME: A couple of minutes or less to check that work is square, plumb, or level.
SKILLS: Use of squares and levels.
TOOLS: Combination, speed, framing squares; 2- or 4-foot level; other levels.

TOOLS TO USE

THE MULTIPURPOSE SPEED SQUARE

Almost every carpenter's belt contains a hammer, utility knife, pencil, and the ever-handy speed square. With a speed square, you can quickly mark 45- and 90-degree angles simply by holding the square with its body firmly against a factory edge. Other angles are marked on the body of the square and can be used with a fair degree of accuracy. In addition, the speed square is handy as a guide for cutting square corners (see page 72).

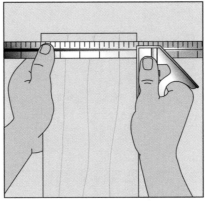

Check board ends for square.
All your careful measuring will be wasted if you start with a piece of lumber that is not square—one edge will be longer than the other. Check the board end by holding a combination square with the body or handle firmly against a factory edge. If the end isn't square, mark a square line and trim the board.

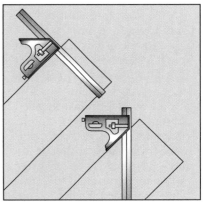

Use a combination square.
With this tool you can easily check for either 45- or 90-degree angles. Also, by sliding the blade, you can check depths. This tool can go out of square if it is dropped, so check it once in a while against a square factory edge (such as the corner of a sheet of plywood).

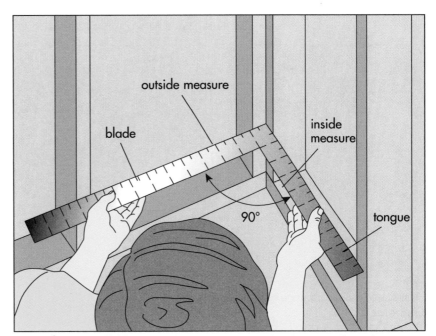

Use a framing square.
For larger jobs, use a framing square. Lay the square up against two members where they meet. If the tongue and the blade of the square rest neatly against the members, the sides are perpendicular. Or, place the square on the outside. Again, if the square touches the members at all points, the unit is square. When using a framing square for measuring, be sure to read the correct scale—inside or outside.

TOOLS TO USE

DRYWALL SQUARE

This tool, sometimes called a T-square, helps you cut drywall much faster than other tools. It is well worth its price if you need to cut a lot of drywall. It also is useful for measuring and marking other sheet goods, particularly plywood and particleboard. Because the blade is a full 4 feet long, you need make only one mark rather than two when marking for a cutoff, and you don't have to align straightedges or mess with chalk lines. A drywall square can get out of square if you're not careful with it. Take care to rest it in places where it won't get banged around. Periodically test it for square by holding it against two factory edges of a sheet of drywall or plywood.

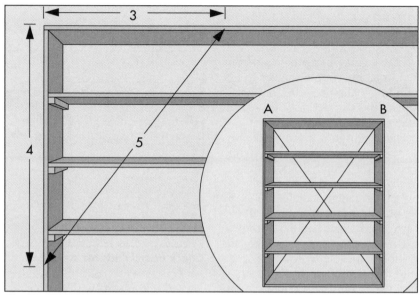

Use the 3-4-5 method.

For large projects, test if a corner is square by using geometry. You don't need to remember the Pythagorean theorem. Just remember "3-4-5." On one side, mark a point 3 feet from the corner. On the other side, mark a point 4 feet from the corner. If the distance between the two marks is exactly 5 feet, it is square. For extra large projects, use multiples such as 6-8-10 or 9-12-15.

As a double check, measure the length of the diagonals. If the project is square, the distance between two opposite corners (marked A in the drawing *above*) will equal the distance between the other two corners (B).

Check for plumb.

To see if a piece is perfectly vertical—plumb—hold a level against one face of the vertical surface and look at the air bubble in the level's lower glass vial. If it rests between the two guide marks, the piece is plumb.

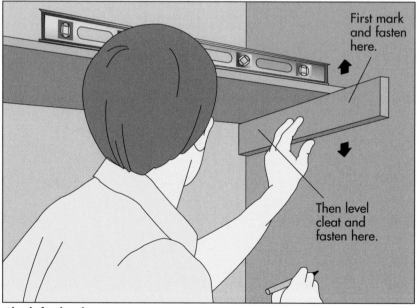

First mark and fasten here.

Then level cleat and fasten here.

Check for level.

In most cases, you can simply set your carpenter's level atop the piece to see if it's level. Raise or lower the piece until the bubble rests between the marks. Mark the position of the piece and remove the level (you don't want to risk knocking it to the floor). Add a fastener to the cleat near the level mark, level the cleat, and finish fastening.

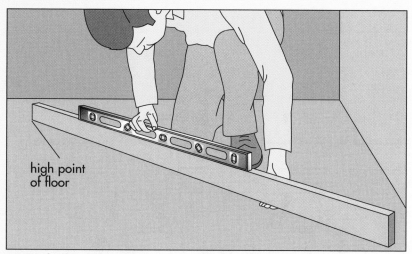

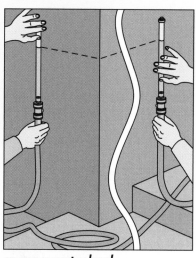

To test for level over long distances, use a board ...

If you need to see if an entire floor is level, select a long, straight board. (Sight down its length to see that it's not bowed.) Place a carpenter's level in the center of the board and raise one end or the other until the bubble is centered between the two lines. Slide the board around until you are sure you have found the high point of the floor. Level the board from this high point and measure the distance from the floor to the bottom of the raised end of the board to see how far out of level the floor is.

or use a water level.

This tool enables you to quickly check for level in awkward situations or over long distances. Basically a long hose and two transparent tubes filled with water, this tool works on the principle that water seeks its own level. Mark at water level.

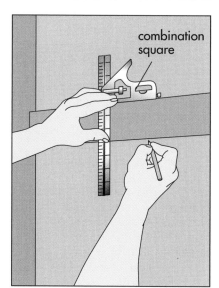

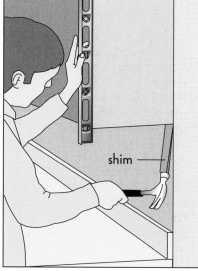

Use small levels in tight spots.

In places where you can't fit in a carpenter's level, use the level that comes on some combination squares or a torpedo level (a short version of a carpenter's level). Or, if you know that an adjoining member or wall is plumb, measure to see that the piece is square to it.

Plumb a cabinet.

When installing cabinets, make sure they are plumb in both directions or the doors will shut or open by themselves. With the cabinet fastened to the wall loosely, hold a level against a vertical framing piece. Tap in shims until the bubble indicates that the cabinet is plumb.

CUTTING WITH A CIRCULAR SAW

Chances are you will do most of your cutting with a circular saw. Whether cross-cutting 1-inch stock, ripping plywood, or cutting bricks with a masonry blade, you'll do the job better if you follow a few basic rules when using this versatile tool.

Whenever you cut, allow the saw to reach full operating speed, then slowly push the blade into the wood. Some carpenters look at the blade as they cut; others rely on the gunsight notch. Choose the method that suits you best. Avoid making slight turns as you cut. Instead, find the right path, and push the saw through the material smoothly. It will take some practice before you can do this consistently. This is a powerful tool with sharp teeth, so take care. It demands your respect.

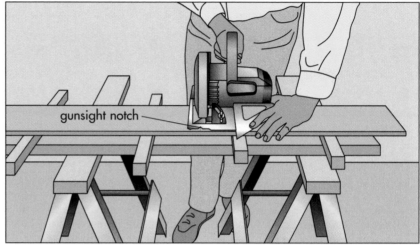

gunsight notch

Support the material properly.
Well-supported work results in clean, safe cuts. If the scrap piece is short, support the board on the nonscrap side. If the scrap is long, it could bind the blade or splinter as it falls away at the end of the cut. To achieve a neat cut and avoid saw kickback, support the lumber in four places. Even with such precautions, you may want to make two cuts: one to cut the work roughly to size, the other for the finish cut.

TOOLS TO USE

CHOOSING A CIRCULAR SAW AND BLADES

■ Choose a circular saw that is comfortable. It should have some heft, but should not be so heavy that it is difficult to maneuver. You should be able to see the blade and gunsight notch easily. Check for ease of depth and angle adjustments. (For more tips, see page 74.)

■ If you buy only one blade for a circular saw, choose a carbide-tipped combination blade that has at least 24 teeth. It works well for rough work and makes cuts clean enough for most finish work. For fine work, buy a plywood blade or a hollow-ground planer blade. For extensive remodeling jobs, get a second carbide-tipped blade that you can use when you may need to cut through nails or other rough materials.

CAUTION!
AVOIDING AND PREPARING FOR KICKBACK

It happens to even the most experienced carpenter: A blade binds, causing a circular saw to jump backward. Kickback can mar the lumber you are working on, and it is dangerous. Unsupported work often is the culprit. But also watch for these situations:

■ A dull blade will bind and cause the saw to kick. Change your blade if you have to push hard to make it cut.

■ Bending or twisting lumber will grab a blade. Sheets of plywood are particularly prone to this. Make sure it is evenly supported, like the 1× above.

■ Kickback also can occur when you back up while cutting or when you try to make a turn. If your cut is going off line, stop the saw, back up, and start again.

■ Occasionally, certain types of wood grain will grab the blade and cause a kickback. There's nothing you can do about this except be prepared.

■ Don't wear long sleeves and don't position your face near the circular saw.

falling scrap

dull blade

bending plywood

EXPERTS' INSIGHT

SET THE BLADE DEPTH CORRECTLY

Before you make any cut, check to see that the blade is set to about ¼ inch deeper than the thickness of the wood. (Be sure to unplug the saw before you do this.) This may seem like a lot of bother, especially if you are constantly switching between 1× and 2× lumber, but here's why it is worth the trouble:

■ A saw blade that extends only slightly below the material will produce a much cleaner cut than a blade that extends way below the material.

■ The deeper the blade is set, the more prone it will be to binding and kickback, jeopardizing the work and your safety.

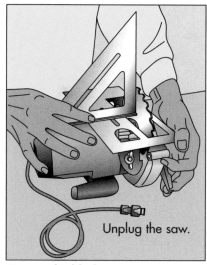

Unplug the saw.

Square the blade.
To square a blade, hold a speed square against the blade and adjust it. (Be sure to position the square between the teeth.) To test if your blade is square to the baseplate, crosscut a piece of 2× lumber. Flip the piece over and press cut edge against cut edge. If you see a gap at the top or the bottom, the blade is not square.

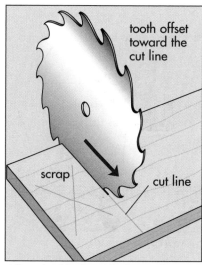

tooth offset toward the cut line

scrap

cut line

Align the blade with the cut line.
Once you have drawn an accurate cutoff line and have properly supported the board, position the saw blade to the scrap side of the line. The teeth on most circular saw blades are offset in an alternating pattern, half to the left and half to the right. When clamping a guide, align a tooth that points toward the cutoff line.

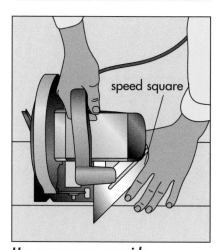

speed square

Use a square as a guide.
With practice, you will learn to cut accurately without using a guide. But for cuts that have to be precise, use a guide. For 90-degree cuts, a speed square works well because it's easy to hold stable. Align the blade, then slide the square into position against the saw's baseplate. Grab the board along with the square, so the square won't slip out of position.

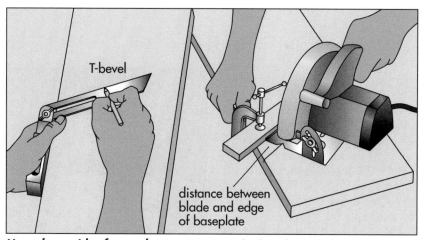

T-bevel

distance between blade and edge of baseplate

Use other guides for angle cuts.
With care, you can improvise a saw guide that will be as accurate as a miter box. Set a T-bevel to the desired angle and transfer the angle to the board.

Select a straight piece of 1× and clamp it along the cutting line as a saw guide. To offset the guide correctly, measure the distance between the blade and the edge of the saw's baseplate and clamp the guide that distance from the cut line. It may take some experimenting before you get this correct. Be sure to align the blade to the correct side of the line.

You can use the same principle for long rip cuts. Clamp a straightedge—the factory edge of a 1× or a drywall square—onto the material, setting it back from the cut line to allow for the width of the saw's baseplate.

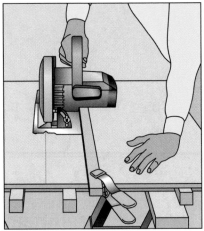

Support sheet goods.
Cut sheet goods with a carbide-tipped combination blade or a plywood-cutting blade for a smoother cut. It is important to support the sheet properly, or the blade will bind. You can do this by setting four 2× support pieces on the floor, a table, or a pair of sawhorses. Arrange two support pieces on either side of the cut line so that when the cut is complete, both pieces of the sheet are stable.

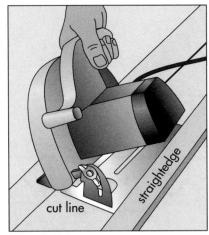

Use a guide.
Use a guide to make a straight, long cut. Get a straightedge that is as long as the material you are cutting—a straight 1×4 or the factory edge of a piece of plywood. Measure the distance from the edge of the saw's baseplate to the blade and clamp the guide that distance away from the cut line. Set the saw in place and check alignment with the cut line. Clamp the opposite end of the guide the same distance from the edge.

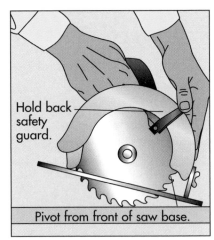

Make a plunge cut.
Use a plunge cut, also called a pocket cut, to make a hole or slit in the middle of a board or sheet. Set the blade to the correct depth. Retract the safety guard and tilt the saw forward, setting the front of the baseplate on your work. Start the saw and lower it slowly into the cut line until the base rests on the stock. Complete the cut.
Note: *Because you will be exposing the blade, any twist could result in a dangerous kickback. Be careful.*

Using a Miter Box

A miter joint is made when two pieces of wood are angle-cut or bevel-cut at the same angle then joined to form a corner. Most often, two pieces that have been cut at 45 degrees are joined to make a 90-degree corner. Miter cuts must be precise. If they are off even one degree, the corner will be noticeably out of true.

The most inexpensive way to make angle or bevel cuts in narrow stock is to use a miter box—essentially a jig for holding the saw at the proper angle to the work. If you have a lot of joinery to cut, consider buying a power miter saw (see page 76).

Before placing the piece in the miter box, support it on a scrap of 1×4 or some other suitable material. This allows you to saw completely through the work

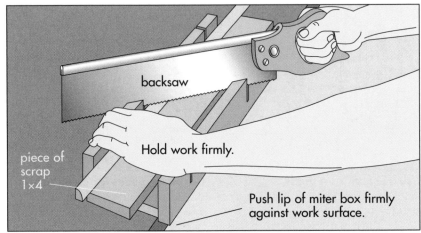

without marring the bottom of the miter box. Place the member against the far side of the miter box, positioned as it will be when in use, and make the cut with a backsaw. Hold the work firmly against the back of the box with your free hand.

If there's any trick to using a miter box, it's not in the cutting technique, but in correctly measuring and marking for the cut. Whenever possible, make your miter cut first, then cut the other end of the piece to the proper length with a straight cut.

MAKING INSIDE AND CONTOUR CUTS

Often you need to make a cut in the center of a piece of lumber or sheet goods or make a curved or irregularly shaped cut. These cuts require two basic steps. First you need to drill or plunge-cut an access hole in the material. Then you need to use a narrow-bladed tool that can handle curved cuts to follow the contours.

To begin an inside cut, you can use a circular saw to make a plunge cut (see page 96). You will need a sabersaw or handsaw to finish the job. If you find it difficult to make a precise plunge cut, use a drill and sabersaw—especially when the finished work will be highly visible.

Note: *Do not attempt to make a curved cut with a circular saw. Such a practice not only can damage your saw and saw blades, but it also can be dangerous.*

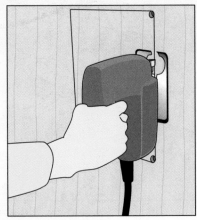

Make an inside cut.
How you start an inside cut depends on the material you're cutting. With lumber and sheet goods, the safest way is to drill a starter hole at each corner of the cutout, as close as possible to the cut lines. Insert the blade of a sabersaw or keyhole saw into one of the holes and complete the cut.

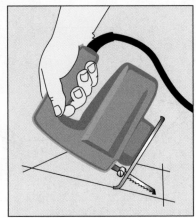

If you are experienced with a sabersaw, make a plunge cut. Tip the saw forward on its baseplate, as shown. Start the saw and slowly lower the blade into the wood along the cut line. A sabersaw blade tends to dance before cutting into the surface, which can badly mar your work. You may want to practice on a scrap of wood first.

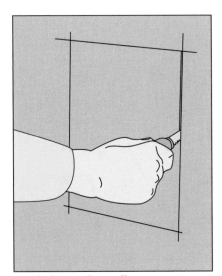

Cut holes in drywall.
For a clean cut, score the paper face of the drywall with a knife before sawing it. Poke the tip of a drywall saw (a type of keyhole saw) into the drywall at a cut line. Either push or punch the saw handle with the heel of your hand.

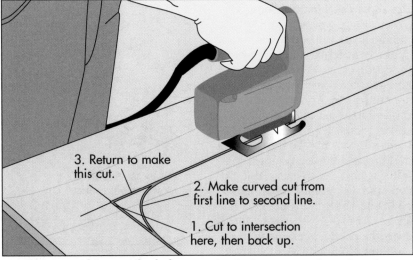

3. Return to make this cut.

2. Make curved cut from first line to second line.

1. Cut to intersection here, then back up.

Cut corners without a pilot hole.
You can maneuver a sabersaw around fairly tight corners, but don't try to make 90-degree turns. Use a three-step procedure to cut such corners. On your first approach to a corner, cut just up to the intersecting line. Carefully back the saw up about 2 inches and cut a gentle curve over to the next cut line. Continue in this direction, supporting the scrap material as you cut, until the scrap piece is free. Then go back and finish trimming the corners with short, straight cuts.

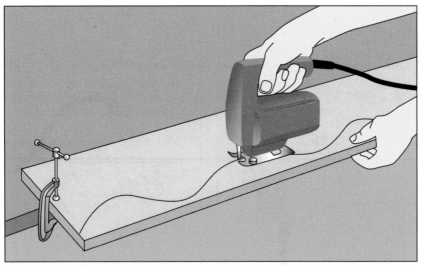

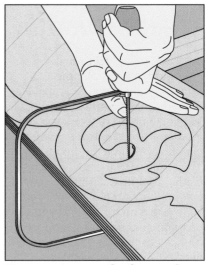

Cut curves with a sabersaw.

For most contour cuts, use a sabersaw. Once you get the knack of using this tool, you can cut curves that are as smooth as any line you can draw. Be sure the piece you are going to cut is stable; clamp it if necessary. Check that nothing is blocking the path of the blade underneath the piece you are cutting.

Turn the saw on, then begin the cut. Guide the saw slowly, without forcing the blade. One sharp turn can break a blade. If the saw begins to bog down or overheat, you're cutting too fast. If you wander from the line, don't try to make a correction with a sharp turn. Instead, back up and start again. Support the scrap material as you reach the end of each cut to prevent it from breaking off.

Use a coping saw for fine work.

For intricate cutting or scrollwork, use a coping saw. This hand tool allows you to set the blade in any direction in relation to its frame. To begin a cut from the inside of a board, remove the blade from the saw frame and reinstall it through a starter hole. For delicate cuts, install the blade with the teeth angled toward the handle so the saw cuts on the backstroke.

Use coping cuts for moldings.

When you're working with moldings, it's difficult to get perfectly matched mitered joints for inside corners, especially because the corners of walls often are not square. That's why professionals usually cope inside corner joints.

Start by cutting the first piece of molding at a 90-degree angle so it butts against the adjacent wall. To cope the overlapping piece, make an inside 45-degree miter cut, as shown. Use a coping saw to cut away the excess wood along the molding profile. Back-cut slightly (cut a little more off the back of the piece than the front) to ensure a neat fit. Whenever possible, make the cut on the coped end first, hold the piece in place, then mark for the cut on the other end.

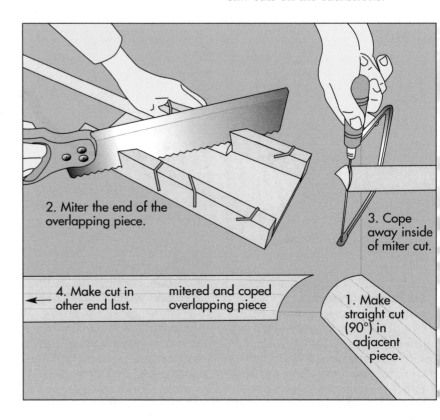

2. Miter the end of the overlapping piece.

3. Cope away inside of miter cut.

4. Make cut in other end last.

mitered and coped overlapping piece

1. Make straight cut (90°) in adjacent piece.

DRILLING

Some carpenters still haul out a brace and expandable auger bit when they can't find a spade bit of the right size. But now the electric drill usually is the tool of choice. Not only can you drill a hole of about any size with a variable-speed power drill, but you also can use a drill to drive screws into wood or metal, buff and grind, and even mix paint or mortar.

Some carpenters keep two drills on hand—one for drilling pilot holes, the other for driving screws. That way, they don't waste time changing bits. A power drill with a keyless chuck speeds up a bit change, although you may find bits slip during heavy-duty tasks.

For perfectly perpendicular holes, you'll need a drill press. But if you learn the techniques here and on the next three pages, you can bore holes that are straight enough for household carpentry.

EXPERTS' INSIGHT

CHOOSING A DRILL

■ Avoid buying a cheap drill with a ¼-inch chuck. It will not have the power you need and will soon burn out. One tipoff to a better-quality tool is the cord. Look for a long cord that flexes more like rubber than plastic.

■ A hammer drill, or a drill with a hammer option, bangs away at the material as it drills. It's useful when boring holes in concrete.

■ A cordless drill can make your work go more easily, but only if it is powerful enough to do most things that a corded drill can do.

■ Some drills are designed specifically for driving in drywall screws. These set the head of the screw at the required depth—deep enough to make an indentation, but not so deep that it damages the drywall.

■ Specialized tasks often require a high-speed drill (one with high revolutions per minute). For example, self-tapping steel stud screws (see page 136) require a drill rated to at least 2,500 rpm.

■ For heavy-duty work, choose a drill with a ½-inch chuck. This will run at fewer revolutions per minute, but will be more powerful than a standard ⅜-inch drill.

For additional information on choosing a drill, see page 74.

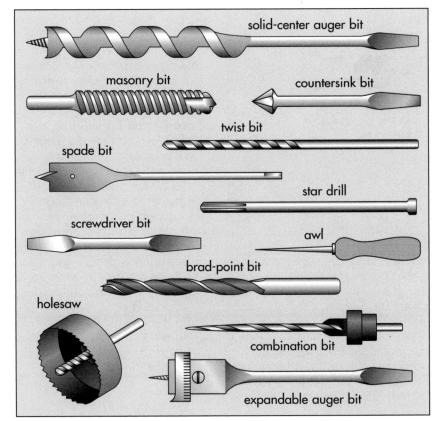

Choose the correct bit.
Shown at *left* are some of the more common drill bits. **Auger** bits, either solid-center or expandable, are designed to be used with a hand brace, as is a **screwdriver** bit. For holes ½ inch or smaller in diameter, use **twist** bits. A **brad-point** bit makes a cleaner hole than a twist bit. For holes from ½ to 1¼ inches in diameter, use a **spade** bit. For making holes in masonry or concrete, use a carbide-tipped **masonry** bit or a **star drill,** which you drive with a hammer. A **countersink** bit bores a shallow hole so you can set screw heads flush with or below the surface. A **combination** bit drills both a pilot hole and a countersink hole in one step. Use a simple **awl** to prepare the way for a small screw. For holes larger than 1¼ inches, and/or for drilling precise holes through tough materials, use a **holesaw**.

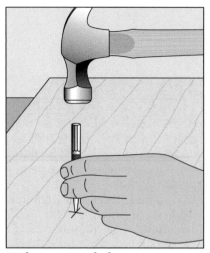

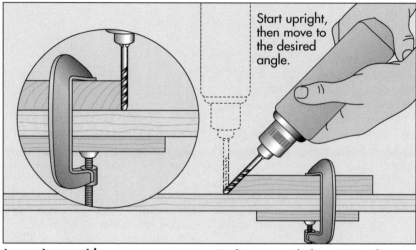

Make a starter hole.

Drill bits tend to skate away when you begin boring holes, so make a shallow starter hole with an awl or a center punch. In softwoods, a gentle tap on an awl with the palm of your hand will do the job. With hardwoods or metal, you may need to tap the center punch or awl with a hammer.

Improvise a guide.

Usually, you'll want to drill holes perpendicular to the board. Check the bit for square as it enters the material by clamping a piece of square-cut scrap lumber in place, as shown. With some drills, you can hold a square on the material and against the body of the drill.

Sometimes you'll want your bit to enter the material at an angle.

Fashion a guide by cutting the edge of a piece of scrap lumber to the desired angle of your hole. Clamp the guide so it aligns the tip of the bit exactly on your center mark. Begin the hole by drilling perpendicular to the surface. Once you have gone deep enough to keep the bit from skating away, shift the drill to the correct angle.

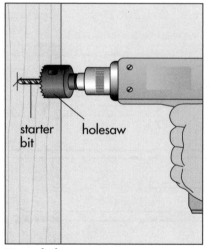

Mark the bit for depth.

When you want to drill one or more holes to a certain depth, wrap masking or electrical tape around your drill bit so the bottom edge of the tape contacts the surface of the material at the desired depth. Drill with gentle pressure. Back the bit out as soon as the tape touches the surface of the material.

Use a holesaw.

When drilling large-diameter holes with a holesaw, make a starter hole on your center mark to guide the starter bit. To ensure that the other side of the material doesn't splinter when the bit penetrates it, clamp a piece of scrap stock against the other side. Or, drill just far enough so the starter bit pokes through, then drill from the other side.

CAUTION!
AVOID DAMAGING YOUR DRILL BITS AND DRILL

Drilling is a simple procedure, but it's easy to dull or break a drill bit. Be careful not to overheat the bit; an overheated bit will become dull quickly. If you see smoke, stop drilling immediately.

Pause once in a while and test the bit for heat by quickly tapping it with your finger.

If you own a homeowner-type drill rather than a professional model, it is not designed for constant use. If you feel the body of the drill heating up, stop and give it a rest, or you could burn it out.

Hold the drill firmly upright as you work. If you tip the tool while drilling, there's a good chance the bit will break.

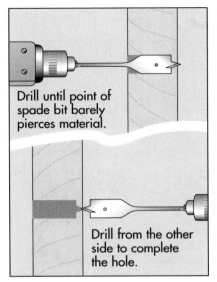

Drill until point of spade bit barely pierces material.

Drill from the other side to complete the hole.

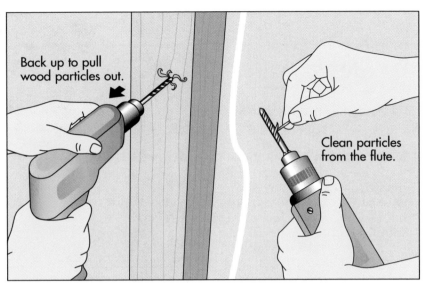

Back up to pull wood particles out.

Clean particles from the flute.

Avoid splinters with a spade bit.

When using a spade bit, drill through the material until the tip of the bit begins to poke out the back side of the material. Carefully reverse the bit out of the hole. Complete the hole by drilling from the other side, using the pilot hole you've just made.

Keep particles from clogging hole.

When you drill deep holes into thick material, wood particles build up in the hole, clogging the bit and causing it to bind. Don't force the bit in farther than it wants to go or you will burn it out. Instead, feed the bit into the wood slowly and back out of the hole frequently with the drill

motor still running. This will pull trapped wood particles to the surface. If you're working with sappy or wet wood, shavings may clog the flute of the bit. If this happens, stop the drill, and use the tip of a nail to scrape out the shavings. If the bit jams, reverse the drill rotation. Pull the bit straight up and out.

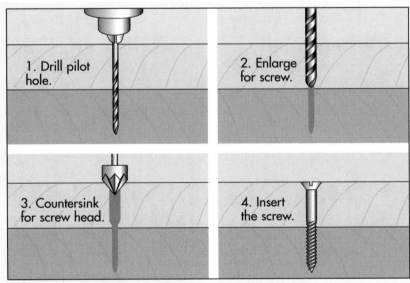

1. Drill pilot hole.

2. Enlarge for screw.

3. Countersink for screw head.

4. Insert the screw.

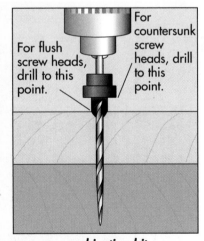

For flush screw heads, drill to this point.

For countersunk screw heads, drill to this point.

For the best fit, drill three holes...

When you use wood screws to fasten two pieces of material together, take the time to provide clearance for the screw to ensure easy driving and to avoid splits. Using a bit that is slightly smaller than the screw, drill through the top and bottom piece. Then select

a bit that is as thick as the screw shank and drill through the top board. The screw should slide easily through this top hole and grip tightly as it passes into the smaller hole. Use a countersink bit to bore a space for the screw head. When you drive the screw, it will fit without cracking the wood.

or use a combination bit.

If you're driving a lot of screws, buy a combination countersink-counterbore bit, which drills three holes in one action. Be sure to get the correct bits for the screws you will be driving. If you want the screw head to be flush with the surface, drill until the spot marked on the bit is even with the surface. To counterbore the screw head, drill deeper.

EXPERTS' INSIGHT

DRILLING THROUGH METAL

If you need to make a hole in metal, it is best to use a high-quality titanium bit. But if you work carefully, you can drill through metal with any sharp twist bit. The trick is to keep the bit and the metal lubricated with light oil at all times. If the bit is dry for even a couple of seconds while drilling, it can burn out and become dull.

Before you start, drip motor oil onto the bit and the spot to be drilled. Add oil as you work. Take your time, stopping often to make sure the bit is oiled and not overheating.

If you need to drill a hole larger than ¼ inch in diameter, drill a smaller hole first, then use a bigger bit.

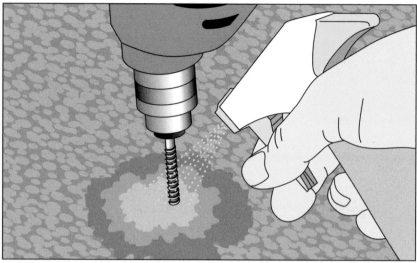

Drill into masonry and concrete.
Use a masonry bit when drilling into brick or concrete surfaces. Usually, brick is easy to drill into and concrete is more difficult. Check the bit often to make sure it's not overheating. If you see smoke, stop immediately.

Here is a trick that works surprisingly well: Spray the bit and the hole with window cleaner as you work. Not only does this keep the bit cool, but the foaming action of the cleaner brings debris up and out of the hole.

Occasionally when drilling into concrete, you will run into an especially hard spot (usually a rock embedded in the concrete). Take the bit out, insert a masonry nail or thin cold chisel, and bang with a hammer to crack the rock and give your bit a place to grab. If you have a lot of masonry drilling to do, buy a hammer drill, which bangs away as you drill.

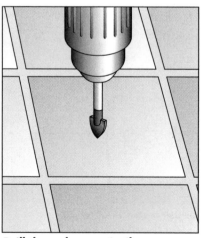

Drill through ceramic tile.
Wall tiles are usually soft, but floor tiles can be very tough. Nick the surface of the tile just enough so the bit will not wander as you drill. Keep the bit and the hole lubricated with a few drops of oil. Use a masonry bit or a special tile bit like the one shown *above*.

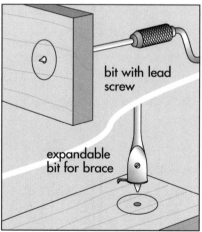

Use a brace and expandable bit.
A brace is an old-fashioned tool that works faster than you may expect. To drill large diameter holes, bore until the lead screw of the bit pokes through the material. Then drill through from the other side. To get more pressure on the brace, hold its head against your body and lean into the work.

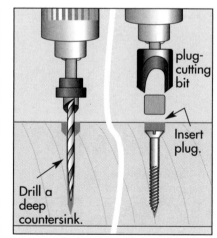

Bore and plug for a finished look.
For a handcrafted appearance, drill pilot holes, then drill a wooden plug using a plug-cutting bit. Drive the screw in, squirt a little white glue into the hole, and tap in the plug. Allow the plug to stick out slightly. After the glue has dried, chisel and sand the plug flush with the surface.

NAILING

The quickest way to make a job look shoddy and amateurish is to make a nailing mistake that mars the wood. All your careful measuring and cutting will be for naught if the wood ends up with "smiles" and "frowns" made by a hammer that missed the nail, or if you bend a nail while driving it.

Professional carpenters make nailing look easy—and for good reason. When properly done, pounding a nail home is not a struggle, but is done with smooth, fluid motions. You may never be as fast at nailing as professionals because they get plenty of practice, but you can learn to drive in nails accurately without damaging the material or yourself.

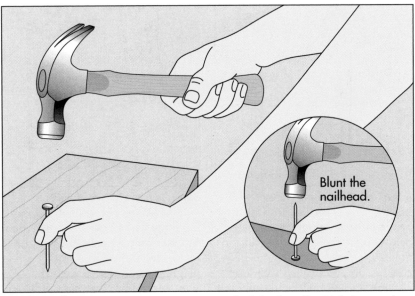

Blunt the nailhead.

Set the nail.
Practice on scrap pieces before you pound nails into finished work. To ensure that the hammer strikes the nail and not your fingers and that the nail will be driven into the board squarely, grasp the nail near its head and the hammer near the end of the handle. Lightly tap the nail until it stands by itself.

If you must drive a nail near the end of a board, drill a pilot hole or turn the nail upside down and blunt its point with a hammer. Either technique will reduce the risk of splitting the wood.

EXPERTS' INSIGHT

GETTING THE HOLDING POWER YOU NEED

■ How well a nail will hold in wood depends on how much of its surface contacts the wood. The longer and thicker the nail, the better it will hold.

■ When possible, use the Rule of Three: A nail should be three times as long as the thickness of the board being fastened. Two-thirds of the nail then will be in the second board to which you are fastening the first one. If the nail must penetrate through dead space or drywall, increase the nail length by that distance.

■ A thick nail holds better, but not if it splits the wood. In that case, most of its holding power is lost. Special nails, such as ring-shank and cement-coated nails, hold better than standard nails. A headed nail holds better than a finish nail.

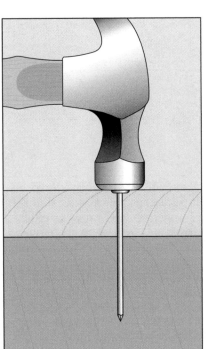

Use proper nailing techniques.
Once the nail is set in place, remove your hand from it. Keep your eye on the nail as you swing the hammer, letting the weight of the hammer head do the driving.

Beginners tend to hold a hammer stiffly and keep their shoulders stiff, swinging from the elbow. This leads to a tired, sore arm and to mistakes. Loosen up. Your whole arm should move as you swing from the shoulder. Keep your wrist loose so the hammer can give a final "snap" at the end of each blow. The entire motion should be relaxed and smooth.

With the last hammer blow, push the head of the nail flush or nearly flush with the surface of the wood. The convex shape of the hammer face allows you to do this without marring the surface.

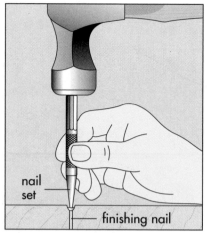

Countersink finishing nails.
In most cases, it's best to drive the heads of finishing or casing nails below the surface. You can fill the hole with wood putty later. This actually doesn't take all that long and leads to a much better-looking finish than nails driven flush. Hold a nail set against the nailhead and tap it in.

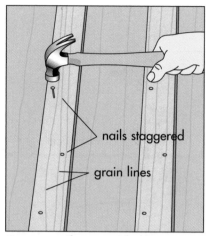

Stagger nails to avoid splits.
When driving several nails along the length of a board, stagger them so you don't split the board. The idea is to avoid pounding neighboring nails through the same grain line; two nails will stress the grain twice as much as one nail. If the work will be visible, stagger the nails in a regular pattern.

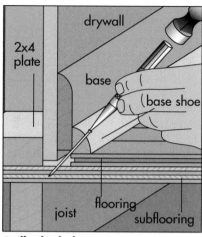

Drill pilot holes.
When you nail within 2 inches of the end of a board or into hardwood, drill pilot holes to avoid splitting the wood. Pilot holes should be slightly smaller than the diameter of the nail. When attaching a base shoe, drive nails into pilot holes so they miss the flooring, which needs room to expand and contract with changes in temperature and humidity.

EXPERTS' INSIGHT

USING MASONRY NAILS

■ Masonry nails offer a quick way to attach materials to concrete, brick, and masonry block. With flat-style masonry nails, be sure to turn the nail in the direction of the grain so it's less likely to split the wood.

■ You can use a standard hammer, but the job is easier with a heavy mallet. Hold the board in place, and drive the masonry nail through it. Once the nail hits the masonry surface, strike it with hard strokes. With subsequent nails, check to see if you have dislodged any nails; you may have to put in more.

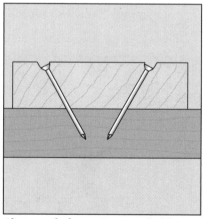

Skew nails for a stronger hold.
In situations where you cannot use as long a nail as you would like, drive nails in at an angle. Drive in one nail at about a 60-degree angle in one direction, then drive in another one in the opposite direction. The skewed nails will work together, making it difficult for the board to pull loose. Set the nailheads into the surface for a finished appearance.

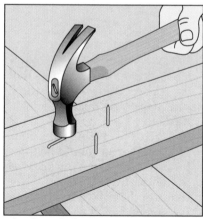

Clinch nails for the best hold.
If looks are not important, but strength is, use nails about 1 inch longer than the thickness of the pieces you're fastening. Drive in the nails, then turn the boards over and bend the exposed portion of the nails so they are nearly flush with the surface and parallel to the wood grain. The resulting joint will be extremely difficult to pull apart.

FASTENING WITH SCREWS

It's not hard to see why screws fasten so well. The threads grip wood fibers in a way that a smooth nail cannot. When the screw is driven home, the threads exert tremendous pressure against the screw head to hold the fastener firmly in place. With the right tools (see box below), driving screws can be almost as quick as nailing. If you make a mistake, it's easy to remove a screw without damaging your work. Screws must be driven with care, however. If you do not start out straight, there is no way to correct the mistake as you continue driving the screw. Without a pilot hole, the screw may split the wood and the screw will not hold securely. If the pilot hole is too large, again, the screw will not grip well.

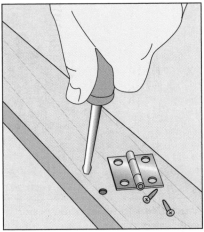

Make a starter hole with an awl.
Small screws seldom require pilot holes (see the box, below right). However, they do need a starter hole. Poke a hole with a scratch awl. Give it a few twists, back it out, and you're ready to drive in the screw.

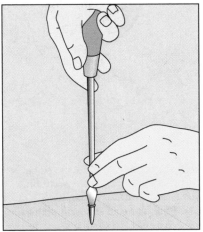

Drive with a hand screwdriver.
Start screws by holding the screwdriver handle with one hand and the screwdriver blade with the other. Don't hold the screw. If the screw is spinning around and not going into the wood, put two hands on the handle to apply more pressure.

TOOLS TO USE

Power-driven screws hold tightly, go in quickly, and are removed easily. Here are some tools that make working with them even more convenient.
■ A variable-speed, reversible drill starts the screws slowly and removes them if necessary.
■ With a magnetic sleeve, screws stick to the bit, making it easy to drive them in hard-to-reach places. Changing bit tips is easy; simply press them into the sleeve.
■ Have on hand a collection of drill bit tips, particularly #1 and #2 Phillips bits and some slotted bits, as well.
■ Consider buying square-headed screws and bits. These bits fit into and grab the screw slot better than Phillips-head and slotted screws.

slotted screw bit

Power-drive slotted screws.
Even a few screws can take a long time to drive by hand, so consider using a drill with a screwdriver bit. When driving slotted screws, take care that the bit does not wander partway out of the slot, or you could damage the surface into which you are screwing. Don't drive screws too quickly, or the bit may slip out of the slot. Maintain firm, even pressure as you work.

EXPERTS' INSIGHT

WHEN DO YOU NEED A PILOT HOLE?

If there is a danger of cracking the wood, you should always drill a pilot hole, no matter how small the screw. For instance, if the wood is brittle or if you will be driving a screw near the end of a board, almost any screw can split the wood. But if you are drilling into a sound board at a spot 2 inches or more from its end, it usually will be safe to drive in a No. 6 or thinner screw without a pilot hole. If you are drilling into plywood or framing lumber, you should be able to drive No. 8 screws without pilot holes. For advice on selecting the correct-size bit, see page 241.

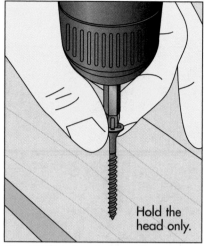

Use Phillips-head drywall screws.
You can buy drywall screws by the pound at bargain prices and drive them into most materials in which you would use nails. If you use a magnetic sleeve, place the screw on the bit first, then set the tip of the screw in place on the material. If you need to hold the screw to keep it from wandering, hold the head only, not the sharp threads.

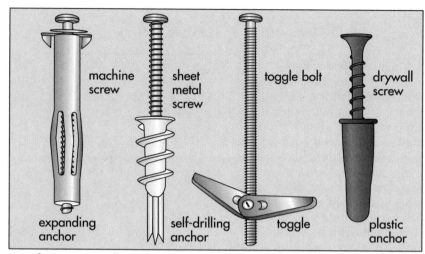

Attach items to walls with special wall fasteners.
If you need to attach something to a wall, the ideal way is to drive a screw into a stud. But often that's not possible. The screws and bolts shown *above* are designed to hold items firmly in drywall or plaster walls. To use **expanding anchors** and **plastic anchors**, drill holes and tap the unit into the wall; the

anchor will spread and grip as you tighten the screw. Use **self-drilling anchors** only in drywall. You don't need to drill a hole; just screw them in and insert a screw. To use a **toggle bolt**, drill a hole large enough for the folded-back toggles to fit through. Push the toggles through the hole, and turn the bolt until the toggles snug up to the back side of the wall.

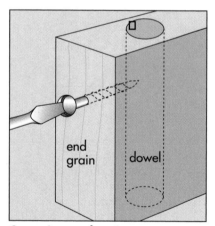

Screw into end grain.
When a fastener is driven into the end grain of a board, it will not hold as well as it does across the grain because it runs parallel to the grain rather than at an angle to it. Use a longer screw than you usually would. Where holding power is critical, drill a hole and install a dowel, as shown, into which you can drive the screw.

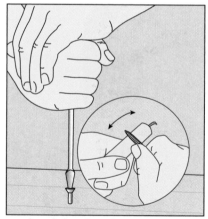

Deal with hard-to-drive screws.
If the going gets tough, the screw may stop turning. Exert pressure on the screwdriver with the palm of one hand and turn it with the other. If you still can't drive it, remove the screw and drill a slightly larger pilot hole. Another solution is to lubricate the threads with candle wax and try again.

EXPERTS' INSIGHT

FASTENING TO METAL WITH SCREWS

■ For fastening thin sheet metal or soft metal, such as brass, you can use one of several types of self-tapping sheet-metal screws (see page 85). Simply drive the screw in; it makes its own path with a metal-cutting point.

■ For heavier metals, drill a pilot hole using the techniques for drilling through metal (see page 102). Then install a sheet-metal screw.

■ For metal $1/8$ inch or thicker and where you want an extra-strong joint, buy a drill-and-tap kit. With this, you can make a machine-threaded hole that will accept a machine bolt.

FASTENING WITH BOLTS

Nails and screws depend on friction between the fastener and the wood to do their job. When you tighten a nut on a bolt, however, you're actually clamping adjoining members together, producing the sturdiest of all joints. All types of bolts require a hole bored through both pieces being joined together. Here's information about installing machine and carriage bolts. For help with toggle bolts and other anchors, see page 134.

> **CAUTION!**
> *Overtightening bolts can strip threads and damage wood, reducing the holding power of the bolt. Tighten the nut and bolt firmly against the wood, give them another half turn, then stop.*

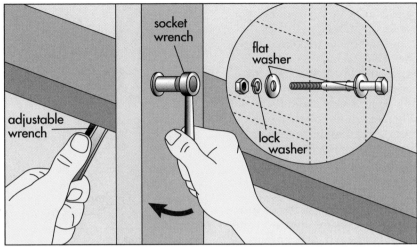

Fasten with machine bolts.
Machine bolts have hexagonal heads and threads running partway or all the way along the shank. When fastening two pieces of wood together, slip a flat washer onto the bolt and slide the bolt through the holes in both pieces of material. Add another flat washer, then a lock washer. Screw the nut on and tighten it. The flat washer keeps the nut and the bolt head from biting into the wood. The lock washer prevents the nut from coming loose. Use two wrenches to draw the nut down onto the bolt: one to steady the nut, the other to turn the bolt head.

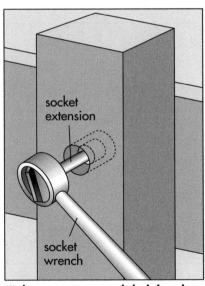

Tighten a countersunk bolt head.
To install a machine bolt in a hard-to-get-at place or when you have to countersink the bolt head, use a socket wrench with a socket extension to reach into the recess. Hold the nut with another wrench.

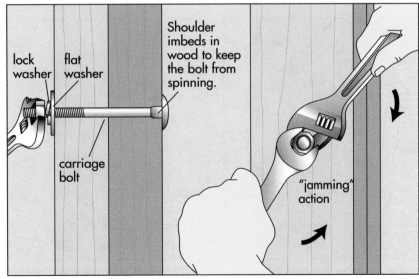

Install a carriage bolt.
A carriage bolt has a plain, round head. Insert it into the hole and tap the head flush with the surface. Slip a flat washer, a lock washer, and a nut onto the bolt. Tighten the nut. The square or hexagonal shoulder under the bolt head keeps the bolt from spinning as the nut is tightened. No washer is needed under the head.

The lock washer should keep the bolt from working loose. As added protection, you can thread another nut onto the bolt, snug it against the first, then "jam" the two together by turning them in opposite directions.

REMOVING NAILS AND SCREWS

Mistakes are a part of every carpenter's day. In fact, knowing how to undo mistakes is one of the hallmarks of an experienced carpenter, and that necessitates a good knowledge of how to remove nails and screws. Whether you're correcting mistakes, disassembling an old structure, or recycling used lumber, you'll find it's worth it to learn how to remove old fasteners quickly and neatly.

Removing screws often is just a matter of reversing your drill and screwing the old fastener out. However, you may be faced with a stripped head or an extra-tight screw (see page 109).

Most commonly, you'll be faced with removing nails. Don't just start whacking away in frustration, or you'll damage the wood. Use these methods and accept that nail removal is a normal part of a carpenter's job.

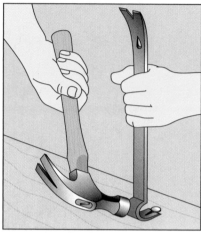

Pry with a flat bar.
If the head of the nail has not been set into the wood, it may be possible to shoehorn a flat bar under it and pry the nail up. Tap the notch of the chisel-like head of the bar under the nailhead and pull back on the bar. Because of its smooth, flat body, a pry bar makes only a slight indentation in the board as you remove the nail.

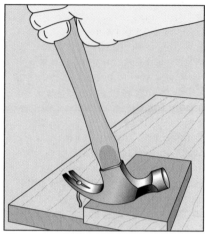

Use a wood block.
There are two good reasons for using a wood block when removing a nail. First, the raised height gives your hammer extra leverage, making it much easier to pull the nail out. Second, the block protects your work. Without it, the head of the hammer would dig in and make an unsightly indentation.

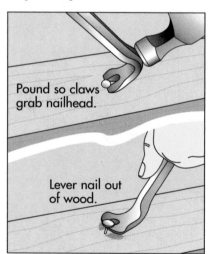

Dig nails out with a cat's paw.
A cat's paw removes nails that are embedded deeply in lumber. Its drawback is that it also must bite deeply into the wood to grip the nailhead. Place the clawed tip behind the nailhead at a 45-degree angle. Pound the claws under the nailhead, pry the nail partway out, then use a hammer and block.

Pound out board to loosen nails.
If you have access to the back side of the joined material, strike the joint from behind, then hammer the members back together from the front. This usually pops the nailheads out far enough for you to get hold of them with your hammer claw.

Cut the nails.
Where access is tight, sometimes you can disjoin two members by sawing through the nails. If you have a reciprocating saw with a metal-cutting blade, this will be easy. Otherwise, use a tight-work hacksaw. After you break the joint, use a nail set to force the heads out, then remove the nails.

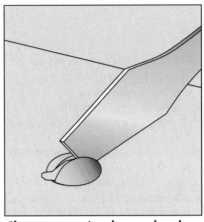

Clean out a painted screw head.
When removing old screws that have been painted, take the time to clean the paint out of the slots. If you don't clean the head, you may strip the screw head, making it even more difficult to remove. Place a screwdriver as shown *above,* and tap with a hammer.

Punch through and pry.
To avoid splitting molding, punch the finishing nails that hold it in place through the molding with a nail set. Try not to make the hole larger; use a small-diameter nail set. Pound the head of the finishing nail deeply into the molding. You'll feel the board come loose. Once the nails are punched through, pry off the molding with a putty knife or chisel, taking care not to mar the wood.

EXPERTS' INSIGHT

REMOVING OLD SCREWS
Here are some tips for removing stubborn old screws:
■ For a slotted screw that has been stripped so much that a screwdriver can't get a good hold, deepen the slot by cutting into it with a hacksaw.
■ Extremely tight screws often can be loosened with heat. Hold the tip of a soldering gun against the screw head for a minute or two, then try it.
■ For stripped Phillips-head screws, it sometimes helps to drill a small hole in the center of the head to give the screwdriver more to grab onto.
■ For an extremely stubborn screw, buy a screw and bolt extracting tool. Drill a small hole in the screw head, insert the tool, turn it with a wrench, and twist the screw out.

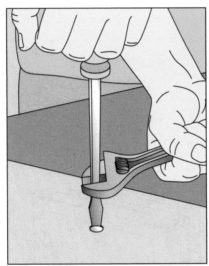

Add force to a screwdriver.
If you need greater turning power, use a screwdriver with a square shank in conjunction with an adjustable wrench. Adjust the wrench so it fits tightly on the screwdriver. Press down on the handle of the screwdriver with the palm of your hand as you turn with the wrench.

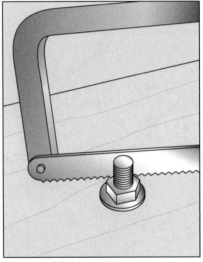

Cut a stubborn nut.
Rusty or damaged bolt threads make it hard to remove a nut. You can solve the problem quickly with a hacksaw. Align the saw blade so it rubs against the threads and cut down through the nut. You will cut off about one-third of the nut. Once you have done this, it will be easy to knock the nut loose or unscrew it.

GLUING AND CLAMPING

A joint will be stronger if you use glue in addition to nails or screws. For some projects that do not require great strength, glue alone will be enough.

Use contact cement to attach wood veneers or plastic laminates to wood surfaces. Apply the cement to both surfaces and let them dry. Align the parts precisely before you join them—the first bond is permanent. Use paneling adhesives to attach sheet goods to walls. For interior projects, use carpenter's glue with aliphatic resin. This is superior to standard white glue because it sets up faster, resists heat and moisture better, and is stronger. For the glue to work, however, the pieces must be clamped together firmly until the glue sets.

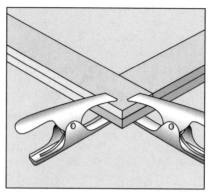

Use speedy squeeze clamps.
For light work, these are the easiest clamps to use. Apply glue to both pieces and place them together in correct alignment. Squeeze the clamp handles to spread the jaws. When you release the handles, the springs will clamp the work together. You may want to have several sizes of these inexpensive clamps on hand.

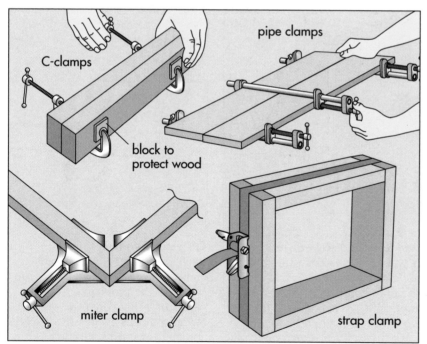

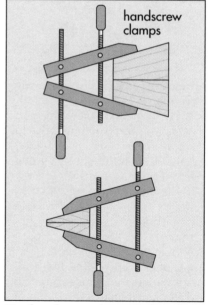

Use the right clamp for the job.
C-clamps are inexpensive and work well when the pieces are not too wide. Use blocks of wood to keep the clamps from marring the boards. For miter joints, use **miter clamps** that hold the boards at a

90-degree angle. For large projects, use **pipe clamps**. You should alternate them to prevent buckling. A **strap clamp** works well for cabinetry projects. It will clamp several joints at once and will not mar the wood.

Use handscrew clamps for angles.
These clamps work well for cabinetmaking and other woodworking projects. Because their jaws are made of wood, you don't have to worry about marring your project. Adjust the clamp to almost any size or angle by simply turning the two handscrews.

CAULKING AND APPLYING MASTIC

It takes practice before you can lay down a clean-looking bead of caulk. Practice on scrap materials or start in an inconspicuous area before you caulk an area that is highly visible.

Choose among a wide variety of adhesives that are designed for particular jobs (see the chart, *below right*). When working with adhesives, be careful to apply the material smoothly and evenly, so the piece will adhere uniformly. Avoid applying too much adhesive; cleaning up messes can take longer than the actual job.

YOU'LL NEED

TIME: About 20 minutes to caulk around a bathtub or countertop; 10 to 30 minutes to adhere laminate or paneling.
SKILLS: Smooth, steady control.
TOOLS: Utility knife, caulking gun, notched trowel.

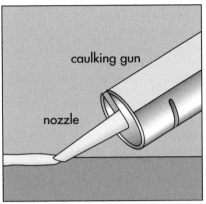

Apply a bead of caulk.
Make sure the joint to be caulked is free of dirt and grease and there are no gaps wider than your bead of caulk. Snip the nozzle of the caulk tube at about a 45-degree angle. The closer to the tip you cut, the smaller the bead will be. You may need to puncture the inside seal with a long nail. Squeeze the handle until caulk starts coming out; move smoothly to apply an even bead.

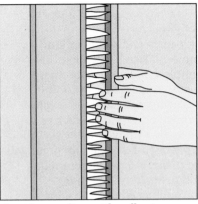

Attach paneling with adhesive.
To attach paneling to walls, apply a bead of adhesive on either the wall or the back of the panel. Use a notched trowel or make a squiggle pattern using a caulking gun. Press the panel against the wall, then pull it out slightly. Wait for a few minutes for the adhesive to get tacky (the manufacturer's instructions will tell you how long), then press the materials together again.

Apply with a notched trowel.
For a smooth, even application, use a notched trowel to apply adhesives. Check the adhesive container for the type and size of notches the trowel should have. Apply the adhesive with the trowel held nearly parallel to the surface to make sure it sticks. Tilt the trowel up at about a 45-degree angle and press firmly as you spread the adhesive.

SELECTING ADHESIVES

Adhesive Type	Primary Use	Holding Power	Moisture-Resistance	Set/Cure Time	Type of Applicator
Contact cement	Applying wood veneer and plastic laminate.	Excellent	Excellent	Must dry first/ 1–2 days	Brush, notched trowel, or paint roller
Epoxy adhesive	Bonding almost any materials. Must mix the parts.	Excellent	Excellent	30 minutes/ 1–10 hours	Throwaway brush or flat stick
Panel adhesive	Attaching drywall or paneling to walls.	Good	Good	1 hour/ 24 hours	Caulk tube or notched trowel
Carpenter's glue	Bonding wood together for small projects.	Good	Fair	30 minutes/ 24 hours	Squeeze-type container
Cyanoacrylate (superglue)	Bonding small items of most any material.	Good	Fair	1–2 minutes/ 24 hours	Squeeze tube

MAKING SIMPLE, STRONG JOINTS

Strong, good-looking wood joints are essential to all carpentry and woodworking projects. Here are some of the simplest and strongest joinery methods. Each of these joints can be made with hand tools, but if you have shop tools, such as a tablesaw or power miter saw, the job will go faster and the joint will be tighter. None of them requires cabinetmaking expertise.

You'll need to hone your measuring, cutting, and fastening skills to make neat, sturdy joints. See pages 88–100 for a review of the basic techniques.

All of the joints shown on this page are **butt joints**—two square-cut pieces joined together by positioning the end of one member against the face or edge of another member. A butt joint can be fastened with nails or screws only. It will be stronger, however, if reinforced with corner braces, T-plates, angle brackets, dowels, a plywood gusset, or a wood block.

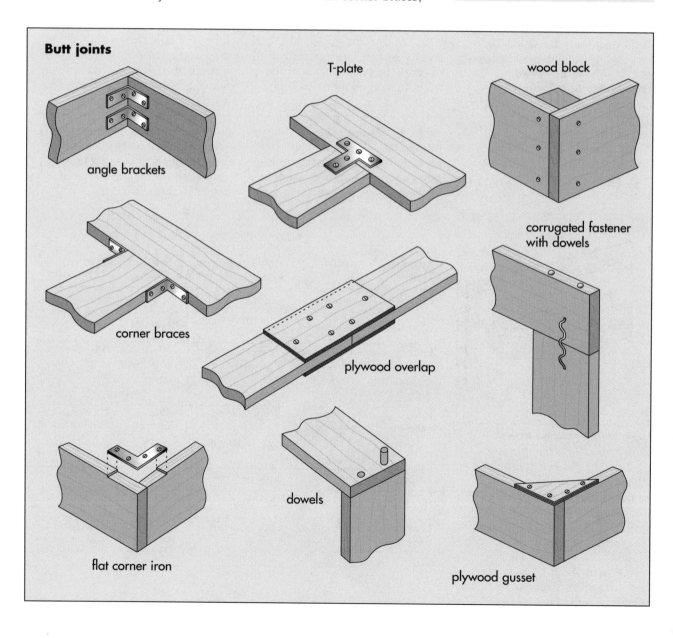

Butt joints

angle brackets

T-plate

wood block

corner braces

plywood overlap

corrugated fastener with dowels

flat corner iron

dowels

plywood gusset

Lap joints are stronger than butt joints and often look better, as well. To make an **overlap joint**, simply lay one of the members on top of the other and nail or screw it in place. For a **full-lap joint**, cut a notch into one member that is as deep as the second piece is thick. Clamp and glue the two pieces together, adding fasteners if you prefer. The **half-lap joint** is the strongest joint.

Dado joints are attractive and strong, but are difficult to make.

A **stopped dado** has the strength of a dado and hides the joinery.

For a finished-looking corner, make a **miter joint**. Cut the pieces at the same angle (usually 45 degrees), then glue the joint and drive in finishing nails.

A **biscuit joint** also is strong and has the advantage of being completely hidden, To make it, however, requires a biscuit joiner power tool.

YOU'LL NEED

TIME About 10 to 30 minutes per joint, depending on complexity.
SKILLS: Ability to make square cuts, drill, use fasteners, and make neat notches.
TOOLS: Square, ruler, pencil, saw, drill and bits, hammer, nail set, screwdriver. The biscuit joint requires a biscuit joiner tool.

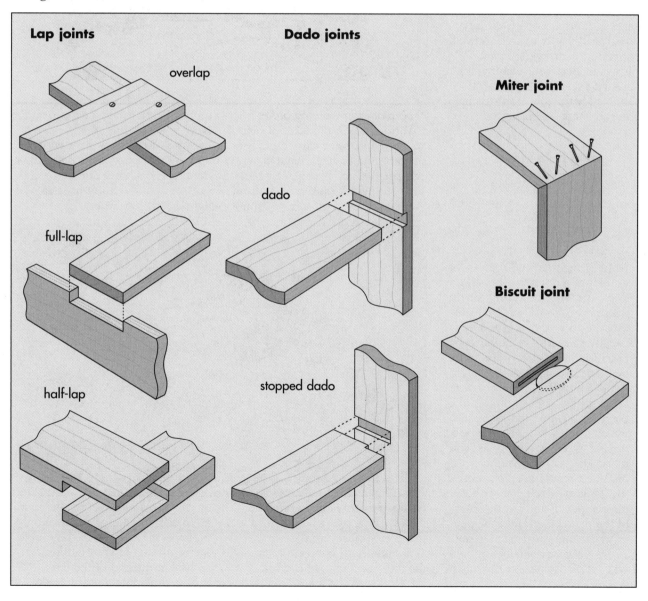

Lap joints

overlap

full-lap

half-lap

Dado joints

dado

stopped dado

Miter joint

Biscuit joint

SHAPING AND PLANING

Beveling edges and corners, planing down doors, trueing edges and ends of lumber—most carpentry projects include at least one of these shaping tasks. Three types of tools work best for shaping wood surfaces: planes, surface-forming tools, and rasps or wood files. With practice and a clean, sharp tool, shaping can be a pleasure rather than a chore.

However, even the sharpest shaping tools are no match for a board that's badly twisted, bowed, cupped, or warped (see page 77). Always inspect your material for flaws and select only the stock suitable for the job. Don't assume you can shape it up later.

SCRIBING A TRUE LINE
■ To straighten out a piece of lumber or a door, you must first draw the line indicating where the piece should end. This is called a true line. A true line is usually straight, but not always. For instance, a door often must be planed to fit an opening that is not straight. To make a true line, scribe it by holding the piece up against the place into which it must fit. Run your pencil along the opening as you mark the piece for planing.
■ When scribing a line, check the angle at which you are holding the pencil and the thickness of the pencil line. Hold the pencil at the same angle at all points along your scribe line or you will cut off too little or too much wood. Decide if you want to cut off all of the pencil mark or just up to the mark.

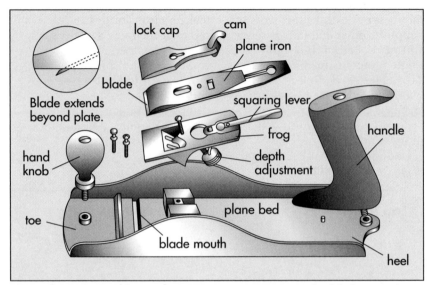

Keep planes in working order.
Various types and sizes of planes are available. Most carpenters use a smoothing plane (shown *above*) or a small block plane (see page 115). To help keep the blade from dulling, lay it on its side when not in use. Retract the blade into the body when storing it. If any parts become rusty, clean them with a little oil and fine steel wool. Adjust the blade so it cuts thin shavings easily; you should not have to fight against the wood.

Use a block of wood to support plane when shaving a narrow edge.

Follow general planing rules.
Follow these tips when using a plane or surface-former:
■ It takes both hands to operate the tool, so clamp your work.
■ Plane with the grain.
■ If you get anything but a continuous, even shaving, the blade is dull or adjusted too thick, or you're planing against the grain.
■ To avoid nicking corners, apply pressure to the knob of the tool at the beginning of your cut and to its heel at the end of the cut.
■ When planing a narrow edge, grip a square-cornered block of wood against the bottom of the plane as you work.

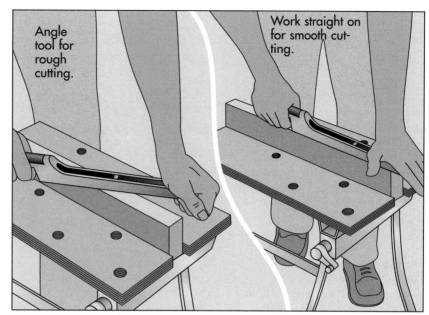

Angle tool for rough cutting.

Work straight on for smooth cutting.

Shape with surface-forming tools.
Surface-forming tools, also known as sure-form tools, come in a variety of sizes and shapes. The one shown, *above,* works much like a plane. You cannot adjust the depth of the cut and it will not produce as smooth a cut as a plane, but it is easy to use.

You can regulate the cut by the way you position the tool against the material. For rough-cutting, hold the tool at a 45-degree angle to the work as you push it. For a smoother result, hold the tool parallel to the board's edge.

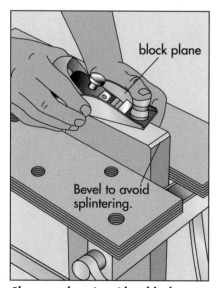

block plane

Bevel to avoid splintering.

Shape end grain with a block.
As long as you're shaping wood parallel to the grain, planing will go smoothly. But when you need to shape the end grain, you will be working at a 90-degree angle to the grain. A small block plane works best on end grain. Bevel the

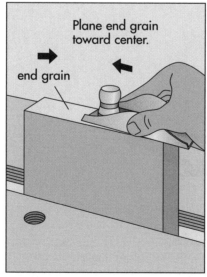

Plane end grain toward center.

end grain

corners first, with the bottom of the bevel at the final cut line. For narrow stock, just plane in one direction. For wider material, shave from each end of the board toward the center. Finish the job by shaving off the hump that remains in the middle.

TOOLS TO USE

POWER PLANER AND BELT SANDER

■ If you have a lot of planing to do, buy a power planer. The depth is easy to adjust, and as long as you hold the base flat against the surface, you will get a smooth cut with little effort. Be sure to use carbide-tipped blades, or you will have to change them often.

■ If you can work carefully, a belt sander shaves material, especially softwoods, with relative ease. Start with a coarse sandpaper. Hold the sanding belt flat to the surface; you'll make gouges if you tip the tool. Once you have taken off almost as much material as you need to, switch to a smoother paper.

SANDING

Once you've taken the time to cut and assemble your project, don't skimp when it comes to the final steps. Do a thorough job of sanding, so the wood will be well prepared for its final finish. Don't expect stain, varnish, or paint to smooth out the surface for you. They will only follow the contours of the wood, and often will accentuate, rather than hide, imperfections. Unless you are using a belt sander with a rough abrasive, don't expect sanding to remove more than ⅛ inch of material; shape or plane instead (see pages 114–115).

> **CAUTION!**
> *Particularly when sanding with power tools, wear a face mask. To avoid difficult cleanup later, seal the room.*

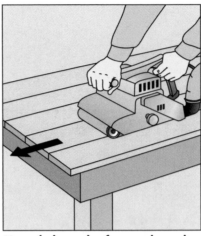

Use a belt sander for rough work.
Use this tool only on rough surfaces and only if you are sure of yourself; it is easy to make gouges if you tip the tool or if you rest it in one spot too long. Always run the sander with the grain, never against it. Don't apply pressure as you work; just let the weight of the sander do the work.

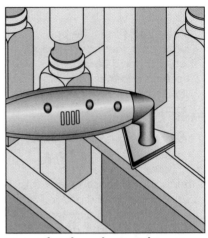

Use a detail sander in tight spots.
For awkward areas, a detail sander can spare you hours of finger-throbbing work. Sanding pads are self-adhesive; just lift one off and put the next one on. Proceed carefully. A detail sander works with an oscillating action. Because it concentrates on such a small area, it takes off material quickly.

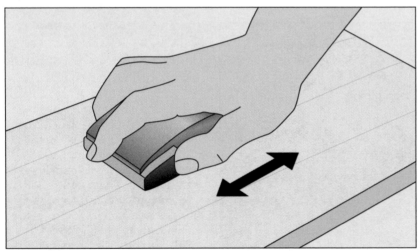

Hand-sand with a block.
Except in hard-to-reach areas, never use abrasive sheets alone—always use some sort of sanding block, either store-bought or improvised. Sanding with a block is less tiring and produces more uniform results.

Tear abrasive sheets to size, rather than cutting them, or you will dull your knife blade quickly.

Check that the bottom of your block is clean and smooth. Any debris can tear the paper and mar your work.

Sand only in the direction of the wood grain. Sanding across the grain or in a circular motion can leave hard-to-remove lines. Don't exert a lot of pressure. If you're using the right grade of paper, light strokes are all you'll need.

EXPERTS' INSIGHT

SAND THREE TIMES
■ Take the time and trouble to sand three times, using progressively finer sandpaper. The wood surface may feel smooth after your first and second sandings, but it will get smoother as you move on to finer-grit sandpapers. A common progression is to start with 80-grit paper, then proceed to 120-, 180-, and possibly even 240-grit abrasives. Clean dust from the wood between sandings.

■ If you can't sand out a stain or discoloration, apply a small amount of laundry bleach to the stain. Try several applications until you get the right color. Dry before sanding it again.

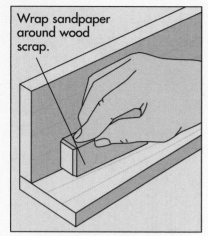

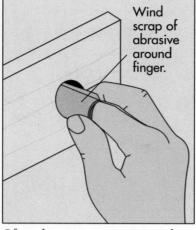

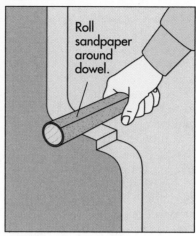

Use ingenuity for tight spots.
When smoothing wood in tight quarters or in unusual situations, special tools can help. Consider buying or renting a detail sander (see page 116) or a contour sanding attachment for your drill.

Often, however, you can get the job done with a sheet of abrasive and a little ingenuity, as these three examples show.

To sand two surfaces where they meet at an inside corner, wrap a creased sheet of abrasive

around a sharp-cornered block. To smooth inside edges of bored holes and small cutouts, wrap abrasive around your finger or a small round object. For sanding outside curves, wrap a sheet of abrasive around a dowel.

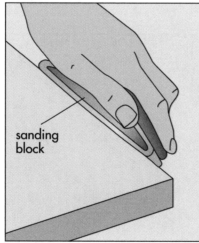

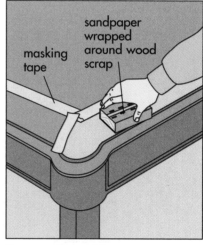

Sand a small piece.
When you need to smooth the surface of a small item, sand it on a full sheet of abrasive held flat with your free hand. This keeps the surface of the piece even and flat. If the abrasive fills with dust, wipe it with a clean cloth or give it a few slaps against your bench.

Round off edges.
Because wood edges are susceptible to nicks and splinters, it is a good idea to blunt them with a light sanding. Hold the sanding block at an angle; use gentle pressure combined with a rocking motion. A molded rubber sanding block like the one shown, *above,* is ideal for this purpose because its base gives slightly.

Protect edges with tape.
Sometimes you'll want to sand one surface without scratching an adjoining surface. To do this, protect the surface you don't want sanded with masking tape. Affix the tape carefully, making sure it is stuck down tightly at all points. Watch closely as you sand and immediately replace any tape that gets ripped or damaged.

FILLING AND FINISHING

Paint, stain, or clear finishes rarely cover up imperfections in wood. Often, they make things look worse rather than better. It pays to prepare your wood carefully before you add a finish.

Fill in holes with wood filler and sand the surface smooth. If you're applying a clear finish, limit your use of putty to small spots; even putty that is made to accept stain never quite looks like real wood. Even if you're going to paint the surface, cover exposed plywood edges. They soak up paint like a sponge and will look rough no matter how many coats of paint you apply to them.

Once the wood surface is prepared, match your paint or clear finish to the intended use of your project. See chart on page 119 for selecting finishes.

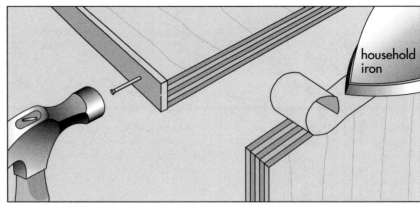

Cover plywood edges.
To conceal a plywood edge, cut a thin piece of molding to fit, apply carpenter's glue to the edge, and fasten the molding with brads (small finishing nails). You also can cover an edge with wood veneer tape. Buy tape that is wider than the thickness of the material and matches its surface. Cut the tape with scissors, leaving at least ¼ inch extra on all edges. Position iron-on tape carefully, so it covers the edge along the entire length. Apply even, steady pressure with a household iron set on high. Use contact cement to apply non-iron-on veneer. Trim the edges with a sharp knife, then sand the corners lightly.

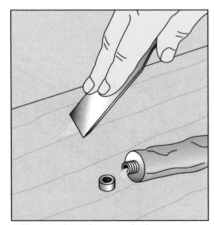

Fill in nail and screw holes.
For small holes, use a dough-type wood filler. Apply filler either before or after staining; experiment to find out which looks best. Begin by tamping a small amount of the filler into the hole with your thumb. Smooth it with a putty knife. Wipe away the excess with a rag dampened with water or mineral spirits, depending on the type of putty (check manufacturer's directions).

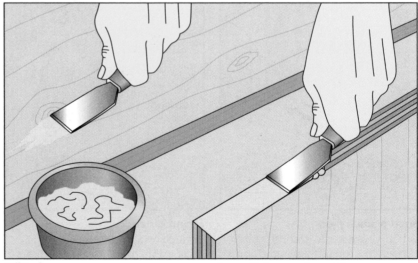

Fill in large areas.
If you're going to paint the entire surface of a project, water-mix putty excels at filling shallow depressions over a large surface area. The putty sets up quickly, so don't mix more than you can use in 10 minutes. To fill cracks around a knot, mix the putty to a pastelike consistency and force it into all the cracks with a putty knife. Feather out the patch to the surrounding wood. To fill edges of plywood or the end grain of boards, mix the putty to a thinner consistency. Sand and apply a second coat if necessary. For deep holes, you may have to apply two layers to allow for any shrinkage of the putty.

SELECTING CLEAR FINISHES

Type	Characteristics	Application and Drying Time
Natural-resin varnish	Resists scratches, scuffs. Spar varnish good outdoors.	Use varnish brush or cheesecloth pad. Dries in 24–36 hours. In humid weather, allow 36 hours.
Polyurethane varnish	Mar-resistant, durable, remains clear.	Use natural-bristle brush, roller, or spray. Let dry 1–2 hours; 12 hours between coats.
Two-part epoxy varnish	High resistance to scuffs and mars. Ideal for floors.	Use brush. Check directions if coating wood filler. First coat dries in 3 hours; second in 5–8 hours.
Shellac	Easily damaged by water. Clear or pigmented.	Use small brush with chiseled tip. Thin with alcohol or recommended solvent. Dries in about 2 hours.
Lacquer	Fast-drying. Ideal for furniture.	Best sprayed in many thin coats. Let last coat dry 48–60 hours, then rub with fine steel wool or hard wax.
Resin oil	Soaks into and hardens grain. Resists scratches.	Usually hand-rubbed in 2–3 coats. Needs 8–12 hours to dry.

Apply penetrating stain.
Apply stain with a brush and wait for a few minutes. The heavier the application and the longer you wait, the deeper the color. Wipe with a clean rag, taking care to make the color even throughout the piece. To make it darker, apply a second coat. If it is too dark, rub with a cloth moistened with the recommended thinner.

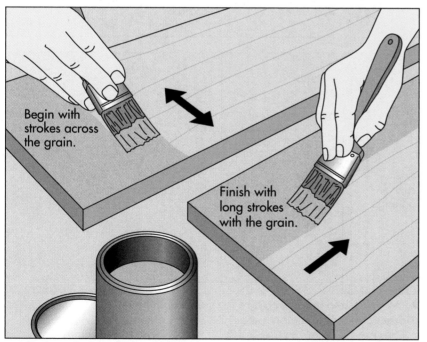

Paint correctly for a smooth look.
Painting with a brush may seem like a simple task, but here are a few tips to keep in mind. Begin applying paint to wood surfaces with short strokes across the wood grain, laying down paint in both directions. Don't bear down too hard on the bristles.

Finish painting with longer, sweeping strokes in one direction only—this time with the wood grain. Use just the tips of the bristles to smooth out the paint.

EXPERTS' INSIGHT

ANTIQUING
■ If you have old furniture or cabinets that are worn or marred, you can avoid all the work of stripping, sanding, and refinishing them by emphasizing the wood's imperfections.
■ If you are new to this process, buy an antiquing kit, which usually includes base and finish coating materials and brushes and applicators. Choose from a variety of finishes: marbleized, distressed, spattered, stippled, crumpled, and others.
■ Remove dirt and wax from the surface, apply the base coat, and let it dry. After sanding, apply a finish coat quickly. Wipe it to achieve the desired finish. Allow it to dry for 48 hours and add a clear, protective finish.

INSTALLING MOLDING

Installing molding to finish off a project can be the most gratifying part of the job. Although it's easier than you might expect, installing molding takes some practice. Start installing molding in an area of the room where it will be the least visible. You'll soon surprise yourself with your speed and neat joinery. The most common mistake is to cut a miter in the wrong direction. Whenever possible, mark pieces clearly, not only for length, but also for the direction of cut.

YOU'LL NEED

TIME: About 10 minutes per piece of molding.
SKILLS: Precise measuring and cutting, figuring out the direction of cuts, nailing.
TOOLS: Tape measure, miter box and backsaw or power miter saw, coping saw, hammer, nail set.

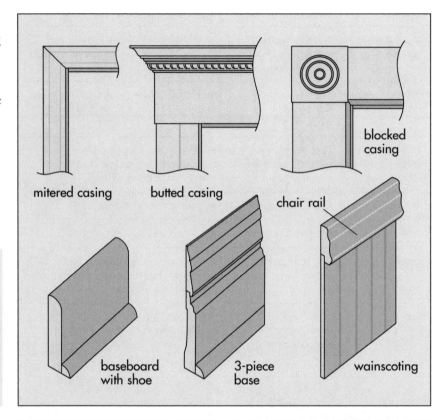

mitered casing   butted casing   blocked casing   chair rail

baseboard with shoe   3-piece base   wainscoting

EXPERTS' INSIGHT

BUYING MOLDING

Molding can be expensive, so determine exactly how many pieces of each size you need. On a piece of paper, make columns for each size—8 feet, 10 feet, 12 feet, etc. As you measure for individual pieces, tally how many you need under each column. If you have an old house, you may need moldings that are not made any longer. A lumber-yard with a mill or a millwork company can make replicas. If the price is too high or you need only a small piece of molding, you can make a reasonable fac-simile using a router, tablesaw, radial-arm saw, and belt sander.

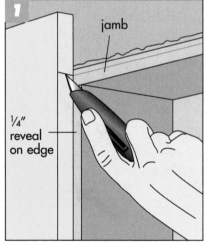

1. Measure and mark precisely.
Whenever possible, hold a piece of molding in place and mark it with a knife, rather than using a tape measure. For window and door casings, take into account the ¼-inch reveal on the edge of the jamb. As a guide, use a compass set to ¼ inch to mark the reveal on the jamb.

2. Cut the miter.
Sight down the blade of the saw and slide the molding until the saw will cut just to the scrap side of your mark. Hold the molding against the back of the miter box, as shown *above*. Grasp it tightly so it will not slide as you cut it. As an alternative, use a power miter saw or radial-arm saw (see page 247).

INSTALLING BASE MOLDING

Install door and window casing and other vertical molding before you install molding at the bottom of your walls. Choose from ranch or colonial base molding or use a three-piece base for a traditional look (see page 120).

It is best to add a quarter round or base shoe as well. These types bend easily with variations in the flooring and buffer scuffs from vacuum cleaners.

You may be tempted simply to miter-cut pieces for inside corners. This often leads to unsightly gaps and misaligned joints because the corners are almost never true 90-degree angles. Instead, cut the first piece to length with a regular 90-degree cut and cope-cut the second piece (see page 98).

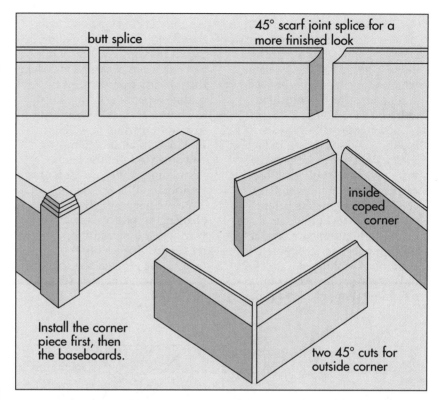

butt splice

45° scarf joint splice for a more finished look

inside coped corner

Install the corner piece first, then the baseboards.

two 45° cuts for outside corner

ACHIEVING THAT PROFESSIONAL LOOK

■ Avoid splits. Thin stock, such as often is used for baseboard molding, is prone to splitting and cracking. Don't take chances. Wherever you will be driving a nail within 3 inches of the edge of a piece, drill a pilot hole. You may be able to simply attach a short piece of molding with construction adhesive.

■ Don't overnail. The most common mistake amateurs make when installing moldings is to put in too many nails. Drive in only as many as you need to hold the piece firmly flush against the wall.

■ Stain first, but paint second. If you will be staining molding, do it before you install it. If you will be painting, install the molding first, then paint.

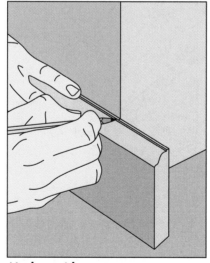

Mark outside corners.
As with all molding, for greater accuracy, hold and mark the pieces in place wherever possible. For an outside corner, butt one end of the molding in place, allowing the other to extend past the corner. Make the mark exactly even with the corner.

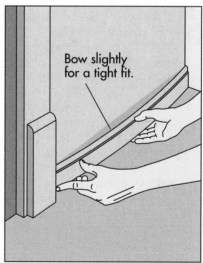

Bow slightly for a tight fit.

Install an inside-to-inside piece.
Mark and cut the piece about 1/16 inch longer than the space. If you are butting against a piece of casing, make sure the casing is well-secured so it does not move when you press against it. Install the baseboard by bending it into position. This will give you a tight fit on both sides.

INSTALLING CROWN MOLDING

Transform a boxy room with the elegant and softening beauty of crown molding. With more and more molding profiles available, you have plenty of options for adding an attractive finishing touch to your home.

Although installing crown molding takes patience and a few tricks of the trade, homeowners who are comfortable with basic carpentry tools and who have coped molding miters before should have few problems. Careful fitting and refitting are crucial to obtaining a close fit between sections of molding.

When working over your head, a solid working platform makes all the difference. Don't try to do the careful fitting and nailing that crown molding requires while working from a stepladder. Make the job easier on yourself by finding a plank and two sturdy sawhorses to make a platform to stand on while installing the molding. In addition, enlist a coworker to hold the lengths of molding while you measure, position, and fasten them.

Before beginning this challenging project, review marking and measuring techniques (pages 88–89), how to use a miter box (page 96), and nailing techniques (pages 103–104).

YOU'LL NEED

TIME: About 4 hours for a 12×12-foot room
SKILLS: Precise measuring, use of miter box or power miter saw, driving nails.
TOOLS: Deep miter box with backsaw or power miter box, drill, hammer, nail set.

CAUTION!
WHICH SIDE IS UP?
Remember to think upside down as you make miter cuts. Double-check which edge of the crown molding goes up— the difference is subtle.

Money $ Saver

PRACTICE MAKES PERFECT
To avoid expensive mistakes with crown molding, you should hone your mitering and coping skills before you plunge into the job. Ask your local home center or lumber dealer for a 2- or 3-foot scrap of molding similar to the type you plan to use. Practice the steps shown on these pages.

It is particularly important to gain some familiarity with the way molding is cut and coped. The more proficient you are at making overlapping joints, the less likely you are to make costly errors.

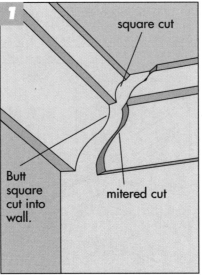

1. Cut the first piece square.
To achieve a mitered look with corners that are seldom perfectly square, run the first piece of crown molding tightly into the corner. Cope-cut the second piece in the shape of the profile of the molding, so it can butt neatly against the face of the first piece.

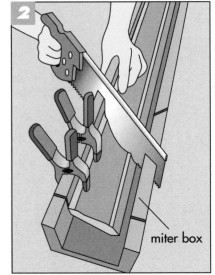

2. Make a miter cut.
Use a deep miter box and a fine-toothed backsaw to make a cut that reveals the profile of the molding. Position the molding so that it is upside down in the miter box. The face of the molding that goes against the ceiling will be on the bottom of the miter box. Remember, for inside corners, the bottom of the crown molding will be the longest edge.

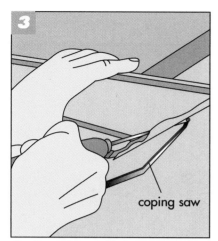

3. Cope the profile.

If the mitered cut is correct, you'll be able to see the profile of the molding. Cut away the excess wood along the back side of the molding with a coping saw. Err on the side of removing too much rather than too little; only the outermost edge of the coped molding will be seen.

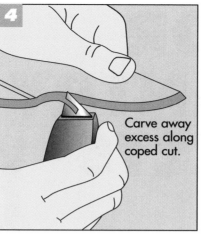

Carve away excess along coped cut.

4. Fine-tune your cut.

Use a utility knife to remove any excess material you missed with the coping saw. Be careful that you do not cut into the exposed face of the molding. Hold the piece in place to test the fit. Take it down and do more carving if necessary.

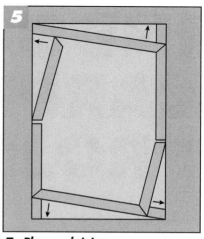

5. Plan each joint.

Map out the job so that one end of each piece of crown molding always will be cut straight and one end will be mitered and coped. Use butt joints for long runs. Save the most visible parts of the job for last, when you've honed your coping skills.

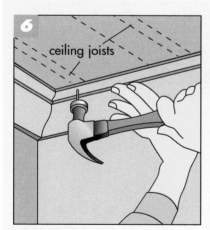

ceiling joists

6. Nail in place ...

If the molding runs perpendicular to the ceiling joists, determine the location of the joists. Drill pilot holes to keep the molding from splitting. As you attach the molding, tack it in place with a few nails. Take a good look at the positioning before completing the nailing.

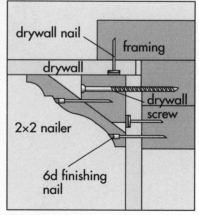

drywall nail
framing
drywall
drywall screw
2×2 nailer
6d finishing nail

or add a nailer.

To provide a solid nailing area where the joists run parallel to the crown molding, cut a beveled face on a 2×2, as shown. Cut the 2×2 to length and screw it to the wall so it's in the corner of the ceiling and the wall. The 2×2 provides a surface, at the proper angle, to which you can nail the molding.

TOOLS TO USE

BE SHARP

The right tools—kept clean and sharp—help make a precise job, such as installing crown molding, easier. Here are some tips:

■ Drop off your saw for professional sharpening well before you begin the job. A sharpened saw provides better control and a cleaner cut, and it makes the job go more pleasantly.

■ Buy new coping-saw blades. They break easily, so have half a dozen on hand.

■ Have plenty of clamps to hold the molding while you cut it. The less you rely on your own holding power, the easier and more accurately you'll be able to make the saw cuts.

INDOOR CARPENTRY PROJECTS

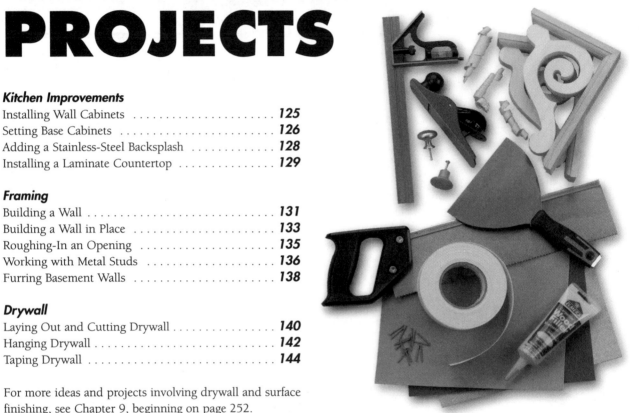

Chapter 4

Kitchen Improvements
Installing Wall Cabinets **125**
Setting Base Cabinets **126**
Adding a Stainless-Steel Backsplash **128**
Installing a Laminate Countertop **129**

Framing
Building a Wall **131**
Building a Wall in Place **133**
Roughing-In an Opening **135**
Working with Metal Studs **136**
Furring Basement Walls **138**

Drywall
Laying Out and Cutting Drywall **140**
Hanging Drywall **142**
Taping Drywall **144**

For more ideas and projects involving drywall and surface finishing, see Chapter 9, beginning on page 252.

INSTALLING WALL CABINETS

*T*ake the cabinets out of their boxes and inspect them carefully; you won't be able to return them once you have driven screws into them. If you are installing undercabinet lighting, you may need to drill holes in the back lower lip of the cabinets for the electrical cable to slip through.

If your walls are not plumb or square, you may end up with a cabinet that doesn't fit. Check in advance and reposition your layout accordingly.

Always work with a helper, and have a stable stepladder on hand. If any of the cabinets are heavy, remove the doors to reduce the weight and lessen the chance of damaging the cabinets.

You'll Need

TIME: Several hours for six or seven cabinets.
SKILLS: Leveling, driving screws.
TOOLS: Level, drill with screwdriver bit, clamps.

EXPERTS' INSIGHT

FASTEN WALL CABINETS TO WALL STUDS

If you've carried a stack of 10 or 12 dishes, you know how heavy they are. Cabinets holding dishes or canned goods bear a surprisingly heavy load. Because wall cabinets do not rest on anything, the screws attaching them to the wall carry all the weight. Make sure you drive screws into wall studs. If you are attaching to a masonry wall, use metal masonry shields.

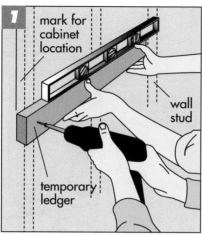

1. Attach a temporary ledger.
Anchor a straight piece of 2×4 lumber to the wall so you can rest the cabinets on it as you work. Level it and attach it with just a few screws or nails, so you won't create a big wall-patching job when you remove it.

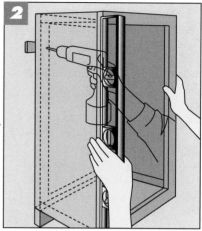

2. Fasten the cabinets.
While a helper holds the cabinet, check for plumb in both directions. Use shims, as shown, if necessary. Once the cabinet is positioned, drive 2½- or 3-inch screws through the cabinet frames and into wall studs. If your cabinet has a lip on top, drive the screws in there so they will not show. Use trim washers for a more finished look on the inside of the cabinet.

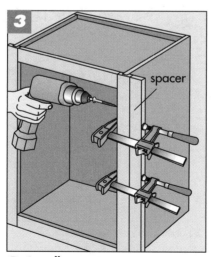

3. Install spacers.
Where the last cabinet meets up against a side wall, hold the cabinet in place and measure for a spacer. Cut it and attach as shown, using clamps to hold it firmly while you drill pilot holes and drive screws from the cabinet into the spacer.

4. Install spacer for inside corner.
If you simply attach two cabinets at an inside corner, usually at least one door will not open fully. Before installing them, attach a spacer to one of the cabinets (see Step 3) and then attach the other cabinet to the spacer. Drill pilot holes and drive in screws.

SETTING BASE CABINETS

Take the time to make sure all the cabinets are level from the beginning. If you give in to the temptation to cheat a little, you will run into frustrating problems, both in installing the other cabinets and in putting on the countertop.

If a baseboard or other piece of molding gets in the way, it is almost always best to take it off the wall and cut it, rather than cutting the cabinet to fit around the trim.

YOU'LL NEED

TIME: Most of a day for an average-size kitchen.
SKILLS: Leveling, driving screws, clamping, cutting.
TOOLS: Drill, level, hammer, chisel, pry bar.

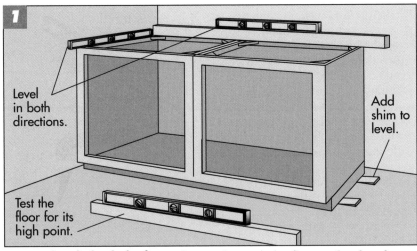

Level in both directions.

Add shim to level.

Test the floor for its high point.

1. Level and plumb the first unit.

Find the highest point on your floor and start there because you can shim up but not down. Set the first cabinet in place and check it for level in both directions. As a further check, make sure the stiles or door faces are plumb. Use shims at the floor to level and solidly support the cabinets. If your wall is out of plumb or wavy, you may need to shim the back of the cabinet as well—make sure when you drive the screws in (see next step) you don't pull the cabinet out of level.

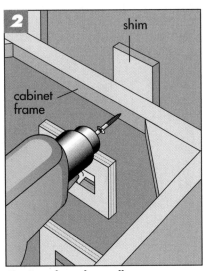

shim

cabinet frame

2. Attach to the walls.

Drive in screws through the back of the cabinet and into the wall studs. When possible, screw through solid framing pieces. After driving in the screws, check to see that the cabinet is still sitting flat on the floor. If not, back out the screws and adjust the shims before driving the screws back in. Check again for level and plumb.

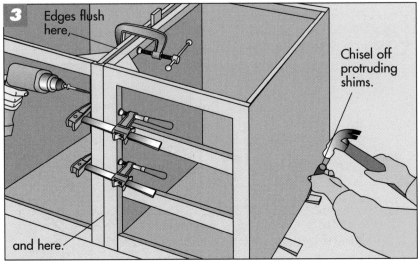

Edges flush here,

Chisel off protruding shims.

and here.

3. Join cabinets together.

After installing the first cabinet, use clamps to hold the next one in alignment as you screw them together. Make sure that their surfaces are flush with each other—not just the face frames, but the top edges as well.

Also make sure the screws are the right length, so they will not poke through the stiles. To keep the surface of the stiles smooth, drill pilot and countersink holes, then drive in the screws.

In most cases, you can use a hammer and chisel to nip off shims that stick out. With layers of shim, use a handsaw.

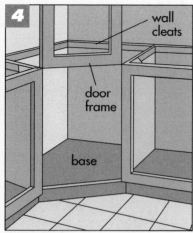

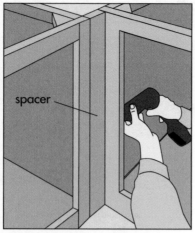

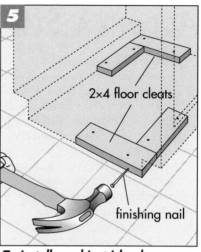

4. Install a corner cabinet...

You may buy a complete corner cabinet with sides or a less-expensive knockdown unit like the one shown above. For this type of corner cabinet, install the base first, then set the two adjoining cabinets in place next to it. Insert the door frame and join it to the adjoining cabinets. Install 1×2 cleats on the walls to support the countertop.

or join two base cabinets.

This method provides you with less usable space, but it may save money. Be sure to install at least one spacer so both doors swing freely. Clamp, drill pilot and countersink holes, and drive in screws.

5. Install a cabinet island.

When there is no wall to attach a cabinet to, as in the case of an island or peninsula, provide strong framing on the floor. Lay the cabinet on its side and measure its inside dimensions. Measure and install 2×4 cleats on the floor carefully so the cabinet slips over the cleats tightly. For exposed areas use finishing nails; otherwise drill pilot holes and use screws.

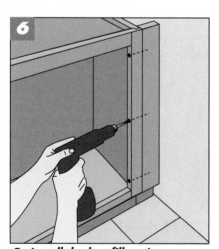

6. Install the last filler piece.

When you come to an inside wall, measure the distance between the cabinet and the wall at both the top and bottom. Rip a filler piece to fit snugly and position it flush with the cabinet face. Drill pilot and countersink holes and drive in screws. Unless the filler piece is more than 4 inches wide, you do not need to attach it to the wall.

7. Install panels.

If your design calls for an exposed edge that is not the side of a cabinet, as is the case when a dishwasher is at the end of a run, purchase an end panel made for the purpose of completing the run. Use clips at the floor, countertop, and wall so the panel can be removed to service the dishwasher.

EXPERTS' INSIGHT

INSTALLATION TIPS

Even durable cabinets made to hold up to decades of normal use can be scratched or dinged easily by carpentry tools. Take special care not to damage cabinets as you work on them. Cover installed cabinets with heavy drop cloths or cardboard from their shipping boxes and keep sharp tools well away from door and drawer faces.

If your floor is out of level or wavy, avoid unsightly gaps at the bottom of your cabinets by installing vinyl cove base. Or remove the kickboard, take out the nails, and reinstall it tight against the floor.

ADDING A STAINLESS-STEEL BACKSPLASH

Here's an unusual touch for a household kitchen—a stainless-steel backsplash. It looks stylish and provides a commercial-grade, easy-to-maintain surface between your countertop and the wall cabinets.

The first step is to find a source of the material. If your home center or hardware store can't help you, check in the Yellow Pages under stainless steel or sheet metal. Find a shop that can provide pieces of stainless steel to the exact length you want. Often, stainless steel has to be ordered from a specialty supplier, so schedule accordingly.

Check your measurements or provide a template to be sure you get the correct sizes of pieces. Although it is extremely hard, stainless steel can be damaged during installation. As you work, support the material so it doesn't crimp or get scratched because stainless steel is expensive.

YOU'LL NEED

TIME: A day for several pieces with a few outlet cutouts.
SKILLS: Measuring, checking for square, drilling, cutting metal.
TOOLS: Square, tape measure, drill, sabersaw

TOOLS TO USE

IF YOU MUST CUT STAINLESS STEEL

You can make rough cuts around outlets because the edges will be covered up. But it's hard to make a straight, smooth cut in this amazingly hard material. Use a drill to start the hole, then cut the opening with a sabersaw with a metal-cutting blade designed for cutting stainless steel.

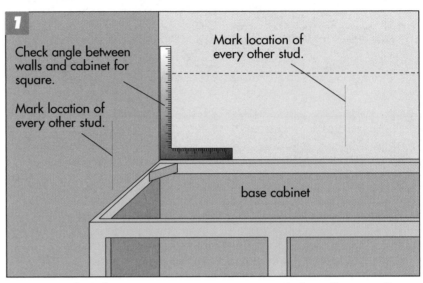

1. Lay out the job.
If possible, do this job before installing the countertop or the wall cabinets. Check the walls for square and measure the lengths you need. Corners are the critical areas; any variation along the length of the piece will be covered by the wall cabinet above and the countertop below. If your walls are plumb, you may be able to get away without the corner trim pieces shown in Step 3. If the walls are out of plumb, you may be able to compensate by cutting a slot in the corner and sliding a bit of one piece of steel into it.

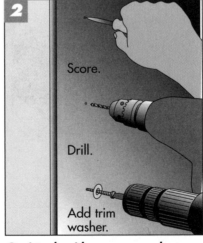

2. Attach with screws, washers.
Set the metal in place and make sure the pieces line up. Drill holes and drive stainless-steel screws, fitted with trim washers, into studs. Because the material is rigid and will be anchored by the cabinets as well, two screws driven in every other stud are adequate.

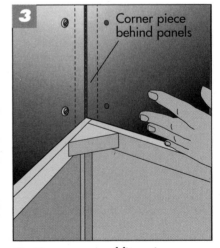

3. Use corner molding pieces.
If you have trouble getting the corners to match up, use a piece of corner molding, attaching it to the wall with clear silicone sealant and butting each panel against it. If one wall is wavy, you can, with patience, scribe and curve-cut one of the pieces using a belt sander.

INSTALLING A LAMINATE COUNTERTOP

You can make your own laminate countertop. Unless you are a skilled do-it-yourselfer, however, it may not be worth the time and effort. If your countertop configuration is fairly typical, you can save money by purchasing post-form countertops from your home center. Made with precut corners, these countertops can be trimmed to fit most base cabinets.

But if you don't like the colors available at your home center or if you have an unusual situation, such as a wide counter for an island or a narrow counter for a tight spot, you will need to have a countertop made for you. You may have a wider selection of color and pattern if you choose a square-edge top rather than a post-form.

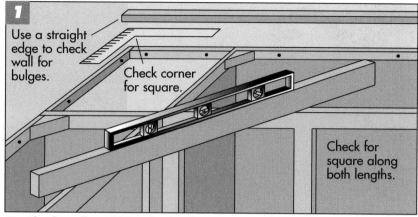

Use a straight edge to check wall for bulges.

Check corner for square.

Check for square along both lengths.

1. Check walls, cabinets for level and square.
Make sure cabinets are level all around so the top will be able to sit flat on them. If necessary, install cleats on walls, as shown, or end panels (see page 127) to support the top firmly. Check walls to ensure they are square with each other and free of major bulges by laying a straightedge down the full length of each. Most post-forms have a "scribe," a lip of laminate that can be trimmed (see below) to compensate for variations of up to ⅜ inch. A square-edged top with a separate backsplash will let you compensate for up to ¾ inch.

YOU'LL NEED

TIME: Half a day to install several tops carefully.
SKILLS: General carpentry, working carefully to avoid damaging the tops as you work.
TOOLS: Level, carpenter's square, drill, circular saw, compass, belt sander, laundry iron.

CAUTION!
BE SURE THE TOP HUGS YOUR WALLS

If you have a wavy wall or if your walls are more than ⅜ inch out of square, a ready-made top may not fit snugly against your walls. Take measures to straighten out your walls or hire a professional countertop maker to come in and take precise measurements so a custom countertop can be made to fit your space.

temporary guide

2. Cut a top to length.
If you purchase a factory-made top that you must cut yourself, do this with great care. Use a fine-cutting blade and cut it with the face side down to avoid nicks. Check that the blade on your circular saw is square to the base and use a clamp-on guide to make sure your cut is straight. Be sure to support the waste side so it does not fall off before you finish the cut—an easy way to chip laminate.

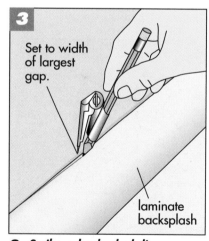

Set to width of largest gap.

laminate backsplash

3. Scribe a backsplash line.
The countertop might not fit tight against the wall, either because the walls are out of square or the wall is wavy. If such is the case, push the countertop against the wall, making sure it is aligned correctly with the base cabinets. Use a compass to scribe a line as wide as the largest gap between the countertop and the wall.

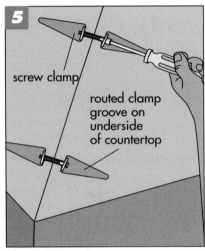

4. Belt-sand to the scribe mark.

Don't attempt to cut to the scribe mark with a sabersaw or circular saw—you'll almost certainly end up chipping the countertop. Use a belt sander with a fairly coarse 36-grit sanding belt. Pressing lightly, slowly sand away material up to the scribed mark.

5. Make a splice.

If you need to splice pieces at a corner or in the middle of a run, have a professional make the cuts and rout the grooves for the clamps. Apply waterproof glue to the edges of the pieces, line up the pieces, and start to tighten the clamps. Check the countertop as you work to make sure it doesn't slide out of alignment.

6. Attach the top to the cabinets.

Screws should extend as far into the countertop as possible without poking through it. Drill pilot holes every 2 to 3 feet along the front and rear of the top and drive in screws upward to hold the counter firmly. Screw into structurally sound sections of the cabinet framing. Make sure the countertop does not move as you work.

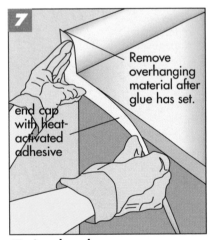

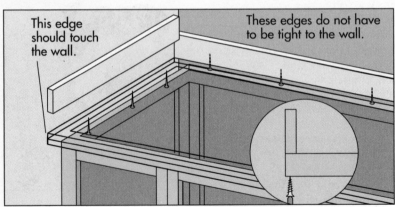

7. Attach end caps.

Buy a precut end cap to cover the end of a post form. If it has heat-activated glue, hold it in place so it overhangs the countertop edge. (You'll remove the excess later.) Slowly run a hot laundry iron along the end cap, being careful not to burn the laminate, until the glue adheres. File, sand, or rout away the excess material.

Install a square-edged countertop.

If you buy a square-edged countertop and your walls are not square, this type of edging covers up the gap. Set the top so it overhangs the cabinets evenly. Cut the backsplash pieces to fit and set them in place. Mark their position on the countertop, then pull the top away from the wall. Run a bead of bathtub caulk along the bottom of the edging, set the edging in place, and fasten it with screws from underneath. Attach the top from underneath as shown in Step 6. If your wall bows, fasten the top in place, then glue the edging pieces to the wall with construction adhesive. Brace them with pieces of 1× or heavy objects so the edging conforms to the wall.

BUILDING A WALL

Behind most finished residential walls lies a rather simple construction. Vertical members, called studs, butt at the top and bottom against horizontal members, called plates. Although it looks straightforward, building a wall takes thoughtful planning. When you cover the framing with sheets of drywall or paneling, the seams between sheets must fall in the center of studs. There must be a nailing surface for the sheets at all the corners (see page 134). And, all framing members must be aligned along a flat plane.

If the floor and ceiling are nearly level, it's rather easy to preassemble a stud wall on the floor and then raise it into position. If the floor and ceiling are uneven, or if you're building the wall in tight quarters, it's best to build the wall in place, custom-cutting each stud to fit and toenailing it to the top and bottom plates (see page 133).

Whichever approach you choose, make sure you have a way to attach your wall to the ceiling. If the wall runs perpendicular to the ceiling joists, simply fasten the wall's top plate with two 16-penny nails at every joist. If it runs parallel to the joists, you will have to install cross braces, so you can nail the top plate into solid material (see page 134).

YOU'LL NEED

TIME: About 2 hours to build a simple 10-foot wall; longer if you need to build it in place or in awkward situations.
SKILLS: Cutting, measuring, fastening with nails.
TOOLS: Tape measure, chalk line, pencil, framing square, saw, speed or combination square, level, hammer.

Use a framing square to establish a perpendicular line.

Pull the line taut and snap it.

chalk line

1. Mark the wall location.
Begin by deciding exactly where the wall will go. Use a framing square and a chalk line to mark its location on the floor. For long walls, check for square using the 3-4-5 method (see page 92).

Using a level and a straight 2×4 that is as high as your ceiling, mark the wall location on the ceiling, joists, or cross bracing. These marks will help you position the wall before you plumb it. Make sure there is adequate framing in the ceiling to which you can nail the top plate.

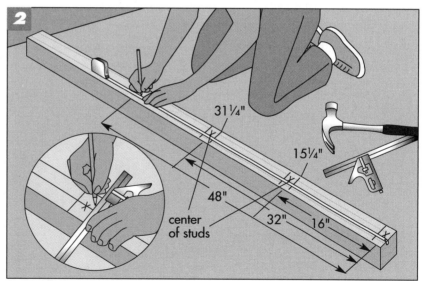

31¼"

15¼"

48"

center of studs

32"   16"

2. Cut and mark the plates.
Using your floor layout as a guide, mark and cut 2×4s for the top and bottom plates (usually the same length). Place them on edge beside each other and mark for the studs. The first stud will be at the end of the wall. The remaining studs should be 16 (or 24) inches on center, meaning that from the edge of the wall to the center of each stud will be a multiple of 16 (or 24). Make a mark every 16 inches; then with a combination or speed square draw lines ¾ inch on each side of your first marks. Draw an X in the middle of the marks to show where to nail the studs.

BUILDING A WALL

3. Provide nailers, cut studs.

If your new wall runs parallel to the ceiling joists, cut pieces of 2× material to fit tightly between the ceiling joists and install them every 2 feet or so. Measure for your studs (see page 131) and cut them to length.

4. Assemble the wall.

Working on a flat surface, lay the studs on edge between the top and bottom plates. It helps to have something solid, such as a wall, to hold the framing against while you assemble and nail the wall.

For speed, nail one plate at a time to the studs. Drive two 16-penny nails through the plate and into the ends of each stud. Because hammer blows tend to knock studs out of alignment, continually double-check your work while nailing. Keep the edges of the studs flush with the plate edges. If any of the studs are twisted or bowed, replace them.

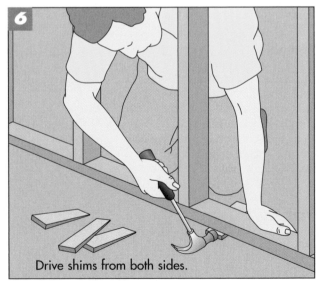

5. Raise the frame.

Framework can be cumbersome, so have a helper on hand. Position the bottom plate about where it needs to go and tip the wall into position. If the wall fits so tightly against the ceiling that you have to hammer it into place, protect the framing with a scrap of 2×4 as you pound. Tap both ends of the frame until it is roughly plumb in both directions.

6. Snug the frame with shims.

If the wall is a bit short in places, drive shims between the bottom plate and the floor or between the top plate and the ceiling joists. Have your helper steady the framework while you drive the pieces in place. Drive shims in from both sides, thin edge to thin edge, to keep the plate from tilting.

7. Fasten frame to wall and floor.
Once the frame is snug, recheck that the wall is plumb in both directions. Check both ends of the wall and every other stud. Fasten the top plate to the ceiling by driving in a 16-penny nail through the plate and into each joist. Fasten the bottom plate to the floor. Use 16-penny nails if the floor is wood; use masonry nails or a power hammer if the floor is concrete.

MEASUREMENTS

GETTING THE STUD LENGTH CORRECT

Few things are more frustrating than building a stud wall only to find that your measurements were off and the wall is ¼ inch too tall. When that happens, the only thing you can do is take the wall down, pull off one plate, remove the nails, cut all the studs, and nail it back together again.

To measure for stud length, nail together two scraps of 2×4 to represent the top and bottom plates. Set this double 2×4 on the floor, measure up to the joist, and subtract ¼ inch for shimming. Take measurements every few feet.

1. Install top and bottom plates.
If building a wall on the floor and raising it into position are not practical in your situation, begin by cutting the top and bottom plates, and marking them for studs (see page 131). Transfer the marks to the faces of the plates, making sure the marks are clear so you can see them easily to align the studs while toenailing.

Nail the top plate to the joists. Use a level and a straight board to mark the location of the bottom plate or use a chalk line case as a plumb bob. Mark the floor in two places and make an X to indicate on which side of the mark the plate should be positioned.

Use masonry nails or a power hammer to fasten the bottom plate to the floor.

16d nails

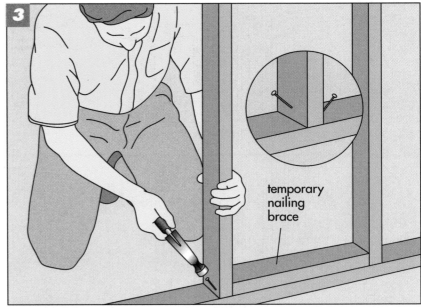

temporary nailing brace

2. Cut and install the studs.

With top and bottom plates installed, measure the required length of each stud individually. Add ¹/₁₆ inch for a snug fit and cut. Tap each stud into place. If you really have to whack it to get it into place, it is too long. Don't risk splitting the stud; take it down and trim it a little.

4. Frame at corners.

When framing corners, make sure there is a nailing surface for every piece of drywall or paneling that will be installed. This means adding nonstructural nailers.

In Situation 1, *right,* the extra stud is turned sideways to offer a nailing surface and strengthen the corner. Drive 16-penny nails first through end stud #1 and into the extra stud, then through end stud #2 and into the extra stud and end stud #1.

In Situation 2, *right,* several foot-long 2×4 scraps (usually three in a standard 8-foot wall) serve as spacers between two full-length studs placed at the end of one wall. Tie the wall sections together with 16-penny nails.

Situation 3, *right,* shows two intersecting walls. Nail three studs together and to the plates, then attach to the adjoining wall.

3. Toenail the studs.

To secure the studs, drive 8-penny nails at an angle through the side of studs and into the plate; this is called toenailing. Tap the nail once or twice while holding it parallel to the floor or ceiling. When the nail tip bites into the wood, change the angle to 45 degrees. Drive four to six nails into each joint, two on each side, with an optional one at the front and back. The first nail may move the stud, but the second nail, driven from the other side, will move it back.

If you have difficulty toenailing, drill pilot holes for the nails, using a ³/₃₂-inch bit. Or, place a 14¹/₂-inch board between studs to serve as a temporary nailing brace.

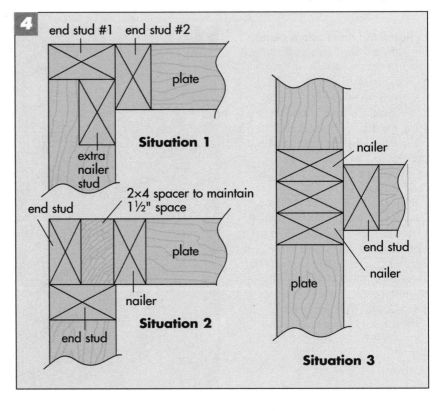

end stud #1   end stud #2

plate

Situation 1

extra nailer stud

end stud

2×4 spacer to maintain 1¹/₂" space

plate

nailer

Situation 2

end stud

nailer

end stud

nailer

plate

Situation 3

ROUGHING-IN AN OPENING

If you plan to install a door in your wall, find out the rough opening dimensions you'll need. For a prehung door, measure the outside dimensions of the jamb and add ½ inch for shimming. With a slab door (one that is not prehung), measure the width of the door, add 2½ inches for the side jambs and shims, and add 2 inches to the height for the head jamb, shims, and flooring. Standard door widths are 24, 26, 28, 30, 32, and 36 inches. Door heights usually are 80 inches.

Once you know the opening's size, build the wall as described on pages 131–133, with the addition of the framing members shown below. These framing members have special names and functions.

Jack studs are the vertical 2×4s on each side of the door opening. They are attached to a **king stud** or to another jack stud. This doubling of studs provides solid, unbending support for the door.

The **header** is made of two 2×6s with a ½-inch plywood spacer sandwiched in between. (The plywood is needed to make the header 3½ inches thick, the same thickness as the wall framing.) The header rests on top of the jack studs and spans the top of the opening, supporting overhead loads. For openings that are less than 3 feet wide, you can use 2×4s instead of 2×6s.

Cripples are the short 2×4s added between the header and the top plate. They maintain a 16-inch on-center stud spacing for nailing the drywall and help distribute the weight equally from above.

A window opening is much like a door opening. You install a sill (much like a header) at the bottom height of the window and add more cripples between it and the wall's bottom plate.

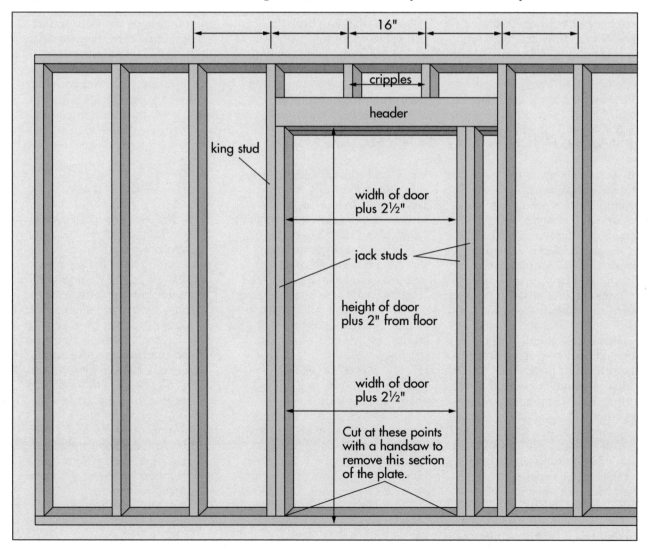

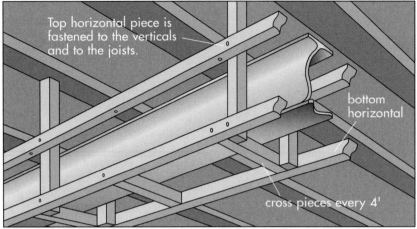

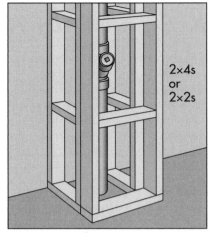

2×4s or 2×2s

Frame around an I-beam.

Use 2×2s to frame around a narrow obstruction, such as a beam. Fasten the frame together with screws rather than nails because the structure will be wobbly as you work. Drill pilot holes whenever you drive a screw near the end of a board.

Make chalk lines on the joists, 1⅝ inches out from either side of the beam. On every other joist,

attach a vertical 2×2 to the joists, cutting them to extend 1¾ inches below the bottom of the beam. Fasten horizontal pieces to the bottom ends of the verticals, then fasten horizontal pieces at the top, driving screws into both the vertical supports and the joists. Finish the framing by installing short horizontal cross pieces about every 4 feet between the bottom horizontal frame members.

Frame around a pipe.

You can cover a soil stack or other tall, narrow obstruction with a frame. Mark lines on the floor and measure for top and bottom plates as you would a regular wall. Draw plumb lines on the walls to use as guides. Build three narrow walls of 2×4s or 2×2s; raise them into position; and fasten them to the floor, ceiling, wall, and each other.

WORKING WITH METAL STUDS

Metal framing costs a good deal less than wood 2×4s, and it is lighter. Metal is not susceptible to rot or insect damage, and the factory-made pieces are free from bows, twists, knots, and other imperfections that sometimes make wood hard to work with.

Working with metal studs takes some adjustments. You can't build walls on the floor then raise them up. Instead, you must install the top and floor runners, then insert the studs. Cut metal studs with tin snips or a circular saw and metal-cutting blade. Fasten the pieces together with self-tapping screws.

If you make a mistake, it usually is easier to move a metal stud than a wood one. Running electrical wiring and pipes for plumbing is easy because punchout holes are precut in the studs.

On the downside, once walls are built, you can't attach items to

metal stud walls as easily as you can with wood walls. You can fasten items to a metal stud with a screw, but not a nail. If you plan to hang cabinets or shelves on the wall, cross-brace the wall with C-runners. Door jambs and windows can be attached to steel framing, but it's easier to shim and attach the units if you use wood framing, fastened to the metal studs, around these openings.

YOU'LL NEED

TIME: 1 to 2 hours to build a basic 12-foot wall.
SKILLS: Measuring and marking for walls, cutting with tin snips, fastening with a drill or screw gun.
TOOLS: Tape measure, level, tin snips or circular saw with metal-cutting blade, drill or screw gun, plumb bob.

CAUTION!
WATCH OUT FOR METAL

■ The ends of metal studs, especially those that you cut, often are very sharp. When working with metal, wear gloves. If you're cutting with a circular saw and metal cutting blade, wear long sleeves that are not loose or floppy.

■ Cutting metal also can be dangerous because small pieces of metal fly through the air. Be sure to wear eye protection whenever you cut metal studs.

■ If you run electrical wiring through metal framing, use sections of plastic foam pipe insulation or specially made plastic grommets to protect wires from damage.

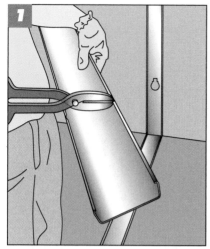

1. Cut the studs.

Lay out framing as you would for a wood wall (see pages 131–134). Cut the runners to be used for top and bottom plates to length with tin snips. Or, use a metal-cutting blade on a circular saw. Using a circular saw is faster, but make sure no one is in the area as you cut, and wear protective eye wear and clothing as you work.

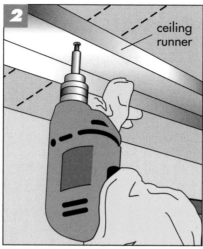

2. Attach the ceiling runner.

Position the ceiling runner and attach it to each joist with a drywall screw. If joists run parallel to the wall, install cross-bracing so there is something to which you can attach the runner. Position the floor runner directly below the ceiling runner, using a plumb bob. Attach it to the floor with screws or masonry nails.

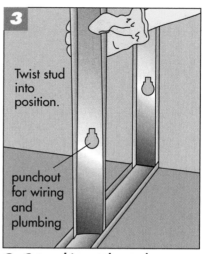

3. Cut and insert the studs.

Cut the studs to length with tin snips. Insert them into the runners, starting at a slight angle and twisting them into place. For easier plumbing or electrical installation, make sure all the stud legs are pointed in the same direction and all the predrilled punchouts line up.

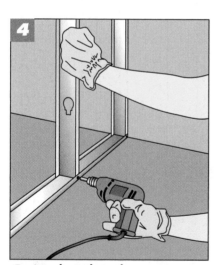

4. Attach studs to the runners.

Once studs are placed correctly, drive in 7/16-inch pan- or wafer-headed screws through the runners and into the studs. Hold the stud flange firmly against the runner as you work. Drive in four screws, one on either side of each runner at the top and bottom.

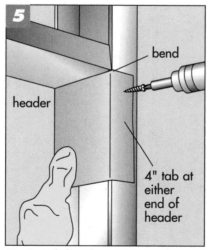

5. Attach headers.

Where you need a door or window header, cut a stud piece 8 inches longer than the width of the opening. Cut the two sides of the stud 4 inches from each end so you can bend back a tab, as shown. Slip the tabs into place and attach with screws.

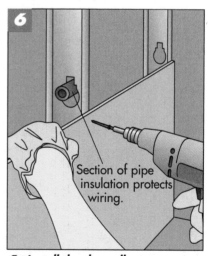

6. Install the drywall.

Inspect the framing to make sure you have a fastening surface for drywall at all points. Attach the drywall with drywall screws placed 8 to 12 inches apart. Install corner beads with screws or staples. Tape and finish the walls (see pages 144–145).

FURRING BASEMENT WALLS

When finishing basement walls, one option is to build regular stud walls (see pages 131–134), and fasten them to the concrete or masonry walls. A stud wall goes up quickly, gives you room to add plenty of insulation, and ensures that the new walls will be straight, even if the existing walls are not. The disadvantage is you lose some floor space because of the thickness of the walls.

If insulation is not a problem and your basement walls are fairly smooth and straight, you may want to save money in materials and preserve some square footage by building the walls with 1×2, 1×3, or 1×4 furring strips.

The layout is the same as for stud walls. The seams between drywall or paneling sheets must fall on a furring strip, and there must be a nailing surface in all corners and at ends of the sheets.

The construction method, however, is much different. Furring strips are shimmed where necessary, then fastened with glue and masonry nails or with a power hammer, which shoots nails with gunpowder charges (see the "Tools to Use" box, *opposite*).

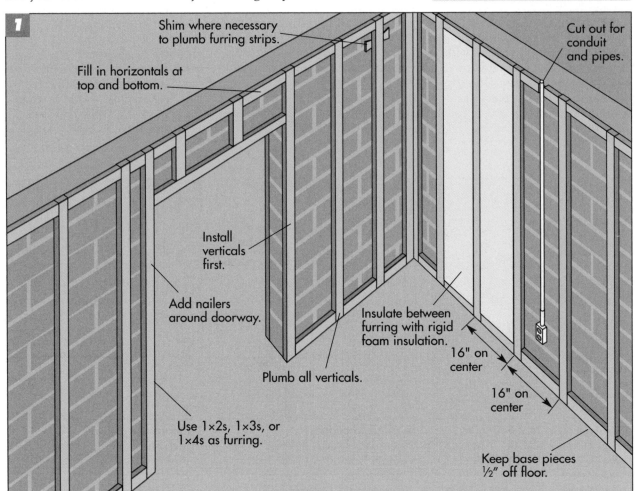

1. Shim where necessary to plumb furring strips.

Fill in horizontals at top and bottom.

Cut out for conduit and pipes.

Install verticals first.

Add nailers around doorway.

Insulate between furring with rigid foam insulation.

Plumb all verticals.

16" on center

16" on center

Use 1×2s, 1×3s, or 1×4s as furring.

Keep base pieces ½" off floor.

1. Plan the furring layout.
Begin the job by marking the locations of the vertical furring strips. One easy way to do this is to position a sheet of your wall material in the corner of the room,

plumb it, and strike a chalk line down its outside edge. Using this line as a guide and 16 inches as the center-to-center measurement, mark the locations of the other vertical strips along that wall.

Measure and cut each strip to fit between the floor and ceiling. Cut each piece ½ inch short, so that it will be fastened a bit above the floor as a safeguard against flooding and settling.

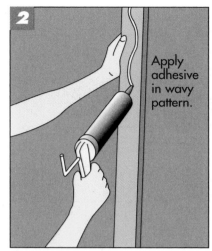

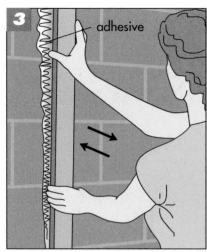

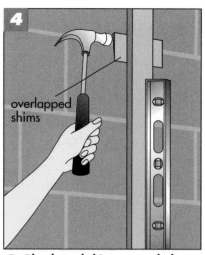

2. Apply adhesive.

With a caulking gun, squeeze a wavy ¼-inch bead of construction adhesive onto the furring strip. As you finish, turn the gun's handle to ease pressure on the adhesive, discontinuing the flow. Push the strip against the wall in its correct location, pressing firmly to help spread the adhesive.

3. Set adhesive.

Pull the strip off the wall and lean it against another wall to dry and let the adhesive begin to set up. After letting it set for the time specified by the manufacturer, press the strip back into place.

4. Plumb and shim as needed.

Check the strip for plumb. If a dip or bulge is noticeable to the eye, tuck pairs of shims behind the strip and wedge it into line. Double-check your work as the job progresses by holding a straightedge horizontally across four or five vertical pieces. Correct any gaps or bulges.

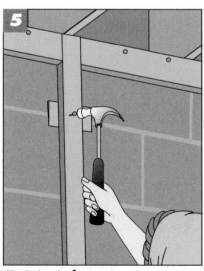

5. Drive in fasteners.

Hammer concrete nails through the strip and the shims and into the masonry wall. On a brick or block wall, it often is easiest to drive the nails into the mortar joints. Use a baby sledge if you have one. Driving nails into concrete walls is extremely difficult; consider a power hammer (see box at *right*).

6. Install the horizontal pieces.

After all the verticals are in place, aligned, and secured, begin work on the top and bottom horizontal pieces. Measure and cut them one at a time. Apply adhesive, shim if necessary, and install them as you did the verticals.

TOOLS TO USE

POWER HAMMER

Choose a power hammer that loads quickly. It usually makes sense to rent a better-quality power tool, rather than buying a cheap one. Experiment with several types of loads to find one powerful enough to drive in the nails completely, but not so powerful as to drive them through the furring strips. *Note: Follow the manufacturer's directions carefully. A power hammer is literally a firearm, and is dangerous if mishandled.*

QUART-SIZE CAULKING GUN

On large jobs, this tool will pay for itself because adhesive purchased in large tubes costs less per ounce. It also will save you time and create less mess because you'll need to change tubes 2½ times less often.

LAYING OUT AND CUTTING DRYWALL

Drywall is inexpensive, and hanging and finishing skills are within the reach of a homeowner. But hanging drywall is difficult work. The sheets are heavy and unwieldy because they are so large. Most rooms are out of square, so cutting is often difficult.

Finishing drywall to a perfectly smooth surface takes three applications of compound and sandings for professionals—four or five for beginners. Finishing success relies in part on careful hanging. So, this is one job you may want to get estimates for hanging and finishing and hire the job out to a professional.

Check framing to make sure you have adequate nailing surfaces (see page 132). Add members that are missing. If you are covering an existing wall, locate all the joists and studs and clearly mark their locations on the walls and ceilings. Draft a strong helper—hanging drywall alone is nearly impossible.

YOU'LL NEED
TIME: With a helper, a day to drywall a 12×12-foot room.
SKILLS: Measuring, physical strength, thoroughness.
TOOLS: Tape measure, drywall square, utility knife, drywall saw, chalk line.

TOOLS TO USE

DRYWALL SQUARE
Don't hesitate to spend the money for a drywall square (see page 71). It quickly pays for itself in time and labor savings. For crosscuts, you simply make one measurement, set the square in place, and run your knife along the square's blade for a square cut. It also simplifies rip cuts.

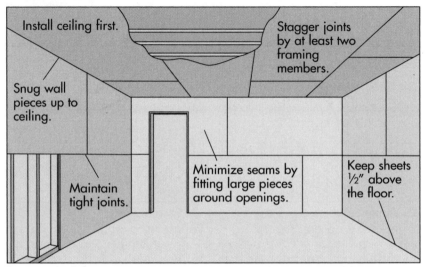

Install ceiling first.

Stagger joints by at least two framing members.

Snug wall pieces up to ceiling.

Maintain tight joints.

Minimize seams by fitting large pieces around openings.

Keep sheets ½" above the floor.

Lay out the job.
Plan where each sheet will go. Begin by hanging sheets on the ceiling, then butt the wall pieces up against the ceiling. Remember that taping and finishing (see pages 144–145) the drywall takes more time than hanging it (see pages 142–143), so minimize seams wherever possible. Sometimes you can eliminate a butt seam, which is the hardest type of seam to tape, by using 10- or 12-foot sheets instead of standard 8-foot sheets. Installing these big sheets may seem like a lot of trouble, but it will save you time and effort in the long run.

Trap with foot.

Cut backing after break.

Make a crosscut.
Store drywall sheets flat or on edge on pieces of 1× or 2× scrap lumber to hold the sheets off the floor. Before cutting a sheet, make sure the finished surface is facing you. Mark your cut line, stand the sheet on edge, and set your drywall square in place. Clasp the square firmly on top, and brace it at its base with your foot. With the edge of the knife blade against the square, cut downward most of the way, then finish by cutting up from the bottom. Snap the segment back away from your cut line. Finally slice through the backing paper with your knife.

Measure for the last piece.
To determine the correct cutoff length of a corner sheet, measure the distance from the last sheet to the corner at both the top and the bottom. If it is more than 1/4 inch out of square, mark both ends of the cut, rather than making a square cut with a drywall square.

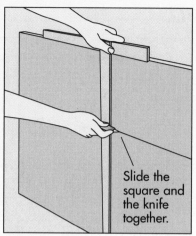

Slide the square and the knife together.

Make a rip cut.
If you need to make a parallel rip cut—one that is the same width all along its length—use your drywall square. Set the square on the edge of the sheet, and hold the knife against it at the measured distance. Slide the square along with the knife in

Use a chalk line for cuts not parallel to the edge of the sheet.

position, cutting as you go.
Often a rip cut will not be square; it will be shorter at one end than the other. In this case, make a mark at each end of the sheet and chalk a line between the marks. Cut freehand or use a straightedge as a guide if you need precision.

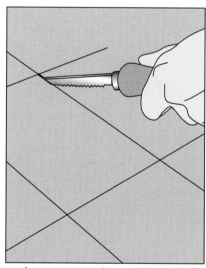

Make a rectangular cutout.
To make a cut for a receptacle box, measure the distance from the box edges to the edge of the last panel. Then measure the distance from the top and bottom of the electrical box to the floor (minus 1/2 inch) or from the piece above it. Transfer the measurements to the sheet and draw a rectangle. Score the surface with a utility knife, then cut it with a drywall saw.

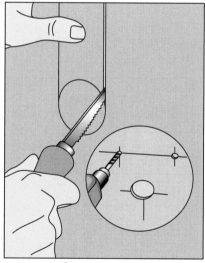

Cut around pipes.
To cut a hole for a pipe, measure and mark the sheet for the center of the pipe. Drill a hole using a holesaw bit that is slightly larger than the pipe diameter. Or, you can draw a circle and cut it out with a drywall saw or a knife.

HANGING DRYWALL

Be prepared for strenuous labor when it comes time to hang drywall. The sheets are heavy, you'll be working in awkward positions, and you'll have to hold the sheets in place while you drive in nails or screws. It's tempting to rush the job, but you'll kick yourself later if you do sloppy work. Wide gaps between drywall sheets take a long time to tape, and nobody wants nails popping out later. Here's how to do the job correctly the first time.

YOU'LL NEED

TIME: 20 minutes per sheet for walls, 30 minutes per ceiling sheet.
SKILLS: A strong back, fastening in difficult circumstances.
TOOLS: Tape measure, good ladders or scaffolding, hammer or drill with drywall-type screwdriver attachment, drywall taping blades.

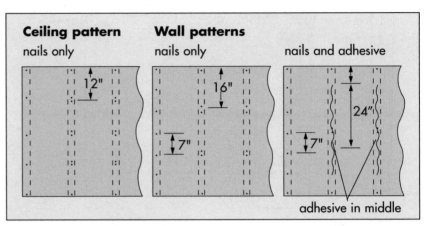

Nail or screw according to code.

Local building codes specify how many nails or screws you should use to hang drywall and in what sort of pattern. Codes vary not only from region to region, but from room to room; for example, more fasteners may be required in bathrooms. Check with your building department.

Many professionals don't nail in pairs, but there is good reason to do so: If one nail pops through the paper, the other will hold.

For ceiling panels, the general practice is to pair nails at 12-inch intervals around the perimeter and 12 inches along each joist. Requirements are less stringent for walls. If you don't use adhesive, install two nails into the wall studs at 16-inch intervals and a single nail every 7 inches along edges. When using adhesive, install two nails at 24-inch intervals and one nail at 7 inches along the edge. Keep adhesive 6 inches away from top and bottom of sheet.

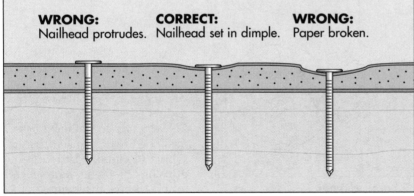

Set nailheads correctly.

If you simply drive in a nail flush, you will not be able to cover over it with joint compound. If you drive the nail too deeply, you will break the paper on the drywall. When the paper is broken, the nail won't hold; it tears right through the gypsum inner core.

Try to drive the nail so the nailhead is set into a slightly dimpled surface. No portion of the nailhead should protrude above the surface of the drywall.

To test if your nails are driven deeply enough, run a taping blade along the surface of the wall. You should not feel any nailheads click against the blade as you pull it across. Pull out any nails that miss a joist or stud. Swat the hole with your hammer to dimple it.

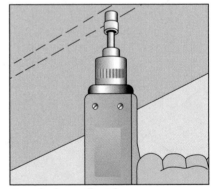

Attach drywall with screws.

If you are using screws, the same principles apply as with nailing: The screw head must be set below the surface, but it must not break the paper. This is difficult to do with a simple screwdriver bit. Use a dimpler bit or a drywall screwdriver (see box on page 143). Always drive in screws perpendicular to the sheet or their heads will tear the paper.

Install the ceiling sheets.

Hang drywall on the ceiling before installing the wall sheets. Start in a corner and against one side of the room and work out from there, keeping the panels perpendicular to the joists. Take time before you start to locate joists and mark their locations on the sheet and the wall. Searching for joists while holding the sheet up with your head is no fun.

The quickest, but most difficult, way to install drywall on a ceiling is to set the panel in place and support it with your head, leaving your hands free to hold and drive nails or screws. Wearing a baseball cap greatly minimizes pulled hair and a sore head.

To make things easier, construct one or two 2×2 T-braces to use as props. Or, rent a drywall hoist. Either solution will make the process easier and result in a much neater job.

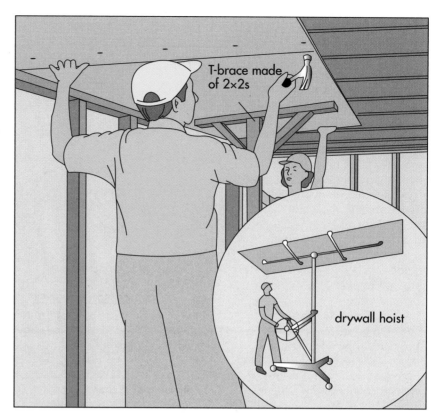

T-brace made of 2×2s

drywall hoist

TOOLS TO USE

DRYWALL HAMMER

There are hammers made especially for drywall installation. They are light, for easy handling; they have wide heads so it's easier to make a dimple without damaging the paper; and their heads are tilted a bit for access into corners. You may not use one very often, but it will make hanging and, subsequently, taping easier.

DRYWALL SCREWDRIVER OR DIMPLER BIT

A drywall screwdriver has an adjustable bit that, once set correctly, will drive the bit to the correct depth, then stop. A less expensive, and just as good, option is a dimpler bit that you can attach to a drill.

Install the wall sheets.

Once the ceiling panels are up, hang sheets on the walls. If you are installing sheets horizontally, begin with the upper sheets, butting them firmly against the ceiling drywall. Make sure all vertical seams hit studs. Butt the lower panels firmly against the upper panels, tapered edge to tapered edge. Raise up sheets tightly with a wedge or lever.

If you are installing sheets

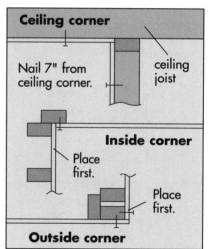

Ceiling corner

Nail 7" from ceiling corner.

ceiling joist

Inside corner

Place first.

Place first.

Outside corner

vertically, check the tapered edges to make sure they fall midway across a stud. If they don't, either cut the drywall or attach pieces of lumber to the stud to give yourself a nailing surface for the next piece.

Overlap pieces at corners, as shown *above*. Finish the job by adding the filler pieces, measuring and cutting each piece to size. Make sure each piece has at least two nailing members to support it.

TAPING DRYWALL

Once you've gained some experience, three coats of drywall compound, with sandings, will produce smooth walls. But as a beginner, don't be surprised if it takes you four or five coats. Unless you have large holes that require patching plaster, use ready-mixed drywall joint compound. Dry-mix compounds provide more strength for trouble areas, but you'll need to work fast if you use them. To hide imperfections, apply texture to your walls with a rented texture gun and hopper.

YOU'LL NEED

TIME: For a typical bedroom, 5 hours for the first coat and 2 hours for subsequent coats, plus time for sanding and drying.
SKILLS: Patience and willingness to learn.
TOOLS: Utility knife; 6-, 10-, and 12-inch taping blades; corner taping tool; pole sander or hand sander; tin snips.

EXPERTS' INSIGHT

DRYWALL FINISHING TIPS

■ Use self-sticking mesh tape on the drywall wherever a tapered edge meets a tapered edge, as shown *above*. Use paper tape everywhere else. Mesh tape requires less joint compound, but does not work as well for inside corners.
■ Rusty, gunked-up tools ruin your work. Scrape, wash, and dry blades after every use.
■ When sanding, control the extremely fine dust by using a fan to pull the dust out a window. Seal doorways and wear a breathing mask.

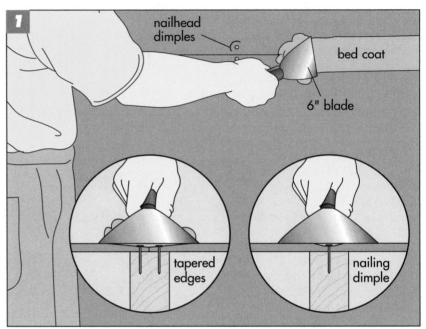

1. Apply a bed coat.
Conceal nailheads by putting compound on a 6-inch taping blade and passing over the spot twice. Make sure you leave compound only in the depression and none on the rest of the sheet. Do this with each coat until the dimple is filled in completely.

Joints are much more difficult— butt joints especially. If you are using self-sticking mesh tape, simply cut pieces to fit, press them into place, and begin applying joint compound. For paper tape, start by spreading a bed coat over the joint with a 6-inch taping blade. Apply just enough for the paper tape to adhere.

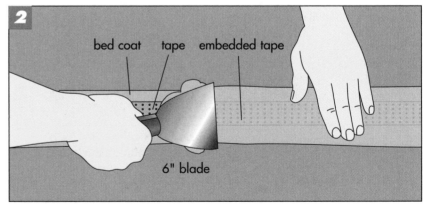

2. Embed the tape in compound.
(Skip this step if you are using mesh tape.) Immediately after applying the bed coat to a joint, center a length of paper tape over the joint and press the tape firmly against the filled joint by running your taping blade along it. If the tape begins to slide, hold it in place with your hand. If bubbles form under the tape, if there are places where the tape is not sticking to the bed coat, or if wrinkles appear, peel the tape back and apply more compound. Then press the tape back again.

3. Apply compound over the tape.

Load a 10-inch taping blade with compound and apply a smooth coat over the tape. Where two tapered joints meet, make sure the blade extends past both tapers. Fill in the tapers only, so you have a flat wall surface. For butt joints, feather out the compound 7 to 9 inches on each side; a small ridge in the middle can be sanded later. After the compound dries, scrape off ridges and bumps, and sand. Apply and sand successive coats until the surface is smooth.

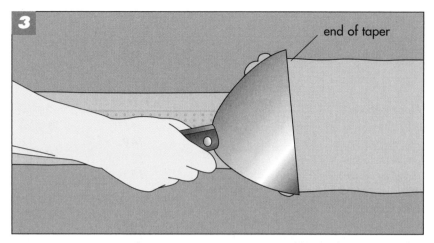

end of taper

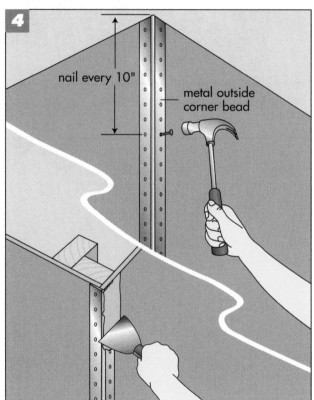

nail every 10"

metal outside corner bead

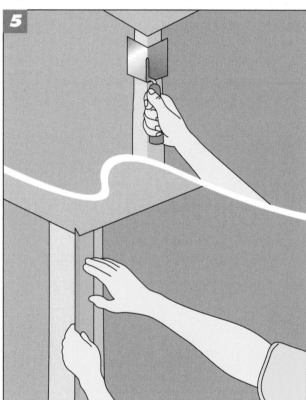

4. Coat outside corners.

To protect and conceal the drywall edges that meet at an outside corner, cut a piece of metal corner bead using tin snips. Fit the strip over the corner and fasten it to the wall one side at a time. Drive in nails or screws at 10-inch intervals. Check to make sure the flange of the corner bead does not protrude above what will be the finished surface by running a taping blade along the length of the corner bead. Fasten down any areas of flange that protrude. Apply a coat of joint compound with a 6-inch blade angled away from the corner. Allow one side of the blade to ride on the bead, the other side on the wall. For subsequent coats, use 10- and 12-inch blades.

5. Tape inside corners.

Outside corners can be almost fun, but inside corners are more difficult. Apply a bed coat of compound to both sides with a 6-inch blade. Cut a piece of paper tape to the correct length, fold it, and place it in position by hand. Keep it straight to avoid wrinkles. Run a corner taping tool along its length to embed the tape in the compound. Lift and reapply compound wherever the tape has wrinkles, bubbles, or nonadhering spots. Once the tape is embedded, apply some compound to the walls and some to the corner tool. Stroke on a smooth coat. This will take several passes and some practice. You may find it easier to feather out the edges with an 8-inch blade.

FLOORING

Chapter 5

Floor Repairs

Silencing Squeaks **147**
Refinishing Wood Floors **149**
Patching Resilient Tile **151**
Patching Sheet Flooring **153**

Stairways

Fixing Stairs **155**
Tightening Rails and Balusters **156**
Silencing Stair Squeaks from Above **157**
Silencing Stair Squeaks from Below **158**

New Installations

Installing Tongue-and-Groove Flooring **159**
Installing Wood Flooring over Concrete **160**

For more tile flooring projects, see Chapter 8, beginning on page 207.

SILENCING SQUEAKS

Most wood floors develop squeaks at some time or another. Temperature and humidity changes cause various floor parts to shrink and swell at different rates. The result: Squeaks develop where loose boards rub against each other or against loose nails.

Modern building codes determine how big the joists must be (typically 2×6 or 2×8), depending on the length they must span. Some older homes, however, were built without benefit of effective codes and may develop sags because the joists are undersized or too widely spaced.

In an older home, the subfloor may be made of 1× planks laid diagonally to the joists; tongue-and-groove softwood strips may be installed over the subfloor. In newer homes, the subflooring may be a single sheet of ¾-inch plywood, or there may be two layers of ⅝-inch plywood.

In other older arrangements, 1×3 "sleepers" are laid across the floor every 12 inches or so. The tongue-and-groove flooring rests on top of the sleepers.

If joists below the squeaks are concealed, repair from above, using the techniques on this page.

If the joists are exposed below, watch while someone walks on the noisy spot. If the subfloor moves, use shims or cleats to support it. Lack of movement may mean that the finished floor is loose and needs to be pulled down with screws. Strengthen any weak joists by installing bridging.

YOU'LL NEED...

TIME: 10 to 15 minutes per squeak.
SKILLS: Basic carpentry skills.
TOOLS: Drill, hammer, and nail set.

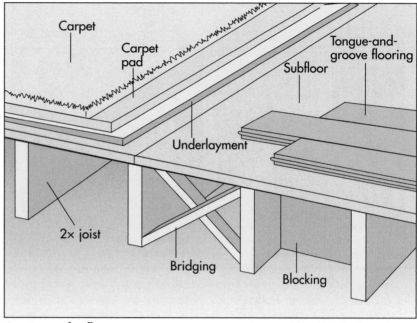

Anatomy of a floor.
Typically a subfloor rests on 2× joists stiffened by bridging or blocking. Underlayment may be used to add rigidity and smoothness for a finished surface, such as carpeting or tile. Tongue-and-groove flooring may rest on a plywood or plank subfloor or on underlayment.

1. To fix a squeak from above, drill pilot holes.
To quiet a loose board from above, nail it to the subfloor. To prevent the wood from splitting, drill pilot holes, angling them as shown.

2. Drive in flooring nails.
Drive ringshank nails or finish-head screws. If your flooring was installed with sleepers, there may be a space between the flooring and the subfloor. If so, you must use longer nails. Sink fastener heads below the surface, then fill with wood putty.

If the subfloor moves and you can work from below, insert a shim...
Use a tapered shim to tighten a loose subfloor board. Dip the tip of the shim in glue and tap it between the joist and subfloor until it's snug.

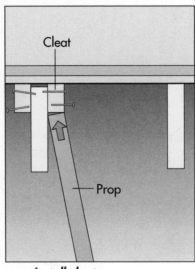

...or install cleats.
To tighten a series of boards, force a 2×4 up against the subfloor using a temporary prop. Nail or screw the 2×4 to the joist. Repeat on the other side.

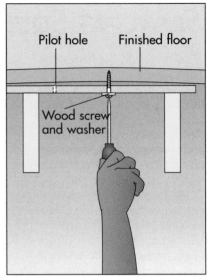

Screw upward.
Pull loose finished boards tightly against the subflooring using 1¼-inch roundhead screws. Drill pilot holes (take care not to drill all the way through the flooring), and use washers so the screws won't pull through the subfloor.

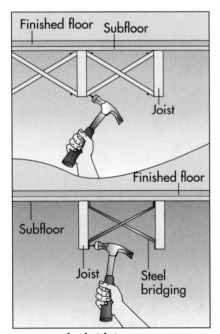

Improve the bridging.
If the bridging isn't tight between joists, drive in new, larger nails or screws at an angle. If squeaks persist, add steel bridging. Push it tight up against the subfloor, then nail it to the bottom inside of the joists.

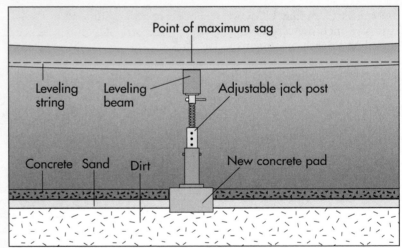

Lift a sagging floor.
If a floor has a major sag, you may have to add a supporting jack post under it. Break out a section of the basement floor, and pour a 24×24×8-inch concrete pad for the post to sit on. Let the concrete cure for a week. Place the jack post on the pad and set a 4×4 pressure-treated beam, long enough to span several joists, on top of the jack. Jack up the beam until it is snug against the joists, then raise it a quarter turn more. Wait a week and make another quarter turn, continuing this process until the sag is gone. Don't lift faster, or you may cause structural damage.

REFINISHING WOOD FLOORS

Refinishing a wood floor is a job that takes care and patience. You'll need to rent a random-orbital sander or upright drum sander and a disc-type edge sander. Ask the rental dealer to demonstrate the machines. A sander that uses 220 volts will work much better than a standard 120-volt machine; be sure you plug it into the correct receptacle.

Sanding a floor with a drum sander requires concentration and smooth movements. If you allow the sander to dig into the floor, it will create an unsightly dip. For floors without heavy finish buildup or deep scratches, an upright random-orbital sander (also called a jitterbug sander) is a better choice. It doesn't work as fast as a drum sander but is less likely to damage the floor.

If only the finish is damaged and you do not need to remove deep scratches, consider "screening" rather than sanding. Rent a janitor's buffing machine, and buy circular screens to fit. If a home center does not have this equipment, check with a flooring supply store.

Do this work on a day when you can open doors and windows to let out the dust. Wear a respirator to contend with fine dust, and seal off adjoining rooms with dampened sheets.

YOU'LL NEED...

TIME: 6 to 8 hours over 2 days for a 10×12-foot room. Allow an additional 2 to 4 days for applying the finish.
SKILLS: Basic carpentry skills.
TOOLS: Hammer, nail set, drum or random-orbital sander, disc-type edge sander, paint scraper or chisel, vacuum, tack cloth, putty knife, and paintbrush or wax applicator.

1. Remove the base shoe.
After you have removed the furnishings, pry off the baseboard shoe molding—the piece at the very bottom. If there is no shoe, remove the baseboard itself. If the pieces are in good shape, number them on the back so you can reinstall them. Otherwise plan to install new molding.

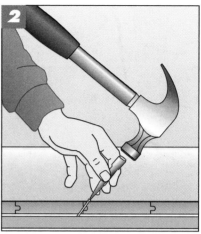

2. Set popped nails.
Any protruding metal will quickly rip up a sanding disc or belt. Use a nail set to drive any popped nails below the surface.

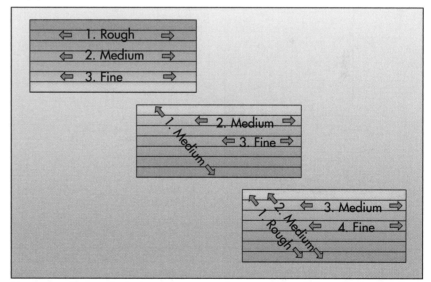

Drum-sanding techniques.
Different situations call for different sanding techniques. For most floors use three sandpaper grits—sanding *with* the grain. It may take several passes with each grit.

Getting nowhere sanding with the grain? Try one diagonal pass, but never sand directly across the grain. Finish up by sanding with the grain.

Badly cupped or warped old floors may require four cuts—two diagonal passes and two with the grain. Be sure to always overlap each pass.

3. Sand the main floor.

Make the first cut with coarse-grit sandpaper. Use coarse grit until you reach bare wood and most of the scratches have disappeared. With a jitterbug sander (as shown above) you don't have to follow the grain of the wood. Use medium- and fine-grit sandpaper for the next two cuts. At each stage expect to use several sheets of sandpaper on each of the four oscillating heads.

4. Sand the edges of the floor.

Use an edge sander for hard-to-reach areas. Work slowly, and finish with a very fine sandpaper so the circular lines will not be visible. In corners that the sander cannot reach, use a sharp paint scraper or chisel, always working with the grain.

Tack cloth

5. Remove dust with a tack cloth.

After each sanding pass, vacuum the floor thoroughly. Use a tack cloth after the last vacuuming to pick up the remaining dust.

WOOD FILLER

6. Apply a filler.

Fill in any holes and gaps between the boards using paste wood filler. Apply it first with a putty knife. Always work with the grain. When the filler begins to set, wipe across the grain with an old rag to remove excess. Let the filler dry overnight.

POLYURETHANE

7. Finish with polyurethane.

Apply two to four coats of polyurethane finish with a brush or a wax applicator, sanding with fine sandpaper between coats. Use a tack cloth to pick up all the dust between coats. Do not apply wax over a polyurethane finish.

PATCHING RESILIENT TILE

Most resilient floor tiles will lift out easily once you apply some heat to soften the adhesive underneath.

If you cannot raise a corner, use a chisel, working out from the center to the edges. Once the tile is removed, scrape or sand all remnants of old adhesive off the floor so the new tile will lie flat.

If you cannot find an exact replacement tile, steal a tile from under the refrigerator or another inconspicuous spot, and replace it with a fairly close match.

Different types of tile require different adhesives. To avoid confusion, ask a tile salesperson to recommend a suitable product.

To make the new tile look less conspicuous, rub off the gloss with fine steel wool.

YOU'LL NEED...

TIME: About 15 to 20 minutes, depending on how hard it is to remove the old tile.
SKILLS: Basic skills.
TOOLS: Putty knife, straightedge, utility knife, sanding block, framing square, clothes iron, chisel, and adhesive applicator.

CAUTION!
ASBESTOS TILE
Some older tiles contain asbestos, which is toxic if inhaled. If you are not sure, call in a pro for evaluation. If you must remove asbestos tile yourself, wear a respirator-type dust mask. Keep the area damp while you pry the tile out so fibers cannot fly through the air. Better yet, hire an experienced pro.

1. Soften the tile with an iron.
Lay a towel on top and soften the tile with a medium-hot iron. Take care that the iron doesn't overlap onto adjacent tiles.

2. Pry out the tile.
While the tile is still hot, slip a putty knife under a corner and pry up. Make sure not to pry against the surrounding tiles.

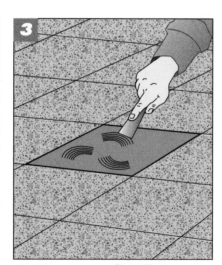

3. Scrape away the adhesive.
Use a putty knife or a paint scraper to remove all of the adhesive. If it does not come up, try heating the area again. You may need to sand away the last remnants of adhesive. Take particular care to remove adhesive from the perimeter of the patch.

Trim line

4. Test the fit of the new tile.
Be sure the new tile will fit and lie flat. If the tile is slightly large and you have to force it in, use a sanding block or plane to shave one or two sides until it fits properly.

5. Cut the tile to fit.
If the new tile is too large, use a utility knife and a straightedge to cut it. Slice with several passes, then bend the scrap back to break it off. Smooth any rough edges with sandpaper wrapped around a scrap of wood.

6. Spread adhesive.
Apply adhesive with an applicator (as shown above), a notched trowel, or a brush (check the manufacturer's instructions). With some types, you must wait until the adhesive has dried to a tacky feel before setting the tile. With other types, the tile should be set while the adhesive is wet.

7. Soften the tile with an iron.
Use the iron to soften the new tile. Protect the tile's surface with a cloth.

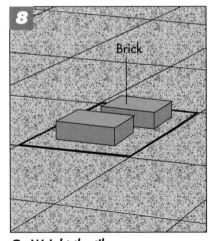

8. Weight the tile.
Set—do not slide—the new tile into position. Wipe away any squeezed-out adhesive using a cloth dampened with water or mineral spirits, depending on the type of adhesive. Weight the tile down for 24 hours before walking on it.

EXPERTS' INSIGHT

SOLVING OTHER TILE PROBLEMS

There are two basic types of resilient tile—commercial tile, which has flecks of color that run through the tile, and surface-printed tile, which has an embossed pattern.

■ **Tears:** Cheaper varieties of surface-printed tiles are easily torn. If this is a recurring problem, remove all the tiles and install tiles of a higher quality.

■ **Lifts:** Surface-printed tiles are often made to be self-sticking, but the self-sticking adhesive is not very strong. When installing a replacement tile, use tile mastic to enhance sticking power.

■ **Scratches:** Scratched commercial tile will often heal itself in time. If you fill a scratch with wax or acrylic finish, the damage will disappear eventually. (See 154.)

■ **Burns:** Scouring—plus some careful scraping with a sharp knife—also will remove shallow burns.

■ **Stains:** You can often remove stains by rubbing them with a mild detergent solution. If that doesn't work, try a white appliance wax. As a last resort, scour stains with very fine steel wool and a household cleanser.

PATCHING SHEET FLOORING

Most sheet flooring is glued to the floor in a bed of adhesive. Some newer types of flooring, designed especially for do-it-yourself installation, require adhesive only at seams and edges.

If the entire floor has been laid in adhesive, you usually can work a putty knife underneath and peel up the damaged piece. You may need to apply heat with an iron (see page 151) to loosen it. To make the patch less conspicuous, take time to carefully match its pattern to the surrounding area. To patch the newer types of flooring, cut out the damaged section and cement a patch as you would the seam of a new floor.

Though it is often referred to as "linoleum," most sheet flooring today is made of vinyl with an embossed surface-printed pattern. This product can be durable but if it is deeply scratched or torn, it must be patched or replaced. (Genuine linoleum, which is making a comeback, has color that runs through its body. That means any scratches will conceal themselves.)

A "no-wax" finish will eventually wear away. Rejuvenate the floor using acrylic finish or a product made specifically for no-wax floors.

YOU'LL NEED...

TIME: 20 to 25 minutes, depending on the time needed to clean the underlayment.
SKILLS: Basic skills.
TOOLS: Utility knife, framing square, putty knife, and adhesive spreader.

1. Mark with a framing square.
Use a framing square to mark and cut around the damaged area. Cut with a utility knife.

Flooring scrap

2. Trace the cutout.
Lay the cutout on a piece of matching material so that the pattern lines up precisely. Use a pencil or felt-tipped pen to trace around it. Accuracy is essential for a good fit.

Framing square

3. Cut with a square.
Either leave the cutout in place and use it as a cutting guide or use a framing square to cut along the trace lines. Place a scrap of plywood under the patching material to prevent damaging the floor.

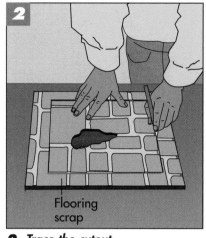

4. Scrape the underlayment.
Clean the underlayment, making absolutely sure to remove all of the adhesive. Then test-fit the patch. If it is too large, sand the edges.

5. Apply adhesive to the new tile.
If the area around the patch is not set in adhesive, lift up its edges and apply adhesive around the perimeter. Apply adhesive to the patch with a serrated spreader or a brush. Align one edge, matching the pattern, and lower the new section into place.

6. Weight down the patch.
Wipe off adhesive that has oozed out from the edges, then weight down the patch evenly for at least 24 hours.

TOOLS TO USE

FLOOR SCRAPERS

■ Vinyl sheet flooring shows even the tiniest imperfection in the underlayment. Use the right tools to make the underlayment perfectly smooth.

■ To remove adhesive or flooring from a large area, buy or rent a floor scraper, which can be operated while standing up. It has removable blades that scrape much more efficiently than a putty knife.

■ Once most of the adhesive has been removed, sand the area. Alternatively, wipe with a solvent-soaked rag to clean up and smooth the adhesive.

EXPERTS' INSIGHT

SOLVING OTHER SHEET FLOORING PROBLEMS

■ **Scratches:** Shallow scratches in wax or a no-wax finish may heal themselves. If you fill shallow scratches with floor wax or acrylic finish, they often seem to disappear. For deeper cuts compress the edges of the torn flooring by dragging a worn coin along—not across—them.

■ **Tears:** If the material has torn all the way through, lift the edges of the wound, scrape away any old adhesive, apply fresh adhesive, and stick the edges down again. For the repair to lie flat, you may need to sand one edge.

■ **Blisters:** If a blister develops in your flooring, flatten it by making a clean cut through its center. Alternating edges, press down on one edge of the cut, work adhesive underneath the other edge, and apply weight.

■ **Holes:** Filling small holes in vinyl flooring is a tougher assignment. The best and quickest way is to fill the void with a special seam-welding product offered by the manufacturer of the flooring. This product dissolves the vinyl, then sets up again to complete the repair.

■ **Patches:** Scrape flakes from a piece of scrap flooring and grind them into a powder. Mix the powder with clear lacquer or nail polish to make a putty-like paste. Work the paste into the hole, packing it well and mounding slightly to compensate for shrinkage. After the paste dries, sand the repair and wax according to the manufacturer's directions.

FIXING STAIRS

The staircases in your home have many parts—all of them interlocked with sophisticated joinery that is usually concealed from view.

A pair of stringers (also called carriages) slopes from one level to the next. The stringers support a series of steps, called treads. A simple staircase—such as one that leads to a basement or deck—consists of little more than stringers and treads (see page 156).

The illustration at right shows both "open-" and "closed-stringer" staircases. An open stringer has notches cut out of it; treads rest on the notches. A closed stringer has a series of grooves into which treads and risers fit.

In most interior stairways, risers fill the vertical gaps between the treads. Risers give a more finished appearance, keep dirt and objects from falling to the floor below, and add strength.

Finally, a balustrade—which consists of a handrail, balusters, and a newel post—provides safety along at least one side. Because all the parts are subject to various stresses, they all must fit tightly.

On most interior stairways, the balusters fit into the treads with dado, dowel, or dovetail joints. Balusters come in many styles, ranging from simple to ornate. On less-formal and outdoor stairways, the balusters may be attached to a bottom rail, which runs parallel to the railing a few inches above the treads.

You can treat most of the ills that afflict staircases using the techniques shown on pages 156–158. If you want to build a basic, open-riser staircase.

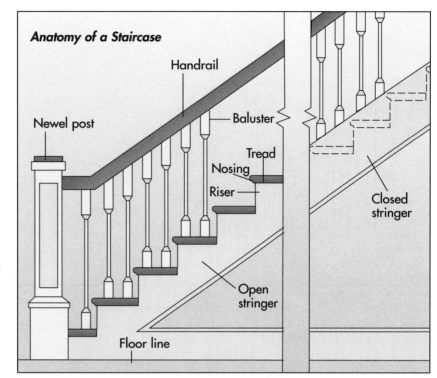

Anatomy of a Staircase

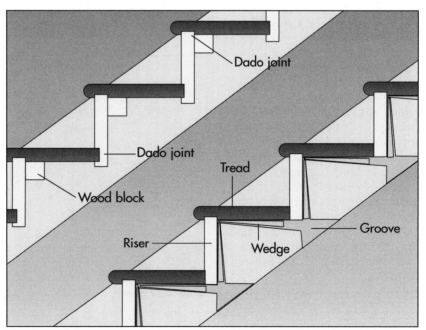

Treads and risers.
Interior stairway construction typically uses hardwood pieces milled to exact specifications and assembled much like cabinetry. Treads and risers usually fit together with dado joints (above left). In some cases wood blocks provide additional support.

In another arrangement (above right), treads and risers fit into grooves cut in a closed stringer. Wood wedges are tapped in and glued snug to the treads and risers.

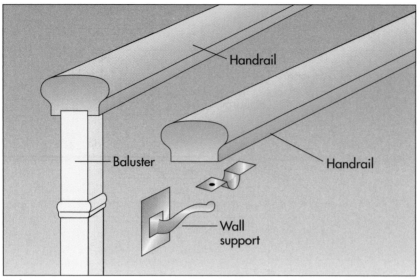

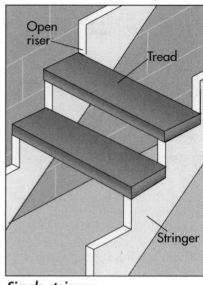

Balusters.

Balusters fit into grooves or holes in the underside of the handrail. At the stairway end, balusters often fit into holes in the stair treads. At the bottom of the stairway, a newel post is firmly anchored to the stair's framing.

If there is a wall on one side of the stairway, it may have a handrail, usually attached to special handrail supports that are anchored to studs in the wall.

Simple stairway.

A stairway for a porch or a basement may consist of stringers and treads. Usually a loose tread can be firmed up by drilling pilot holes and driving new screws. Even the simplest stairway should have a solid handrail.

Tightening Rails and Balusters

Wobbly handrails call for detective work. Is the handrail working loose from the balusters, or are the balusters parting company with the treads or bottom rail? If the handrail is pulling away from a newel post, use the technique at right.

A newel post handles a lot of stress. It is usually attached to the stringer, and may be attached to the house's framing as well. Unless you see an obvious solution to a wobbling newel post, call in a pro for help.

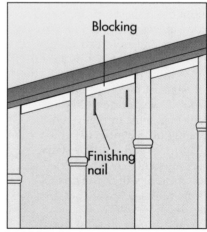

Screw and glue.

Drill a pilot hole at an angle through the baluster into the rail or tread. Countersink a trimhead screw in the hole. Alternatively, drill pilot holes through the railing and into the baluster. Work wood glue into the joint, and drive finishing nails or finishing screws.

Add blocking.

If the entire railing is loose, add blocking as shown. Use a T-bevel and a miter box (see page 96) or a power miter saw to cut angles for a snug fit. Drill pilot holes, apply wood glue, and drive finishing nails or trimhead screws.

SILENCING STAIR SQUEAKS FROM ABOVE

Most staircase squeaks result from a loose tread rubbing against the top or bottom of a riser or a stringer. To locate the problem, watch as someone rocks back and forth on each tread. If the tread moves, it's time to take corrective action.

You can stop a squeak by forcing the tread either down or up, and wedging it firmly in place.

A small problem can sometimes be solved using finishing nails. However, take care: If you drive a nail near the edge of a tread or riser, continued flexing of the riser could cause the wood to crack.

Work from below if you have access to the underside of the staircase. Otherwise you'll have to attack the situation from above. A few well-placed nails, screws, or hardwood wedges will usually solve the problem.

The directions on these pages enable you to repair several squeaky treads. If the stairway squeaks or groans at many points, however, the problem is likely structural. Go under the stairway and look for a cracked stringer, a closed stringer that is pulling away from the wall, or treads that are pulling away from a closed stringer. To correct a major problem, call in a pro.

YOU'LL NEED...

TIME: About 15 minutes per tread.
SKILLS: Basic carpentry skills.
TOOLS: Backsaw, coping saw, hammer, pry bar, drill, utility knife or chisel, screwdriver bit, and nail set.

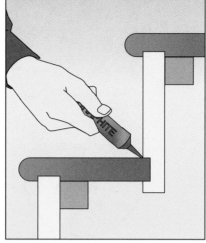

Powdered graphite.
Lubricating squeaks with powdered graphite may quiet them, but only temporarily. Squirt graphite into suspect joints and wipe away any excess graphite.

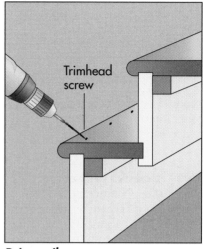

Drive nails or screws.
If the front of a tread is loose and you don't mind the appearance of small holes in the tread, drill pilot holes at opposing angles. Drive in ring-shank flooring nails or trimhead wood screws. Countersink the fastener heads and fill with wood putty.

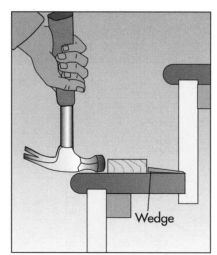

Install glued wedges.
If the tread is loose at the back, coat hardwood wedges (not softwood shims) with glue, tap into place, and let dry. Cut off exposed wedge ends with a utility knife or a chisel.

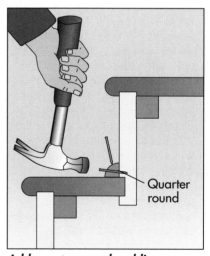

Add quarter-round molding.
For uncarpeted stairs, you can tighten joints with molding. The larger the molding, the better—¾-inch quarter round works well. Apply glue, drill pilot holes, and drive finishing nails into both risers and treads. Use a nail set to sink the nail heads.

SILENCING STAIR SQUEAKS FROM BELOW

Usually repairs made from underneath the stairs will be stronger and more durable than repairs made from above. The problem is getting there. Stairs leading to a basement may be exposed on the underside. Most other interior stairs are not so easy to access.

EXPERTS' INSIGHT

GAINING ACCESS

Removing one or more treads or risers may give you enough room to work. Because one stair part is often set into another part's groove, disassembly is often difficult. But as long as one side of the stairway is open, you should be able to take things apart. Often it helps to cut through nails or screws using a reciprocating saw. When you reassemble the stairs after the repair, the last tread will probably need to be fastened from above.

If the area under the stairway is covered with drywall and extensive repairs are needed, consider removing the drywall, even though replacing and finishing the drywall will be a substantial job.

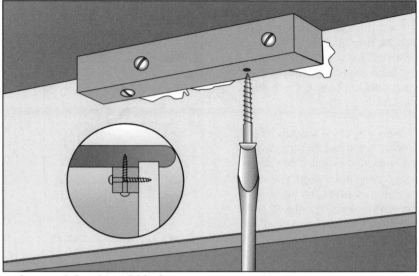

Tighten with hardwood blocks.
Purchase a length of 2×2 oak, birch, or other hardwood, and cut it into pieces about 4 inches long. Drill four pilot holes, running in two directions (see inset).

Where a tread or riser needs support, apply wood glue to the wood block, press it firmly in place, and drive wood screws to fasten it. Make sure the screws are not long enough to poke through the surface of the tread.

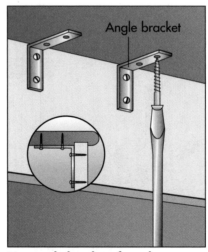

Use angle brackets for a loose tread.
If the entire tread is loose, use two or three metal angle brackets to tighten it down to the riser. Small brackets act much like wood blocks; larger brackets support the entire tread.

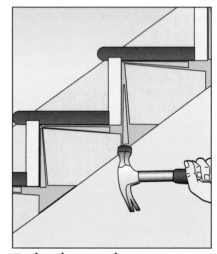

Replace loose wedges.
If old wedges are loose, remove and replace them. If a wedge comes out easily and in one piece, apply wood glue and hammer it back tightly into place. If a wedge is stuck but not supporting the stairway, chisel it out and replace it with a new wedge.

INSTALLING TONGUE-AND-GROOVE FLOORING

If you need to firm up a floor, install sheets of plywood. If the new flooring will be too high compared to nearby floors—most people find a height difference of ¾ inch to be a tripping hazard— you may need to remove old flooring before installing the new.

Sweep the floor well, set any popped nails, and remove the baseboard shoes or moldings. If the molding is in good shape, write numbers on the backs so you can remember where the pieces go. Otherwise plan on installing new moldings.

Level any bad dips by pulling up the old flooring, nailing shims to the joists, and renailing the old boards. Staple one or two layers of roofing felt (tar paper) onto the subfloor. This will help prevent squeaks.

Use spacers to create a ⅜-inch gap between the flooring and walls or baseboards. This is important; boards that are installed tight against the wall may buckle. Shoe molding will cover the gap when you're done.

YOU'LL NEED...

TIME: A day for a 12×14-foot room if the subfloor is prepared.
SKILLS: Intermediate carpentry skills.
TOOLS: Square, compass, string line, hammer, pry bar, drill and drill bits, power flooring nailer and mallet, power miter saw, saber saw, and nail set.

1. Nail the first board into place.
Place the grooved edge of the first board ⅜ inch from the wall. The power nailer will not be able to reach this close to the wall. Drill pilot holes and drive flooring nails at a 45-degree angle through the tongue every 12 inches.

2. Tap the boards together.
To keep the courses parallel, tap the boards together before nailing. Use a wood scrap as a driving block to protect the flooring. Or use the neoprene head of the power nailer mallet. For a professional appearance, offset all neighboring joints by at least 2 inches.

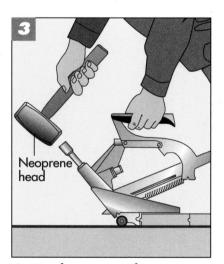

3. Use the power nailer.
Load the power flooring nailer with staples recommended for your type of floor. Experiment with depth settings; the staple heads should just barely sink below the wood surface. Fit the nailer to a tongue, make sure it rests flat, and hit it with the mallet.

4. Measure for cut pieces.
Measure before cutting the last piece in each course, and cut with a power miter saw or a circular saw. Don't cut off the edge with the tongue or the groove that you'll need. About every six courses , stretch a string line to check for straightness.

5. Scribe around irregularities.
Cut casings at the bottom, using a scrap of flooring as a guide. To fit around other irregularities, scribe with a compass and cut with a saber saw.

6. Secure the last rows.
You may need to ripsaw the last course. Protecting the wall with a wood scrap, push the last courses tight with a pry bar. Drill pilot holes and drive finishing nails through the face of the boards. Set the nails and fill with wood putty.

EXPERTS' INSIGHT

STRAIGHTENING BOARDS

■ If tapping (Step 2) does not tighten a warped board, pounding the driving block hard with the mallet will probably move it over the last ¼ inch or so, but no more.

■ If a board is warped on the side toward the board you are butting against, start nailing at one end and straighten the board by nailing as you go.

■ If the warped edge is away from the board you are butting to, fit the board as tight as possible and drive nails hard into the middle of the board until it is tight.

LAYING WOOD FLOORING OVER CONCRETE

Strip or plank flooring can't be attached directly to concrete. Seal the concrete against moisture with a layer or two of plastic sheeting, and then provide a wood surface to attach the flooring to. Laying strip or plank flooring over concrete requires a vapor barrier, sleepers, and a subfloor.

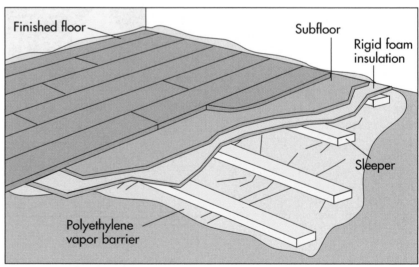

YOU'LL NEED...

TIME: 2 days to install a vapor barrier, sleepers, subfloor, and finished flooring for a 12×14-foot room.

SKILLS: Intermediate carpentry skills.

TOOLS: Hammer, nail set, pry bar, power flooring nailer, power miter saw, and saber saw.

Build a subfloor over the concrete.
Lay a polyethylene vapor barrier over the concrete; consult with a carpenter or a building inspector to make sure the barrier will be effective in your conditions.

Install 2×4 sleepers, allowing 14½ inches of space between them. To attach the sleepers, drive masonry nails or screws every 16 inches (see page 190). Lay rigid foam insulation over or between the sleepers. Then screw a ¾-inch plywood subfloor to the sleepers. Install the flooring as shown at on these pages.

DOORS AND WINDOWS

Chapter 6

Window Repairs

Freeing a Balky Sash *162*
Replacing a Sash Cord *163*
Repairing Sliding Windows *165*
Repairing Casement Windows *166*

Door Repairs

Understanding Interior Doors *168*
Correcting Strike Problems *170*
Lubricating Balky Latches *171*
Repairing Bifold Doors *172*
Repairing Sliding Doors *173*

Installation

Installing Handles and Locks *174*
Installing a Prehung Door *176*

Glass

Replacing Windowpanes *177*
Replacing Sills and Saddles *179*

Screens and Storms

Maintaining Screening *180*
Repairing Screens and Storms *181*
Replacing Screening *182*
Installing New Storm/Screen Windows *183*
Installing a Storm Door *185*

FREEING A BALKY SASH

When a double-hung window binds or refuses to open, don't try to force it. Take a look around the sash, both inside and out. Chances are you will find that paint has sealed the sash shut or that a stop molding has warped. The steps shown here will enable you to gently pry and free the sash, preventing damage. If the top sash is painted shut, you may choose to leave it that way, unless you need to move it for cleaning.

YOU'LL NEED...

TIME: 30 minutes or more, depending on the cause.
SKILLS: Basic skills.
TOOLS: Sash knife or utility knife, flat pry bar, and hammer.

1. Break the paint seal.
To break a paint seal, use a sash knife, which is specially designed for this purpose. Or run a sharp utility knife several times between the sash and stop. Be sure to cut through the paint at every point.

2. Pry the window open.
Pry from the outside edges with a pry bar and a protective block of wood. Take your time, using gentle to moderate pressure at several points. Alternating sides, work inward from the edges until the sash pops free.

3. Spread the stops.
If a sash is binding between its stops, try separating the stops slightly by tapping along their length with a hammer and wooden block that fits tightly between the stops. If the binding is severe, you may need to pry the stop off and nail it in a new position.

4. Lubricate the sash.
Once you get the window moving, scrape or chisel any built-up paint off the edges of the sash or between the stops. Lightly sand its jambs; then lubricate with a candle or with paraffin, paste wax, or bar soap.

EXPERTS' INSIGHT

OTHER DOUBLE-HUNG MECHANISMS

The spring lift and the weight-and-pulley system, shown on pages 163–164, are the most common mechanisms for double-hung windows. Another type uses a tension spring—a flat metal strap that attaches to a spring-loaded drum unit in the sash. Finding replacement drum units may be difficult. A friction sash is made of vinyl or aluminum; it grabs the sash tightly enough that it does not slide down when raised.

REPLACING A SASH CORD

Each sash in an old double-hung window is connected to two weights that run through channels in each side of the window. A sash cord or chain is secured to the sash and runs through a pulley near the top of the jamb. Sometimes a window binds because the cord has come out of its groove in the side of the sash; if so, force it back into position. If a cord or chain has become detached from the sash, reattach it with a short screw. If the cord is broken, replace it. A cord will not last as long as a sash chain, which also looks better.

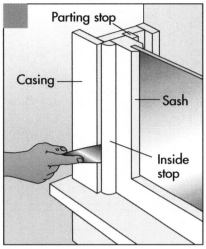

1. Pry out the stop.
Usually you need to remove only one inside stop. Cut through the paint using a utility knife. Using a putty knife, pry carefully at several points to loosen the stop, and then remove the stop with a flat pry bar.

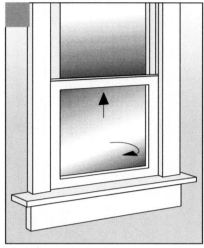

2. Lift out the sash.
Lift the sash and swing it clear from the frame. One or both cords may still be connected. Take care that a cord does not come loose and suddenly fly upward.

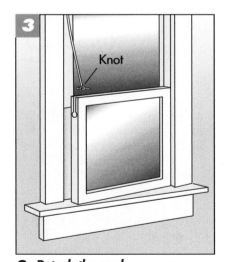

3. Detach the cord.
Hang on to the cord and pull it out of the sash; you may need to pry out a nail or unscrew a screw.
NOTE: *Be careful never to let go of the cord. Pull it out and slip a nail through the knot so that the cord cannot slip through the pulley.*

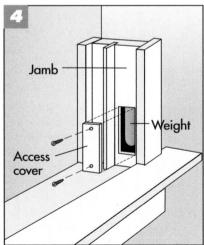

4. Open the access cover.
There will probably be an access cover at the base of the jamb; unscrew the fasteners that hold the cover in place. Gently pry it out to reveal the weights. If there is no access cover, you may have to pry off the jamb.

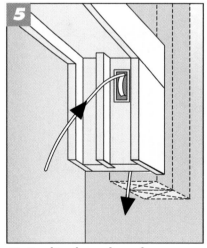

5. Feed in the sash cord.
Untie or cut the cord off of each weight and pull the weight out. Cut new cords or chains longer than they need to be. Feeding new sash cords or chains over pulleys calls for patience. Replace the cords or chains on both sides.

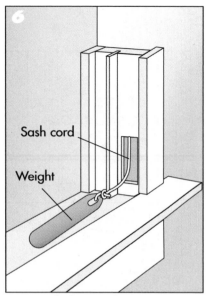

6. Attach the weight.
Once the new cord or chain is visible through the access hole, tie a knot in the other end so that it cannot slip through the pulley. Tie the cord or chain to the weight and tug to make sure the knot is secure. Slip the weight back in place.

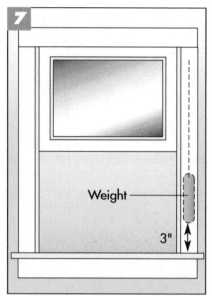

7. Check the weight's position.
Weights should hang 3 inches above the channel bottoms when the lower sash is raised fully. Once you have determined the correct length, knot the other end of the cord or chain and fit it into the groove. Secure the cord or chain with a short screw—don't drive the screw into the windowpane.

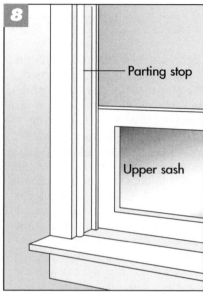

8. Remove the upper sash.
To replace the cords on an upper sash, you have to remove the lower one, then one of the parting stops. Use the same techniques as for the lower sash.

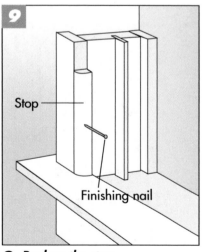

9. Replace the stop.
When you replace stops, partially drive in longer nails, or drive in nails at different points. Raise and lower the sash to check the stop positioning; it should be fairly tight, yet allow for smooth operation.

EXPERTS' INSIGHT

REHABBING AN OLD DOUBLE-HUNG WINDOW?

An old window will probably never insulate as well as a newer window. The cavity that houses the weights cannot be filled with insulation, and the panes are single-glazed. So installing new windows may save money in the long run.

However if you have the time and energy, you can plug most of the leaks and make the window a smooth operator. Remove the sashes and sand their edges smooth. Repair the glazing and paint the glazing so that it is sealed with the glass (see pages 177–178). Caulk around all the casing and apron edges, both inside and outside.

If you install a friction sash channel, you can remove the pulleys and fill in the cavity with insulation. Adding combination storm/screen windows will add a great deal to the insulating ability of a window.

REPAIRING SLIDING WINDOWS

Tracks for sliding (or gliding) windows are notorious collectors of dust and grit, which make for rough opening and closing. Keep tracks clean with regular vacuuming and scrub them when grime starts to build up. Scrape any paint away. To improve performance, spray with a silicone lubricant. If a slider jams, binds, or jumps loose, something may be lodged in the track or the track may be bent. If all seems clear, lift out the sash and check its grooved edges. Clean and lubricate these, too, if needed.

YOU'LL NEED...

TIME: About 30 minutes per window.
SKILLS: Basic skills.
TOOLS: Hammer, screwdriver, and large pliers.

EXPERTS' INSIGHT

HARDWARE REPAIRS FOR SLIDING WINDOWS

■ If a latch does not close readily, remove it and clean it with a brush and vacuum, then spray with silicone lubricant. Also check the strike, where the latch attaches, and clean away any obstructions. If the latch is broken, replace it.

■ To replace a roller or track, look for the manufacturer's name on the window's frame or the sash, and contact them by phone or on the web. A local hardware store may stock hardware for a window that's common in your area.

Remove a sash.
To remove a sliding sash, partially open the window, then lift it up and pull its lower edge toward you. The second sash may be fixed in place, or you may need to remove some hold-down hardware before it can be slid over and removed.

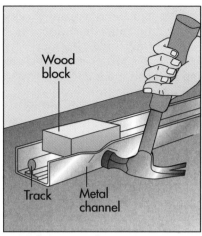

Straighten a track.
To straighten a bent track, cut a wood block to fit snugly in the channel and carefully tap the track against it. Or place a piece of metal on either side of the track and squeeze with a large pair of pliers.

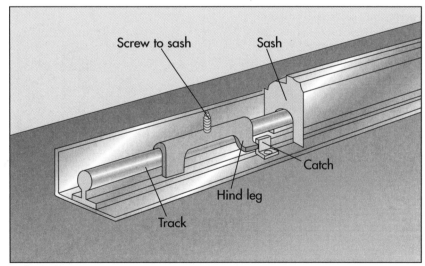

Adjust dogs.
"Catch-and-dog" window latches can get bent. Adjust them so that the dog's "hind leg" hits against the catch. Bigger windows roll on sets of nylon wheels called sheaves, which are self-lubricating and rarely need attention. If a sheave is mangled, remove the assembly and replace it.

REPAIRING CASEMENT WINDOWS

Accumulations of paint, grease, or dirt cause most casement window difficulties. If your casement is malfunctioning, check all sash and frame edges. A few minutes with a wire brush or scraper may remove the debris that is causing the rub.

Examine the unit's mechanical components. Lubricant may be all you need. Use automobile grease or oil for parts that are encased in a housing (such as the crank operator). Where parts will be exposed to the elements and dust, use graphite, paste wax, or silicone lubricant to avoid attracting dust.

If an arm is bent, remove it and set it on a hard, flat surface. Place a piece of metal on top, and tap with a hammer to straighten the arm. Or use a large pair of pliers.

If a sash binds, partially close it and look for places where the window rubs against the sash. On a metal unit, scraping away excess paint may solve the problem.

Wood casements sometimes suffer the same problems that bedevil doors. Solve these problems by adapting the door-fitting and planing techniques illustrated on pages 168–169. Remove about ¹⁄₁₆ inch extra wood, then apply primer and paint.

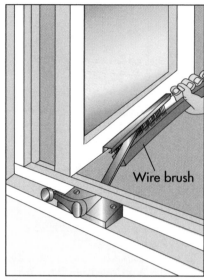

Clean the arm mechanism.
If the sash is difficult to close, try cleaning the sliding arm mechanism with a wire brush. Lubricate with graphite or silicone.

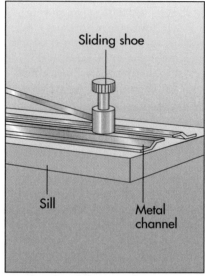

Service the sliding mechanism.
Sill-mounted sliding shoes trap dirt. Unscrew the channel, clean it and the sill, and then lubricate with paste wax.

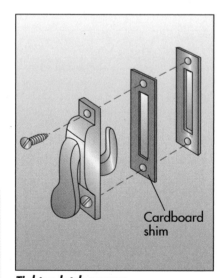

Tighten latch screws.
Tighten any loose latch screws. If a screw won't tighten, tap slivers of wood into the screw holes and drive the screws again. If a handle won't pull its sash snug, shim under it or add weather stripping.

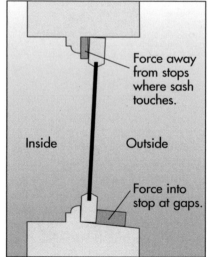

Unwarp.
If a wood sash has warped, counter-warp it with wood strips. Temporarily screw or nail the pieces so they warp the window in the opposite direction. Leave the strips in place for a couple of weeks.

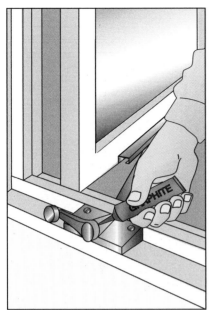

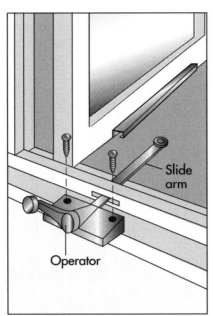

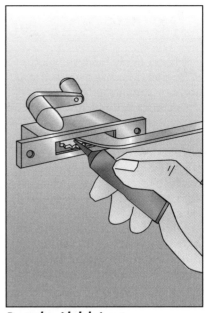

Lubricate a crank.
To keep cranks turning freely, apply graphite or a light oil. With some cranks you may need to take off the handle first.

Dismantle an operator.
To dismantle an operator, disconnect the slide arm from the sash, then unscrew it from the frame.

Repack with lubricant.
If the gears are encrusted with old grease, soak the operator mechanism in a solvent, then repack it with a multipurpose lubricant or automobile grease.

INSULATION ABILITY OF WINDOW TREATMENTS

Treatment	Description	Summer Reflective Efficiency	Winter Insulating Efficiency
Venetian blinds	Multiple parallel slats	Effective when closed	Virtually none
Draperies	Tightly woven white fabric	Effective when closed	Fairly effective if tight-fitting
Shades	White shade cloth	Effective when closed	Virtually none
Double-glazing	Insulating glass or single-glazing plus storm window	Not very effective	Cuts heat loss by 50%
Triple- and Low-E glazing	Insulating glass plus storm or coated glass	Low-E is fairly reflective	Cuts heat loss by 70%
Thermal shades	Quilted, fiber-filled material sealed tightly to a window frame	Very effective	Cuts heat loss by 80%

UNDERSTANDING INTERIOR DOORS

Almost every modern wood panel door has a vertical-stile and horizontal-rail framework. This construction helps counteract the wood's tendency to shrink, swell, and warp with humidity changes. With a panel door (right), you can see that framing. Spaces between frame members are paneled with wood, louvered slats, or glass.

Smooth-surfaced "flush doors" hide their framing beneath two or three layers of veneer. Alternating the veneer directions minimizes warping. A solid-core flush door has a dense center of hardwood blocks or particleboard; a hollow-core door uses lighter material in the interior, such as ribbons of corrugated cardboard or rigid foam insulation.

For sliding and bifold doors, spages 172–173.

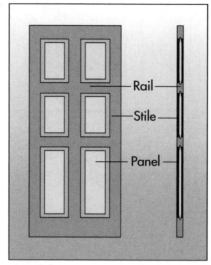

Panel doors.
Made of milled pine components, panel doors are easy to plane and, if necessary, cut down to fit an opening. Cheaper types are made of molded hardboard.

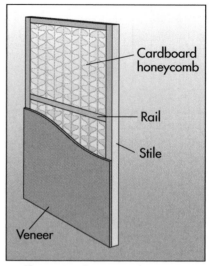

Hollow-core doors.
Covered with oak, birch, or lauan-mahogany veneer, hollow-core doors are inexpensive. They are difficult to cut down, though, because there is only 2 to 3 inches of framing at the top and bottom.

FREEING A BINDING DOOR

When a hinged door sticks, don't be too quick to take it down to plane its edges. Many difficulties are better corrected by making minor adjustments with the door in place.

Most problems result from one or more of the following causes: loose hinge screws, paint that is too thick on the jamb and/or door edge, improperly aligned hinges, an improperly aligned strike plate, a frame that is out of square (usually because the house has settled), or warping of the door.

YOU'LL NEED...
TIME: 30 to 90 minutes, depending on whether you have to plane the door
SKILLS: No special skills needed.
TOOLS: Hammer, nail set, chisel, wedge, plane, and screwdriver.

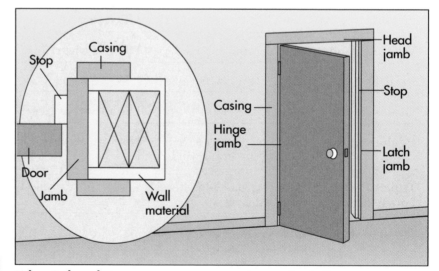

Where's the rub?
If a door sticks or refuses to fit into its frame, open the door and pull up on the handle, then let go. If either hinge is loose, screws need to be tightened. Next close the door as far as it will go without forcing it, and carefully examine the perimeter. Look for an uneven gap along the hinge jamb; this means that the hinges need attention. If the door seems too big for its frame—or out of square with it—mark the tight spots, then sand or plane those spots.

1. Shim the door.

Loose hinge screws can cause sags. To tighten them, first wedge the door open under the latch edge. (Hinges usually come loose for a reason—often because the door binds when it is closed. After tightening the screws, take steps to make sure that the door does not bind.)

2. Plug the screw holes.

Remove the screws and plug their holes with glue-coated golf tees, wood splinters, or dowels. Drive new screws into each plug. If this does not work, try driving longer screws. Make sure the screws are driven straight, so their heads are flat; angled screw heads can cause the door to bind.

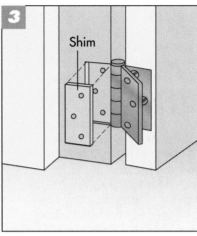

3. Shim out a hinge.

If the door binds on the hinge side, scrape and sand away any built-up paint on the edge of the door and the jamb. A hinge leaf should be flush with the surrounding surface. If either leaf is set in, remove the screws, insert a cardboard shim, and rescrew.

1. Plane the door top in place, if possible.

If the door binds, gently close the door and scribe a cut line at all points where binding occurs, using the jamb as a guide. Usually you won't have to remove the door from its hinges to plane the top or the latch side. First bevel any edges to prevent splintering. For instructions on planing, see pages 114–115.

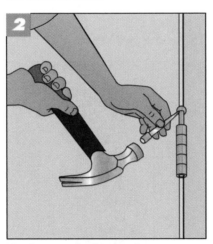

2. Tap out the hinge pins.

To trim the bottom or an edge you can't reach with the door in place, remove the door. Shim the bottom of the door so it is stable. Use a nail set or screwdriver to hammer out the hinge pins, bottom first, then the top. If the hinge is rusty and the pin is stuck, try squirting with penetrating oil. If that doesn't work, you may need to remove the screws from one hinge leaf.

3. Plane the door.

Brace the door for planing. Avoid planing the hinge side, if possible. If you must do so, first remove the hinges. You may have to reset the hinges afterwards.

CORRECTING STRIKE PROBLEMS

When a door will not latch, or if it rattles when latched, examine the strike plate attached to the jamb. Minor adjustments often will solve the problem.

If the latch does not engage the strike plate, determine if the latch is too far from the strike. Scratches on the strike plate probably mean the latch is hitting the strike but missing the hole.

A door that does not fit snugly against its stop molding almost certainly will rattle. To silence it, move the strike plate or reposition the stop.

YOU'LL NEED...

TIME: About 30 minutes to adjust a strike plate.
SKILLS: Basic carpentry skills.
TOOLS: Screwdriver, file, drill, and chisel.

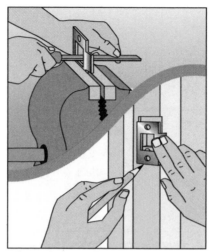

File and move the strike plate.
If the strike plate is off only ⅛ inch or so, remove the strike plate and enlarge its opening with a file. You may need to chisel away some wood when reinstalling. For bigger shifts, relocate the strike. You'll need to extend the mortise (see page 174).

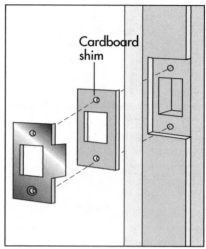

Shim the strike.
If the strike is too far away to engage the latch, first check if the hinges need to be shimmed out (see page 169). If the hinges fit properly, shim out the strike using thick cardboard.

Cardboard shim

SILENCING SQUEAKY HINGES

If a hinge squeaks, it may be under extra pressure because the door is binding (see pages 168–169). Or the hinge may be rusty because of damp conditions. Cleaning and lubricating may solve the problem; but in the case of bad rust, you're better off replacing the hinge.

You might solve the problem by oiling with the pin in place. Spread a cloth on the floor and squirt some penetrating oil into the moving parts. Open and close the door to work the lubricant in.

YOU'LL NEED...

TIME: About 15 minutes per hinge.
SKILLS: Basic carpentry skills.
TOOLS: Hammer, nail set, drill, steel wool, and wire-brush pipe cleaner.

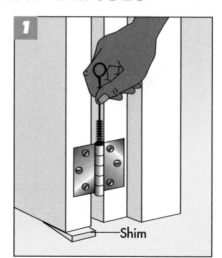

1. Clean the pins.
If oiling does not quiet a rusty hinge, shim the bottom of the door so it is stable. Remove the hinge pin. Clean the pin with steel wool. Poke out the pin hole with a wire-brush pipe cleaner.

Shim

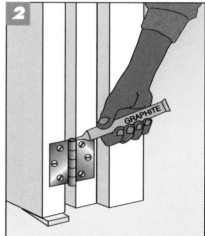

2. Put graphite on moving parts.
Coat moving parts with graphite. When you replace the pin, don't drive it tight; leave space for prying it out again and adding more graphite in the future.

GRAPHITE

LUBRICATING BALKY LATCHES

Old latches have springs that may break. If lubricating a latch does not free it, remove the unit and take it to a locksmith, who may be able to repair it. Or consider buying and installing a replacement (see pages 174–175).

A latch that has been painted is in danger of binding. Remove all paint by carefully scraping with a chisel or by using a wire-brush attachment on a drill.

If you're going to use powdered graphite to lubricate the lock, place a newspaper under the area to protect carpeting.

YOU'LL NEED...
TIME: 10 to 15 minutes per latch.
SKILLS: Basic skills.
TOOLS: Screwdriver.

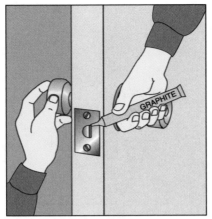

Apply graphite to latch.
Turn the handle to retract the latch bolt, then puff powdered graphite into the works. Turn the handle repeatedly to work the bolt back and forth, and apply more graphite if needed. If this does not solve the problem, you may need a new latch.

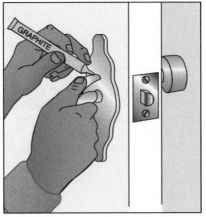

Apply graphite to thumb latch.
Lubricate a thumb-operated latch lever by puffing graphite powder into the lock body. Move the latch up and down to work in the graphite. Wipe away any excess.

DEALING WITH A WARPED DOOR

If a door rattles when closed, or if you have to press hard to get the latch to engage, the door may be warped. Close the door until it just touches the stop, then check to see if the door meets the stop all along its length (see page 168). If there is a gap at either end or in the middle, the simplest solution is to reposition the stop rather than trying to straighten the door.

If a door is badly warped yet valuable, try straightening it out: Remove the door, set it on pieces of wood, and weight it to counter-warp it. Give it at least a week to straighten.

YOU'LL NEED...
TIME: 2 hours to add a hinge; a week if you weight the door.
SKILLS: Basic carpentry skills.
TOOLS: Hammer, nail set, chisel, pry bar, and screwdriver.

1. Move the stop.
To reposition a stop, cut through the paint lines (if any) and gently pry the stop away. Close the door, and scribe a line on the jamb to indicate where the stop should be. Drill pilot holes and drive new finishing nails to reattach the stop.

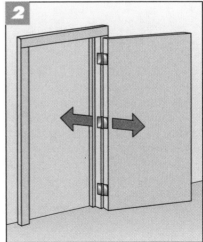

2. Add a hinge.
If a door is warped along the hinge side, you may be able to straighten it by adding a hinge in the middle. Install the jamb side hinge and trace the door hinge. Remove the door and chisel the mortise. Rehang and attach the hinge. With a helper, force the door straight and insert the pins.

REPAIRING BIFOLD DOORS

Bifold doors are commonly used for closets. Because they don't swing far outward, they save space in a bedroom.

Most bifold doors are light-weight, with light-duty hardware to match. Roughhousing kids can easily break slats or bend a hinge or a track. Straighten a bent track by placing a strip of wood inside and tapping with a hammer; or use a pair of pliers and two strips of metal.

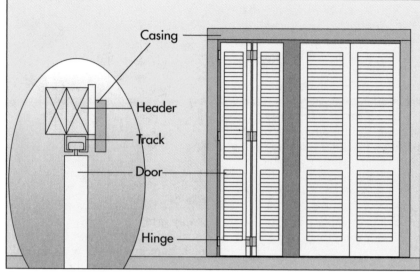

YOU'LL NEED...

TIME: 15 to 30 minutes for most repairs, as long as you have the necessary hardware.
SKILLS: Basic carpentry skills.
TOOLS: Open-end wrench, screwdriver, and drill.

Anatomy of a bifold door.
A bifold door has two halves that are hinged together. One half of the door pivots on fixed pins that attach to holders with slots at the floor and the header jamb. The other half of the door slides along a header track—secured to the header jamb—as the center hinges open or close. The pin that runs in the header track does not support the door; it only guides it.

EXPERTS' INSIGHT

INSTALLING A NEW SET OF BIFOLDS

Installing a new bifold door is straightforward. A unit comes as a kit, with the doors hinged and the hardware supplied. Bifolds typically fit into 24-, 30-, 32-, and 36-inch openings. A typical closet has two bifolds in a 6-foot-wide opening. Flush, panel, and louvered doors are available. Painting can take a long time, especially if the bifold has louvers. Consider buying a prefinished door, or purchase a unit with good-looking wood so that you need only apply a clear finish. More expensive units are available with mirror panels, minimizing the surface area of wood to be finished.

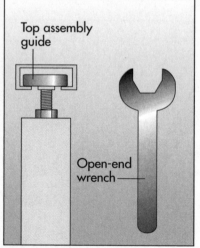

Adjusting the hardware.
Ideally when a bifold door is closed, it should be aligned with the jamb on all three sides. However if the opening is out of square, you may need to compromise on one side. In a typical arrangement, the top assembly guide (above left) fits into a hole and can be adjusted

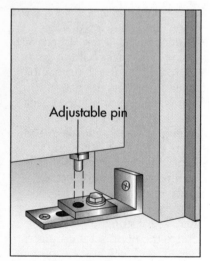

out or in. At the bottom of the door you may find an adjustable pin-and-slot arrangement (above right); loosen the nut to slide the slot. On other models you simply pick the door up, move it over slightly, and set the bottom pin in a different part of the slot. Use an open-end wrench to make adjustments.

REPAIRING SLIDING DOORS

Sliding doors, also called bypass or gliding doors, come in pairs, and slide past each other to open or close. Though flush bypass doors are the most common, paneled and louvered models are also available.

Exterior glass patio doors roll on wheels along a bottom track. Adjust and maintain these as you would a sliding window (see page 165). Be aware, however, that these doors are quite heavy.

Interior bypass doors are usually easy to maintain. However if the door itself is warped, it should be replaced.

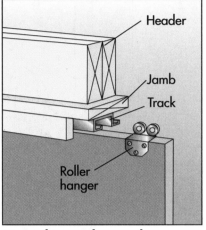

How a bypass door works.
At the top of an interior bypass door, a roller hanger glides through a metal track. Rollers are typically nylon and need no lubrication. The track must be attached firmly to the header because it is the door's sole support. At the bottom of the door opening, a floor guide (see below) provides only guidance.

Removing a bypass door.
To remove a bypass door, lift it above the floor guide and tilt it out slightly. Then pick the door up and guide it out of the track. Be careful; some units are heavy.

You'll Need...

TIME: About 15 to 20 minutes per door.
SKILLS: Basic skills.
TOOLS: Slot and phillips screwdrivers, and pliers.

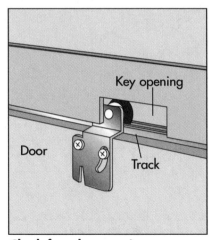

Check for a key opening.
With some models you can free the door only when its wheels are at a key opening in the track.

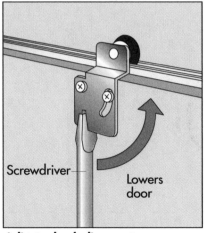

Adjust wheel alignment.
Raise one side or the other by adjusting the roller hanger. In the type shown above, first slightly loosen the two screws. Then insert a screwdriver into the slot and pry the hanger up or down. Tighten the screws.

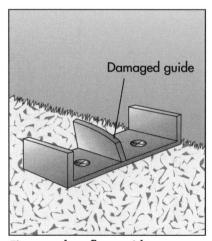

Fix or replace floor guides.
If a floor guide is bent, try bending it back into position with a pair of pliers. If it is broken, or if it is difficult to straighten, replace it.

INSTALLING HANDLES AND LOCKS

Once the door has been hung so that it swings freely and closes snugly against the stop, the next step is to install the handle. An entry handle simply opens from either side; a privacy handle can be locked from one side. Purchase drill bits in sizes recommended by the manufacturer.

YOU'LL NEED...

TIME: About 45 minutes.

SKILLS: Measuring precisely, chiseling, drilling, and fastening with screws.

TOOLS: Drill with hole saw and bits (see lockset instructions), utility knife or butt marker, tape measure, center punch, awl, screwdriver, hammer, and chisel.

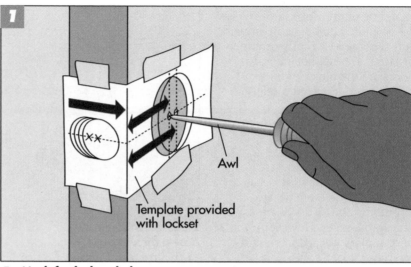

Awl

Template provided with lockset

1. Mark for lockset holes.

The handle set or dead bolt will come with a paper or cardboard template. Tape it or hold it against the door. If a strike already exists in the jamb, align the template with it so you won't have to cut a new mortise for the strike. With an awl or the point of a spade bit, mark for the two holes by piercing through the template.

Hole saw

2. Drill the large hole.

Use a hole saw to drill the larger hole through the face of the door first. To avoid splintering the veneer, drill just far enough that the pilot bit of the hole saw pokes through. Then drill from the other side.

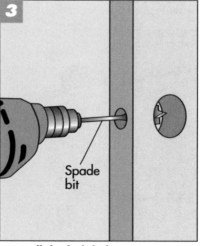

Spade bit

3. Drill the bolt hole.

Use a spade bit to drill through the edge, taking care to hold the bit parallel to the surface of the door. Some types of locksets require that you continue drilling into the rear of the large hole approximately ½ inch.

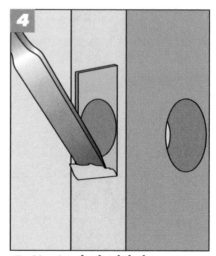

4. Mortise the latch bolt.

Insert the bolt through the smaller hole. Temporarily screw it centered in the door, and mark for its mortise with a sharp pencil or a knife. Cut and chisel a mortise as you did for the hinges. Depending on the type of bolt, this mortise may be deeper near the center than at the edges.

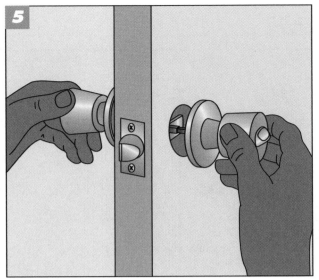

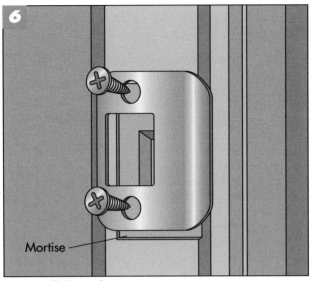

5. Install the handle.

Install the bolt by setting it in the mortise, drilling pilot holes, and driving the screws provided. Then install the lockset or handles according to the manufacturer's directions. Tighten all screws. Test the mechanisms from both sides of the door to make sure they operate smoothly; you may need to clean out or widen your holes.

6. Install the strike.

Mark the jamb for the correct location of the strike. The latch or bolt should be vertically centered in the strike opening. Horizontally, make sure the latch or bolt will enter the door while holding it fairly tight against the door stop. Mortise the jamb, drill pilot holes, and install the strike with the screws provided.

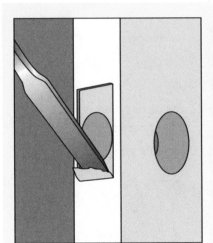

Assembling a dead bolt.

Install a dead bolt much as you would a handle. Mark for the position of the two holes and drill them. Insert the bolt and latch face, mark for the mortise, and cut it with a chisel.

Screw the latch face (above right) into the mortise. For many lock types, you'll need to use a screwdriver to partially extend the bolt. Insert the lock tailpiece through the slot in the bolt. Slip on the interior turn bolt or lock until the two pieces sit flush against the door. Fasten the retaining screws and install the strike plate.

INSTALLING A PREHUNG DOOR

Building a custom door saves money, but takes time and expertise. Prehung units cost more, but you get everything you need—door, hinges, jamb, stop and casing moldings, and even a latch if you want it—all in one accurately made component.

See page 135 if you need to frame for the door. Before you buy a prehung unit, measure the thickness of the wall; plaster and drywall surfaces call for different jamb widths.

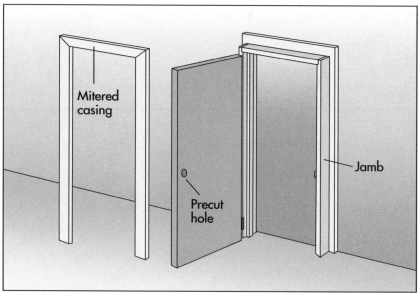

Choosing a prehung door.
A prehung door comes already assembled, with the holes precut for the handle and the strike plate. The casing can be removed from either side of a prehung door. A standard jamb is 3⅝ inches wide to fit into a standard stud-and-drywall wall; in an older home, you may need a wider jamb.

1. Shim a prehung door.
Remove the casing on one side. Set the door into the opening, with the other casing (not visible above) flush against the wall. If necessary shim the hinge side to make it plumb. Check the other two jamb pieces for square by closing the door; the gap should be even all around.

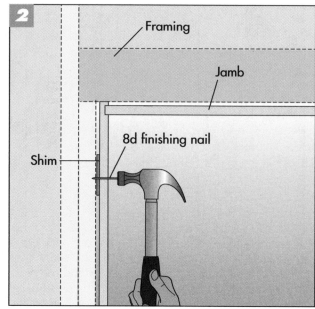

2. Drive nails.
Open the door and shim it at the bottom so it is stable. Anchor the hinge jamb securely with 8d finishing nails that enter the framing. To hide nails, simply remove the stop, drive the nails, then replace the stop. Drive nails to attach the latch jamb, and check again for square.

REPLACING WINDOWPANES

Faced with a broken window, you have three options: Remove the sash and take it to a hardware store or glass shop for reglazing; buy a new pane that is cut to size, and install it yourself; or cut the glass yourself from standard-sized sheets kept on hand for such emergencies.

Dismantling a window is sometimes far more work than simply replacing the glass. Cutting glass isn't difficult, but you might break a pane or two before getting the knack. A hardware store will cut glass to the size you need.

YOU'LL NEED...
TIME: About 30 minutes a pane.
SKILLS: Basic skills.
TOOLS: Putty knife, scraper, caulking gun, and paintbrush.

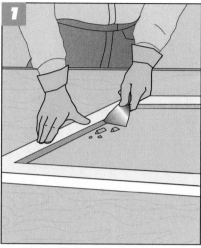

1. Chip off the old glazing.
NOTE: *Wear heavy gloves and long clothing when handling broken glass.* Carefully pull out all the pieces of the old pane. Chipping off old glazing compound can be the hardest part of the job. Use a putty knife or old chisel, or soften old glazing with a soldering iron or heat gun.

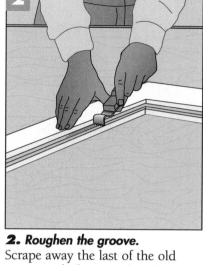

2. Roughen the groove.
Scrape away the last of the old compound, then roughen the groove with a scraper so the new glazing compound will adhere properly. Be sure to remove all the old glazier's points, which may be tiny metal triangles instead of the push-type points shown in Step 6.

3. Measure the sash.
Sashes aren't always perfectly square, so measure at several points, then subtract ⅛ inch from each dimension to determine the glass size. Have the glass cut at a hardware store or glass shop, or cut it yourself.

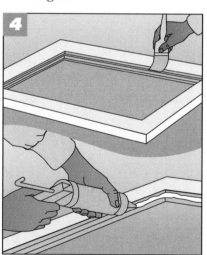

4. Prime the groove and apply a bead of glazing.
Prime the groove with linseed oil, turpentine, or oil-based paint. Untreated wood will draw oil from the glazing compound, shortening its life. Before you insert the new pane, apply a ⅛-inch-thick bead of caulk or glazing compound. This helps seal and cushion the glass.

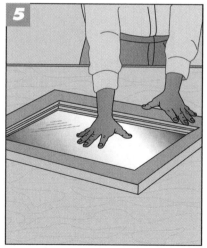

5. Press the pane into place.
Line up one edge of the pane in the sash, lower it into place, and press gently with your palm or fingertips to seal it into the glazing compound.

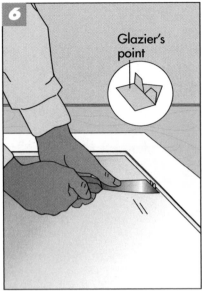

6. Add glazier's points.

Approximately every 12 inches around the perimeter, press a glazier's point (see inset) into the sash with a putty knife. Don't push too hard—you may crack the glass.

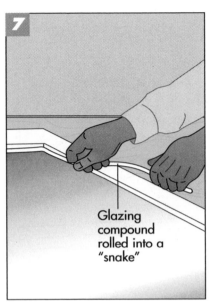

7. Apply glazing compound.

If the glazing compound is in a can, grab a hunk and roll it into a "snake." Alternatively, use glazing compound in a caulk tube. Apply a generous bead of glazing compound. Press it into place to make sure it sticks to both the glass and wood.

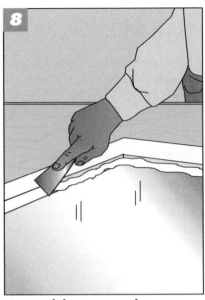

8. Bevel the compound.

Working in only one direction, firmly draw a putty knife all along the bead. If the compound sticks to the knife, wet the knife with turpentine. If small ridges appear, lightly run your finger in the opposite direction to smooth the compound.

9. Paint the compound.

Let the compound dry for a week before painting. Paint should overlap the glass about 1/16 inch for a tight seal.

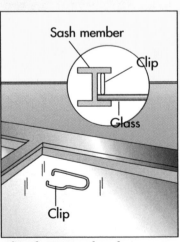

Clips for a metal sash.

Spring clips substitute for glazier's points in steel sashes. Install as shown here. Metal windows needn't be primed before installing the glass.

Gasket for storm window.

In an aluminum storm window, a rubber gasket, forced into place with a putty knife, holds the glass. If the gasket is cracked or broken, replace it.

REPLACING SILLS AND SADDLES

Windowsills take a terrific beating from both rain and the sun. Alternate soaking and baking can make them veritable sponges.

The best preventive is a couple of coats of paint applied annually. If a sill is too far gone for that, consider repair options (see the "Experts' Insight" box below).

If the sill is heavily damaged, you may need to install a new sill. Door sills, called saddles or thresholds, also fail over time. Replace either by following the procedures illustrated here.

Determine if the sill or saddle fits under the jambs on either side, then measure, and buy a new piece of sill stock. The drawings at right show how to install a new piece of wood in either situation—but you might opt to replace a saddle with a preformed, predrilled metal or plastic unit.

If you can get the old sill out intact, use it as a template for marking the replacement. If not, measure exactly for a snug fit.

For more about how windows and doors are put together, see page 168. To learn about weather-stripping-type thresholds, see page 181.

If the window has problems in addition to the sill, it's probably time to consider installing a replacement window.

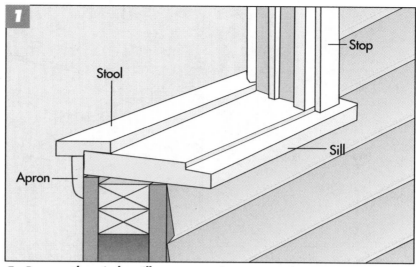

1. Remove the windowsill.
Removing the sill will probably be the most difficult part of the job. You'll have to take off the apron, the stool, and stop molding to remove a sill.

Use a chisel or old screwdriver to probe for nails that may be holding the piece in place.

If you can't get the nails out, saw out a section as shown below. You can also demolish it by splitting it along the grain with a hammer and chisel, then pulling out the splintered remains.

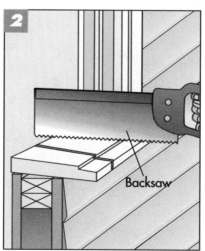

2. Saw the sill if needed.
If the sill is embedded on either side, saw out a section from the center. Use a handsaw (a backsaw is shown) or a reciprocating saw, taking care not to damage underlying wood. Remove the middle piece, then drive the end pieces inward and pry them out.

YOU'LL NEED...
TIME: 1 to 2 hours per sill.
SKILLS: Basic carpentry skills.
TOOLS: Backsaw, chisel, hammer, nail set, flat pry bar, drill, and caulking gun.

EXPERTS' INSIGHT

REPAIRING A SILL
Replacing a sill, though sometimes necessary, is a difficult and demanding task. Before you start removing pieces, consider the possibility of repair. New products make it possible to repair wood pieces that are heavily damaged.

If the wood is cracked and weak, apply liquid hardener, which strengthens the fibers.

If an area is rotted, use a hammer and chisel to carve away the rotted material. Mix and apply two-part epoxy wood filler. Once it dries, the filler can be planed, sanded, and painted like wood.

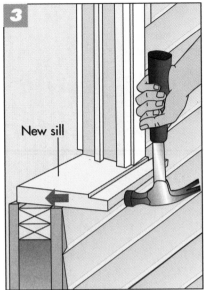

3. Tap the new sill into place.
Gently tap the new sill or saddle into place. Don't force it. If it resists, remove and sand the ends, beveling them slightly.

4. Nail the sill from underneath.
Using rust-resistant nails or deck screws, secure the windowsill from underneath. Countersink the fasteners, then caulk the holes and the ends of the sill.

Nail door saddles onto the framing sill.
Nail or screw a saddle at both ends and in the middle. Countersink fastener heads with a nail set and hide with putty. Caulk both ends of the saddle.

MAINTAINING SCREENING

Even rustproof screening materials (see page 182) require occasional attention. Check the caulking around the frames of combination units, and replace any worn-out gaskets. Vacuum dirt that collects on the screening. Clean oxidized aluminum with car polish.

Older wood-framed screens require careful monitoring and diligent maintenance. Repaint the frames as soon as the old paint starts to fail. Check each unit when you take it down and set aside those that need repair.

Consider how many windows you actually open up during the summer months. Leaving a storm window in place not only saves you some work, it also helps keep an air-conditioned room cool—as long as the window does not receive direct sunlight.

Clean screens.
Remove dust and debris by spraying a screen with a blast from a hose. Scrub metal screens with a stiff brush. Clean the frames as well as the screening.

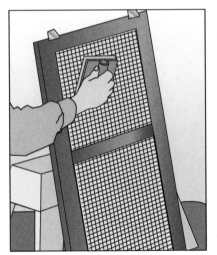

Paint steel screens.
If older steel screening is heavily rusted, replace it. If the rust is only modest, apply paint that is made to go over rusty metal. A paint pad is the easiest method. Paint one side, let it dry, then paint the other side. To unclog holes, gently rub the back side with a dry pad.

REPAIRING SCREENS AND STORMS

The little parts on an aluminum storm/screen—the splining, gaskets, plastic pins, and sliding clips that hook to the storm's frame—are notoriously fragile. To find replacements, look for the manufacturer's name on the frame, or bring broken parts to a hardware store.

Wood storm or screen frames that have been painted too many times may need to be sanded or planed, then repainted. Installing weather stripping can make wood storms more energy-efficient. Position felt or rubber weather stripping on the window's frame or the frame of the storm to create a tight seal when the storm is attached. You may need to move the closing hardware in order to accommodate the thickness of the weather stripping.

Adjust or replace screen/storm door closers as soon as they begin to malfunction; doors that slam or flap in the breeze wear out quickly. A closer should shut the door slowly but completely. Replacement closers are inexpensive and easy to install.

YOU'LL NEED...

TIME: 10 minutes to 2 hours, depending on the damage.
SKILLS: Basic skills.
TOOLS: Needle-nose pliers, hammer, drill, shears, and screwdriver.

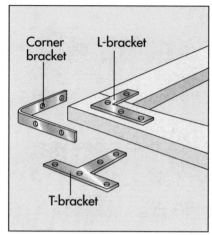

Repair a wooden frame.
Reinforce corner joints in a wooden frame using mending plates. Position a plate, drill pilot holes, and drive screws to fasten the plate. When possible install a plate on both sides; offset the plates so the screws don't run into each other.

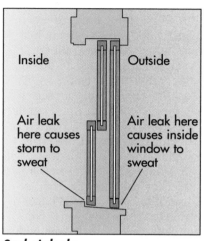

Seal air leaks.
Air leaks around interior sashes or storms cause condensation to form on the sash that's not leaking. The solution is to caulk the air leak.

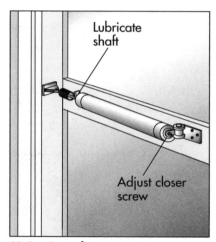

Maintain a closer.
Every autumn, lubricate door closers by wiping the shaft with oil. Check the adjustment for proper operation. Once a closer starts to fail, replace it.

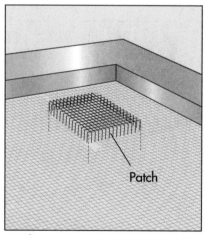

Patch a screen.
Mend a small puncture with a dab of superglue. To patch a hole in a metal screen, cut a patch, unravel a few strands, fit the patch over the hole, and bend the strands toward the hole. Repairing fiberglass screening is difficult; you're better off replacing the entire screen.

REPLACING SCREENING

Install screening much as an artist stretches a canvas—fasten it at one end of the frame, pull the material taut, then secure it at the sides and the other end.

With wood frames, pry screen moldings loose with a putty knife. Work from the center to the ends, applying leverage near the nails. If molding breaks, replace it.

Standard aluminum screening is subject to staining; "charcoal" or "silver-gray" aluminum is easier to maintain. Fiberglass won't stain, but its filaments are thicker, which affects visibility.

YOU'LL NEED...

TIME: 30 minutes per screen.
SKILLS: Basic skills.
TOOLS: Putty knife, shears or scissors, utility knife, staple gun, saw, and spline roller.

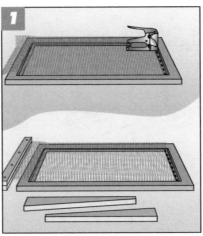

1. Attach the screen at the top.
With shears, cut the screening slightly wider and at least 1 foot longer than the frame, then staple the top edge. Nail a strip of wood to the bench or floor, roll the screen over it, and nail another strip on top of the first.

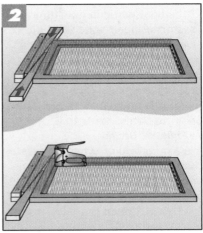

2. Insert wedges and fasten screening.
Rip-cut two wedges and insert them between the cleats and frame on each side. Tap the wedges until the screening is tight. Staple the screening to the bottom edge, then the sides. Trim the excess and refit the screen moldings.

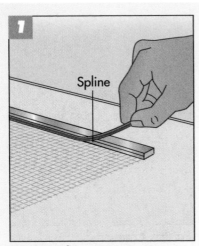

1. To replace screening in an aluminum frame, pry out the spline.
For aluminum frames, remove the old mesh by prying out the spline. You may need to buy new splining.

2. Cut new screening.
Square up the frame, lay new screening over it, and cut it the same size as the outside of the frame.

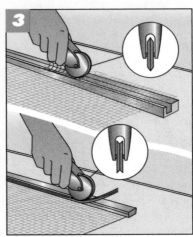

3. Push the screening into place and install the spline.
Bend the screening edges and force them into the channel with the convex wheel of the spline roller. Force the tubular spline into the channel with the concave wheel of the spline roller, tightening the screening.

Installing New Storm/Screen Windows

Door and window units for new construction arrive with doors or sashes already hung in their frames. Carpenters build "rough" openings, tip the units in place, and add trim.

Combination screen/storm doors and windows also arrive assembled. Because openings for these units are already finished, combinations usually are made-to-order. Installation may be included in the purchase price, but you can save 10 to 15 percent by installing units yourself.

Professional installers are usually paid by the piece, rather than by the hour. This can lead to shoddy installation. If you hire pros, make it clear that you will not write the check unless the windows are installed correctly.

You'll Need...

Time: 2 to 4 hours for a window.
Skills: Moderate carpentry skills.
Tools: Hammer, drill, screwdriver, and caulking gun.

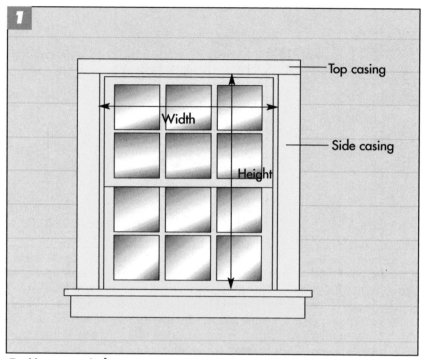

1. Measure window.
A storm/screen unit has a flange that fits over the window casing. This allows some leeway, so the unit does not have to fit precisely. Check the casing for square, and take into account any out-of-squareness. Measure the width between the inside edges of the side casings, and measure the height between the top casing and the sill.

Experts' Insight

Buying Storm/Screen Windows

Combination windows and doors pay for themselves with energy savings, but beware of shoddy products. Poorly made or poorly fitted units can leak air, are difficult to operate, and eventually turn into eyesores.

■ It's worth the extra expense to buy units that are made of thicker-gauge aluminum with an anodized or powdered coating.
■ See that the pins and sliding clips are strong and that replacement parts are available. Consider buying some replacement parts up front; they may be difficult to find later.
■ Better units have warrantees against defects. Choose a company that has been around for a while; a fly-by-night outfit may not be there when you need a part or service.
■ Check the corners of the frames. Lapped joints are stronger and tighter than mitered joints. If you can see light through the joints, you can be sure that they'll admit air.
■ Combinations come in double- or triple-track designs. With double-track units, you must seasonally remove and replace the bottom sash (either storm or screen). Triple-track units have tracks for the top and bottom storm sashes and the screen sash, and are self-storing—you don't have to remove the storm or screen sash you are not using. The deeper the tracks are, the higher a unit's insulation value will be.

2. Trace the outline.

Place the combination unit on the sill; center it between the side casings. The units should be installed square, even if the opening is not square. To check for square, slide a sash nearly all the way up, and see that it aligns with the frame. Sashes should glide smoothly; any binding means the frame is not straight. Trace the outline of the unit with a pencil.

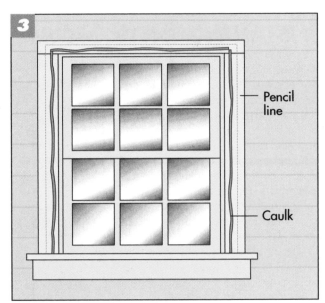

3. Caulk the casing.

Scrape and clean away any debris that could inhibit a tight seal between the combination and the casing. Using a caulking gun, run a bead of latex/silicone caulk around the casings about 1 inch inside the pencil lines. Also run a bead along the sill.

4. Drive screws.

Align the frame with the pencil line, press the frame into the caulk, and drive several screws. Test that the sashes operate smoothly and make adjustments if needed. Drive a screw into every available hole. If screws are difficult to drive, or if you are within 2 inches of the end of a piece of casing, drill a pilot hole before driving the screw.

5. Caulk the outside.

Caulk around the outside of the frame where it meets the top and side casings. Also caulk the bottom where it meets the sill.

INSTALLING A STORM DOOR

Assuming your exterior door is a standard 80 inches tall and 3 feet wide or narrower, you can choose standard-size prehung storm doors.

A combination storm door features interchangeable glass panels for winter and screen panels for summer. Some have both upper and lower interchangeable panels. These maximize solar gain during the winter and allow ventilation during the summer. Others have solid lower panels, which are more practical if you have children and/or animals that constantly push against and damage the lower screen unit.

Don't be too frugal when it comes to doors that handle a lot of traffic. Only the highest-quality door will withstand children running in and out, and adults carrying grocery bags in both arms.

A storm/screen security door has an attractive grate and a sturdy lock, so you can leave the door open to summer breezes.

A combination door typically attaches to the brick molding. Measure the inside dimensions of the molding and purchase a door designed to fit.

YOU'LL NEED...

TIME: 2 hours.
SKILLS: Basic carpentry skills.
TOOLS: Hacksaw, drill, screwdriver or screwdriver bit, caulking gun, hammer, level, and tape measure.

1. Temporarily attach the drip cap.
Unpack all the parts and remove the storm and screen panels from the door. Position the drip cap in the center of the top brick molding with the fuzzy gasket pointing out. Drill pilot holes and attach the drip cap with two screws.

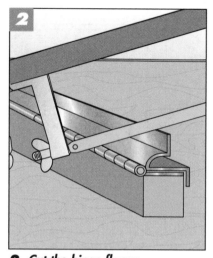

2. Cut the hinge flange.
Make sure you know which side of the hinge flange (also called a Z-bar) is up. Measure the opening height on the hinge side, from the bottom of the drip cap to the door sill. Set the hinge flange on a scrap of wood and cut it to the measured length, minus ⅛ inch.

3. Attach top of the hinge flange.
Apply a bead of caulk to the back of the hinge flange. Have a helper hold the door in position while you work. Align the hinge flange according to the manufacturer's directions. At the top screw hole, drill a pilot hole and drive a screw.

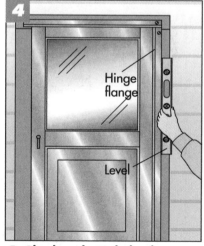

4. Plumb and attach the door.
Check that the hinge flange is plumb. If it is not, loosen the top screw to reposition the flange. Drill pilot holes and drive screws to attach the door.

5. Install the drip cap.

Remove the drip cap. Apply a bead of latex/silicone caulk to its back and reinstall it so that the gap between the top of the door and the cap is even. Drill pilot holes and drive the screws.

6. Install the latching flange.

Install the storm or screen panels in the door. Check that the door swings freely. Measure, cut, caulk, and install the latching flange (or Z-bar) so that the gap between the door and the flange is even.

7. Install the sweep.

Peel off any protective film from the bottom of the door and the sweep. Slide the rubber gasket onto the bottom of the sweep. Slip the sweep onto the bottom of the door. Slowly close the door and adjust the position of the sweep so it seals at the sill without binding. Drive screws to secure the sweep.

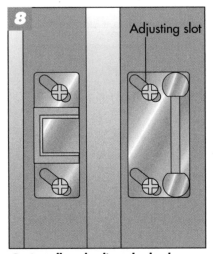

8. Install and adjust the latch.

Assemble and install the latch as instructed by the manufacturer. If the latch does not close easily and latch snugly, loosen the screws and adjust the latching pin.

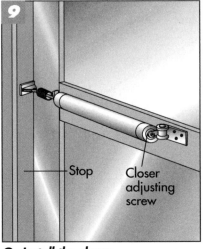

9. Install the closer.

Install and adjust the pneumatic door closer. Hold the closer in place and drill holes in the door (some units will have predrilled holes). Fasten the closer to the door and mark for the bracket that attaches to the stop. Drill holes and fasten the bracket in place.

EXPERTS' INSIGHT

STORM/SCREEN DOOR OPTIONS

Those flimsy aluminum combination doors of yesteryear are still sold, but more substantial units are available. A door with a foam or wood core is difficult to dent. Scratch-resistant surfaces withstand the attentions of pets wanting to come in. Better doors have gaskets that seal storm sashes tight to keep out the cold. Many sweeps have rubber flanges at the bottom that seal just like a standard door threshold.

ROOFING, SIDING, AND WEATHERIZATION

Chapter 7

Understanding Roofs **188**
Understanding Exterior Walls **189**
Inspecting a Roof **190**

Roofing Repairs and Improvements
Solving Roof Problems **191**
Repairing Asphalt Shingles **192**
Repairing Wood Shingles **193**
Repairing and Replacing Flashing **194**
Cleaning and Repairing a Masonry Chimney **195**
Repairing and Maintaining Gutter Systems **196**

Siding Repairs and Improvements
Where Sealing Is Needed **198**
Repairing Wood Siding and Shingles **199**
Replacing a Section of Aluminum Siding **201**
Preplacing Aluminum End Caps **202**
Repairing Dented Aluminum Siding **203**
Replacing a Vinyl Siding Strip **204**
Repairing Stucco Walls **205**

UNDERSTANDING ROOFS

A pitched roof sheds water much the same way a duck's feathers do. Courses of roofing material—most often some variation of the **shingle**—lie one atop the other and overlap, like a bird's feathers. Shingles on a roof are layered at least two deep, with exposed portions slightly smaller than half the total area of the shingle. At the top, a **ridge vent** or an extra layer of shingles covers the ridge.

Valleys, the places where two slopes meet, direct runoff into gutters, which in turn direct the water into downspouts. For additional protection against leakage, metal or composition flashings are placed under the shingles at the roof's most vulnerable points. Typically these include valleys, dormers, vents, and chimneys, or anywhere the roof's surface is penetrated.

Valleys are notorious problem areas; the flatter the roof, the greater the potential for leaks. Metal **valley flashing** must be wide enough and the pieces must overlap correctly. If no flashing is used, roofing must be woven together seamlessly—a job that's definitely for pros. A valley that does not have metal flashing is vulnerable to damage; avoid walking on it.

Any area with flashing—especially around a chimney—is liable to leak. **Chimney flashing** must be installed correctly and sealed tightly against the vertical surface that it abuts.

Vents, whether they are plumbing pipes or exhaust fans, usually come with integral flashing. Typically, the lower half of the flashing is exposed, and the upper half is covered with roofing.

Beneath the roofing material lies a house's most complex structure, framing (typically **gable** or **hip**). The framing ties together the wall structures and supports not only the weight of the shingles but also other loads, such as snow and ice in colder climates. **Rafters,** rising from the top plate of the wall to the **ridge board,** define the roof's pitch. **Collar ties** in the attic help keep the rafters from spreading; **headers** box in any openings.

Deck sheathing, usually plywood, goes on top of the rafters to give the structure rigidity. A layer of **roofing felt** seals the sheathing against moisture. Rafter ends are trimmed at the eaves with a **fascia board** (to which a **gutter** is fastened) and along the rake with **rake boards.** Once the trim is protected with drip cap, the shingles can go on.

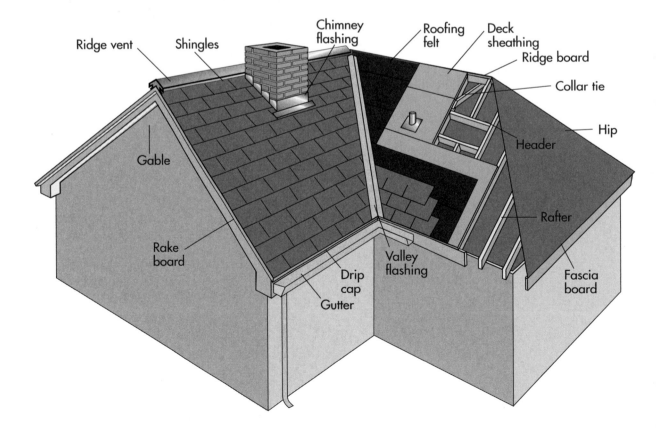

UNDERSTANDING EXTERIOR WALLS

Regardless of your home's exterior skin (siding or brick), its skeleton probably looks like the one shown here. The **sill plate** rests on the masonry foundation. **Rim joists,** collectively called a box sill, rest on the outside perimeter of the sill plate. Floor joists (which also act as ceiling joists for the basement, if there is a basement) attach to the rim joists. In some cases a short framed wall rises from the **foundation,** and the joists rest on this wall. If your basement ceiling is open, periodically check the rim joists, the sill plate, and the **sill seal**.

Attend to any moisture immediately because rot here could cause structural damage. It is also here that termites and other wood-boring insects often enter the house.

Exterior wall framing is made of 2×4 or 2×6 lumber (2×6s are common in newer homes in cold climates because they accommodate thicker insulation). A **sole plate** rests on the joists. Vertical **studs** are usually spaced 16 inches on center (sometimes they are 24 inches on center). The **top plate** is usually doubled to ensure that it can support second-story joists or the roof.

Over a door or window, a header carries the load and must be as strong as the rest of the wall.

Insulation between the studs conserves heat. Wood or composition board **sheathing** adds insulation and strength. Then a layer of **building wrap,** either asphalt-saturated building paper or plastic, seals the sheathing. It is essential that the building wrap be installed correctly so that moisture is sealed out rather than trapped inside the wall.

Outside, **siding** faces the elements and gives your home its visual character. Shown here is horizontal lap siding, named because the boards overlap each other. Other types of siding may be vertical or horizontal, but all overlap in some way in order to seal the exterior. Vinyl and aluminum siding often give the appearance of wood, but with differing maintenance requirements. Siding made of pressed board needs to be kept well protected or it will disintegrate quickly.

Regardless of its composition, siding deserves a careful semiannual inspection. Scan its surface systematically, using binoculars for closeups of high

places if necessary. Look for cracks, splits, peeling paint, and evidence of rot or insect damage. Any breaks in your home's skin—no matter how small—will eventually admit water into wall cavities. If you neglect the repairs explained in this section (see pages 198–206), moisture could wreck insulation, framing, or even **interior wall surfaces.**

If a new paint job is imminent, see pages 261–268. To learn about basic wall-building techniques, turn to pages 131–139.

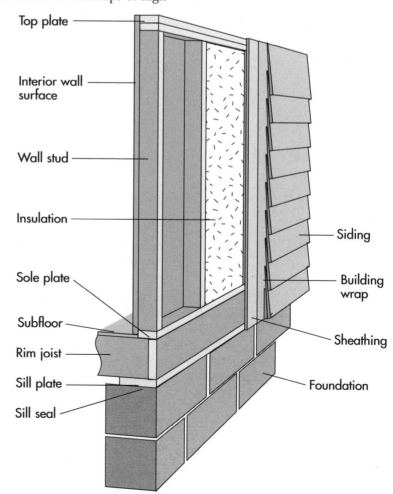

Top plate —
Interior wall surface —
Wall stud —
Insulation —
Sole plate —
Subfloor —
Rim joist —
Sill plate —
Sill seal —
— Siding
— Building wrap
— Sheathing
— Foundation

INSPECTING A ROOF

To ensure a tight roof overhead, you should examine it every spring and fall. You don't have to haul out the extension ladder and risk life and limb crawling onto the roof. Just scan it from all sides through binoculars, paying special attention to the problem areas illustrated here.

If you do decide to climb up for a closer look, exercise caution. Also bear in mind that the sun does more damage than the wind and rain combined, so you may want to focus most of your effort on the sunny side of the house. Don't mount a roof on a hot, sunny day. Shingles (especially asphalt shingles) are easily damaged when hot.

If a number of shingles are broken, blistered, or balding and many have lost their luster, prepare for a reroofing job.

Clean the gutters.
Keep your hips between the rails, and don't overreach; erect ladders are easily tipped with little motion. For solutions to gutter problems, see pages 196–197.

Use a stabilizer.
For roof work, buy a pair of metal roofing jacks, which are held in place with nails driven under a shingle. Install two jacks and stretch a 2×4 between them. Or secure the ladder with ropes tied to a tree on the other side. Or hook a stabilizer over the ridge.

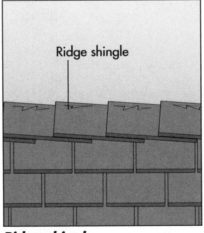

Ridge shingle.
Ridge shingles often fail first. Look for cracks and wind damage. In the case of asphalt shingles, the mineral granules may be worn away. A leak here can show up anywhere inside.

Valley.
Valleys are another place where deterioration causes problems. Make sure any flashing is sound. Shingles should lie flat on top of the flashing. If leaks occur during windy rainstorms, the shingles that lie on the flashing may not be cut correctly; ask a pro.

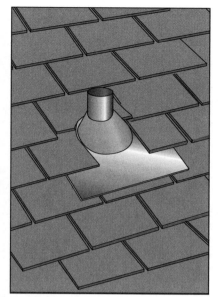

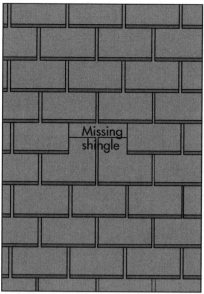

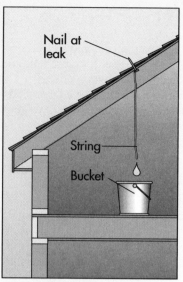

Flashing.

Check other flashing too. It should be tight, rust-free, and sealed with pliable caulking or roofing cement. Installing a new vent like the one shown above is not difficult, but other types of flashing require a pro.

Missing shingle.

Loose, curled, or missing shingles leak moisture that weakens sheathing and harms walls and ceilings. If individual shingles have been damaged by a falling branch, replace them singly. If shingles show general wear and tear, it's time for a reroofing job.

Pinpoint leaks.

Water that gets through a leak in your roof will often follow a meandering, brooklike course. It can travel under sheathing, down a rafter, even along an electrical cable, before showing up as a drip or damp spot on a ceiling or wall.

You may be able to trace the trickle to its source from the attic. Look for water stains on framing and sheathing. Keep in mind that a leak will originate higher than the area where it first appeared. Even then the cause of the leak may be above the point of entry into the attic. Often the culprits are damaged flashing and damaged or mis-applied shingles.

On a sunny day, a leak may appear as a pinhole of light in the attic. If you find one, drive a nail up through it from the attic to mark the spot on the roof itself. Attach a string to guide water to a bucket until you can make the repair.

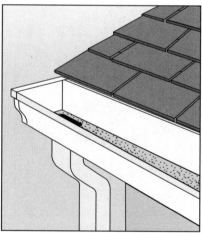

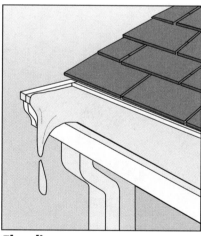

Granules in the gutter.

A large accumulation of granules in the gutter means your roof is losing its surface coating. Expect problems soon.

Flooding gutter.

Watch during a heavy rain to see if gutters are free-flowing. Flooding can work up under lower shingle courses.

REPAIRING ASPHALT SHINGLES

*B*uy roofing cement in caulking tubes to seal minor cracks and holes and to glue down curled shingles. If you have a larger job, buy the roofing cement in larger containers—1-gallon or even 5-gallon buckets.

If the damage is extensive, replace the shingle. When working with asphalt shingles, wait for a warm day when the shingles will be flexible and easier to work with. Avoid ending up with exposed nails as much as possible. If you must leave an exposed nail, cover it well with roofing cement.

YOU'LL NEED...

TIME: About 30 minutes.
SKILLS: Basic roofing skills.
TOOLS: Hammer, pry bar, putty knife, utility knife, flat shovel, caulking gun.

1. Remove the nails.
Loosen the nails in the shingle above by slipping a flat shovel underneath. Lift the shingle above carefully, to avoid cracking it. Pull all four of the nails with a pry bar and slide the bad shingle out.

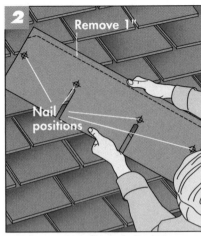

2. Cut a shingle and slip it in.
Remove 1 inch from the top edge of the new shingle by cutting the nongranular side with a knife. Bend the strip back and forth until it snaps. Slip the new shingle into place under the shingle above. Note the positions of the nails.

3. Drive nails.
If possible, lift the shingle above and drive nails close to the old nail holes. The nailhead should cover the old hole, but be far enough away that the nail bites into the sheathing. It may work to push the nail in place, slip a pry bar over the nailhead, and pound on the pry bar.

4. Cover heads with cement.
Coat the nailheads with roofing cement, then firmly press the upper course back into place. If necessary, seal the old holes as well. If the shingle curls up, weight it down temporarily.

Repair with flashing.
You also can back up a damaged shingle with a piece of metal flashing. Secure the flashing by setting it in a bed of roofing cement. Then cover the top of the metal with more cement and press the shingle into the cement.

REPAIRING WOOD SHINGLES

A new replacement shingle may differ in color from the surrounding shingles. In time it will weather and look the same.

Choose grade #1 shingles, made of heartwood, which resists insects and fungi. They will last far longer than less expensive shingles made from sapwood.

When replacing shingles, be sure to match the spacing between the existing shingles. Butting the replacement shingle against the old shingles may create a tight joint that traps moisture, which will encourage rot and decay.

YOU'LL NEED...

TIME: About 30 to 60 minutes per shingle.
SKILLS: Basic carpentry skills.
TOOLS: Hammer, chisel, pry bar, utility knife, saw, nail set, drill, caulking gun.

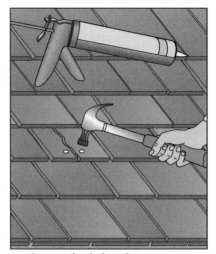

Nail a cracked shingle.
Mend splits by drilling pilot holes and driving shingle or siding nails, which have smaller heads than roofing nails. Seal the gap and the nailheads with roofing cement or butyl caulk (which can be purchased in a color to nearly match the shingles).

Back a hole with flashing.
If a knothole has opened, drive a sheet of aluminum flashing material under the shingle. Be sure that it extends several inches above the hole. If the spot is highly visible, paint the metal to resemble the shingles.

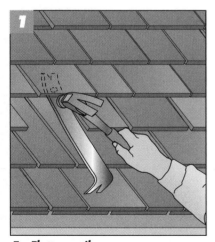

1. Flatten nails.
To remove a damaged shingle, split it along the grain with a chisel and pull the pieces out. The nails that held it in place will remain. Place the flat end of a pry bar over the old nailheads and strike with a hammer to drive the nailheads flush.

2. Tap in a new shingle.
Cut a new shingle to width so that there are appropriate gaps on both sides. With a block of wood and a hammer, drive the new shingle until it is flush with the row and the nailheads are covered.

3. Nail and seal.
Drive two shingle nails into the new shingle at 45 degrees, close to the butt of the shingle above. Use a nail set to drive nailheads flush; seal with caulk.

REPAIRING AND REPLACING FLASHING

Think of flashing as a special-purpose shingle. Like a shingle, flashing overlaps and interweaves with other roofing materials to shed water.

Flashing is made of thin-gauge metal that is bent and formed to fit angled joints where two or more surfaces abut. Because these intersections are vulnerable to leakage, flashing deserves closer scrutiny than the rest of your roof.

Look for flashing that has pulled away from adjoining surfaces and for roofing cement or caulk that has dried and cracked. Even tiny holes can leak; when in doubt, apply new cement or caulk.

Rusted, cracked, or corroded flashing around chimneys, dormers, and plumbing vents will last for a few more years if you trowel on a coat of fibered asphalt-aluminum roof paint. If there is widespread deterioration or valley-flashing failure, call in a roofer or sheet-metal specialist to replace these sections entirely.

You can replace small flashing pieces as long as you buy precise duplicates and replace them in their exact original positions.

Take care that two types of metal do not come in contact with each other, or corrosion could result. For durability at a reasonable price, choose aluminum flashing. Vent flashing comes as a single molded piece of metal or plastic. Simply fit the piece over the pipe and cover with roofing on the uphill side.

YOU'LL NEED...

TIME: 4 to 6 hours.
SKILLS: Moderate carpentry skills.
TOOLS: Tin snips, putty knife, hammer, cold chisel, trowel, joint strike, caulking gun, ladder, rope.

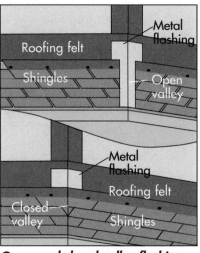

Open- and closed-valley flashing.
Because it is visible, open-valley flashing is easy to inspect. Cement down any shingles that are even slightly curled or loose.

Closed-valley flashing hides beneath the roofing. In some cases shingles are so interlaced on top that it is impossible to check the flashing.

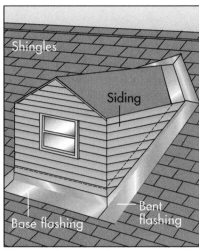

Flashing for a dormer.
To reflash dormers buy pieces of flashing bent at 90 degrees. Using the old flashing as a guide, tuck the flashing under the siding on the dormer. Use valley flashing along the peak. For brick use step flashing capped with counter-flashing let into mortar joints.

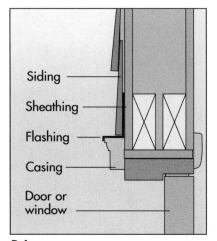

Drip cap.
Drip cap flashing keeps water from seeping under the frames over windows and doors. The drip cap should be several inches high so that water cannot work its way up and around it. Check drip caps periodically for damage.

Replace a vent.
Don't bother repairing faulty vent flashing. Just install a new neoprene and aluminum replacement. You'll need to replace only a few shingles (see pages 192–193).

CLEANING AND REPAIRING A MASONRY CHIMNEY

Chimneys have two enemies: heat and water. The crackling fire you enjoy on winter evenings subjects masonry to temperature extremes that can chip out mortar, especially at the top where the flue penetrates the cap.

Most chimneys have a ceramic flue liner running up through the center. Concrete blocks surround the liner, and bricks cover the blocks. Other chimneys are all brick; a few use firebrick instead of a ceramic tile flue liner. Many also include a chimney cap to keep out rain, nesting birds, and downdrafts. Regardless of your chimney's construction, it pays to inspect it every fall. Examine every visible surface, including the attic. Look for cracks and deteriorated mortar.

Occasionally test for hot spots by feeling with your hand. These may indicate a broken flue—a definite fire hazard that a mason should fix before you use the fireplace again.

How often a fireplace flue needs cleaning depends on how much you use it and the type of wood you burn. Pine and other sappy species produce creosote, which cakes the flue and constricts the opening. The result: smoking and a possible chimney fire. Hire a chimney sweep to clean your chimney, or do the job yourself, as shown here. A faulty firebox design or downdrafts also cause smoking.

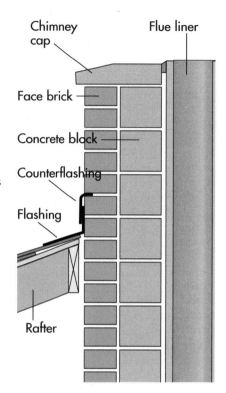

Chimney cap

Flue liner

Face brick

Concrete block

Counterflashing

Flashing

Rafter

YOU'LL NEED...
TIME: 2 to 8 hours.
SKILLS: Basic masonry skills.
TOOLS: Hammer, cold chisel, caulking gun, sweep tools.

1. Seal the fireplace.
Before brushing, open the damper and seal the fireplace opening with a wet sheet, canvas, or polyethylene sheeting. Be sure the opening is sealed very tightly and firmly. Measure the diameter and length of your chimney, and buy chimney brushes and extension handles to fit.

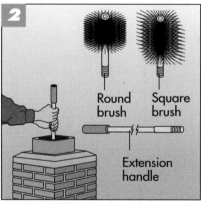

Round brush
Square brush

Extension handle

2. Brush the chimney.
From the top, insert the brush, moving it up and down to dislodge debris from the flue liner. Add an extension and repeat until you reach the damper at the bottom. Wait approximately a half hour for the dust to settle. Slowly remove the sheeting. Wet down the soot before you clean out the firebox. Vacuum around the damper before closing it.

3. Repoint and apply caulk.
Rain erodes mortar joints. Chip away loose material. Apply a generous bead of masonry or butyl caulk around the flue for a flexible seal that rides out expansion and contraction. If the area is badly damaged with large, loose pieces, call in a pro.

REPAIRING AND MAINTAINING GUTTER SYSTEMS

Your roof's drainage system diverts thousands of gallons of water away from your house annually, so you can see why it merits a semiannual inspection.

Here's how the drainage system works: All gutters slope slightly toward their outlets. From there two elbows connect to the downspout; at the bottom a third elbow directs the spout outlet away from the wall.

Check gutters and downspouts every spring before heavy rains begin and late in the fall after leaves have fallen. Remove all debris logging the system, look for rust or corrosion, and be vigilant in looking for low spots where water may pool.

Standing water is the cause of most gutter problems, so check that gutters slope down toward their outlets. Pour or spray water into a gutter and watch what happens. Eliminate sags by lifting the gutter section slightly. Look for and repair loose hangers, or bend up the hanger with a pair of pliers. If this doesn't do the trick, install an additional hanger.

If you have widespread drainage problems, call gutter companies for prices on replacing the entire system. They can install seamless aluminum gutters with leaf protectors for virtually maintenance-free operation.

YOU'LL NEED...
TIME: 4 to 6 hours for a medium-size house.
SKILLS: Basic carpentry skills and comfort working on heights.
TOOLS: Hose and sprayer, wire brush, putty knife, ladder, hammer, hacksaw, pliers, drill.

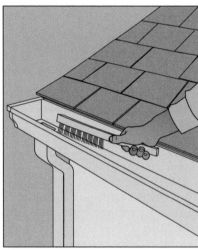

Clean a gutter.
Debris clogs up gutters and downspouts and holds moisture that causes rust, rot, and corrosion. Clear away debris by hand (wear gloves). Finish up by using a wire brush to scrape away caked-on debris.

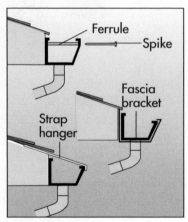

Gutter hardware.
There are three forms of gutter hangers: a spike and a ferrule driven through the gutter into rafter ends, a strap nailed to the roof sheathing, or a fascia bracket attached to the fascia. If a gutter sags, add a strap hanger.

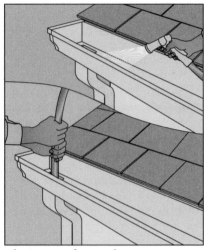

Blast water from a hose.
Hose your gutters clean, beginning at the high end of each run—or in the middle of runs having spouts at both ends. Often you can blast out spout blockage with water pressure or a plumber's snake. Otherwise you may have to dismantle the downspouts.

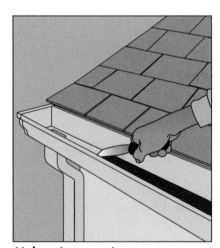

Make minor repairs.
If the inside of a gutter is rusting, scrape and wire-brush it clean, then apply a thin coat of roofing cement. Seal any cracks or gaps at joints using gutter caulk. If sections of a downspout are coming loose, drill pilot holes and drive short sheetmetal screws.

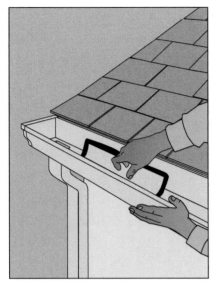

Patch a gutter.
Patch a rusted-out gutter with metal flashing. Bend a piece of sheet metal so it can rest in the opening. Spread a layer of roofing cement and set the patch into the cement. Then coat the patch with more roofing cement.

Install a screen guard.
Screen guards keep out leaves. Buy guards made to fit your size of gutter. Slip the inner edge under the first course of shingles and bend the screen into place.

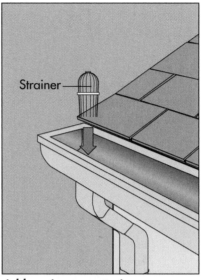

Add a wire-cage strainer.
Wire-cage strainers eliminate downspout clogging. However, you will still have to clear debris from around the cages.

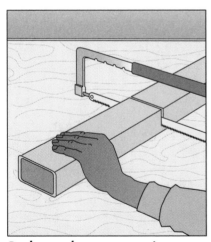

Replace a downspout section.
Cut downspouts with a fine-tooth hacksaw. Mark a line around the circumference so the edges will be square. Use a file or sandpaper to remove any burrs.

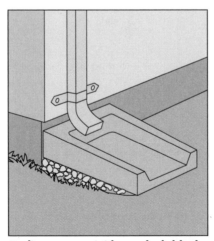

Redirect water with a splash block.
Splash blocks must be pitched away from the foundation walls. Use gravel to raise and shim a splash block.

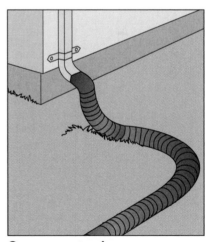

Or use an extension.
If water puddles near the house, or if your basement leaks during rainfalls, take steps to move the water at least 8 feet away from the house. A corrugated plastic extension stays in place; a perforated roll-up hose extends like a party noisemaker when the water comes down.

WHERE SEALING IS NEEDED

Different building materials swell and shrink at different rates. This results in cracks where siding meets masonry, where siding butts trim, and where flashing contacts roofing. Use caulk wherever unlike materials meet. The illustration below shows typical spots to check.

Caulking material falls into two categories—rubber-derived formulations, such as latex and butyl, and synthetic-based, high-performance materials. The type you select depends upon the job you want it to do.

Before buying, read the product data for preparation requirements, materials the caulk will adhere to, and paintability. The chart below compares the common sealants.

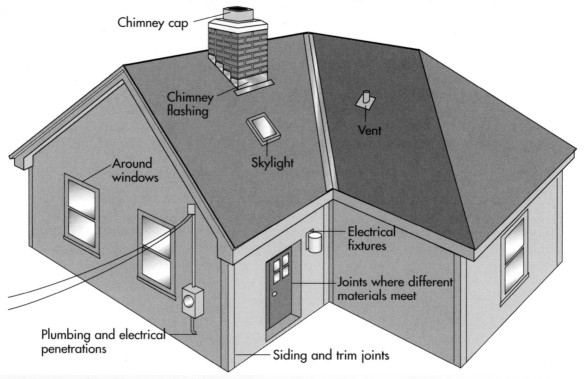

Chimney cap

Chimney flashing

Vent

Skylight

Around windows

Electrical fixtures

Joints where different materials meet

Plumbing and electrical penetrations

Siding and trim joints

CHOOSING SEALANTS

Type	Characteristics	Cost
Latex	Inexpensive and easy to work with; liable to shrink and crack in time	Inexpensive
Latex/silicone or latex/acrylic	Good general-purpose, fast-drying sealant; remains flexible for years; ideal for filling small cracks and joints; paintable	Moderate
"Tub and tile" caulk	Highly adhesive and waterproof; good for wet areas, such as tubs and showers	Moderate
Butyl or "gutter"	Excellent exterior caulk for gutter seams, flashings, storm windows, and large joints; paintable	Moderate
Silicone	The most durable caulk; remains flexible, but many types do not stick well; water-based products perform better and are paintable	Most expensive
Foam	Quickly fills wide cracks and openings; remains flexible; paintable, but impossible to smooth out; "non-expanding" type is easier to control	Moderate

REPAIRING WOOD SIDING AND SHINGLES

Damaged siding permits moisture to enter exterior walls, where it can rot the sheathing and even the framing. It needs quick attention.

Keep exterior walls well covered with quality paint (see pages 262–269). Make repairs as soon as you spot damage. Pack small cracks, splits, and open seams with latex/silicone or butyl caulk.

You may be able to repair splits and holes using epoxy wood filler (see page 203). If not, you'll have to replace the damaged board or shingle. If more than a few boards or shingles are failing, consider re-siding the entire wall.

YOU'LL NEED...

TIME: 1 to 3 hours for one course.
SKILLS: Moderate carpentry skills.
TOOLS: Chisel, hammer, pry bar, close-work hacksaw, square, putty knife, utility knife, plane, backsaw, drill, caulking gun.

1. Loosen the board.
To remove a length of siding, cut through the paint along its bottom edge. Work a chisel under its lower edge, then switch to a flat pry bar. To keep from damaging the surrounding siding, pry by pulling away from the house rather than pushing toward it.

2. Pry it away.
Each course of lapped siding is held in place by nails driven through the course above it. First deal with the lower nails. If the nails begin to come out with the board, jam the nail with a pry bar and tap the board down. This may cause the heads to pop out, making them easy to pry away. The same can be done for the nails in the course above.

3. Cut nails that won't pop out.
If the nails aren't cooperating, or if they are not accessible from the surface, slip a hacksaw blade underneath the siding and cut them. A close-work hacksaw works well for this. Be careful not to scrape the siding beneath the damage.

4. Prepare to cut out the damaged area.
To cut a piece to length, tap wedges under the course above and use a square to mark the cut lines. Cut first with a utility knife to diminish splintering.

5. Saw the siding.
Use a backsaw or fine-toothed handsaw to cut the face of the siding. Use short strokes, holding the top of the blade to keep it from buckling. As you finish each cut, be careful not to cut siding below the damaged area.

6. Split away the damage.
Split the damaged area along the grain and remove a piece at a time. Carefully pry away all remnants under the board above. Pry away or pound down all nails. Check that the replacement piece can slide all the way up into position.

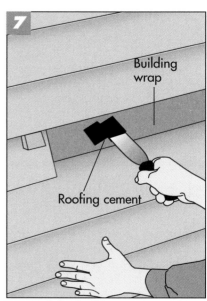

7. Seal the building wrap.
If you puncture the building paper underneath, seal it with roofing cement. Or cut a piece of roofing felt (tar paper) slightly larger than the opening and shoehorn it in. Fasten any loose paper with roofing nails or staples.

8. Slip in the patch.
Cut the replacement for a snug fit, then slide it under the board above, tap it into place, and remove the wedges. Avoid too tight a fit, however. Use a block plane to skim off one edge if you have to force the patch.

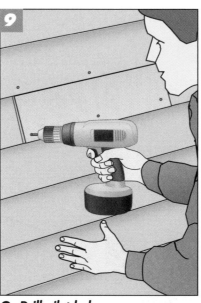

9. Drill pilot holes.
Wherever you will drive a nail less than 3 inches from the end or edge of a board, drill a pilot hole first to prevent splitting the board.

10. Nail, and caulk the seams.
Finally nail the new board at the top and bottom. Use siding nails, which have thin shanks. Fill nail holes and the vertical seams with caulk, then prime and paint.

REPLACING A SECTION OF ALUMINUM SIDING

Most aluminum siding is shaped like beveled wood siding and installed horizontally, as shown here. The less common vertical aluminum siding interlocks in much the same way, so repairs are essentially the same.

Because siding pieces are very long, it usually is easier to patch a damaged spot rather than replace the whole piece. The patch fits over the existing siding, so the cut does not have to be precise. A repair like this will result in joints that look nearly the same as other joints.

YOU'LL NEED...

TIME: An hour to cut and replace a section.
SKILLS: Basic cutting skills.
TOOLS: Square, utility knife, perhaps a circular saw, tin snips, flat pry bar, pliers, caulking gun.

1. Cut out the damaged section.
Using a square as a guide, cut a rectangle around the damaged area. It will take several passes with a utility knife to cut through the siding; you may need to change blades partway through.

2. Finish the cut.
You may find it easier to finish the cut using a pair of tin snips. A circular saw with the blade installed backwards makes cutting easy, but take care not to damage nearby pieces. Pull the cutout away and unsnap it from the wall.

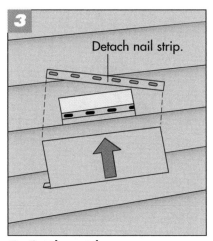

3. Cut the patch.
Cut a patch of matching siding at least 3 inches wider than the cut-out area. Cut off its nailing strip along the top. Test to see that the piece will fit. Its top should slip at least ¼ inch up under the piece above, and its bottom should be able to snap into place.

Detach nail strip.

4. Apply caulk.
Clean the area of all residue. Use a caulking gun to apply clear silicone sealant to the perimeter of the hole.

5. Lock the patch in place.
Slip the patch into place and slide it up until it locks in place. Press the sides flat and wipe away any squeezed-out caulk.

Wipe excess caulk.

REPLACING ALUMINUM END CAPS

Corners of a house often get bumped, so it's common to see aluminum end caps that are dented. Replacing them is not difficult.

The original installer may have left some end caps in your garage or basement. If not, bring an old end cap to your supply source to find an exact replacement.

Chances are that the old siding has faded, so you may not be able to get an exact color match. If so, paint the pieces to match the siding before installing them.

You'll Need...

Time: About an hour to replace six or seven end caps.
Skills: Basic cutting, fastening, and caulking skills.
Tools: Hacksaw, hammer, flat pry bar, drill, blind pop riveter.

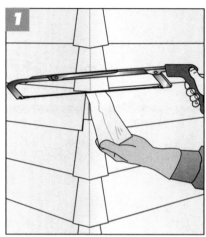

1. Cut damaged caps.
In some cases broken or dented corner caps will pull out easily. However, you may need to pry out the siding above to get at the nails. If you cannot pull out the nails without damaging the siding, cut through them with a hacksaw. If you can't get to the nails, cut through the corner piece itself.

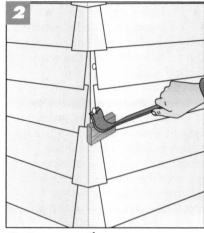

2. Remove nails.
Remove the damaged corner caps, then take out the remaining nails with a flat pry bar. Use a scrap of wood to prevent denting the siding as you pry.

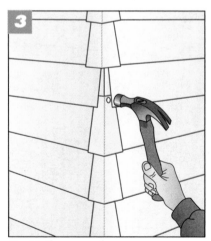

3. Nail new end caps.
Starting at the bottom, slide each replacement cap under the bottom lip of the course above, and slide it up until it snaps into place. Taking care not to dent the siding, attach each cap with one or two nails or screws. You may need to angle the fastener in order to hit solid wood.

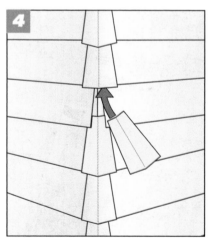

4. Install the last piece.
Cut the nailing strip off of the top replacement cap so it can slip under the course above by about 1/4 inch. Test to see that it fits snugly and can snap into place at the bottom. Apply silicone caulk to the back side of the cap, slide the cap into place, and wipe away any excess caulk.

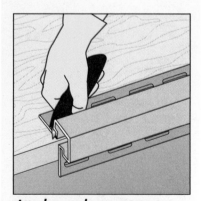

Attach a replacement post.
If you have to replace a dented corner post (a problem common to aluminum and vinyl siding), cut through the sides with a knife; it will take several passes. Cut the flange off a replacement piece and test to see that it fits. Apply clear silicone caulk to the flanges and attach using screws or blind pop rivets.

REPAIRING DENTED ALUMINUM SIDING

This technique is more time-consuming than patching with a replacement piece (page 201), but it's useful if you have a hard time finding siding to match.

Automobile-body filler is available at an auto parts store. It comes as a two-part epoxy; add a bit of hardener and mix with a small scrap of plastic or wood. It quickly hardens to the point where it can be planed or sanded. An hour or two later, it can be painted.

You'll Need...

TIME: Several hours, including time for the material to harden.
SKILLS: Basic patching skills, spraying paint.
TOOLS: Lock-joint pliers, drill, wide putty knife, sanding block, spray paint can, painting tools.

TOOLS TO USE

BODY REPAIR TOOLS

If you have a number of dents to patch, invest in some tools that will enable you to quickly make and smooth the patches.

■ Self-tapping screws with large heads can be quickly driven into the soft aluminum and pulled out.

■ A pull-style paint scraper (with removable blades) makes it easy to scrape away excess body filler when it is partially hardened.

■ To grind down the patch after it has fully hardened, use a vibrating or random-orbit power sander.

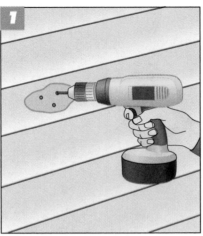

1. Drill a series of holes.
Equip a drill with a ⅛-inch bit, and drill several holes in the middle of the dented area. One or two of these will be pilot holes for the pull-out screw (Step 2), and the others will help the body filler to grab tightly onto the siding.

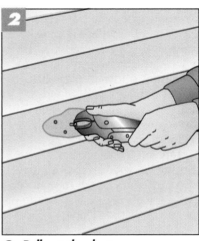

2. Pull out the dent.
Drive a No. 8 screw slightly into the deepest point of the dent. Grab the screw head with lock-joint pliers, and pull the dent partway out. Do not pull the siding out beyond the surrounding surface. If the dent is large, repeat this process with other screws in other locations.

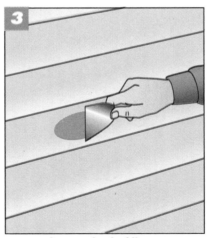

3. Apply auto-body filler.
Sand the dented area until it is bare of paint. Mix and apply two-part auto-body filler using a wide putty knife or the plastic scraper that comes with the filler. Smooth the patch so it is slightly higher than the surrounding siding. Once it has started to harden, scrape it down further.

Foam painting pad

4. Finish the patch.
Sand the area with 120-grit paper until it is smooth and level with the surrounding surface. Spray on metal primer, then apply color-matched paint suited for aluminum siding.

REPLACING A VINYL SIDING STRIP

*I*n some cases you can repair a section of vinyl by slipping a patch over the damaged area, in much the same way as shown for aluminum siding on page 201. However, many types of vinyl siding do not allow you to slip the top edge of the patch securely under the course above. Fortunately vinyl bends without denting, so you can pry out the top course far enough to remove existing nails and fasten the top of the repair piece.

YOU'LL NEED...

TIME: An hour for most repairs.
SKILLS: Basic carpentry skills.
TOOLS: Zip tool (made especially for vinyl siding), pry bar, utility knife, square hammer.

EXPERTS' INSIGHT

PAINTING VINYL SIDING

Vinyl siding is advertised as eliminating the need for painting. But some types (especially older and less expensive vinyl siding) may fade significantly in the sun. If you prepare carefully, you can apply paint to vinyl. First rough the vinyl with a hand or power sander and 60-grit sandpaper. Then apply a coat of alcohol-based primer, followed by exterior paint.

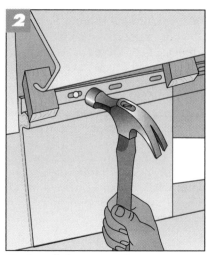

1. Pry out the damaged strip.
Unless you want to replace the entire strip, use a utility knife to cut it in place (see page 201). To remove a strip, insert a Zip tool under the lower lip, pull down, and slide the tool to the left or right. Also pull out the bottom of the course above.

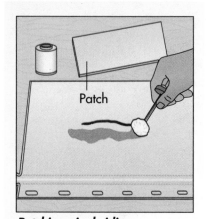

2. Install the new strip.
Carefully pry the upper course back, and use blocks to hold it away from the house so you can get at the nails. Remove the nails and the damaged piece. Fasten the new strip by nailing through the centers of the nail slots. Do not drive the nails tightly.

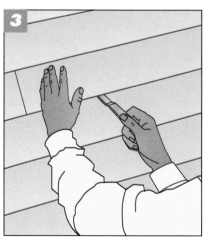

3. Finish the patch.
Relock the new strip by pulling down and sliding the Zip tool while pressing in along the bottom edge.

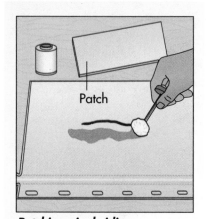

Patch

Patching vinyl siding.
To fix a tear, you needn't replace the piece. Cut a piece of plastic slightly larger than the damaged area. On the back side of the siding, apply PVC pipe primer, then cement. Press the patch into the cement and hold it for a few seconds.

REPAIRING STUCCO WALLS

Small cracks in stucco can be filled with butyl or silicone/latex caulk and then painted. But if there are many cracks or if a section is coming loose, you must chip away the old material down to the lath or masonry underneath, then build up a new surface in two or three layers. Problem areas larger than 8 feet square usually require restuccoing of the entire wall. This is a major job that you may want to leave to a professional.

Make repairs during mild weather when there's no danger of freezing. Plan on the project taking at least three days. Wait at least six weeks before painting, then prime and apply paint recommended for concrete and stucco.

Colored stucco is difficult to match. Experiment with pigments, keeping in mind that colors will fade as much as 70 percent by the time the stucco dries. Never let the coloring pigment exceed 3 percent of the batch's total volume.

Blending the patch's final surface with the surrounding area can be difficult. Consult with a pro to find out (or guess at) the technique and tool used by the original installer.

YOU'LL NEED...

TIME: 3 working days for a large patch, extended over 10 to 12 days to cover drying time.
SKILLS: Moderate to advanced masonry skills; knowledge of the special technique used by the original stucco contractor.
TOOLS: Cold chisel, pry bar, hammer, stapler, trowel, hawk, improvised rake, spray hose, metal straightedge.

1. Prepare the area.
Chip away loose stucco using a cold chisel, pry bar, and hammer. You may need to use wire cutters or tin snips to cut the metal lath. Staple new roofing felt and metal lath onto the sheathing. Make sure the surrounding stucco is firmly attached to the wall; if not, chip away some more.

3. Scarify.
When the stucco begins to firm up, scratch it with a scarifying tool, or an improvised rake made by driving nails through a piece of wood every inch. The scratches should be about ⅛ inch deep.

2. Trowel the first coat.
Mix a batch of stucco base coat, following directions on the bag. Place a dollop of stucco on a hawk or a piece of plywood, and push the stucco into the metal lath using a straight trowel. Apply the first coat to a depth of about ¼ inch below the surrounding surfaces. Smooth the area.

TOOLS TO USE

FINISHING STUCCO

Stuccoers use a variety of tools to achieve the final surface. If you are unsure how to mimic the surrounding area, spread stucco on a plywood scrap and practice using these methods:

■ Dab at the stucco with your palm or a trowel and pull straight back to achieve peaks. Perhaps "knock down" the peaks by lightly passing over the surface with a trowel.

■ Produce a basically smooth surface. Dip a whisk broom in a bucket of stucco and dash it at the wall to produce hills. Perhaps knock them down.

■ Make a swirled surface by brushing with a whisk broom using wavy or arcing strokes.

4. Cure the base coat slowly.

The more slowly the stucco cures (dries out), the stronger it will be. Mist the scratch coat with a fine spray as often as necessary to keep it damp for two days. In windy or sunny weather, repeat several times a day. If the air is dry, tape a piece of plastic over the patch while it cures.

5. Add the brown coat.

Some installations omit this step and go straight to the finish coat (Step 7). Mix a batch of stucco for the second or "brown" coat. Apply this coat to within about 1/8 inch of the surface, and level it off with a metal straightedge or a large trowel.

6. Float the surface.

"Float" the brown coat by working it with a trowel until bleed water comes to the surface. Avoid overworking; stop once the water has appeared.

7. Texture the finish coat.

Mist the brown coat for two days and wait a week. While you are waiting, practice applying finish stucco to a scrap of plywood until you can achieve a texture that blends in with the rest of the wall. Moisten the brown coat and mix a batch of finish stucco. Smooth on the finish coat. Texture it within a half hour.

TILING

Chapter 8

Tile Basics
Planning Your Tiling Project **208**
Selecting the Right Tile for the Job **210**

Tiling Tools and Materials
Selecting Installation Tools **214**
Choosing Grouting Tools **215**
Using Tile Spacers **216**
Selecting Adhesives **217**
Choosing Setting Beds **218**
Selecting Grout **219**
Selecting Membranes **220**
Choosing Caulk and Sealers **221**
Assessing Substrates **222**
Calculating Materials **223**
Preparing the Site **224**
Laying Out the Job **225**

Tiling Techniques
Cutting Backerboard **228**
Installing Backerboard **229**
Mixing Thin-Set Mortar **230**
Spreading Thin-Set Mortar **231**
Cutting Tile **232**
Trimming Tile **233**
Setting Tile **234**
Setting Mosaic Tile **236**
Grouting Tile **237**
Caulking and Sealing **240**

Tiling Projects
Tiling Floors **241**
Tiling a Kitchen Floor **245**
Tiling a Bathroom Floor **247**

PLANNING YOUR TILING PROJECT

Good architectural design often goes unnoticed. A well-proportioned house or intelligently laid-out kitchen simply has a natural rightness about it. In the same way, instead of shouting for attention, a well-designed tile installation should just fit in. When a surfacing material jumps out at you, the design probably has failed.

The age of your house, the decorating style you seek to capture, and your budget all affect the design you choose. Books, magazines, and tile brochures are probably the best sources of ideas. However be sure the types and patterns of tile that you find attractive suit your space.

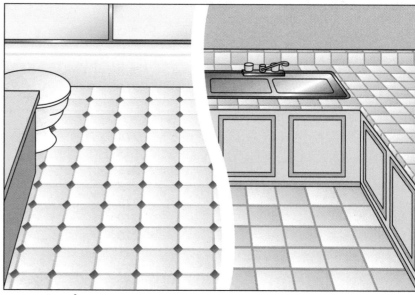

Proportion tile to room size.
As a general rule, tile size should be proportional to the size of the room. That is, small tiles generally work best in small rooms and large tiles look better in large rooms. Larger tiles seem less large when used on horizontal surfaces. Use larger tiles on lower surfaces; wall tiles or countertop tiles that are bigger than the floor tiles tend to make a room top-heavy.

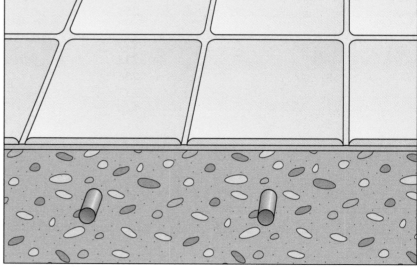

Plan for comfort as well as style.
Radiant heating systems in which heated water passes through tubing embedded in or under the floor surface are becoming increasingly popular. Tile is a great choice for the finish surface on a radiant floor. Because the tubing usually is embedded in concrete, the concrete pad can be used as an ideal setting bed for tile. Also tile is a highly conductive material that transmits heat quickly and efficiently. If you are tiling a new addition or need to improve heating in a room, consider incorporating a radiant heating system into the design.

EXPERTS' INSIGHT

DESIGNING WITH COLOR

With so many stunning tile colors readily available, it's tempting to wield a broad brush and let the color fly. But because today's fashionable color is often tomorrow's eyesore, white and almond tend to be the tones of choice for most homeowners. These light neutral tones help brighten up rooms and can coexist with almost any other colors as your decorating schemes change. But many people think too much white or off-white is monotonous. Accent and border colors often cancel out this impression. In rooms with plenty of windows, consider using darker tiles to offset the ambient lighting.

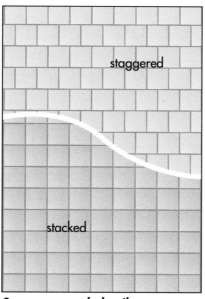

Stagger or stack the tile.

Area tiles usually are installed in a grid pattern or a staggered pattern. A stacked pattern is the easiest to install, and the clean straight lines appeal to many people. Although they require careful alignment, staggered joints have a pleasingly retro look.

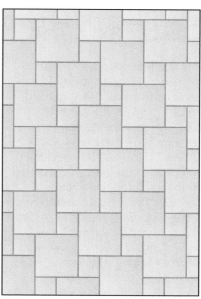

Make the most of one color.

Using only one color of tile does not have to result in a plain-looking installation. Use tiles of different sizes to add a level of contrast. Consider different grout colors and grout joint sizes. Or, use tiles with only small variations in color.

Consider herringbone.

Plain rectangular tiles gain a new dimension when installed in a herringbone pattern. As a variation, wrap a small square tile with rectangular tiles.

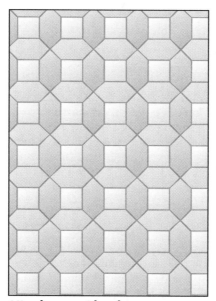

Mix shapes with colors.

Manufacturers offer tiles purposely sized to allow for mixing different shapes into a coherent whole. You can add further interest with this approach by using two or more colors as well.

Define your space.

Borders help define the perimeters of a tile installation and can add a whole new level of interest to the surface. Here, variously colored and sized tiles create a border surrounding a field of tiles installed diagonally.

SELECTING THE RIGHT TILE FOR THE JOB

Although simplicity is part of the universal appeal of ceramic tile (it is essentially a thin a slab of baked clay), don't assume that just any tile will suit your project. You'll have to consider several factors as you select the right tile for the job: The material from which the tile is made (ceramic tile is made from clay; some tiles do not use clay at all but are actually slabs of stone milled into regular shapes), the degree of firing, the type of glaze, and the shape of the tile.

If you are planning several tiling projects for your home, you may want to contact one of the associations created by tile manufacturers, designers, retailers, and installation contractors. These groups have developed standards and acceptable practices relating to tile and tile installations.

The American National Standards Institute (ANSI) has prepared a list of minimal standards that are followed by all professionals in the industry. The Tile Council of America (TCA) publishes the inexpensive annual *Handbook for Ceramic Tile Installation*, which sets forth the ANSI standards. Contact the TCA at P.O. Box 1787, Clemson, SC 29633 or at www.tileusa.com/publication_main.htm.

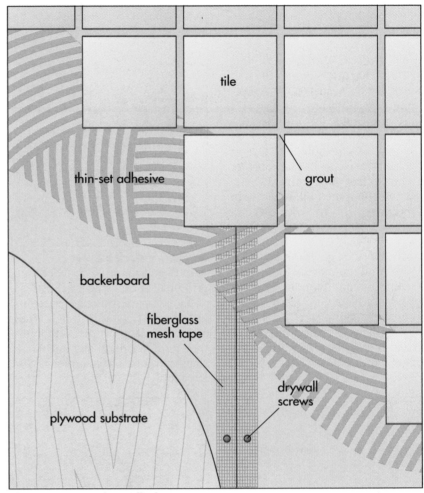

Plan out a typical installation.
Installing tile is a bit like making a sandwich: You proceed one layer at a time. The substrate, often plywood, is the layer in direct contact with the framing (studs for a wall installation or joists for a floor installation). Backerboard serves as the setting bed for the tiles themselves. Tiles form the outer layer. Adhesive is used to bond each layer.

TILE INSTALLATION CHECKLIST

The ANSI standards cover proper materials and installations for just about any type of tile job you can imagine. Use this simple checklist as a design and shopping guide.

Type of Tile
- ☐ glazed wall tile
- ☐ glazed floor tile
- ☐ ceramic mosaic tile
- ☐ paver or quarry tile
- ☐ natural stone

Location of Installation
- ☐ always dry or limited water exposure
- ☐ frequently wet
- ☐ interior
- ☐ exterior
- ☐ subject to freezing

Special Requirements
- ☐ fire resistant
- ☐ stain resistant
- ☐ crack resistant
- ☐ color
- ☐ heavy use

WATER ABSORPTION

Clay absorbs water, and water can cause cracks in tiles and create damage beneath the surface. Ceramic tiles that have been kiln-dried longer and at higher temperatures absorb less water, but they also cost more. So it makes sense to choose tiles precisely rated for the protection you need.

Tile Rating	Best Uses
Nonvitreous	This tile typically is used for decorative purposes only. It is intended for use indoors, in dry locations, such as a fireplace surround or a decorative frieze in a dining room
Semivitreous	This type of tile is used indoors in dry to occasionally wet locations, such as a kitchen wall or behind a serving area in a dining room.
Vitreous	This multipurpose tile is used indoors or outdoors or in wet or dry locations for anything from bathroom floors or walls to a patio surface.
Impervious	Such tile generally is used only in hospitals, restaurants, and other commercial locations where the ability to thoroughly clean is important.

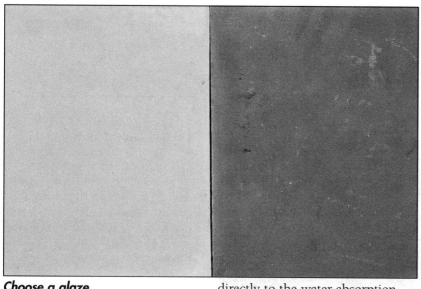

Choose a glaze.
A glaze is a protective and decorative coating, often colored, that is fired onto the surface of tiles. Glazes can be glossy, matte, or textured. Glazing is not related directly to the water-absorption categories listed above. Although glazing does keep moisture from penetrating the top surface, the unglazed sides and bottoms of the tile don't have the same protection.

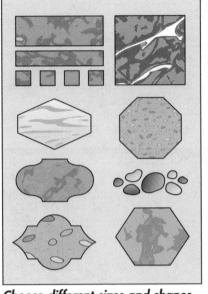

Select the type of ceramic tile.

Modern ceramic tile is made from refined clay, usually mixed with additives and water. It then is hardened in a kiln. Several different types of tile are created through that process. Quarry tiles are unglazed and vitreous tiles, usually ½ inch thick and used for flooring. Pavers are ⅜-inch-thick vitreous floor tiles and are available glazed or unglazed.

Choose different sizes and shapes.

Square tiles are the most common and the easiest to install. But rectangles, hexagons, and other shapes are readily available. An easy and inexpensive way to add interest to a tile installation is to mix shapes, sizes, and colors; tile retailers and home centers offer a wide range of options.

Consider stone tile.

Use natural stone tile on floors, walls, and countertops. Marble, granite, flagstone, and slate are widely available; other types of stone may be available in your area. Dimensioned (or gauged) stone is cut to a uniform size and thickness and can be installed much like ceramic tile. Hand-split (or cleft) stone tiles vary in size and thickness.

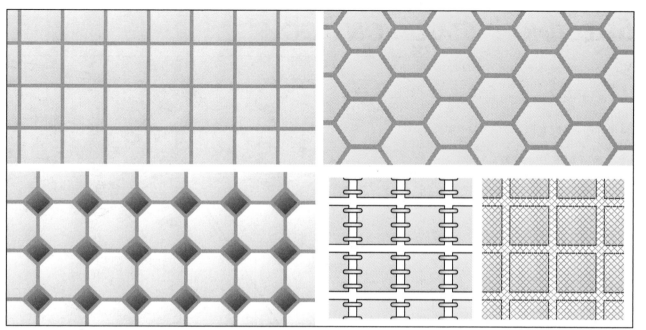

Use mosaic tile.

Mosaic tiles are 1- or 2-inch squares or similarly sized hexagons or pentagons mounted together as a larger unit. Most commercially available mosaics are vitreous and freeze-thaw stable and can be used on most tiling projects. Mosaic tiles are sold almost exclusively mounted on sheets or joined with adhesive strips. Back-mounted mosaic tiles are much easier to install than individual tiles. They can be mounted with standard thin-set adhesive and grout.

MEASUREMENTS

NOMINAL VS. ACTUAL SIZE

Most do-it-yourselfers learn quickly that when buying lumber, a 2×4 doesn't measure 2 inches by 4 inches. The tile trade has a similar discrepancy. Individual ceramic tiles are often sold with dimensional names that describe their installed size, that is, the size of the tile plus a standard grout joint. Thus, 6×6-inch tiles measure $\frac{1}{8}$ inch shorter in each direction. The actual size will be $5\frac{7}{8} \times 5\frac{7}{8}$ inches. Only when installed with a $\frac{1}{8}$-inch grout joint will the installed size of the tile be about 6×6. Always check the actual size of the tiles before you buy them.

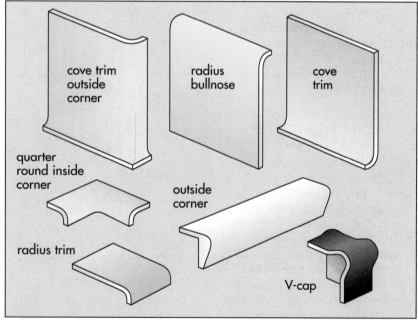

Determine the right trim tiles.

In general, tiles are divided into field tiles, which are flat, and trim tiles, which are shaped irregularly to turn corners or define the edges of an installation. There are dozens of trim-tile profiles, and the names of each can be confusing. When choosing tiles, be sure to check the availability of these specialty tiles and select a style with trim tiles suitable for your project.

SELECTING INSTALLATION TOOLS

For mixing thin-set mortar and grout, you need a sturdy bucket. An empty, clean **drywall-compound bucket** will suffice for relatively small jobs, but a **mortar-mixing box** is better for larger jobs. A **mortar mixer** is a great time saver for mixing two or more gallons of thin-set mortar or grout. The mixer is mounted, like a drill bit, on an electric drill.

Notched trowels have two smooth sides for spreading adhesive and two notched sides for combing the adhesive to the right depth. Check the tile and adhesive manufacturers' recommendations for the proper notch size.

You'll need a **beating block** to press the tiles evenly into the adhesive. Use a piece of 2× lumber covered with terrycloth or buy a rubber-faced model. With Mexican pavers and other irregular tiles, use a **rubber mallet** instead.

A canvas **drop cloth** readily absorbs moisture and has enough heft to protect surfaces from dropped tiles. Use **masking tape** to cover plumbing fixtures.

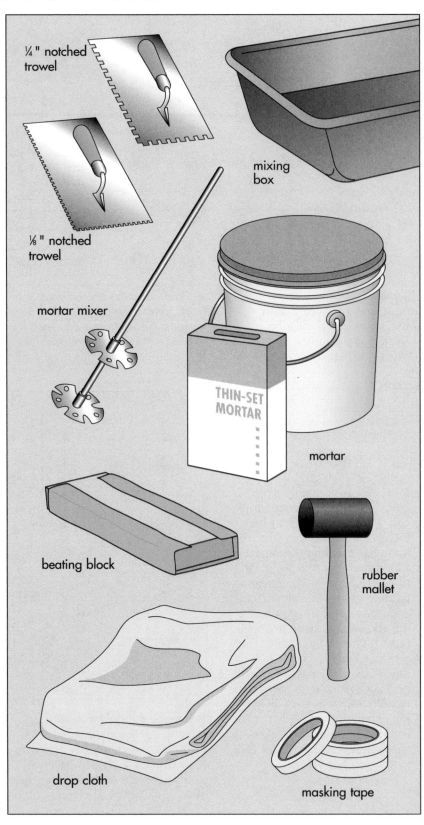

¼" notched trowel

⅛" notched trowel

mixing box

mortar mixer

THIN-SET MORTAR

mortar

beating block

rubber mallet

drop cloth

masking tape

CHOOSING GROUTING TOOLS

Many of the tools used for applying thin-set mortar also can be used for spreading grout. A **grouting float** is a rubber-backed trowel used for pressing the grout into the joints. It also removes excess grout from the tiling surface, although a **squeegee** may be more thorough. A **mason's trowel** is handy for finishing grout joints, although you also can use a **putty knife** or the handle of an **old toothbrush**. A **margin trowel** is used to mix small batches and for scooping adhesive or grout onto the setting surface. A **grout bag** is useful when you need to force grout into joints that can't be reached easily with a grout float.

Good-quality **sponges** are best for cleaning grout off the tile surface. Look for sponges made especially for tiling work. Use **cheesecloth** to remove the haze left on the tile after the grout has set for a while. For applying caulk and sealant around edges, you will need a **caulking gun**.

EXPERTS' INSIGHT

DRESS FOR SUCCESS

Tile setting is a messy business, so wear clothes that you won't mind ruining. When working with adhesive or grout, wear short sleeves because long or baggy sleeves tend to fall into the muddy mix. Protect your hands with rubber gloves when using any product with concrete. When you are installing a tile floor, wear knee pads. They cushion your knees and protect them from sharp objects.

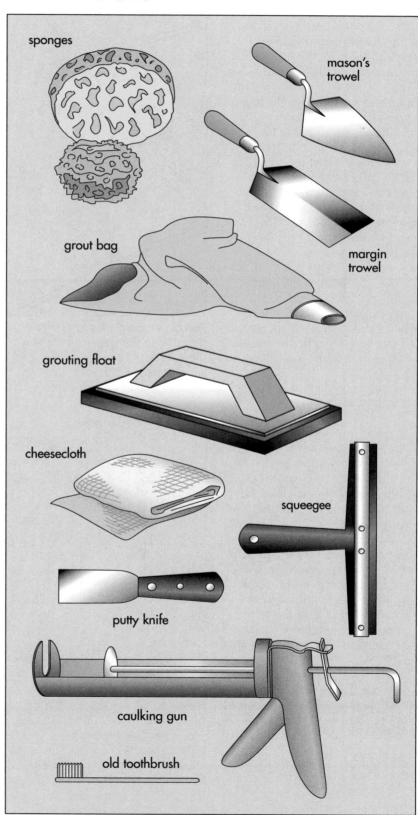

sponges

mason's trowel

grout bag

margin trowel

grouting float

cheesecloth

squeegee

putty knife

caulking gun

old toothbrush

USING TILE SPACERS

The space between tiles serves two important functions: It provides room for the grout essential to any tile job, and it allows for some creativity in your design. You can change the look of a finished tile installation significantly by changing the width of the grout joint or by altering the color of the grout.

Tile spacers are small pieces of plastic used to ensure consistent width of the grout joints. They come in a variety of sizes and shapes to match different types of tile and tile installations. Many types of ceramic tile today are self-spacing, that is, they have small lugs along their sides that ensure proper spacing. If you use self-spacing tiles, you need not use tile spacers unless you prefer a wider grout joint than the lugs allow.

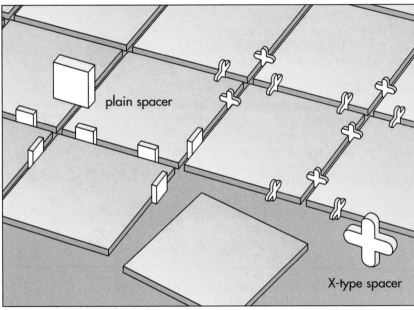

Purchase manufactured spacers.
Buy plastic tile spacers from your tile supplier. They are available in sizes from $1/16$ inch to $1/2$ inch. X-shaped spacers are the most common. They are placed at each corner. Though less common, plain spacers often are preferred for spacing and holding wall tiles firmly in place.

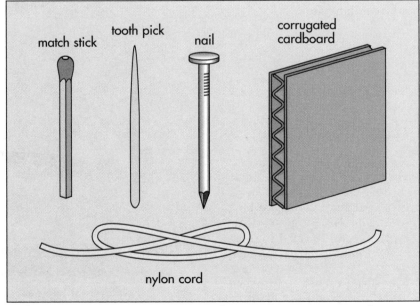

Make your own spacers.
Plastic spacers are one of the least expensive materials used for tile installation. But for a small job or in a pinch, you may use an alternative. Look for objects that have a consistent size, such as wooden matchsticks, toothpicks, or nails. Nylon cord can be used over a long run. Remember to remove the spacers before grouting.

SELECTING ADHESIVES

The setting adhesive bonds the bottom of the tile with the setting bed. Recent improvements in setting adhesives make it easy for do-it-yourselfers to set tile with professional results. Although adhesives fall into the broad categories of organic mastic and thin-set mortar, in reality there are many types of products and manufacturers. The first step in choosing an adhesive is to determine what kind of installation you are doing (wet or dry? indoor or outdoor? floor or wall?) and to what substrate the tile will be applied.

Organic mastics are popular because they require no mixing. However, they are not suitable for areas exposed to heat or for exterior installations. Thin-set mortars usually are mixed by the installer. A variety of thin-set additives are available to create an adhesive best suited to specific installations. The chart below offers general guidelines.

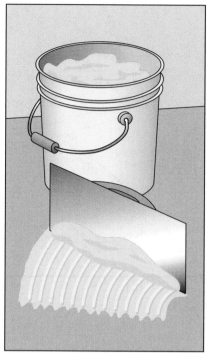

Buy ready-mixed organic mastic.
Organic mastic is a premixed adhesive that is easy to use. It is especially popular for use on walls because tiles will not slip when set in place.

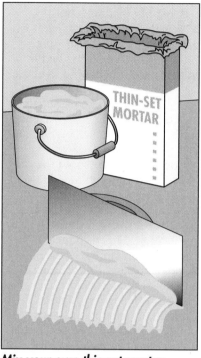

Mix your own thin-set mortar.
Thin-set mortar requires more work than does organic mastic, but offers superior bonding strength and flexibility.

CHOOSING THIN-SET MORTARS

Type	Description and Uses
Water-mixed mortar	Also referred to as *dry-set mortar,* this is a blend of Portland cement, sand, and additives. Mix with water.
Latex- and acrylic-mixed mortar	Also referred to as *latex mortar,* this mortar is similar to water-mixed mortar, but has latex or acrylic added to it. The additives improve adhesion and reduce water absorption; they may be premixed with the mortar in dry form or added as a liquid by the installer. It's an excellent choice for wet and dry installations.
Epoxy mortar	This is a mixture of sand, cement, and liquid resins and hardeners. It's costly, but effective with any setting material and is good choice when the substrate is incompatible with other adhesives.
Medium-bed mortar	This adhesive remains stronger than regular thin-set mortar when applied in layers of more than ¼ inch. It's useful with tiles that do not have uniform backs, such as handmade tiles.

CHOOSING SETTING BEDS

A tile installation is only as good as the surface to which it is applied. Investing in adequate materials for the setting bed is as important as buying the right tile for your project. Tiled floors, in particular, require an extremely stiff setting bed; any imperfection in the subfloor can crack tiles and ruin your project.

You may be able to set the tile over an existing subfloor or wall surface, or you may want to add a layer or two of setting material to ensure a stiff and durable installation. The introduction of cement-based and gypsum-based backerboard has dramatically simplified tile installations without compromising strength and durability. Previously tile was applied over thick beds of mortar, almost exclusively by trained professionals. The process was time consuming and required skill and experience.

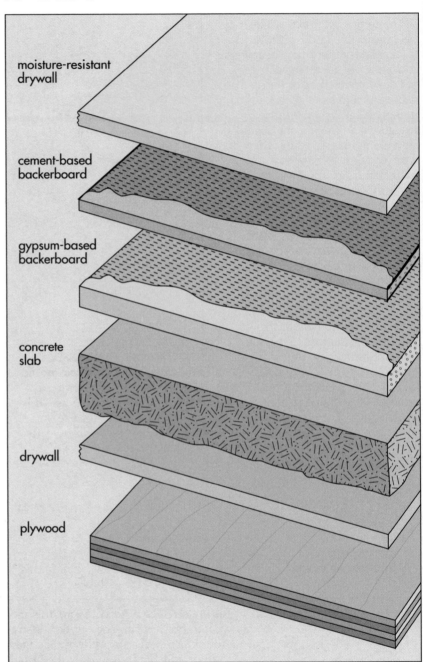

EXPERTS' INSIGHT

MORTAR-BED INSTALLATIONS

Modern thin-set mortars are typically applied in a layer only ⅛ to ¼ inch thick; that's how they get their name. Traditional (mudset) tile installations use thick mortar as the setting bed. Mortar, with wire-mesh reinforcement, is poured over tar paper to a thickness of 1 to 2 inches. Then the tiles are set on the mortar before it cures. Mortar-bed installations are strong and particularly useful on shower floors.

Choose a setting bed.
Backerboard often is called cement board, although some products contain no cement. Sold in varying thicknesses and sizes, backerboard is easy to install and provides a ready-made surface for setting tile. Cement-based backerboard has a mesh coat and is cut using a carbide-tipped scoring tool.

Gypsum-based backerboard can be cut with a utility knife.

Concrete slabs (old or newly poured) are ideal setting beds for tile floors. With suitable adhesives, tile can be installed over plywood. A double layer of drywall (regular or moisture-resistant) is a suitable setting bed only in dry areas.

SELECTING GROUT

Grout is a mortar used to fill the joints between tiles. It stiffens the tile installation and helps prevent moisture from penetrating the joint. Grout usually is sold with all of the dry ingredients mixed together; the installer adds the liquid. It also is available in caulking-gun tubes with all of the wet and dry ingredients already mixed and ready for application.

Grout not only seal joints, it plays an important role in the overall design. The width and color of the grout joint can radically alter the finished look of a tile installation. Choose a grout color to complement, match, or contrast with the tile. Increase or decrease the joint size to provide the most appropriate balance for that size room.

CHOOSING GROUT

Type	Description and Uses
Plain grout	Also referred to as unsanded grout, this is a mixture of Portland cement and additives chosen to achieve specific characteristics. It is used for grout joints of $\frac{1}{16}$ inch or less. It's also recommended for absorptive tile and marble.
Sanded grout	This is similar to plain grout but has sand added. It is used for grout joints greater than $\frac{1}{16}$ inch. The ratio between sand and cement varies, depending on the size of the joint.
Epoxy grout	This grout contains epoxy resin and hardener. It's used when chemical and stain resistance are required or where high temperatures are likely.
Colored grout	Offered in premixed packages in a wide assortment of colors and formulations, you can usually find a colored grout to match any need and fill any typical grout joint. Natural grout can be used if you prefer the look of cement.
Mortar	This is similar to sanded grout, but is used for joints between brick pavers, slate, or other masonry materials.
Premixed grout	Some grouts are available premixed and ready to use out of the container. Choices are smaller, and the cost is high, but it may be a good choice for small jobs.

Know your grout.

Grout and tile are the two visible materials on a tiled surface. A good tile installation requires a good grouting job. Use the best ingredients, mix them right, and apply the grout so it completely fills the joints between tiles. Although tile is completely inflexible, you can achieve some flexibility in the grout joints by adding latex or acrylic additives to the grout. Additives also can increase water and stain resistance. When grout joints begin to fail, they should be repaired immediately or water damage could occur behind the tile.

SELECTING MEMBRANES

In addition to backerboard or other setting bed materials (page 218), some installations call for use of a membrane. The two types are waterproofing membranes and isolation membranes.

Waterproofing membranes are used to prevent moisture from penetrating through the surface (usually the grout joint). If water will often sit on your floor tiles, or if your wall tiles will be in a room that often becomes very humid, moisture can seep through grout or unglazed tiles and cause serious damage to the substrate and even the structural wood. A sealer (page 221) may solve the problem for wall tiles, but floor tiles that will get soaked need a membrane.

Tar paper (that is, felt paper saturated with tar) has long been the standard waterproofing membrane. Polyethylene sheeting is another inexpensive option. The most effective waterproofing membrane is chlorinated

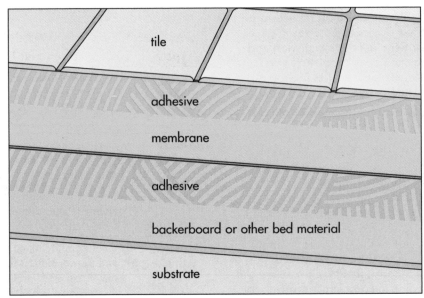

polyethylene (CPE), a strong and thick sheet that is joined to the substrate with adhesive. Liquid membranes are applied with trowel or brush.

The function of an isolation membrane is to protect the tiled surface from damage due to

movement in the underlying surface. Use one when you tile over an existing floor that shows signs of movement from seasonal changes or settling of the house. Chlorinated polyethylene sheets are often used as isolation membranes.

Tar paper waterproofing.
Tar paper is an inexpensive and easy-to-install membrane. It is sold in rolls of varying widths and lengths and can be stapled or nailed to studs or drywall.

CPE waterproofing.
Chlorinated polyethylene is a durable and flexible product that offers the best water resistance of any available membrane. It is particularly effective on floors that will be wet on a regular basis.

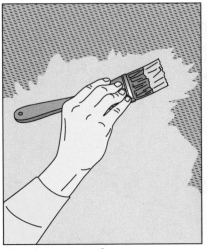

Liquid waterproofing.
Single-component liquid membranes are spread on the setting bed. Once cured, they form a reasonably waterproof layer. Multicomponent membranes require liquid and fabric installed in layers.

CHOOSING CAULK AND SEALERS

Tiles may last centuries, but a tile installation has no chance of reaching such a ripe age unless it is maintained regularly. Some components of the installation need to be replaced or renewed every few years. *Caulk* refers to a variety of flexible products used to fill joints that should not be grouted for one reason or another. *Sealers* are protective coatings applied over the entire tiled surface or all the grout lines; they prevent staining and protect tile and grout from water infiltration.

The best choice for a long-lasting, mildew-free joint in high-moisture installations is silicone caulk. Latex caulk is not suitable for tile jobs. Use siliconized acrylic caulk in areas exposed to only minimal moisture. Tub-and-tile caulk contains a mildewcide, but it is not always effective.

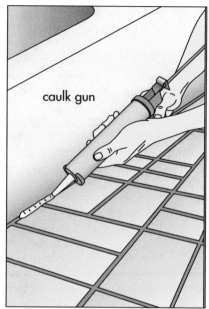

Where to caulk.
Use caulk instead of grout in expansion joints (see box below), between dissimilar materials, and around penetrations in the tiled surface such as between tiles and a

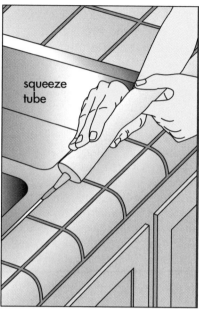

sink. Like grout, caulk is available in sanded and plain formulations, and in colors that match the grout. Caulk tubes used with a caulk gun are the easiest to use. Buy a squeeze tube for small jobs.

TILE AND GROUT SEALERS

Sealers are used on unglazed tile and stone products. They are also applied to grout. *Penetrating sealers* are intended to be absorbed beneath the surface of the tile and grout. They reduce the absorbency of the surface without necessarily adding a sheen. *Coating sealers* are formulated to remain on the surface, where they generally add a glossy or semiglossy sheen. Use a *grout sealer* on a wall with glazed tile. It will keep your grout watertight and make it easier to clean. Usually, you must wait two weeks after tile installation before applying grout sealer.

EXPERTS' INSIGHT

EXPANSION JOINTS

■ Tile and grout generally don't expand and contract with seasonal and temperature changes, but the materials beneath and around them may. Expansion joints are safety features that anticipate that movement and prevent the tile and grout from being damaged by it. On most installations, expansion joints are intended to look like grout joints, but they are filled with a flexible material such as silicone caulk.

■ Use expansion joints around the perimeters of all tile installations, especially where the tile edges meet a different material. Use them where floors meet walls, countertops meet backsplashes, and where tile meets wood or another material. Any runs of tile on a floor that exceed 24 feet must be interrupted with an expansion joint.

■ The most typical method of creating an expansion gap is to leave a ¼-inch joint between the tile and the adjoining surface, then fill the joint with caulk. The setting bed should also be designed with expansion joints.

ASSESSING SUBSTRATES

The *substrate* of a floor or wall includes the setting bed (page 218) and any other layers beneath the tile surface. Even if tile adheres firmly to its setting bed, it won't last long if that setting bed isn't part of a completely sound and sturdy substrate.

The structural needs of your substrate may change when you add a new type of surface. For example, if you are planning to install ceramic tile on a floor that currently is covered with resilient sheet flooring, you will be adding a lot of weight to the underlying framing. If you doubt that the joists and subfloor are strong enough, consult a professional.

A quick way to tell if a floor is firm enough to handle ceramic tile: Jump on it. If it feels springy, there's a good chance that your tiles or grout lines will crack in time. Add a layer of plywood or backerboard to strengthen it, or consult a professional.

Walls should be firm to the touch. New tiles will not add significant strength.

SUBSTRATE RECOMMENDATIONS

Substrate	Preparation
Exposed joists	▪ Verify that the framing will support the new floor. ▪ Install ¾-inch CDX plywood. ▪ Install backerboard or underlayment-grade plywood.
Concrete slab	▪ Repair cracks or low spots in the concrete. ▪ Ensure that the slab is flat, clean, and dry. ▪ Roughen the surface to improve adhesion.
Finished floor	▪ Verify that the framing will support the new floor. ▪ If necessary, remove the finish flooring. ▪ Install backerboard or underlayment-grade plywood over suitable subfloor, or over the old finish flooring.
Wall paneling	▪ Remove thin sheet paneling. ▪ Install backerboard, plywood, or drywall.
Drywall	▪ Scrape away any loose paint and roughen the surface with sandpaper. ▪ Clean the surface or apply deglosser. ▪ Add a second layer of drywall for added strength.
Masonry or plaster walls	▪ Repair cracks and level indentations. ▪ Ensure that the surface is sound, not soft and crumbling or springy when pressed. ▪ Clean the surface or apply deglosser.

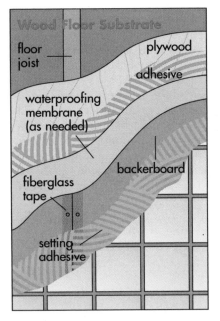

Wood Floor Substrate

floor joist — plywood — adhesive — waterproofing membrane (as needed) — backerboard — fiberglass tape — setting adhesive

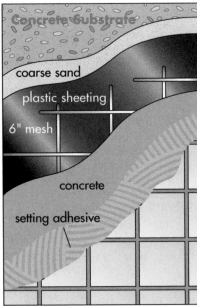

Concrete Substrate

coarse sand — plastic sheeting — 6" mesh — concrete — setting adhesive

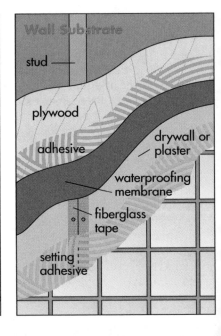

Wall Substrate

stud — plywood — adhesive — drywall or plaster — waterproofing membrane — fiberglass tape — setting adhesive

CALCULATING MATERIALS

Before you go shopping for tile and setting materials, determine how much of each material you need. Fortunately that doesn't mean that you have to count every last tile you intend to install. Tiling materials are usually sold by the square foot, so for most jobs, all you have to do is measure the surface to be tiled, then take that number to the store with you.

Buy more tile than you plan to use. Expect to break a few tiles, and to need a few more than anticipated. It's handy to have a few extra tiles should you need any replacements someday. So get an extra 5 to 10 percent more than your estimate.

Where to Buy

Tile and setting materials are widely available. Small lumber yards and hardware stores may carry a limited selection, while home centers and tile outlets offer a much wider choice. It pays to shop around, because prices and selection can vary significantly. Of course you should shop for a good price, but also look for a retailer who is knowledgeable and willing to answer questions. A little good advice might save you plenty of time and money. Be sure to ask about the store's policy on returns. In the event that you buy considerably more than you need, you should be able to return unopened boxes and packages for a refund.

Metrics

Tiles are manufactured and sold all over the world. So the tiles you choose may have been manufactured to a metric size, which was then rounded off to inches. So, for example, you may have a "13-inch" Italian tile that actually measures $13^3/_{16}$ inches.

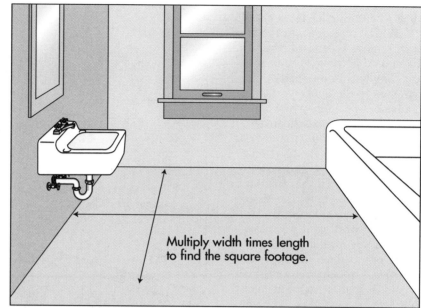

Multiply width times length to find the square footage.

Determine square footage.
If you are tiling a single rectangular surface, simply measure the width and the length (in feet), and multiply the two numbers to determine the square footage. For multiple surfaces, calculate each one separately, then add the results. When a door or a window interferes, include it in your initial calculation, then find the square footage of the obstruction and subtract it from the overall total.

If you will be installing large, expensive tiles, make a drawing of your space, with exact dimensions, and bring it to your dealer, who can help you to determine the most economical layout.

ESTIMATING GROUT AND ADHESIVES

The amount of grout you need depends on the size of the tiles and on the width and depth of the grout joint. Packages of grout often include tables for estimating the amount needed. This chart gives you a rough idea of how many square feet can be covered with one pound of grout. The figures should be treated only as estimates, but they do show how much the coverage changes depending on tile size.

Tile Size	Joint Width	Coverage per Pound of Grout
$2"\times2"\times^1/_4"$	$^1/_{16}"$	24 square feet
$4^1/_4"\times4^1/_4"\times^5/_{16}"$	$^1/_{16}"$	16 square feet
$4^1/_4"\times4^1/_4"\times^5/_{16}"$	$^1/_8"$	8 square feet
$6"\times6"\times^1/_4"$	$^1/_{16}"$	28 square feet
$6"\times6"\times^1/_4"$	$^1/_8"$	14 square feet
$12"\times12"\times^3/_8"$	$^1/_{16}"$	37 square feet

When applied with the trowel notch size recommended by the manufacturer, one gallon of adhesive will cover 30 to 50 square feet of wall and 20 to 40 square feet of floor.

PREPARING THE SITE

When tiling floors or installing wall tiles down to the floor line, remove baseboard trim. If the baseboard is trimmed with shoe molding (a thin rounded strip attached to the floor), you probably need only remove the shoe, leaving the baseboard in place, in order to tile the floor. If you plan to reuse the trim, take care not to damage it as you remove it. Insert a thin pry bar or stiff putty knife to lift the shoe or pull the baseboard from the wall. Gradually work your way along the molding until it comes off. Write numbers on the backs of the pieces to help you remember where they go. Remove as many obstacles as possible so you will not have to make many precise tile cuts. When preparing to tile a floor, set a tile on the floor and use it as a guide for cutting the bottoms of casing molding.

If you are tiling a bathroom, remember that removing and replacing a toilet is easier than tiling around it, and will lead to a much cleaner-looking job. (Be sure to stuff a rag in the soil pipe to prevent sewer gas from backing up

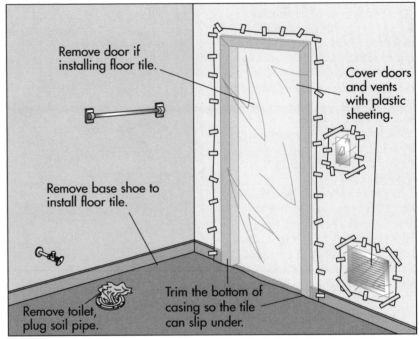

Remove door if installing floor tile.

Cover doors and vents with plastic sheeting.

Remove base shoe to install floor tile.

Remove toilet, plug soil pipe.

Trim the bottom of casing so the tile can slip under.

into the bathroom.) You may want to remove the vanity as well as doors. (You may also need to trim the doors after the tile is installed.)

When preparing to tile walls, remove electrical outlet covers (the outlet box may have to be adjusted before replacing the covers), and fixtures. Sinks and appliances may have to be

removed, depending on your installation. Because the tiles add thickness to the wall, it is usually best to leave window and door casings in place. Keep dust and odors from spreading throughout the house by taping plastic sheeting over doorways. Cover vents with plastic as well.

PREPARING SURFACES TO BE TILED

Floors
■ Remove the original flooring, if it is not firmly stuck to the subfloor, if it is uneven, or if the thinset mortar will not adhere to it.
■ Make sure that the subfloor is at least $1\frac{1}{8}$ inch thick and composed of suitable materials (usually a combination of plywood, backerboard, or concrete).
■ If a plywood floor seems loose in spots, drive nails or screws through it into floor joists.
■ Fill low spots in the subfloor, then smooth the surface and clean it thoroughly.

Walls
■ Remove wallpaper, thin paneling, or anything else that flexes when you press it.
■ When tiling over new drywall, don't bother taping the joints but do seal the surface with a thin coat of adhesive applied with the flat side of a trowel.
■ Scrape away loose paint.
■ Lightly sand glossy surfaces to remove the sheen.
■ Patch holes and cracks, and sand smooth.
■ Thoroughly clean the wall and allow it to dry.

Countertops
■ Remove sink or faucets, and other obstacles.
■ Remove old tile if it exists.
■ To tile over a square-edged laminated countertop that is sound, give it a thorough sanding and remove the backsplash.
■ If you have a post-form countertop with curved edges, remove it and install a new substrate of plywood and backerboard.
■ Make sure the substrate is thick enough for trim pieces and that the trim won't prevent drawers from opening.

LAYING OUT THE JOB

Tile looks best when it is set in a straight line and at least appears to be square and level with adjacent surfaces. Laying out the installation is the most important step for ensuring such an outcome. Tile is an unforgiving material, and floors and walls are rarely as square and level as you might think—or hope. One of the secrets to a successful layout, therefore, is learning how to fudge the installation so the fudging isn't apparent. The other secret is to plan for as few cut tiles as possible. Adjust the layout to minimize cuts and hide those cut tiles along less conspicuous walls and under baseboard trim. Don't be surprised if your house exceeds some of the tolerances recommended here. Tile setters have had to deal with such irregularities for centuries, and cures are plentiful.

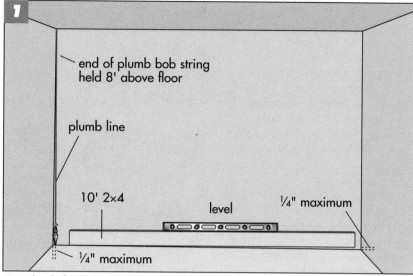

1. Check for tolerances.
Check tiling surfaces for square, level, and plumb using the techniques shown below. If a surface is out of alignment in excess of the amounts shown above, the best solution is to change the surfaces—for instance, fur out a wall, or shim up a subfloor. If this is not feasible, make the unevenness less visible by avoiding narrow tile pieces at the corner. You might be able to split the difference, making two edges slightly out of line instead of having one edge that is way off.

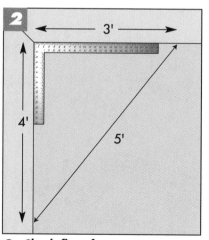

2. Check floor for square.
For small rooms, check the squareness of the floor by setting a framing square at inside and outside corners. For larger rooms, use the 3-4-5 method: Measure along one wall exactly three feet from the corner, and along the other wall four feet. If the distance between those points is exactly five feet, the floor is square.

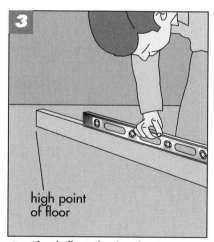

3. Check floor for level.
Use a 2- or 4-foot level to check along each wall. To check for level over a longer span, place the level on the edge of a straight 6- or 8-foot board. If the floor is only slightly out of level, and you are not planning to run tile up the wall, this should not affect your installation.

4. Check walls for plumb.
Place a level vertically on the wall at various spots, or use a plumb bob. Set the level horizontally on the wall to see how flat it is (you can also stretch a string tightly along the wall). A wavy wall, even if it is plumb, should be corrected before tiling.

EXPERTS' INSIGHT

PLANNING FOR FOCAL POINTS

When you walk into a room for the first time, chances are there is something there that catches your eye immediately. As you stand in the room, other areas may become more noticeable. It might be another doorway, a fireplace, a window, counters, or appliance groupings. Plan your layout so that the installation looks best in these focal areas. For example, cut tiles placed around a sink should all be of equal size. If your floor is out of square so that you must have a line of cut tiles that grow progressively smaller, plan so it will be behind a couch or in an area that is not a focal point. Use perpendicular lines and full tiles at focal points.

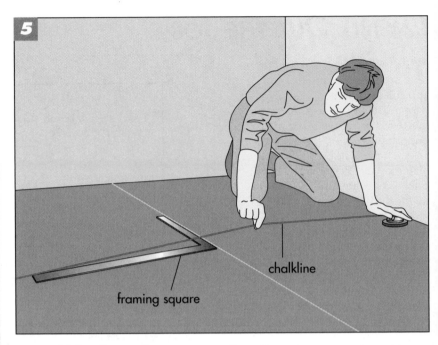

framing square

chalkline

5. Establish reference lines.

Accurate reference lines are critical to the success of a tile installation. Trace around a piece of plywood with two factory edges, or chalk two lines that are perfectly perpendicular. You will place the first tile at the intersection; this tile establishes the alignment and position of the rest of the tiles. (For instructions on your specific tiling project and more information on how to plot reference lines see page 246.)

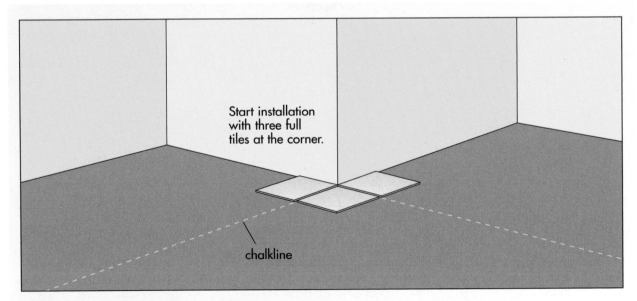

Start installation with three full tiles at the corner.

chalkline

Laying out an L-shaped room.

Often, the outside corner of an L-shaped room will be a focal point, so start there. Here's the simplest way to lay it out: From the corner, extend two straight lines along the floor to the opposing wall. Plan to set three full tiles at the corner, then extend the layout. This will not work, however, if the outside corner is seriously out of square. Also if this method results in very small pieces along a wall, it may be best to modify it.

6. Do a dry run.
With reference lines drawn, you can measure from the lines to the walls and calculate how the tiles will be arranged. However, the safest method is to set tiles in place along the reference lines.

For this dry run, don't use any adhesive, but be sure to space the tiles properly. Take your time, and find out how each edge will look. Don't hesitate to change the entire layout if it will make for a more attractive appearance.

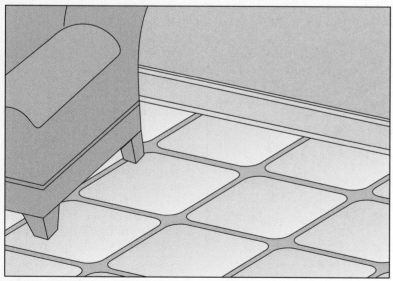

Hiding cut tiles.
One big advantage of a careful and thorough layout is that you can plan where cut tiles will go. A simple rule of thumb is to place cut tiles in the least visible areas. On a floor installation, for example, one wall may be largely covered with furniture. If you place cut tiles under or behind the furniture, they are not likely to be seen. On other installations, you may prefer to adjust the layout so that it has evenly sized cut tiles along the opposite edges.

Cutting Backerboard

Backerboard usually has to be cut to size before it can be installed. You may also have to drill holes in the board so that it will slide into place. If you have ever installed drywall, you will find the score-and-snap method to be very familiar. There are several types of backerboard on the market, and new materials are introduced from time to time. Be sure to follow the manufacturer's instructions if they vary from the process described here. You can cut backerboard with power tools, but it will be messier, not any faster, and may damage your blade or motor.

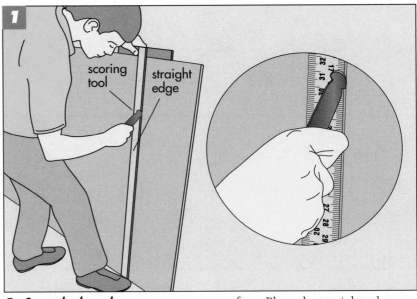

You'll Need

SKILLS: Measuring, cutting.
TIME: Each cut requires no more than 5 to 10 minutes.
TOOLS: Drywall square or straightedge, utility knife or scoring tool, and rubbing stone.

1. Score the board.
For cement-based board, measure carefully and mark cut off lines on both sides of the backerboard. Align a straight edge with the line on one side. Pull the scoring tool along the straight edge; make as many passes as are necessary to break through the mesh on the surface. Place the straight edge on the other side and repeat the process. The mesh must be completely severed on each side. (A faster but somewhat riskier method: Proceed as you would for drywall, cutting one side, snapping the cut edge over, then cutting the other side.)

2. Snap.
Place the backerboard on a flat surface. Press down with your hand on one side of the cut line. With the other hand, lift up just enough to snap the board along the scored edges. Some types of backerboard may break easier if you elevate the board on one side of scoring line, then press down.

3. Smooth edges.
Be careful when handling the cut board. Some types of backerboard may leave a sharp edge along the cut line. The best way to smooth the edge is to use a rubbing stone.

TOOLS TO USE

A HOLE SAW

Cement-based backerboard is often used under tiled surfaces in wet areas. That means you may have to fit it over plumbing protrusions in the wall, countertop, or floor. Most holes can be drilled quickly and effectively using a power drill equipped with a carbide-tip hole saw. The hole saw should be available where you buy your tile or at any large home center. Another method is to mark and score a circle on both sides of the board, then tap through with a hammer.

INSTALLING BACKERBOARD

If it has been cut correctly, backerboard is fairly easy to install. Each type is installed with screws or nails, then the seams are joined with fiberglass tape and mortar. If you are planning to tile in a wet area, remember to take proper waterproofing steps. Cement-based backerboard itself is not damaged by moisture, but it is not waterproof. Water can permeate the board and the underlying framing, causing serious damage. For best results, install a waterproofing membrane behind the backerboard (page 220). Use the type of fasteners recommended by the manufacturer. Roofing nails work, but corrosion-resistant screws offer superior holding power. Edges of backerboard must by supported by studs or joists, or glued with construction adhesive to a sound wall surface.

1. Attach to walls.
Attach backerboard directly to bare studs or over an existing layer of drywall. In either case, make sure the drywall screws or nails are long enough to penetrate the framing at least ¾ inch.

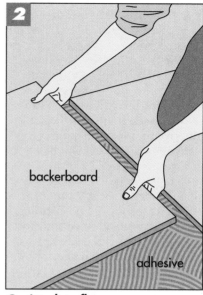

2. Attach to floors.
Coat the clean subfloor with adhesive applied with a notched trowel. Set the boards so that all joints fall over floor joists. Press the board into the adhesive before fastening with screws.

EXPERTS' INSIGHT

EXPANSION GAPS BETWEEN BOARDS

One of the most important steps you can take to ensure a long-lasting tile installation is to plan for some movement on and below the finished surface. Expansion gaps, filled with a flexible material, allow for normal movement without jeopardizing the integrity of the tile and grout. Each manufacturer has specific recommendations for expansion gaps around board edges. As a general rule, you should leave a ⅛-inch gap between boards and a ¼-inch gap around bathtubs and shower pans.

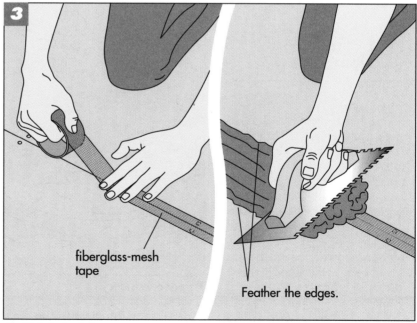

fiberglass-mesh tape

Feather the edges.

3. Finish the joints.
With all boards fastened, apply adhesive-backed fiberglass-mesh tape to the joints. Holding a trowel nearly flat, spread adhesive over the tape, pressing it into the mesh. Feather the edges of the adhesive for a smooth finish. Make sure there are no high spots; shallow low spots are not a problem.

MIXING THIN-SET MORTAR

With the setting bed in place—cleaned, and marked for the layout—it is time to prepare the adhesive. For tiling walls, you will probably use an adhesive that does not have to be mixed. For tiling floors, you can use premixed thin-set or floor tile adhesive, but the thin-set mortar that you mix yourself will be the strongest (see page 217).

Mixing will be easier if all the ingredients are at room temperature; buy the powder and any additives in advance and store them overnight in a heated part of the house. Mixing can get sloppy, especially if you are using a power mixer. Place the bucket in the middle of the area to be tiled, or on top of a drop cloth.

Use a heavy-duty, ½-inch drill for power mixing, as a smaller drill may burn out. Keep a second bucket on hand, about half full of water, for cleaning your mixer.

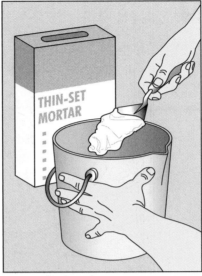

Mixing by hand.
Mix small batches of thin-set mortar (less than two gallons) by hand. Use a trowel or a stiff piece of wood, and make sure you scrape the bottom of the bucket as you stir.

Using a mortar mixer.
Mix larger batches with a mortar mixer mounted on a powerful drill. Clamp the bucket with your feet to keep it from spinning. Set the mixer in and start mixing with short bursts of power to keep the mixture from spilling.

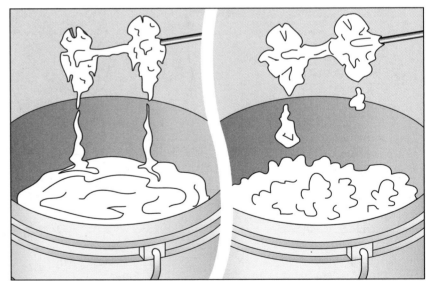

Proper consistency.
It takes some practice and experience to know when the mortar has just the right amount of ingredients. The mix is too loose if it runs off the mixing tool. Add more dry ingredients and mix some more. Lift the mixer again.

The mortar is ready when it falls off, but no longer runs off, the mixing tool. If the mortar starts drying out before you've used it up, discard the batch and mix a new one. Adding more liquid at that point will make the mortar less adherent.

SPREADING THIN-SET MORTAR

After mixing the mortar, let it rest for 10 minutes before applying. Scoop a small amount onto the setting surface and comb it with a notched trowel. If the ridges hold their shape and do not flatten out, the batch is ready to spread. Begin spreading mortar at the intersection of your reference lines. Take care not to cover up the lines. Work in small areas. If you've never tiled before, spread only enough to cover 2 or 3 square feet. As you gain experience, you can expand the size of the working area. Packages of thin-set mortar refer to the *open time*—the amount of time you have to set tiles on combed adhesive. Use a margin trowel (see page 215) to scoop adhesive onto the bottom of your notched trowel, or drop dollops of mortar onto the floor and then spread them out. Give the thin-set mortar a quick stir from time to time.

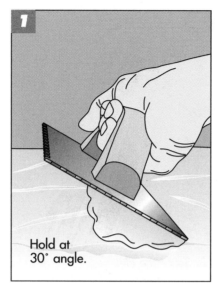

Hold at 30° angle.

1. Apply the thin-set mortar.
Hold the smooth edge of the trowel at a 30-degree angle to the surface. Press adhesive firmly onto the surface. Use sweeping strokes to spread to a consistent depth. Don't cover reference lines.

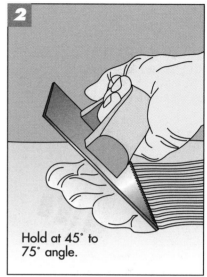

Hold at 45° to 75° angle.

2. Comb the thinset mortar.
Turn the trowel to the notched edge. Hold the trowel at a 45- to 75-degree angle to form the proper depth of ridge. Comb over the entire surface to produce equally sized ridges.

CAUTION!
WORKING WITH EPOXY ADHESIVE

Epoxy-based adhesives are expensive and tricky to use. Fortunately, they are usually not needed for residential tile jobs. But if you have a setting bed that is incompatible with other adhesives, or are installing tile in an area likely to receive extreme heat, epoxies may be necessary. Read all instructions carefully. Wear a charcoal-filter mask, work in a well-ventilated area, and avoid skin contact with the mixed solution. Mix epoxy adhesive by hand and carefully follow the manufacturer's instructions about the proportion of wet and dry ingredients.

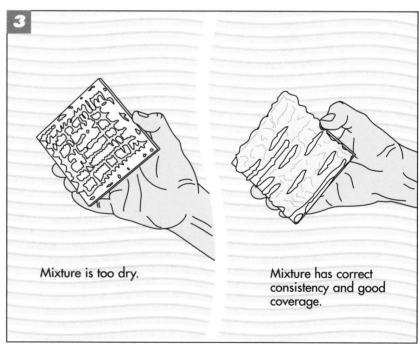

Mixture is too dry.

Mixture has correct consistency and good coverage.

3. Check the coverage.
After spreading and combing a small amount of the mortar, press a tile in place. Twist it a bit so that it is set in the adhesive, then pry it up and look at the bottom. About 75 percent of the surface should be covered. If too little adhesive has stuck to the tile bottom, the mixture is probably too dry.

CUTTING TILE

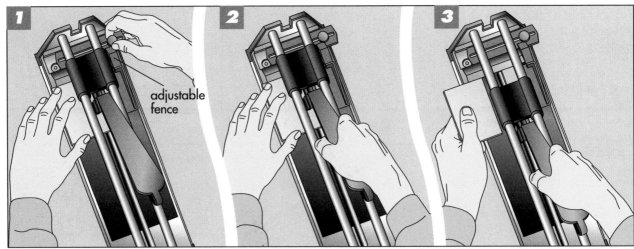

1. To use a snap cutter, mark and position the tile.

Mark a cut line on the tile with a pencil or felt-tipped pen. Place a tile in the cutter, glazed side up, aligning the cut line with the cutting wheel. Set and lock the fence on the cutter to hold the tile in place.

2. Score the tile.

Hold the tile in place with one hand and the handle with the other. Set the cutting wheel on the top of the tile. Pull or push (depending on your model) the handle while maintaining steady pressure on the tile. Try to score the tile evenly on the first pass.

3. Snap the tile.

When the tile has been scored, press back on the handle just enough to snap the tile along the score line. If the tile will not break, the score line was probably incomplete or not deep enough.

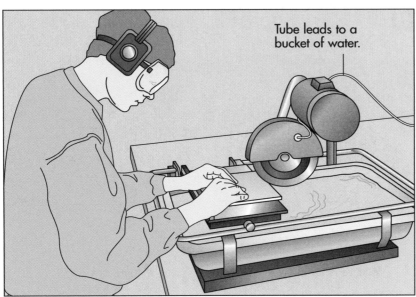

Tube leads to a bucket of water.

Use a wet saw.

Wear safety glasses and hearing protection. See that the blade is in good condition and that the water bucket is full. Place the tile on the sliding table and lock the fence to hold the tile in place. Turn the saw on, and make sure water is running onto the blade. Press down on the tile as you slide it through, taking care to keep your fingers out of the way. When the water runs out, refill the bucket; do not cut with the saw for even a few seconds unless water is running onto the blade.

CAUTION!
BEWARE OF EDGES

One of the advantages of a wet saw is that it makes very smooth cuts. When using a snap cutter or tile nippers, however, the resulting edges can be razor sharp. After cutting the tile, immediately smooth those edges. Grasp the tile on an uncut edge. Move a rubbing stone back and forth over the cut side, smoothing and rounding over the edge as you go. If you do not have a rubbing stone, you can achieve the same result with carbide-grit sandpaper. Use a sanding block, or wrap the sandpaper around a block of wood.

Trimming Tile

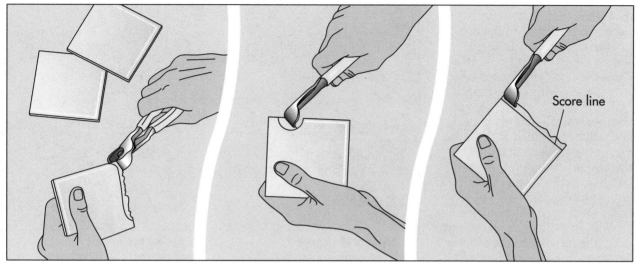

Score line

Use tile nippers for a curved cut...

For cuts that are not straight, use a rod saw (see below right) or tile nippers. (Most floor tiles cannot be cut with a rod saw, so you will need to use nippers.) Practice on scrap pieces of tile to get the hang of it. Hold the nippers roughly parallel to the cut line, and bite away small chunks.

...for a notch...

If the notch will have square corners, use a snap cutter to score at least some of the lines; this will make it a bit easier to nibble precisely up to the lines. Nibbling a notch requires patience. Bite away only a little at a time or you may break the whole piece.

...or for a sliver.

Nippers are also useful for very narrow straight cuts when you do not have a wet saw. Use the snap cutter or a glass cutter to score the glaze on the tile. Place the jaws close to, and parallel with, the score line. Take a series of bites along the cut line.

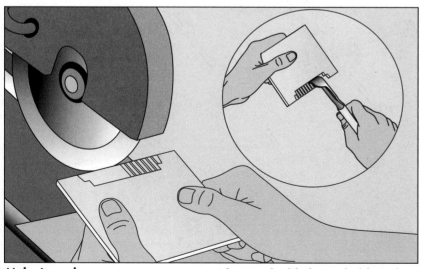

Make irregular cuts.

Use a wet saw to make irregular cuts that would take a long time to accomplish with nippers. To make a series of closely spaced, parallel cuts with the wet saw, hold the tile in your hands. Rest your hands on the sliding table as you move the tile into the blade. By holding the tile at the correct angle, you can produce a series of cuts that all end at the cut line. Break off the tile pieces with your fingers or nippers, then clean up the cut edge with a rubbing stone.

TOOLS TO USE

THE ROD SAW

A rod saw is a cylindrical hacksaw blade made of tungsten carbide. If you are on a tight budget or do not have very many odd-shaped cuts to make, this tool can be a handy accessory. Set the rod saw snugly in the hacksaw body, firmly support the tile, and cut using a sawing motion. With a rod saw you can cut fairly quickly through wall tiles, but it will be rough going—and perhaps impossible—with floor tiles. A rod saw is useful for cutting tight curves.

SETTING TILE

When the adhesive has been combed to the right thickness, immediately begin setting tiles. The most important tile is the first one you set; make sure that it is aligned perfectly with your layout so that the rest of the tiles will fall into place nicely. You will be rewarded at this stage for having spent all that time on the layout. Your reference lines will help to guide you through the entire process; take care not to cover them over with adhesive.

Work in sections small enough to set the tiles before the adhesive begins to dry out. Start by spreading adhesive in a 2- to 3-square-foot area; set the tiles and remove excess adhesive before moving on to the next section. With practice, you can work in larger sections. If the adhesive has begun to skin over, do not set tiles in it. Rather, scoop up and discard the adhesive and apply a fresh layer.

Whenever possible, set all full tiles first, then set the cut tiles. But also avoid kneeling on top of just-set tiles in order to lay the cut ones. On a large job, you might want to set all of the full tiles one day, then handle the cut tiles the next day.

Take care not to tile yourself into a corner. Set tiles so that you can leave the room without walking on them. Don't disturb floor tiles until the adhesive has cured—preferably overnight.

YOU'LL NEED

TIME: About one hour for every 3 to 5 square feet of field tiles; small, complex installations take two to three times as long.
SKILLS: Setting tiles into the adhesive and cutting tiles to fit.
TOOLS: Beating block and hammer, putty knife or trowel, sponge, and tile cutter.

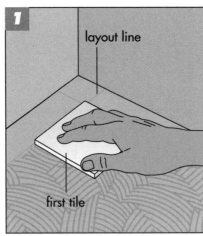

1. Begin at the corner.
With the adhesive spread, place the first tile at the intersection of the reference lines. Press and twist it slightly into place, aligning tile with both lines. Do not slide the tile through the adhesive.

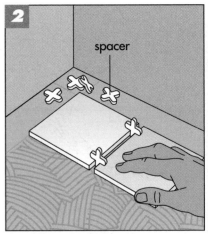

2. Follow the layout.
Place another tile next to the first. Use spacers unless the tiles are self-spacing. Press and twist the tile to ensure that it is fully embedded in the adhesive. Accurate placement of the first few tiles is critical.

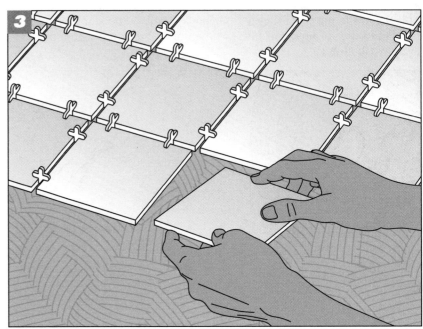

3. Fill in the field.
Continue setting tiles along the layout lines in the section. Then set the tiles in the field, working out from the corner. Insert spacers as shown. (Spacers can also be laid flat at the intersection of the grout lines, but must be removed before grouting.) If the tiles are self-spacing, keep an eye on the gaps between tiles to make sure that they remain uniform. Avoid sliding the tiles once they have been set in the adhesive. Check the backs of the tiles from time to time to see that they are adhering properly.

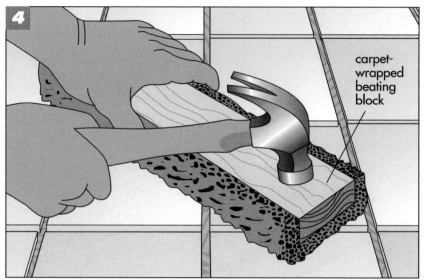

4. Use a beating block.

After setting tiles in one section, use a beating block (see page 214 for tips on making a beating block) to ensure a level surface and full adhesion. Place the beating block so that it spans several tiles, and give it a few light taps with a hammer. Make sure each tile gets tapped this way.

Remove excess adhesive.

5. Clean the joint.

Immediately after setting tiles in each section, remove excess adhesive before it starts to dry. Clean the tile with a damp sponge, and use a putty knife, utility knife, or margin trowel to remove excess from between tiles.

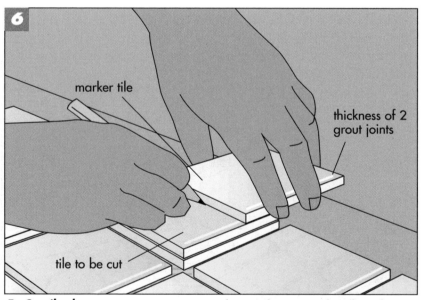

marker tile

thickness of 2 grout joints

tile to be cut

6. Cut tiles last.

When all of the full tiles have been set in the field, begin setting cut tiles around the perimeter. Because walls are rarely square, it is usually best to cut one tile at a time. The safest method is to measure each tile "in place." Set the tile to be cut directly on top of the adjacent tile. Then set another full tile on top, two grout joints away from the wall. Use the top tile to mark the cut line.

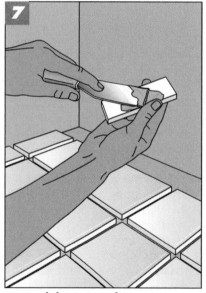

7. Back-buttering tiles.

When you are unable to use a trowel to apply the adhesive on the setting surface, *back-butter* individual tiles: Use a notched trowel or a putty knife, depending on the size of the tile, and spread adhesive on the back. Use enough adhesive so that the tile will be level with other tiles.

SETTING MOSAIC TILE

Historically tile mosaic has been an elaborate decorative technique using small pieces of tile, stone, and shells set one by one to produce unique patterns. Today mosaic tiles are almost always sold in sheets, with small tiles held together by a mesh or paper backing or with small adhesive dots. These sheets make installation much quicker than setting tiles individually. You can find mosaic tiles in a variety of patterns, glazed and unglazed. Glass mosaic tiles are available in 1-inch squares. Mosaic tiles are particularly suitable for use on floors, but are also popular for walls and countertops.

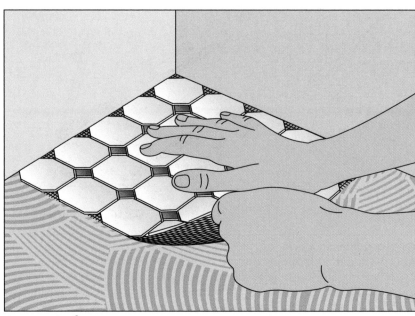

Set mosaic tiles.
Back-mounted mosaic tiles should be set in thin-set adhesive. Because various backing materials perform differently, check with the supplier for any special instructions. Take care to ensure that each individual tile on a sheet is fully embedded in the adhesive. Move a beating block (see page 214) slowly across the whole sheet, lightly tapping it as you go.

EXPERTS' INSIGHT

ARRANGING PATTERNS

Sheets of mosaic tiles are sometimes composed of randomly arranged tiles in a variety of colors. This randomness looks best when it has a balance to it; colors should be scattered around the surface, not clumped together. You can control the balance somewhat by planning the arrangement of the tile sheets. Before you start spreading adhesive and setting the tiles, take time to study the patterns on individual sheets. You may find that some sheets look better than others when placed next to each other. Some mosaic sheets are set according to a pattern. In that case, install the tiles so that you continue, rather than disrupt, the pattern.

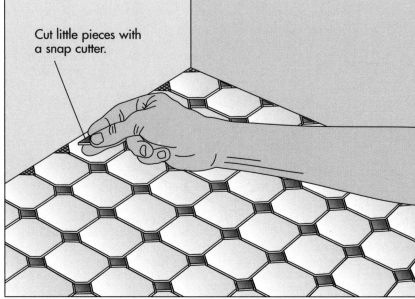

Cut little pieces with a snap cutter.

Cut mosaics.
One advantage of small mosaic tiles is that you can often manage an installation without having to cut individual tiles. Use a utility knife to cut strips of tiles away from the sheet. If you do need to fill in spaces with small, cut tiles, remove the tiles from the backing and cut them with a snap cutter or nippers. Back-butter the tiles with adhesive before setting.

GROUTING TILE

Grout is a thin mortar mixture that is used to fill the joints between tiles. It protects tile edges from nicks and cracks, and it helps keep water from working its way below the tile surface. The size and color of the grout joint can be as important to the finished appearance of a floor as the tile itself. So it pays to choose and apply the grout carefully. (See page 219 for more on grout selection.) Do not apply grout until the adhesive has set, which normally takes up to 24 hours. If you are tiling more than one surface, such as a bathroom floor and walls, set the tiles on all the surfaces before you begin grouting. Then grout the walls before the floor. For stronger and less permeable grout, mix the powder with latex additive rather than water.

YOU'LL NEED

TIME: Several hours for a typical bathroom floor.
SKILLS: Mixing and spreading grout, shaping grout joints, and careful cleanup.
TOOLS: Bucket, trowel or mortar mixer; awl; rubber gloves; grout float; sponge; and joint shaper.

CAUTION!
USING COLORED GROUT
If you are using colored grout, mix a small test batch. Let it dry so you can see the finished color. Also spread some of the grout on a scrap tile to see if it stains the tile surface. When adding color additive to grout, mix it in before adding the liquid. And make note of the exact quantities of ingredients used so that you can mix consistent colors from one batch to the next.

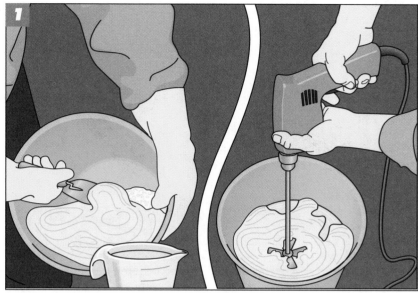

1. Mix by hand...
Measure the liquid and pour it into the bucket. Add the dry ingredients a little at a time. Stir cautiously with a clean trowel or piece of wood. Add more dry ingredients as needed.

...or use a mortar mixer.
For preparing large amounts, use a mortar mixer attached to an electric drill. Set the blade in the mixture, then mix at a slow speed. Don't lift the blade out until it has stopped turning.

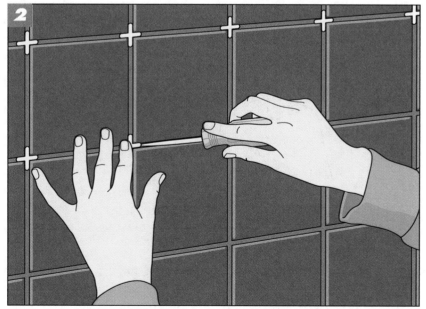

2. Remove spacers, clean joints.
Before you begin spreading grout, remove all of the spacers between tiles. An awl or some other thin tool will make removal easier. Also remove any adhesive that was squeezed into the joints between tiles. A razor blade or grout saw will speed this process. Vacuum the joints and put masking tape over all expansion joints, which will be caulked later.

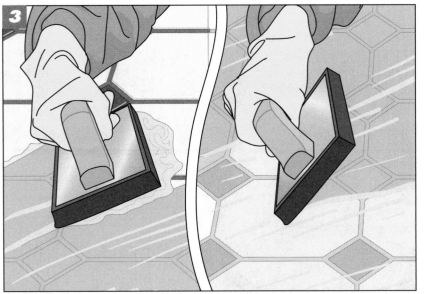

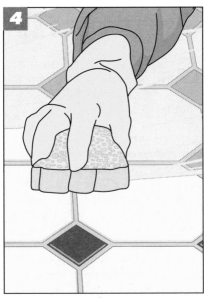

3. Apply the grout.

For a floor, dump enough grout on the tiles to cover about 3 square feet. For a wall, scoop a good-sized dollop up with the float. Hold the grout float at about a 35-degree angle, and spread the grout diagonally across the tiles. Press the grout firmly and completely into the joints. Make two or three passes, working in a different direction for each pass.

Tilt the float up so it is nearly perpendicular to the surface, and wipe away excess grout. Move diagonally to the joints, to avoid digging into them with the float.

4. Wipe away the excess.

When you have finished grouting one area, use a dampened sponge to wipe the tiles. Use a circular motion. If the grout is hard to wipe from the tiles, don't wait so long next time. Take care that the joints are consistent in depth. Rinse the sponge often.

TOOLS TO USE

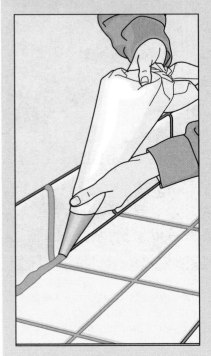

A GROUT BAG

A grout (or mortar) bag looks a bit like a pastry bag used for decorating cakes. It is useful for grouting joints that can't be reached with a trowel, or for particularly porous tiles that soak up grout quicker than you can clean it off the surface. Use a tip on the grout bag no wider than the width of the joint. Fill the bag with grout, then place the tip in the joint. Move the bag as you squeeze grout into the joint. Grout the full length of joints rather than grouting around each tile. Let the grout harden a little, then shape the joints. Once the grout has set for 30 minutes or more, sweep the joints with a broom or stiff brush to remove the excess.

EXPERTS' INSIGHT

WATCH THE GAPS

Don't forget about the expansion joints. These joints at corners and edges must be filled with expandable caulk, which allows the surfaces to expand and contract without cracking or damaging the tiles. Use masking tape to keep grout out of the expansion joints. Some grout will still seep under the tape and into the joint. So when you have finished grouting, remove the tape and clean out the grout. Or wait for it to dry, and cut it out with a grout saw or utility knife. Let the joint dry completely, and vacuum before caulking.

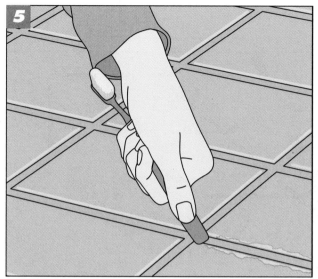

5. Shape the joints.

After wiping the tiles, clean and shape the joints. Pull a barely dampened sponge along grout lines, removing high spots as you go. Some people like thick grout lines that are nearly flush with the surface of the tile, while others prefer grout lines that recede. The important thing is that they be consistent. Buy an adjustable grout shaper, or use a toothbrush handle or a wood dowel. The shaper should be a bit wider than the joint.

6. Fill the gaps.

If you notice a gap or inadvertently pull grout out from a joint, fill it right away with grout. Wearing rubber gloves, press a small amount into the void, filling it completely. Then shape the joint and remove any excess grout.

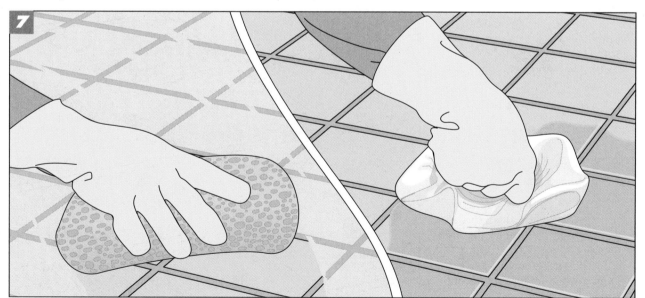

7. Remove the grout film.

Once you have cleaned the tile surfaces of grout and shaped the joints, let the grout set up for another 15 or 20 minutes. With your sponge and a bucket of clean water, and wearing a rubber glove, start the final cleaning of the tiles. Timing is critical: The grout should be dry enough to not be affected by the sponge, yet haze on the tile surface should be not so dry that it is difficult to remove. Rinse the sponge and wring it out. Pass the sponge slowly over a line of tiles. Flip the sponge over and make another straight run. Rinse the sponge and continue. With proper timing and careful execution, this process should remove nearly all of the grout residue from the tile surface. After another 15 minutes, polish the tiles with a dry piece of cheesecloth or a clean rag.

CAULKING AND SEALING

Caulk fills expansion joints around the perimeter of a tiled surface. Its flexibility allows adjacent surfaces to expand and contract without damaging tile; and it won't crack, as grout would. Many fine tile jobs have been marred by ugly caulking, so take the time to do it right. (See page 221 for information on choosing caulk.) Practice on scrap pieces until you feel you've got the knack. Place the tube in the gun, cut the tip, and puncture the seal with a long nail. Some people like to cut the tip at a severe angle, while others like to cut it nearly straight across. Have a damp rag handy, soaked with water or mineral spirits, depending on the type of caulk you are using.

YOU'LL NEED

TIME: Less than an hour for most projects.
SKILLS: Applying and smoothing caulk, and using a paint roller.
TOOLS: Caulk gun, paint roller and tray or paintbrush, and rag.

EXPERTS' INSIGHT

GROUT SEALERS

You can significantly improve the durability of grout joints by sealing them. Wait until the grout has fully cured—a week or two—before applying grout sealer. Use a disposable foam-rubber paintbrush, which allows you to cover the grout without getting sealer on the tile. Allow the first coat to dry, then apply a second. Renew the grout sealer from time to time.

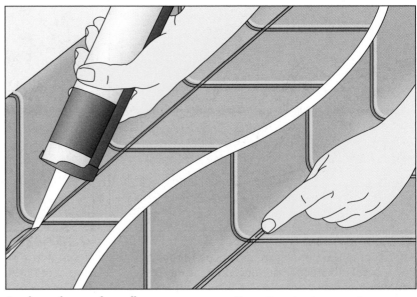

Apply and smooth caulk.
Position the tip of the tube on the surface to be caulked, and get yourself into a comfortable position. Squeeze the trigger carefully until caulk begins to flow. Continue squeezing as you pull the gun along. Either leave the bead of caulk as it is, or use a wet finger or damp rag to smooth it. Strive for a consistent-looking line.

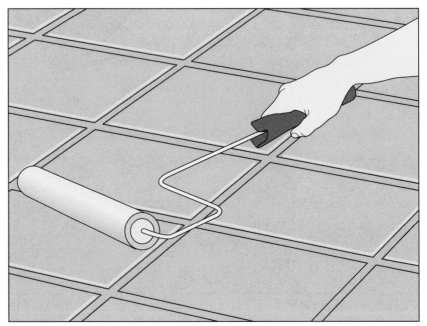

Seal the tile.
Some tiles must be sealed when they are installed; others must have a sealer reapplied every few years. Check with the tile manufacturer for specific instructions. If you are installing unsealed tiles, you may have to apply the sealer before grouting. Renew the sealer as needed. A foam-rubber paint roller works well for most types of tile sealer.

TILING FLOORS

Unless your home was seriously underbuilt, your floors are strong enough so that you can install carpeting or another type of resilient flooring with confidence. But ceramic tile has much more demanding requirements. The weight of the tiles is not usually the problem; deflection is. If a ceramic tile floor flexes, grout and even tiles can crack. If you have any doubts about the strength of the floor, ask a contractor to inspect it before you begin tiling.

Sometimes a bouncy floor can be firmed up by driving screws through the subflooring and into joists. Or, you may have to add another subfloor layer, or even beef up the joists. However, if you build up the floor so much that the new tile surface will be a half inch or more higher than an adjacent floor surface, it will look and feel awkward. That's why in some situations it is simply not practical to lay a ceramic tile floor.

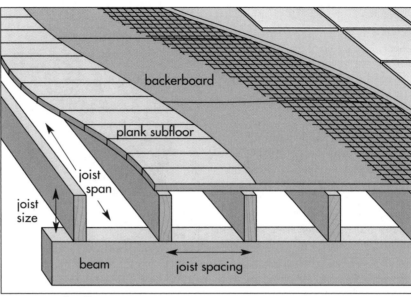

Anatomy of a floor.
Floor joist strength is determined by the size of the joist, the length of the joist's span between supports, and the amount of space between joists. If your joists have spaces larger than 16 inches between them, for instance, then you will need an extra strong subfloor. Plywood is the best subfloor material, but many older homes have strong subfloors made with planks of 1× lumber.

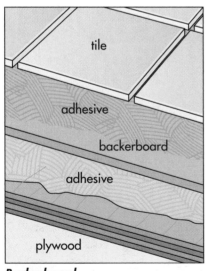

Backerboard
Older installations set tiles on a thick bed of mortar. Backerboard is an excellent modern day substitute. Use as thick a board as possible, installed over a plywood subfloor. See pages 228–229 for cutting and installation help.

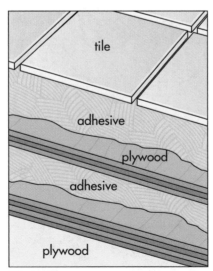

Plywood
Although plywood is somewhat soft and flexible, it also has great strength. When two sheets are laminated together, the result is a very firm surface.

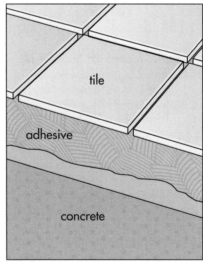

Concrete
Concrete is the best subsurface and works well for straightening out-of-level floors. Do not use curing or acceleration chemicals if you pour a concrete floor. An older concrete surface must be sound; tiling will not strengthen it.

Preparing a wood floor for tile.

If you will be tiling directly over plywood, it is best to install two layers of ⅜-inch-minimum plywood, rather than one thick sheet. Use exterior-grade plywood for the top layer. The edges should always fall over a joist, but stagger the sheets so that the joints do not fall directly over each other. Coat the bottom sheet with construction adhesive before setting the top sheet in place. Leave a gap of ⅛ inch or more around all edges of the top sheets, including at the joints. Fasten the plywood with screws or ring-shank nails. If an existing plywood subfloor is strong enough, sand the surface thoroughly, then vacuum. Talk to your tile dealer about the best adhesive to use.

If the existing floor is composed of 1× or 2× planking in good condition, drive screws into joists wherever it seems at all loose, and perhaps install a layer of plywood over it. If it has cracks and does not feel strong, remove the planking and install plywood.

Preparing a concrete floor for tile.

Concrete is a great base for tile, as long as it is structurally sound and flat. Some slabs may actually be too smooth, and should be scruffed up a bit by grinding with an abrasive wheel. Do not install tile over concrete that was treated with a curing or acceleration chemical when it was poured. These additives will prevent adhesive from bonding properly. If you are uncertain about whether or not such additives were used, try to locate the builder of the house or the concrete contractor. They may have a record. You can also test the slab yourself by sprinkling water on it. If the water isn't absorbed, the concrete was probably treated. Apply a latex bonding agent or add a subfloor.

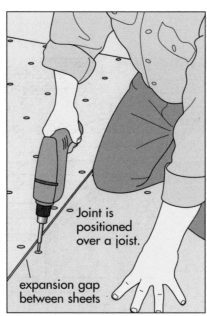

- Joint is positioned over a joist.

expansion gap between sheets

Install plywood.
For the top layer of plywood, leave ⅛-inch gaps between the sheets. Fasten with screws or ring-shank nails in a 6-inch grid in the field, and every 4 inches at the joints and around the perimeter.

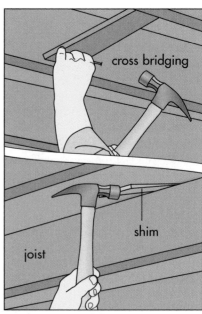

cross bridging

shim

joist

Beef up a wood floor.
Strengthen a weak subfloor by installing wood or metal cross bridging between joists. Close small gaps between joists and the existing subfloor with shims, or drive screws from above.

Don't try to tile over irregular surface.

Crack can be contained with isolation membrane.

Fill in low spots.
Clean out low spots in a concrete slab and fill with thinset mortar. Use a trowel or straightedge to level the surface.

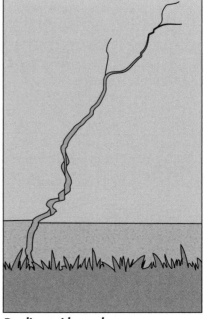

Dealing with cracks.
Cover small cracks in concrete with an isolation membrane (see page 220). Cracks that result in uneven surfaces indicate underlying structural problems; do not tile over such a surface.

EXPERTS' INSIGHT

REPLACING BASEBOARD

■ As long as you're tiling your floor, you may want to update your baseboards as well. New tile may well emphasize your old baseboard's imperfections.

■ Old vinyl cove base can get pretty ratty-looking. Install new cove base after the tile job is done. Make sure that the new material is as wide as the original stuff or you will have an ugly line on the wall. Apply with cove base adhesive or latex silicone caulk.

■ The base shoe gets banged up in time, too, so go ahead and replace it as well. Use stain or paint on it, then cut it with a miter box and fasten it with finishing nails.

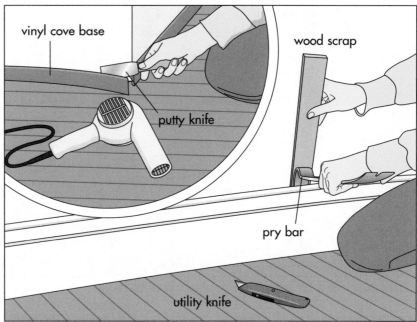

Remove the baseboard.

Before tiling a floor, remove the baseboard from the surrounding walls. If the joint between the baseboard and wall is sealed with paint, score it with a utility knife first. Pull vinyl cove base away with a putty knife. If it resists removal, try heating the vinyl with a hair dryer to loosen the adhesive. Use a pry bar to remove wood baseboard. Protect the wall with a thin piece of wood. If your baseboard has a *shoe*—a small rounded molding at the bottom—remove that piece.

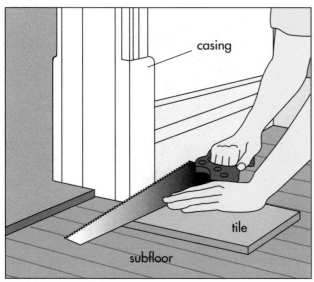

Trim casing and doors.

It is usually not a good idea to remove door casings. But cutting tile to fit around casing is difficult, and usually leads to a sloppy-looking job. So trim the bottom of the casing, and fit the tiles beneath it. With the subfloor installed, place a tile up against the casing. Lay a handsaw on the tile as you cut through the casing.

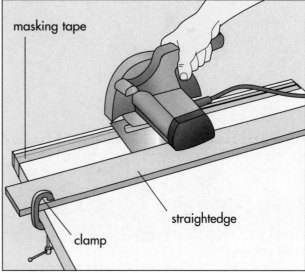

To make sure a door will swing freely after the tiles are installed, place tiles on the floor nearby. If not, use the tiles and a pencil to scribe a cut line at the door's bottom. Allow for a gap of at least ¼ inch. Remove the door by popping out the hinge pins. Place masking tape along the bottom of the most visible side of the door, and mark a cut line. Cut through the tape using a circular saw with a clamped straightedge as a guide.

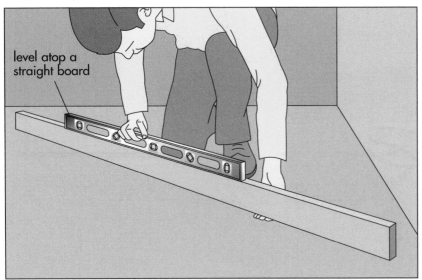

Check floors for level.

Use a carpenter's level and a straight board to check the floor for level and to find any spots that are not flat. If the entire floor is out of level with the wall, it can still be tiled. If you plan to extend tile up the wall, however, you should consider leveling the floor or using tapered baseboard to make the transition attractive.

EXPERTS' INSIGHT

PLANNING TRANSITIONS

A newly tiled floor may be higher than the adjoining floor. Plan your approach to these transitions before you begin any work. The most common technique is to install a transitional piece called a threshold. You can buy metal or wood thresholds that are sloped to ease the transition. Some are designed to be installed after the tile is laid and grouted, and others should be installed at the same time as you lay the tile. Using a table saw, you can make your own threshold out of oak or another hardwood.

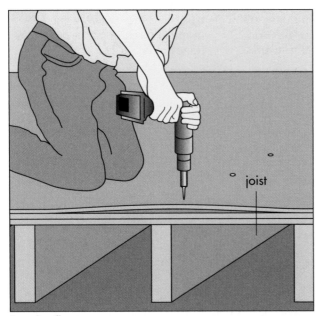

Level a floor.

Small bumps in the floor must be dealt with before you begin tiling. If the wood subfloor comes up in places, try driving screws through the flooring and into a joist to level it out. You may be able to take out small high spots with a belt sander.

To straighten out dips and low areas, or to level out an entire floor, use a self-leveling floor patch. These are made by manufacturers of tile adhesive.

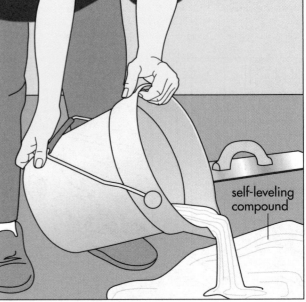

Place barriers where necessary to keep the compound where it belongs. Mix the dry ingredients with water, then pour it on the floor. The mixture will level itself out to a certain degree, but use a long flat trowel to help things along. The compound should be cured and ready for tiling within a few hours. Most self-leveling compounds are intended to function at depths no greater than 1 inch. If the work seems intimidating, talk to a contractor about preparing a level subfloor for you.

TILING A KITCHEN FLOOR

Tiling a kitchen floor can be a major disruption to any household. This project may affect access to food, meal preparation, and upset traffic patterns through the kitchen. Some preparation can be done well in advance of the tiling; some cabinets can be removed, new subflooring applied, and doors removed. For the tiling itself, set aside a long weekend so that the kitchen can be back in operation as quickly as possible.

YOU'LL NEED

TIME: 3–4 days to prepare, lay out, and tile an average-size kitchen.
SKILLS: Disconnecting and removing appliances, removing base cabinets, preparing a subfloor, and tiling the floor.
TOOLS: Screwdriver, hammer, pry bar, and putty knife.

TOOLS TO USE

KNEE PADS

Tiling floors is hard on your knees. In addition to the stress of kneeling much of the time, your knees are vulnerable to injury from tools and pieces of material left around the work area. That's why contractors who spend a lot of time working at floor level consider knee pads essential. For occasional use on wood or tile floors, non-marring foam, rubber, or rubber-capped pads are a good choice. (You'll find these useful for gardening as well.) For heavy-duty protection, but less comfort, buy the skateboarder-type knee pads that have a hard nylon shield on the front.

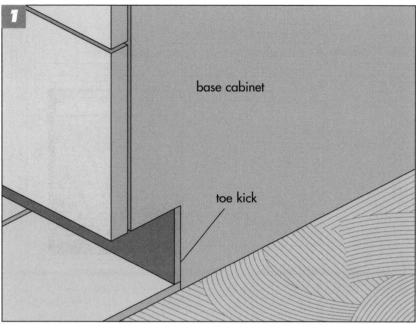

1. Assess the cabinets.
As a general rule, there is no need to install tile where it will be covered by cabinet bases or other permanent fixtures. Instead, use a thin pry bar and stiff putty knife to remove the toe kick and any molding along the floor. Set tile up to the cabinet. After all the tile is installed and grouted, trim the upper edge of toe kick to fit and reinstall it and the molding

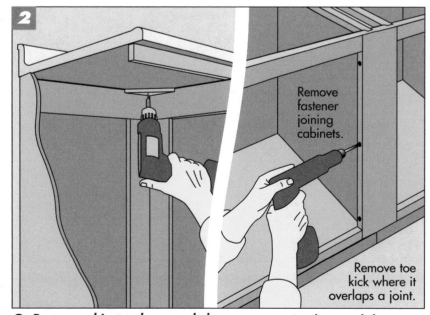

2. Remove cabinets where needed.
Sometimes cabinets must be removed to take out the old flooring or to replace the subfloor. Remove fasteners holding the countertop in place, and the screws that join cabinets to each other and to the wall. In addition, remove overlapping pieces of toe kick and other molding.

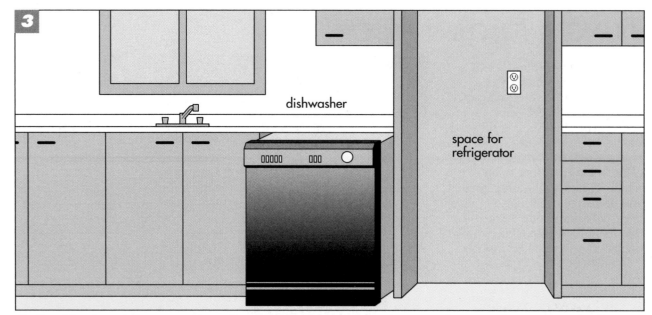

3. Consider the appliances.

One of the issues you will have to address is whether or not to tile beneath appliances. Think of how your kitchen floor would look if your home were empty and up for sale. Untiled spaces where appliances usually sit would be unattractive to potential buyers.

Freestanding appliances, such as refrigerators, ranges, and dishwashers, should be removed from the kitchen to install tile underneath the appliance location. It is also best to tile beneath built-in appliances, although the work can be trickier. Often, when you tile beneath a built-in dishwasher,

for example, you raise the floor level such that the dishwasher will no longer fit under the countertop. You can raise or notch out the countertop a bit to accommodate the appliance. Adjustments may also have to be made in the plumbing connections.

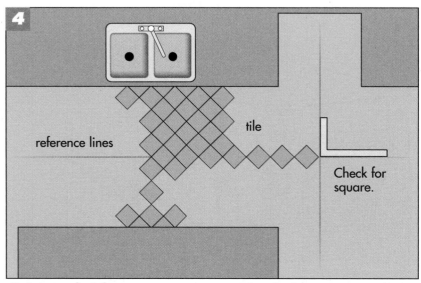

4. Lay out the job.

At the center of the floor, mark perpendicular reference lines with a pencil or chalk line. (In odd-shape rooms you may want to center the layout on the most visible section of the floor rather than in the center of the room.) Check to make sure that the lines are square (see pages 225–227). Using appropriate spacers if needed with your tile, dry set tiles along the reference lines to check the layout. Adjust the layout to minimize the number of cut tiles and to avoid creating any extremely small pieces.

5. Set the tiles.

Begin at the intersecting reference lines and spread thin-set mortar over a small area. Do not cover the lines. Set properly spaced tiles. Use a beating block (see page 214) after setting each section of tiles. Check alignment as you go.

TILING A BATHROOM FLOOR

*T*ile is a great material for bathroom floors: tough, attractive, and easy to clean. Many bathrooms have tile on every surface; plan ahead if you want to resurface your walls, countertops, or tub and shower areas. One of the great joys of tiling a bathroom is the chance to experiment with bold colors and unusual designs.

A typical bathroom floor does not require a waterproof installation, although you should choose tiles and setting materials that are suitable for a surface that will get wet from time to time.

YOU'LL NEED

TIME: A full weekend for an average bathroom floor.
SKILLS: Removing and resetting a toilet, preparing a subfloor, and laying out and tiling a floor.
TOOLS: Wrench, hacksaw, and tiling and grouting tools.

EXPERTS' INSIGHT

REMOVING SINKS

If you have a pedestal or wall-mounted sink with legs sink, remove it before you start to tile. Shut off the water supply and disconnect the supply lines. Remove the trap with a pipe wrench. Unbolt and remove the top of a pedestal sink, then unbolt and remove the pedestal. (One-piece pedestal sinks are bolted to the floor and wall.) Remove the legs of a wall-mounted sink and pull the sink up and off of the mounting bracket. You may also want to remove a vanity, depending on its position.

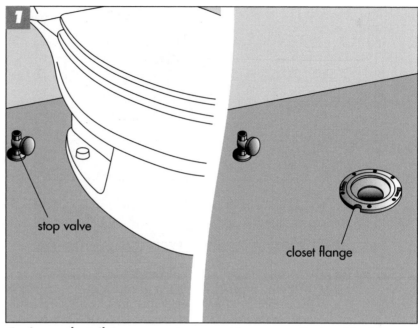

stop valve

closet flange

1. Assess the toilet.
When tiling over a finished bathroom floor, the toilet can be left in place. But you will have to cut tiles to fit all around the base, which will probably leave you with an unprofessional-looking job. It is easier in the long run to remove the toilet and tile up to the closet flange. With fewer cut tiles, the job will look better and pose fewer maintenance problems.

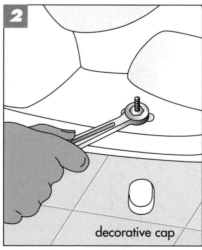

decorative cap

2. Remove the toilet.
Shut off the water supply and disconnect the supply line. Flush the toilet, then sponge the remaining water from the tank. Pry off the decorative caps, then unscrew the flange nuts. If the nut is rusted tight, cut through it with a hacksaw; the easiest way is to

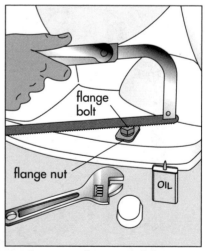

flange bolt

flange nut

OIL

cut down, as shown, and then unscrew it. With a helper, lift the toilet off the flange, and carry it to another room. Stuff a rag in the closet flange (make sure it's large enough so it won't fall down the hole) to contain sewer gases, and scrape off any wax, putty, or caulk.

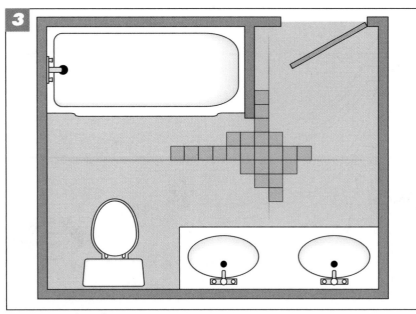

3. Lay out the job.

Small, rectangular bathroom floors are relatively easy to lay out. Arrange grout joints so that they are parallel to the most visible straight edges in the room, such as along counters and tubs. Hide cut tiles in less exposed spots. In such a small area, it is worth your while to check the layout by dry-setting all of the tiles before you begin the installation. See pages 225–227.

4. Set the tiles.

Set full tiles as close as possible to the closet flange. Use nippers to cut tiles to fit around the flange. You don't have to worry about precision here, since the toilet will cover the area.

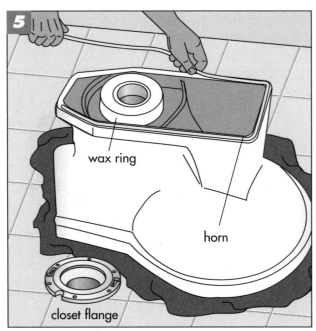

5. Reset the toilet.

After the tile has been grouted, reset the toilet. Install new bolts in the flange; they may need to be longer than the old ones to compensate for the height of the tiles. Clean the horn of the bowl and install a new wax ring. If the flange is well below the tile surface, you may need a second wax ring to seal the gap. Set the toilet over the bolts, then tighten the nuts.

EXPERTS' INSIGHT

TILING OVER TILE

■ When remodeling a bathroom, you may want to replace an old tiled floor with new tiling. Removing the old tile can be a major headache, and it may not be necessary. Instead, you can use the existing floor as a setting bed for the new tile.

■ First, make certain that there are no structural problems with the floor—if the grout is significantly cracked and tiles are loose, it could signal underlying problems that need to be addressed before proceeding. Talk to your tile dealer about the best products and techniques to use over a tiled floor. Normally, the old tiles will need to be sanded heavily, to rough up the glazed surface. You may also need to fill in old grout joints if they aren't level with the tile surface.

■ Keep in mind that the new tile will add to the height of your bathroom floor. Place tiles on top of your existing floor to find out whether this new height will make it awkward to move from the hall into the bathroom. Usually, a threshold will smooth the transition.

TILING A TUB SURROUND

*I*n a tub that also contains a shower, plan to install tile from the top of the tub to about 6 inches above the shower head. If the tub doesn't have a shower, tile at least one foot above the tub (more if you anticipate a lot of splashing). If you want to tile the ceiling as well, use a fast-setting adhesive; it will hold the tiles in place without support. (Install ceiling tile so that it doesn't have to line up with the wall tiles—say, diagonally—because getting it to fit will be very difficult. If an end wall continues out past the tub, continue the tiles at least one full vertical row beyond the tub, and run it down to the floor. Use bullnose cap tiles for the edges.

Set the tile on a backerboard substrate (see pages 228–229 for information on backerboard). The backerboard itself should be installed over a waterproofing membrane of 15-lb. felt paper or 4-mil polyethylene. Overlay the edges of the membrane and seal the seams of the backerboard with fiberglass mesh tape bedded in adhesive.

If you have a window with wood casing and jambs, consider tearing it out or cutting back the casing and tiling the recess). You can eliminate the problems of a wood window altogether by installing glass block.

YOU'LL NEED

TIME: A day to prepare the substrate, most of a day to tile, and a few hours to grout.
SKILLS: Cutting and installing backerboard, patching walls, cutting and installing tile.
TOOLS: Drill, hole saw, scraping tool, wall patching tools, level, a straight board, notched trowel, snap cutter, nibbler, hacksaw with rod saw, grouting float.

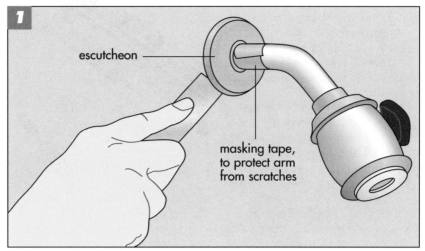

1. Remove the hardware.
You don't want to cut tiles to fit precisely around hardware. Pry the shower-arm escutcheon away from the wall, and perhaps remove the shower arm as well. Remove the tub spout; most can be unscrewed by sticking the handle of a screwdriver or hammer in the spout and turning counterclockwise. Remove the faucet handles and escutcheons.

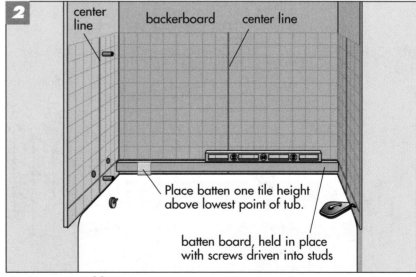

2. Prepare and lay out.
The walls must be solid, and at least close to plumb and square (see page 225). If necessary, remove the existing substrate and install a waterproofing membrane and backerboard. Be sure that the new surface is flush with any adjoining surface.

Establish a vertical reference line by laying the tiles in a row on the tub and making sure you will either have the same size tile on each end, or that you will not have any very narrow pieces. If the end walls are out of square with the rear wall, factor in how the pieces will change size as you move upward. Measuring from the low point of the tub if it is not level, establish a horizontal reference line and tack a very straight batten board along its length.

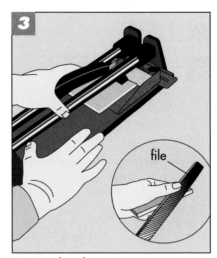

3. Cut the tile.
Use a snap cutter for the straight cuts. Hold the tile in place and mark it for cutting. Align it on the cutter, score the surface by pushing down while sliding the cutter once across the tile, then push down on the handle. For a series of cuts of the same size, use the adjustable guide. Smooth the ragged cut edges with a rubbing stone or file.

4. Set the tile.
Apply adhesive with a notched trowel, taking care not to cover your layout lines. Set the tiles, giving each a little twist and pushing to make sure it sticks. Start with the row sitting on the batten. Most wall tiles are self-spacing. Once you have several rows installed, remove the batten and install the bottom row.

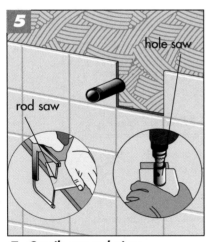

5. Cut tile around pipes.
Cuts around pipes usually do not have to be precise because the opening is covered with an escutcheon. Use a nibbler to eat away at a curved cut, or a hacksaw equipped with a rod-saw blade. To cut a hole, use a tile-cutting hole saw. Or, set the tile on a piece of scrap wood, drill a series of closely spaced holes with a masonry bit, and tap out the hole.

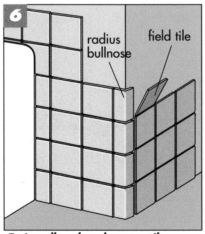

6. Install end and corner tiles.
Cut the curved piece at the corner of the tub with a hacksaw fitted with a rod-saw blade; it may take several attempts to get it just right. Use radius bullnose tiles everywhere there is an exposed edge. (Do not use a field tile edged with grout—it will look very sloppy.)

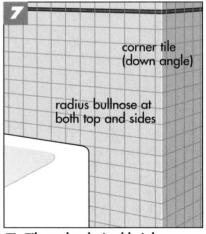

7. Tile to the desired height.
When you reach your top row, wipe away excess adhesive from the wall as you install bullnose caps. Use outside corner pieces ("down angles"), which have two cap edges, at all outside corners.

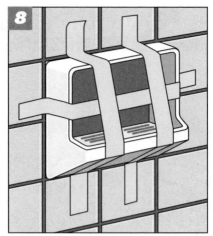

8. Attach ceramic accessories.
Apply adhesive and use masking tape to hold soap dishes and other accessories in place until they are set. Take the tape off after a day or two and apply grout, but wait a week or so before using.

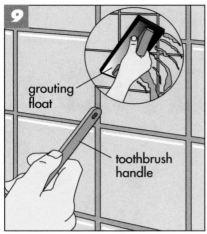

9. Grout, caulk, and seal.
Mix the grout with latex additive, and push it into the joints with a grouting float held nearly flat. Tip the float up and wipe away the excess. Carefully wipe the surface to produce consistent grout lines. Use a toothbrush handle or other tool to shape the joints. Caulk the corners and edges. Wipe and dry-buff the haze.

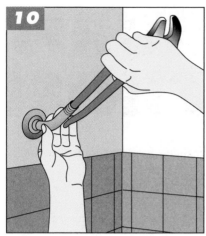

10. Reattach the hardware.
Reattach the plumbing hardware. If you need to install a shower arm, use a thin tool handle to tighten it. If the new tile has caused valves or nipples to be recessed too far and you can't install a faucet or spout, visit a plumbing supplier and pick up suitable extensions. Once the grout has cured, apply sealer.

TILING AN ACCESS PANEL

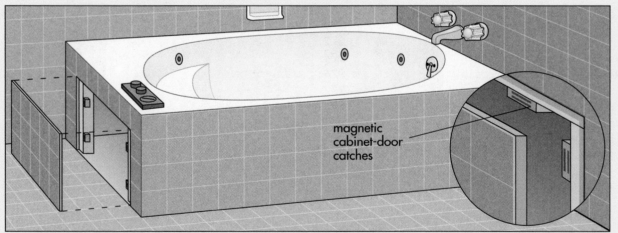

Plumbing access panels are usually located in an adjoining room, but yours might be in the bathroom. The panel may have been installed when the bathroom was built, or it might have been built out of necessity when a plumber needed to gain access to the pipes and valves supplying the tub. Don't just tile over the panel; a plumber may need to get in there again someday. The easiest solution is to cover the panel with a piece of plastic, well-painted plywood, or a plastic access panel made for the purpose (available at home centers).

Or, make a tiled access panel. Cut a piece of plywood sized to hold full tiles. Install tiles on it so they will align with the surrounding tiles, and trim the edges with painted wood molding; drive screws through the molding to hold the panel in place. Or skip the molding, and attach with magnetic cabinet door catches, as shown *above*.

SURFACE FINISHING

Chapter 9

Painting Tools and Materials
Choosing Exterior Paint *253*
Choosing Interior Paint *255*
Choosing Brushes *257*
Using and Caring for Brushes *258*
Choosing Rollers and Pads *259*
Using a Roller *260*
Using a Power Roller *261*

Exterior Preparation
Removing Old Exterior Paint *262*
Preparing Exterior Surfaces *264*
Preparing and Planning to Paint *265*

Exterior Painting
Painting Siding *266*
Painting Trim *267*
Painting Masonry *269*

Interior Preparation
Repairing Drywall *270*
Patching Holes in Drywall *272*
Repairing Cracked Plaster *274*
Repairing Holes in Plaster *276*
Repairing Paneling *277*
Preparing Interior Surfaces for Paint *278*

Interior Painting
Painting Ceilings *280*
Painting Walls *281*
Painting Woodwork *282*

CHOOSING EXTERIOR PAINT

House paints made to cover siding and exterior trim tend to be more durable and more expensive than interior paint. That's because exterior paints contain additional resins and other ingredients that make them last longer and resist moisture. Also many have a larger amount of pigmenting, which gives them a deeper, more vivid color.

Like interior paint, exterior paint comes in two basic varieties: water-thinned (latex) and solvent-thinned (oil- or alkyd-based). Those with oil and alkyd bases dry slowly, making them susceptible during application to being marred by insects and sudden rainstorms. Once they set up, they develop a hard surface that is resistant to water. However, unless the surface is very well prepared, they are prone to flaking.

Properly applied, modern latex exterior paint (though not porch and deck paint) is more durable than solvent-based paint. Latex paints are easier to work with, dry quickly, and have a porous, "breathing" quality that makes them less likely to flake. They will likely peel, however, if applied over an improperly prepared oil- or alkyd-based finish.

Chalking-type latex paints shed dirt by gradually eroding with each rainfall. Usually you can see the "chalk" on foundation walls, shrubbery, and your coat sleeve if you brush against a painted surface. Newer formulations achieve durability without this chalking feature.

Latex paints tend to show brush marks, while solvent-based paints "level" to a more even surface. If a surface will be often handled or walked on (as is the case with a porch), solvent-based paint provides a more durable surface.

Do not use latex paint over a surface covered with solvent-based paint, unless you first apply a primer or thoroughly sand the surface. To find out which type of paint is present, remove a flake or chip and see whether it is flexible. Latex paint will bend slightly before cracking; a flake of solvent-based paint will snap readily. If you bring in a chip, a paint dealer can tell you for sure. If you're not certain what type of paint was used before, it's safest to apply a solvent-thinned paint.

Most people prefer a flat, eggshell, or satin finish for large exterior expanses. Reserve semigloss and gloss for areas subject to hard use or for trim.

What about one-coat house paints? If you plan to match or approximate the present color, any paint will cover in one coat. However, products sold with a one-coat guarantee are thicker, with more resins and pigments. Most guarantees specify that the paint must be applied over sound existing surfaces or primed new wood. You will pay more for a one-coat paint, but the extra money spent might pay off handsomely, especially in terms of time saved.

The chart on the opposite page will help you sort through the often-confusing array of products found in paint stores. As a general rule, the more expensive the paint, the more durable it will be.

ESTIMATING PAINT NEEDS

How much paint you need depends upon the type and condition of the surfaces that you'll be covering, the method of application, and the paint itself. Conditions vary considerably, so read the manufacturer's coverage figures, then buy a little more than you need.

If your home has narrow lap siding, add another 10 percent to your estimate. For textured materials, such as shingles or shakes, add 20 percent. Masonry and stucco—both porous surfaces that soak up lots of paint—can take up to 50 percent more.

To compute surface area, measure from the foundation to the eaves and multiply by the distance around the house. For each gable end, measure the distance from eaves to the peak, measure the width of the wall, and multiply the two. Then divide the result by two.

If you buy paint of a standard color, most stores will let you return unopened cans. Check with your retailer about return policies for custom-mixed paint.

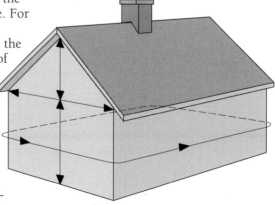

COMPARING EXTERIOR PAINTS

Type	Characteristics/Uses	Application
Vinyl latex	Easy cleanup, durability, and fast drying make latex the choice for amateurs. It can be applied over damp surfaces. Latex is naturally mildew-proof but is incompatible with a previous solvent-based finish.	Don't thin latex. Apply with one stroke of the brush or roller; if you work it out too far, you'll get thin spots.
Acrylic latex	The highest-quality latex paints contain 100 percent acrylic resins; vinyl resins are not as durable. It dries faster than most and will cover just about any building material, including masonry and properly primed metal.	Application technique is about the same as vinyl latex paint.
Alkyd	Alkyd, the most common type of solvent-thinned paint, has most of the same properties as oil-based types, but dries more rapidly; good over old oil- or alkyd-based coatings; excellent hiding power.	Thicker consistency makes alkyd more tiring to apply, but it levels smoother than latex.
Oil	Slow drying times (12 to 48 hours), strong odors, and messy cleanup make oil a less popular choice for amateurs, though some pros swear by its durability.	Drying time makes marring by bugs and rain real perils.
Primers	Use a recommended primer to seal new wood or metal, to kill stains, or prior to applying latex paint over existing solvent-based paint. Alcohol-based primer is the most effective, but solvent and latex types also work.	Priming usually is easier than finishing, but porous surfaces can soak up a lot of primer.
Stains	Solvent- or latex-type stains provide transparent, semi-transparent, or opaque finishes for natural wood siding and trim; some include preservatives or offer a weathered look.	Brush, roll, or spray on almost any way you prefer.
Porch and deck	Alkyd and polyurethane types are the most durable because they produce a hard, washable surface. Some types are formulated for concrete floors. Surface preparation varies; colors are limited.	With most types, you just pour the paint on the floor, then work it outward with a long-handled roller or applicator.
Metal	Solvent- or water-thinned types include rust-resisting priming ingredients so you needn't worry about small bare spots. All-bare metal should be primed separately. Rusty-metal primer seals a rusty spot.	Brush, roll, or spray on for a broad range of finish effects.
Marine	Formulated especially for boats, marine paint provides a super-durable finish on wood and some metal trim. It's expensive, so it's generally inappropriate for large areas.	A gooey consistency makes it difficult to apply.
Masonry	This category includes latex, epoxy, Portland cement, rubber, and alkyd. Some serve as their own primers. Seal masonry with clear silicone. For basement waterproofing techniques.	Latex is easy to apply; other types can be a lot of work.

CHOOSING INTERIOR PAINT

Many people consider interior painting an easy chore requiring no particular skill. As a result, they may plunge in unprepared and produce a botched job that haunts them for years. While it is true that almost any handy person can learn to paint well, it takes practice and attention to detail to produce smooth walls with evenly distributed color. This section will help you learn the correct way to paint or wallpaper a room, seal wood grain, and apply special finishing treatments.

Start by choosing the right paint. A well-informed salesperson can answer your questions, as long as you give the necessary information—the type and color of paint that's on the wall, the condition of the wall, and what sort of wear you expect the wall to endure. If a salesperson is not helpful, go to a different store.

A close reading of the paint can will tell you a few key things. The chart on the opposite page compares paints you're most likely to use.

Whichever type you choose, it's wise to spend more for high-quality paint. Cheaper paint may not cover in one coat, may be more likely to peel in time, and could fade, especially in direct sunlight. Given the amount of time you will spend preparing and painting your walls, it even makes sense to throw out a can of paint if you are displeased with the color.

The most common choice for interior painting is latex. High-quality latex paints are nearly as durable as solvent-thinned products. Latex cleans up with water, has less of an odor than solvent-thinned paint, is environmentally friendly, and dries to the touch quickly, so you can usually put furniture back in the room in an hour or so. However, dried latex paint takes weeks to completely cure. Handle it with care during that time because it can be easily stained or damaged.

If latex paint is applied over solvent-thinned paint, it will likely peel off in time—a disastrous result that will require hours of tedious scraping to remedy. If you suspect that the existing paint may not be latex, take a chip to a salesperson for testing. A latex paint chip will bend a bit before breaking; a solvent-based chip will be more brittle. If you have solvent-thinned paint on the wall, either cover it with a new coat of solvent-thinned paint or apply primer first (see box below).

Solvent-thinned paints, usually alkyd-based, require a solvent, such as mineral spirits (paint thinner), for cleanup. Spend more for odorless thinner; smelly products are unpleasant to breathe. Solvent-based paints generally are more durable than water-thinned paints.

Interior paints come in different sheens. From dullest to shiniest, the most common designations are: ceiling paint, flat, eggshell, satin (or low-luster), semigloss, and high-gloss. The glossier a finish, the harder and more durable it will be—and the more imperfections it will show.

Flat paint is generally considered "washable" but not "scrubbable." Eggshell or satin finishes have a low sheen but can be scrubbed occasionally. Semi- and high-gloss paints are popular for woodwork, kitchens, baths, and other areas that endure hard wear or in which there is high humidity. Again, higher-quality paint is more washable than cheap paint, no matter what the sheen.

Colors are notoriously tricky to choose. They react to each other and cast reflections that may change the appearance of everything in a room. Colors vary under different lighting, and large areas might become far more intense than you imagine when you are looking at small paint-sample chips. Consider buying a quart of the hue that catches your eye and trying it out on a sizable area before you invest in several gallons of paint that may not be returnable.

EXPERTS' INSIGHT

TO PRIME OR NOT TO PRIME

If the wall to be painted is in sound condition, if the new color is close to the existing color, and if you are sure the new paint will stick, then no primer is needed. However, you will need primer for the following conditions:

■ Stains—either localized or spread throughout the room because of smoke—may bleed through repeated coats of paint. The solution is to apply a stain-killing primer. For small spots, you can use a spray-on primer.

■ If the existing paint is solvent-thinned and you want to apply latex paint, apply an appropriate primer first. Solvent-thinned or alcohol-based primers work best.

■ If a wall has been patched, or if new drywall needs to be covered, apply latex primer first.

■ If your paint will not easily cover the existing color, purchase primer and have it tinted to approximate the paint color.

COMPARING INTERIOR PAINTS

Paint	Uses	Features/Characteristics	Thinner/Primer
Latex	The choice for most interior paint jobs; don't use it over unprimed wood, metal, or wallpaper.	Glosses vary from flat to high. It adheres to all but slick surfaces. Latex usually dries fast enough to apply two coats in one day. It is less durable than alkyd-base paints.	Latex is easy to clean up with water and soap. Prepare raw surfaces with a latex or alkyd primer.
Alkyd	Use alkyd for a rough surface or super hiding power. Don't apply over unprimed drywall—it will roughen the surface.	Dries somewhat more slowly than latex and has a slightly stronger odor. Alkyd might be banned in some areas.	For thinning and cleanup, use solvents. Coat unfinished surfaces with alkyd primer.
Oil	Natural-resin oil paints have all but disappeared.	Oil dries slowly, gives off flammable fumes, and doesn't stand up as well as alkyds.	Thin and clean up with mineral spirits, low-odor thinner, or turpentine.
Oil-based primer	Good all-purpose primer	Oil-based primer dries slowly and gives off fumes.	Thin and clean up with mineral spirits.
Latex primer	Prepares patched areas and new drywall	Inexpensive, dries quickly	Easy to clean up with water and soap
Alcohol-based primer	Best primer for most purposes	Kills almost any stain and gives tooth to slick surfaces	Thin and clean up with denatured alcohol.
One-coat	Use it only if surface is sealed, is of a similar color, and doesn't have a lot of patchwork that needs to be covered.	One-coats are ordinary latex or alkyd paints with additional pigment to increase hiding power and are therefore more expensive.	Thinning lessens paint's ability to hide flaws. Clean up with water or solvent, depending on whether latex or alkyd.
Texture paint	Designed to cover up imperfections and give the look of stucco-finish plaster	Some premixed; with others, you must stir in "sand." Application is moderately difficult; paint a section at a time, and keep the desired effect consistent.	Thinning defeats the purpose; stirring can be arduous. Check label for compatible primers.
Acoustic	Coats acoustic tiles without affecting their sound-deadening qualities	Apply acoustic paint by spraying or use a special roller. Color choice is limited.	Thin and clean up with water; no primer is necessary.
Metal	Use over primed or bare metal surfaces; "rusty-metal primer" can be applied over rust.	Self-primers are designed to adhere to bare surfaces. Preparation depends on the type and condition of metal.	Some are thinned with water, others need solvent or mineral spirits. Primer depends on the metal being covered.

CHOOSING BRUSHES

Selecting the right brush for a paint job isn't difficult. Except for foam types, all brushes fall into one of two categories: natural-bristle brushes and synthetic-bristle brushes. Natural-bristle brushes are made with animal hairs and formerly were considered the finest type available. However, some of today's synthetic varieties perform just as well.

If you're using an oil-based paint, choose a natural-bristle or a quality synthetic-bristle brush. Never use a natural-bristle brush with water-thinned finishes. The bristles will become mop-like, resulting in a streaked finish. Many paintbrush manufacturers label the brush package or handle with the type of finish for which the brush is designed.

Disposable brushes come in a wide range of widths and sizes and are suitable for many painting projects. Because they are inexpensive, they can be tossed when the job's done, saving considerable cleanup time. However, painting with a disposable brush may mean you have to apply two coats of paint, where a high-quality brush would cover with one coat. Also a cheaper brush may shed some bristle hairs, which are tedious to remove.

Should you spend extra for a quality brush, or are the inexpensive ones the better buy? If you're willing to take the time to clean your brush after using it, buy better quality. It will serve you well for years. However, if you paint only occasionally and don't like cleaning up, a less-expensive brush is the wiser investment.

To test a brush for quality, spread the bristles and inspect their tips. Quality natural-bristle brushes will have little "flags," like split ends, on the bristle ends. The more the better. On better-quality synthetic brushes, you'll see fuzzy-looking tips.

Check the brush's ferrule, the aluminum or stainless-steel band near the handle. It should be wrapped tightly and neatly around the brush and solidly secured to the handle.

Among your first buys should be a 4-inch wall brush, a 2-inch trim brush, and a 2-inch sash-trim brush. Later you might want to add a 6-inch wall brush for masonry paint jobs and a round brush for delicate work. A brush spinner speeds cleanup jobs.

The four handle styles shown below serve different functions. A beaver-tail handle lets you grip a wider brush in the palm of your hand; pencil and flat handles allow greater fingertip control; the kaiser handle also offers good control, plus a grip that's comfortable to your hand.

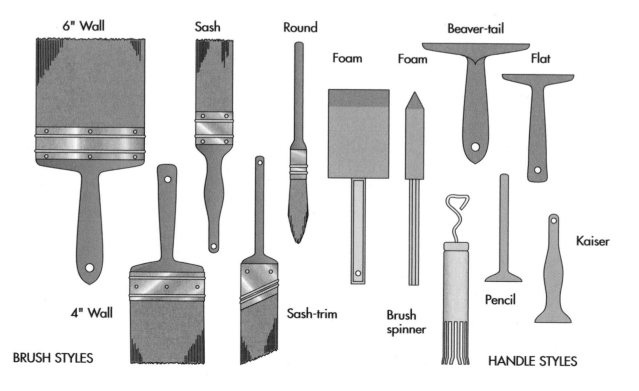

6" Wall   Sash   Round   Foam   Foam   Beaver-tail   Flat   Kaiser   Pencil

4" Wall   Sash-trim   Brush spinner

BRUSH STYLES   HANDLE STYLES

USING AND CARING FOR BRUSHES

Your brush will be a pleasure to use as long as you pay attention to proper loading, cleaning, and storing recommendations.

Before you use a new paintbrush for the first time, spin it by the handle between your hands, then slap it against the edge of a table to remove loose bristles. Work the bristles against a rough surface, such as a concrete wall, to soften the ends. To condition a natural-bristle brush, soak it 24 hours in linseed oil.

When you start painting, you may find more loose bristles and stray ones that stick out from the sides of the ferrule. Pick out loose bristles. Remove stray bristles by using a putty knife to force them against the ferrule so you can snap them off.

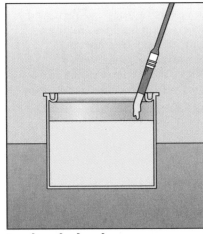

Loading the brush.
Dip the brush into the paint to only one-third the length of its bristles. If you go deeper, you'll waste paint and create a mess. Squeeze the excess paint from the bristles by scraping them lightly against the side of the container as you remove the brush.

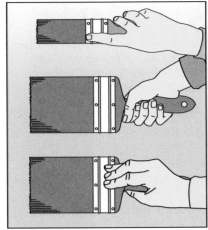

How to hold it.
Hold small brushes between your thumb and your index finger. For larger brushes, use a palm grip or lay your fingers on the ferrule. Some people prefer to hold a large brush with three or four fingers on the ferrule.

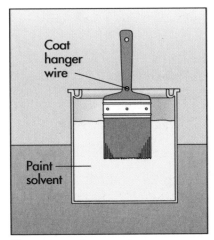

Temporary storage.
If your work is interrupted for an hour or less, leave the brush in the paint. Position it so the paint covers the bristle tips only. For longer interruptions, wrap the brush in foil or plastic. If you'll use the brush within a day or two, immerse it in solvent or water, as shown above. Drill a hole in the handle for hanging.

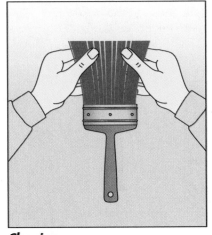

Cleaning.
To clean a brush, work out the remaining paint by firmly stroking the brush back and forth on newspaper. Work until the brush is dry. Before storing a brush for an extended period, remove all the paint you can with the appropriate thinner. Work the bristles, as shown.

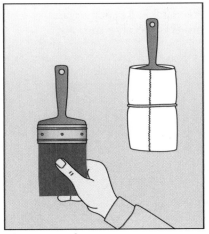

Shaping and storing.
Wash the brush in soap and water, shape the bristles, and let them dry. Then wrap the brush in the cardboard cover it was sold in. Or wrap it with several layers of paper toweling. The bristles should be held in shape but not squeezed.

CHOOSING ROLLERS AND PADS

Most people find it efficient to paint trim and edges (such as where the ceiling meets the wall or where the wall meets the trim) with a brush, and then paint the large expanses of walls and ceilings using a roller. But don't hesitate to try different tools and techniques.

Rollers range in width from 4 to 18 inches. They have a plastic or wooden handle (often machined to accept an extension handle) and a metal frame on which the roller cover is inserted.

Spend more for a professional-quality roller frame that rolls smoothly. A cheaper model may make it difficult to load the roller cover. Buy an extension handle that allows you to easily reach the ceiling—it will save you plenty of time and energy. Some extension handles are adjustable for length.

Trim rollers reach into small and hard-to-get-at areas. Once you get the knack of using a trim roller, they're as easy to control as trim brushes. Trim rollers come in varying widths and configurations. The 3-inch-wide version gets into areas too tight for a full-size roller. Cone-shaped types are used for inside corners, around door and window casings, and almost any point where two surfaces intersect. Doughnut-style rollers paint moldings and other fine work.

A high-quality roller cover (also called a roller sleeve) has a lint-free pile that is uniform in texture and securely fastened. Cheaper covers tend to apply paint unevenly or shed fibers onto the wall. Buy a cover made for the type of paint you will apply.

Mohair covers are designed for gloss finishes and varnishes; they produce a smooth finish because the nap is short and tightly woven. Dynel, acetate, and polyurethane foam covers can be used with all paints. Use a lamb's-wool roller cover for solvent-thinned paint.

Choose a cover with a thick nap—say, 3/4-inch—for rough surfaces and to achieve one-coat coverage. A thick nap will produce a slight pebbly stipple. Use a short-nap cover, either 3/8- or 1/4-inch, to produce a smoother surface. If you're using water-thinned paint, buy a cover with a plastic sleeve. For solvent-thinned paint, use a cardboard sleeve.

Pad painters are also handy. The pads may be a carpetlike material or plastic foam inserted in a plastic mop-like applicator or a paint-brush handle. Although excellent for applying paint to almost any surface, they really earn their keep when you have to paint shakes, fencing, screening, and shutters.

A paint tray, either metal or plastic, completes the system. If you'll be working on a stepladder, buy a paint tray that has ladder hooks to keep the tray secure. To save on cleanup time, purchase plastic tray inserts, which you throw away once the painting is done. With these, the paint never touches your tray.

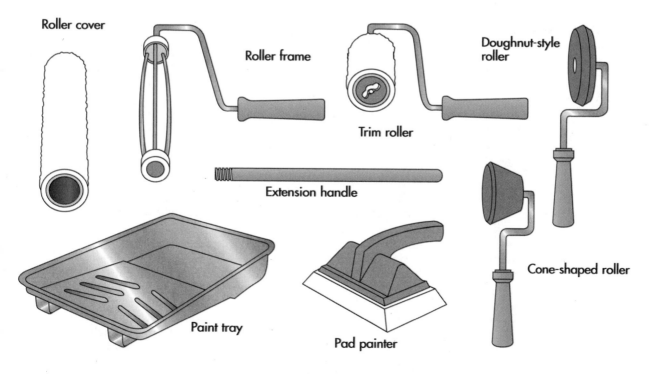

Roller cover

Roller frame

Doughnut-style roller

Trim roller

Extension handle

Cone-shaped roller

Paint tray

Pad painter

USING A ROLLER

Anyone who has ever painted with rollers or pads will vouch for the ease with which these lay down paint.

However, an even application does not come automatically. Keep your eyes peeled for skid marks on the painted surface. Rollers tend to slide as they move, causing small tracks in the finish, which will show when the finish has dried.

Most surfaces are irregular to some extent. To achieve the best coverage when using a roller or pad, lay on the paint from several different directions. In this way, you won't miss shallow depressions, such as joints between drywall panels. After applying paint to an area, go over it again with light vertical passes, taking care to even out thick spots.

Cover the floor and any furniture with a heavy drop cloth. Even when used carefully, rollers do scatter paint speckles.

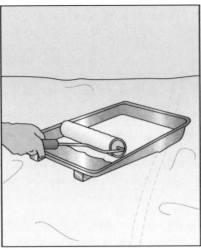

Loading a roller.
Fill the well of the tray, but not the slanted portion. Push the roller into the paint, pull it back a bit, then repeat until paint covers the entire roller. Even out the paint on the slanted part of the tray.

Rolling a wall.
For the best coverage, apply the paint in two or more directions. Minimize dripping by starting the roller on the upstroke. Don't work a roller too quickly, especially when the roller cover is loaded with paint: You'll splatter, which wastes paint and makes a mess.

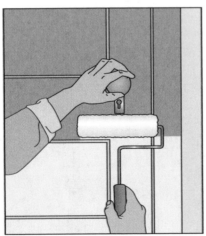

Rolling woodwork.
Rollers work well on wide, flat woodwork, such as raised-panel doors. Paint the recesses first, then finish the flush surfaces. If you do not like the pebbly stipple that the roller produces, run a brush over the paint immediately after using the roller.

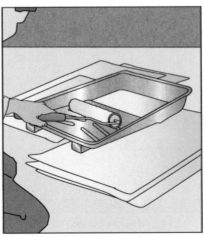

Cleaning solvent-thinned paint.
To clean a roller cover, work out all the excess paint you can on newspaper. Turn to fresh pages as needed. With solvent-thinned paint, pour solvent into the tray and work the roller back and forth. Repeat until the solvent remains clear.

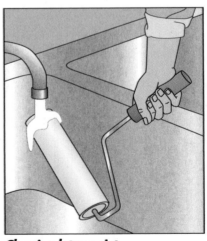

Cleaning latex paint.
Wash out water-based paints in a sink. Let water run over the roller until it is clear. Squeezing the roller speeds things. Wring the cover dry by squeezing it between your hands. Wrap clean, dry roller covers in aluminum foil or plastic bags. Clean pad painters as you would roller covers.

USING A POWER ROLLER

If you have ever painted a room with a roller, you know that most of your time is spent loading just the right amount of paint onto the roller. After about every 50 to 100 square feet, you have to pour more paint into the paint tray.

Power paint rollers and pads eliminate both of these steps and more than double your speed. The power equipment will pump from a 1-gallon can or a 5-gallon can.

Before purchasing a power roller, see that it will be reasonably easy to clean; most are designed for latex paint and water cleanup. Choose a model with few parts to disassemble.

Before painting, practice on a large scrap of cardboard. Turn on the paint control for a few seconds at a time until you get a sense of how much on-time is required. Rollers generally require on-times of about 5 seconds; pads require 1 to 2 seconds.

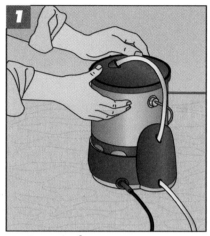

1. Prepare the can.
After opening the paint container and stirring the paint, put the special cover on the paint can. Set the can into the base of the paint pumping unit and then lock it securely in place. Insert the suction tube into the hole in the cover. Push it to the bottom, then raise it ½ inch.

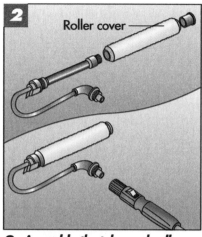

2. Assemble the tube and roller.
Hook up the parts according to the manufacturer's directions. Especially if the parts are all plastic, take care not to cross-thread when screwing the pieces together. Some types have a long handle that fills with paint and makes it easy to reach the ceiling.

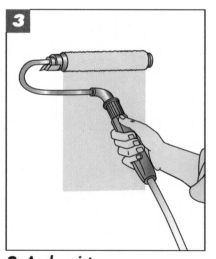

3. Apply paint.
Turn the flow on and off with the switch on the handle. Don't overload the roller or it will leak and spatter.

4. Clean the parts.
When you're finished painting, run the roller or pad dry, remove the arm, and purge the paint from the hose, letting it run into the paint can.

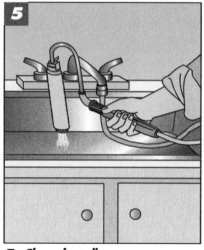

5. Clean the roller.
Attach the paint hose to a faucet adapter—if there is one—and run water through the roller until it is clean. Squeeze the excess water from the roller and stand it on end to dry. Clean the seals on the roller arm.

REMOVING OLD EXTERIOR PAINT

Many of the problems described on the preceding pages require you to strip down the defective areas to bare wood and prime them before painting. Unfortunately, there's no easy way to do this tedious job. A variety of stripping techniques are shown on these pages. Often it takes a combination of techniques to tackle a job. Experiment to find the mix that works best.

If paint is peeling from very large areas, get advice from a local painter. Preparation of old wood can be tricky, and sometimes homeowners spend tons of time stripping and repainting, only to have the new paint peel. If possible, strip and paint a small area and wait a year to see how well the paint sticks.

Old paint comes off most readily when it's dry. Start in the worst spot, work a scraper underneath, and lift off as much of the old finish as you can. You'll have better luck chipping from the edges of bad spots, rather than trying to wear through an unbroken surface.

Once you master a pull scraper, it's possible to get down to bare wood with a single stroke. Hold the blade at an angle and apply firm pressure as you drag it along. When a blade stops cutting well, either change it or sharpen it as you would a knife or chisel.

When you reach tight-sticking paint, feather the edges by sanding. Then spot-prime all bare areas, slightly overlapping the sound paint.

Remove paint from metal surfaces with a wire brush attachment on an electric drill. Don't worry about baring the metal; just remove rust, as well as the loose or caked paint, then prime it.

Chemical paint strippers should be your last alternative. Although effective, you risk dripping the remover on sound paint, creating more problems.

If you have large areas of masonry to strip, consider hiring a professional contractor to sand-blast them. Make it clear that the contractor will clean away all dust and sand when finished.

YOU'LL NEED...

TIME: Several days for an entire house.

SKILLS: Basic skills.

TOOLS: Putty knife, scraper, pull scraper, electric paint softener, wire brush, drill with wire brush attachment, propane torch or heat gun, and power sander.

Removing loose paint with a putty knife.
Remove what paint you can by scraping with a putty knife. Scrape in at least two directions at all spots to make sure you're getting all the loose stuff. Then go over the area with a wire brush. This combination works well for small areas or places where the paint is very loose.

Using a sharp pull scraper.
Most jobs call for harder work. Purchase a pull scraper with multiple replacement blades. Experiment to find which angle works best; you want to remove the paint without digging into the wood. Press down hard as you scrape; it sometimes helps to push on the tool with one hand while you pull with the other hand.

Removing paint with a power sander.
Power-sand large areas with an orbital sander
equipped with fairly rough sandpaper—60- or 80-
grit. Change the paper once it stops being effective.
If you are skillful, you may want to try a belt sander,
which removes paint more quickly. Be careful: It is
easy to dig into the wood when using a belt sander.

Using an electric paint softener.
For heavy paint deposits, use an electric paint
softener. Hold the tool on the paint until it starts to
bubble or wrinkle, then scrape off the paint. A paint-
removing heat gun, shaped much like a blow dryer
for hair, works similarly.

Using chemical paint removers.
Chemical paint removers are best for heavy paint
deposits on small areas. Follow the manufacturer's
directions to the letter.

Using a propane torch to soften paint.
A propane torch with a spreader tip "cooks" paint fast
so you can scrape it off. Be careful not to start a fire,
and have an extinguisher handy. The resulting surface
may be slightly charred in places. Be sure to seal it
with a high-quality primer before painting or the
paint may peel from the charred areas.

PREPARING EXTERIOR SURFACES

If your siding and trim is in good shape, you can happily sidestep the most maddening part of an exterior paint job—removing chipped or peeling paint (see pages 262–263). But don't get out your paint clothes and brushes quite yet.

Go around the house and take off all screens, storm windows, and hardware that can be removed. Inspect the exterior and replace damaged siding materials (see pages 199–203). Use a nail set to drive protruding nails below the surface.

Give your house a bath. You'll need a garden hose and a car-wash brush attachment, a scrub brush or sponge for stubborn dirt, and a mixture of water and trisodium phosphate (TSP) to remove dirt and reduce the gloss of existing oil- or alkyd-based paints.

Remove loose and cracked glazing from the windows and reglaze them (see pages 177–178). Glazing should dry a week before painting. Also caulk all cracks and gaps in the siding; around porch columns; and under, over, and around windows and doors (see page 198).

If you're using an oil- or alkyd-based paint, wait at least a week after the bath before you paint the house. You can paint with latex the next day. When the siding is dry, spot-prime all bare areas. Don't miss exposed metal surfaces on gutters, downspouts, and windows.

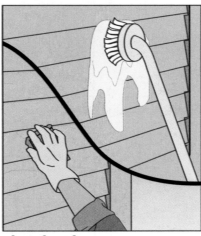

Clean the siding.
Wash the house from the top down, using a mixture of trisodium phosphate (TSP) and water. Rinse well. Let dry one day for latex or one week for oil paint. For mildewed areas, scrub with household bleach and water or a commercial cleaner. Repaint with mildewcide paint.

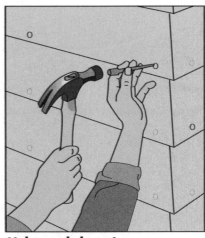

Make needed repairs.
Set popped nails and spot-prime them. Also caulk cracks, replace damaged siding, and prime bare metal spots.

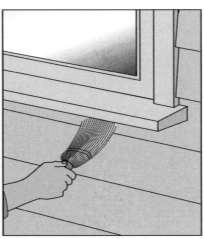

Brush away dust.
With a whisk broom or a paintbrush, flick off the dust you missed with the hose. Keep this brush handy as you paint, to clear away other debris.

Remove obstacles.
Take off fixtures or cover them the day you paint. Remember to take down other accessories, such as house numbers and the mailbox. To speed up the job, remove, clean, and paint screens, storm windows, shutters, and other detachable components separately.

YOU'LL NEED...

TIME: 5 to 6 hours to thoroughly wash and rinse a house.
SKILLS: Basic skills.
TOOLS: Whisk broom, hose, scrub brushes, car-wash brush, hammer, nail set, screwdriver, and a caulking gun.

PREPARING AND PLANNING TO PAINT

Begin exterior painting when the sun has dried off the prepared surfaces. Follow the sun so you're working in the shade; this gives the paint a chance to cure slowly and adhere better.

Work from the top to the bottom of the house to avoid the mess caused by spilled or splattered paint. For a one-story house, do the siding first, then go back and paint the windows, doors, railings, steps, and so forth. If you're painting a two-story structure, do the trim as you go to avoid leaning your ladder against fresh paint.

Always paint above the top of the ladder. Don't try to paint under it, or you'll have ladder tracks where the rails touched the siding.

Protect nearby foliage.
A little paint spattered on grass will disappear with the next mowing, but it will remain on mulch and taller plants. Protect shrubs, flowers, patios, and walks with drop cloths. Use rope and canvas or old sheets to tie tall bushes back out of the way.

Safely set up ladders.
Set ladders on sure footing—never a plastic drop cloth. If the ground is uneven, dig a small hole for one of the legs, or place a wide board under a leg, positioned so that the ladder does not wobble. Use a ladder brace for stability and to hold the ladder away from the side wall for more painting room.

Hang the paint with a bucket hook.
To keep the paint bucket from spilling, hang it from a ladder rung with a bucket hook, which you can buy or make from heavy-gauge wire.

Work close to the ladder.
For safety's sake, don't stretch more than an arm's length on either side of the ladder—it's just not worth the risk. Move the ladder instead.

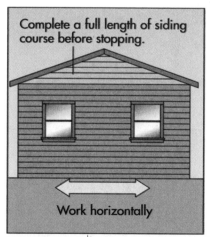

Time the work to avoid lap marks.
Plan the work so that sundown does not catch you in the middle of several courses of siding. Otherwise you will get lap marks.

PAINTING SIDING

Horizontal or vertical siding can be covered quickly, especially if it has a smooth surface. It is usually most efficient to paint siding first, then trim.

If you're applying primer, follow the same procedures as for the finish paint. You may notice lap marks with the primer as it sinks into the wood or other material to seal it. These won't show after you've applied the finish coat.

Remove lighting fixtures and turn off electricity so you can safely paint behind and below them. Let the paint dry before replacing the fixtures.

YOU'LL NEED...

TIME: 4 to 6 days for a small house.
SKILLS: Basic painting skills.
TOOLS: Brushes, ladder, screwdriver, and drop cloths.

Hit the siding bottoms.
Start by painting the underside of a horizontal siding course. If you do the faces first, you'll be touching up continually. Coat the undersides of three or four courses, using plenty of paint so the wood seals properly. Level out the paint with the tip of the paintbrush.

Stab into corners.
When painting next to a casing, paint the corner first, then the underside of the siding. Stab the bristles up into the corner.

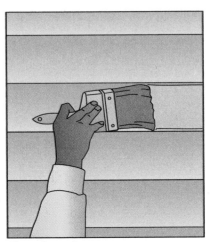

Flow the paint.
Apply plenty of paint to the surface of the course and don't worry about lap marks yet. Just cover and seal the surface thoroughly. Fill in the face of the siding courses, flowing the paint onto the surface with fairly short horizontal strokes. You needn't exert much pressure on the brush.

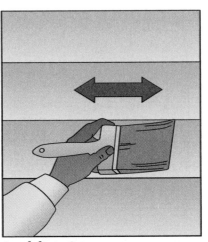

Level the paint.
When the surface is covered with paint, level and smooth it with a horizontal stroke. Make sure tiny cracks are filled. Don't try to save money by brushing the paint thin; even it out on the surface, using fairly long brushstrokes.

Take care at the edges.
Tip the bristles downward as you cut in along the bottom of the last course of siding. This keeps paint off the foundation.

PAINTING TRIM

*I*f someone gives you the choice of painting the siding on a house or the trim, choose the siding. Although it doesn't consume much paint, trimming out a house takes an inordinate amount of time. Using the same paint color for the trim as the siding helps some, but the job is tedious, nonetheless.

Before you get out your sash brush and begin work, study the illustrations on this page for some of the situations you'll encounter.

YOU'LL NEED...

TIME: 45 minutes to an hour for a window.
SKILLS: Intermediate painting skills.
TOOLS: Sash brush, screwdriver, masking tape.

EXPERTS' INSIGHT

USING MASKING TAPE

Applying masking tape can make for clean paint lines at joints between two different surfaces. However, because slight flaws in exterior painting will not be as noticeable as they would be in interior painting, most house painters do not use it. After a few hours of practice, you can learn to cut a clean line using a brush alone. You may, however, choose to use masking tape on windowpanes and to cover hardware.

Seal the joints between trim and siding.
Paint a tight seal between the trim and siding material, especially over the tops of doors and windows. This seal is best made by slightly overlapping the siding paint (see page 266). That allows you to cut a clean line between the trim and the siding.

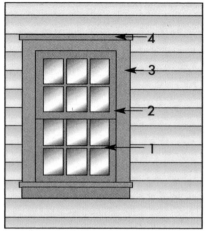

Paint a window.
Paint the outside of windows in the order indicated above, starting with the muntins and then working outward.

Protect windowsills.
Windowsills take a beating from the elements. If they're weather-worn, give them several coats of paint. Stop applying coats only after the paint has stopped soaking into the wood.

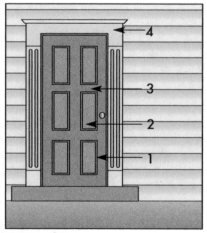

Paint a door.
Mask or remove the knob set and other hardware before painting doors. Paint the door in the order shown above.

Spray hardware.

To save time and create a professional appearance, remove hardware that is to be painted or covered with clear finish, and position it on a sheet of newspaper. Spray-paint it using a can. Keep the nozzle moving at all times and use light applications to prevent buildup and drips.

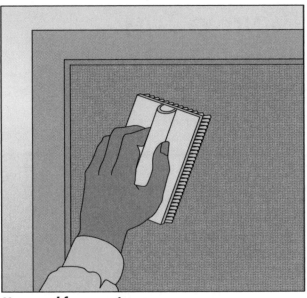

Use a pad for screening.

Paint or varnish screening first, then the frame. Use a special applicator pad to paint the screening—it is designed to apply paint without filling in the screen. (Spray-painting is another option for painting screening.)

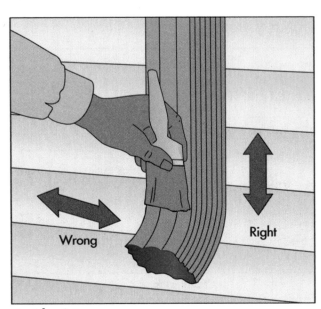

Wrong

Right

Avoid paint runs.

It takes concentration and a methodical approach to erase all paint drips and runs. Every few minutes, when your brush is fairly dry, look back at your work and brush away imperfections using light, even strokes. When painting a downspout, be sure to paint parallel to the flutes. If you don't, you risk messy drips and sags.

Finish with the railings.

Do ornamental metal and wood last. Prepare the surfaces properly and use the correct primer. It's difficult to paint small intersecting members (like those of a railing) without creating drips. If possible, use spray paint for these.

PAINTING MASONRY

Several types of paint will adhere to masonry. A paint dealer will carry paints designed for many types of surfaces and situations. Because they dry to a very hard finish, epoxy paints are probably the best all-around choice for floors, walls that are washed frequently, and exterior applications. Portland cement paint is another good choice; it works well on all walls except those previously painted with another type of finish. Latex paint, probably the easiest to apply, also adheres to foundation walls. Check with your paint dealer for other types suitable for specific applications.

Before painting a masonry surface—especially basement walls and floors—be sure to correct any existing moisture problems. If you don't, no paint will adhere. Also, remove peeling paint with a wire brush, and make necessary masonry repairs.

To finish the prep work, degrease the surface using detergent and water. Then etch the surface with a mixture of 1 part muriatic acid to 3 parts water. This removes and neutralizes alkaline material in the mortar joints. (Be sure to wear rubber gloves and a long-sleeved shirt to protect your skin from the acid.) Finally, rinse the surface with clear water.

After the surface has dried thoroughly, apply the finish with a wide short-bristled brush or a roller cover with a long nap.

YOU'LL NEED...

TIME: 6 to 8 hours to paint a basement.
SKILLS: Basic painting skills.
TOOLS: Scrub brush, paintbrush, roller with an extension handle.

Painting a floor.
Apply a degreasing solution to an oily garage or basement floor. Some products spray on; others require a scrub brush. Use a roller with an extension handle to paint a floor—to prevent backache from bending over. Paint one section at a time.

Fill in a pitted surface.
Smooth a rough-textured wall (but not a floor) with a 1:1 Portland cement and tile-grout mix, scrubbing it into depressions. To smooth a light texture, use an abrasive tool.

Apply the paint.
Apply paint with an old or cheap stiff-bristle brush. You'll have to push hard on the brush and even scrub it into very porous surfaces. If you want a rough texture, use a long-nap roller to apply the finish.

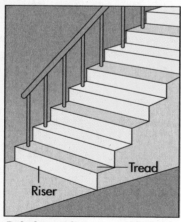

Painting stairs.
To paint steps that are used daily, paint the risers and every other tread. When the finish is dry on those, paint the treads you skipped.

REPAIRING DRYWALL

Drywall—also known as plasterboard and by trade names such as Sheetrock®—consists of big sheets of pressed gypsum faced with heavy paper on both sides. After the sheets have been nailed, screwed, or glued to studs, the joints are covered with a perforated paper or fiberglass mesh tape. Joints are then filled and smoothed over with joint compound, often referred to as mud, to create a smooth surface.

Drywall repairs are easy once you get the knack of working with the material, especially the joint compound. See pages 140–145 for more about working with drywall.

You'll Need...

TIME: 10 to 20 minutes, depending on the size of the repair.
SKILLS: Basic skills.
TOOLS: Drywall taping knives, sanding block, sponge, putty knife, paintbrush, hammer, drill.

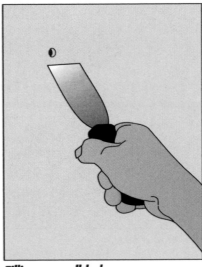

Filling a small hole.
For very small holes, apply joint compound to the void with a putty knife. Allow the compound to dry. If it shrinks, you may need to apply a second coat. To smooth the patch, either sand it or wipe it gently with a damp sponge.

EXPERTS' INSIGHT

JOINT COMPOUND

Ready-mixed joint compound comes in buckets; just scoop it out and apply it. Ready-mix is easy to sand, but it dries slowly and is not strong.

Dry-mix joint compound comes in bags of powder that you mix with water. Bags are typically labeled 90, 45, or 20; the compound will harden (though not dry) in roughly that many minutes. Regular dry-mix is stronger than ready-mix; "easy-sand" dry-mix is not.

Use ready-mix for small repairs. For substantial patches, or to speed up the drying time, apply one coat of dry-mix and use ready-mix for the top coats.

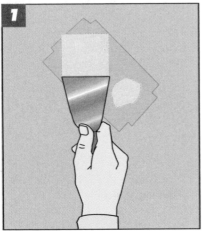

1. To fill a dent, apply joint compound.
Brush away any loose material. Use a taping blade to first pack the dent with joint compound and then to level it off. If the patch shrinks after drying, apply a second and perhaps a third coat.

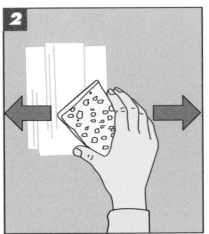

2. Smooth the compound.
Sand the surface very lightly—or smooth it by wiping with a damp sponge.

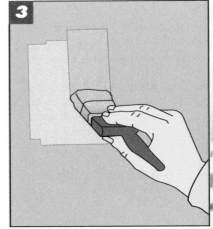

3. Prime and paint.
Joint compound must be primed before you paint. Just about any type of primer, including latex, will do the job. Some paints are self-priming.

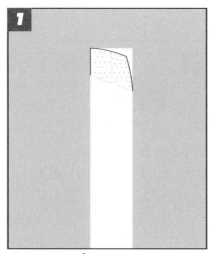

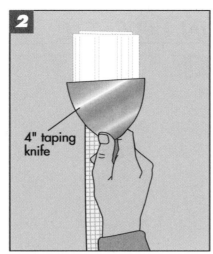

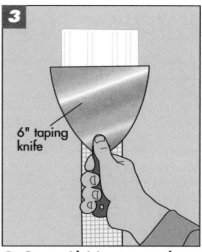

1. To repair loose tape, remove the tape.

If drywall tape is peeling, pull it gently off; you may need to pry it up with a putty knife first. Use a sharp knife to make a clean break at the point where the tape becomes firmly embedded. If the tape has a bubble, cut around the area with a utility knife, and pry out the damaged tape.

2. Install new tape.

Wipe away any dust and debris. Cut a piece of fiberglass mesh tape to roughly fit; it's all right if it is a bit short at either end. Press the tape into place. Apply joint compound over the tape and use gentle strokes of a 4-inch taping knife to cover the tape.

3. Cover with joint compound.

If you are applying ready-mix, or "easy-sand" compound, mound the compound up a bit. If you re-apply regular dry-mix compound, level it with the knife. Let it dry, then apply one and perhaps two more coats, feathering the edges. The patch should look and feel even with the surrounding wall. Sand, prime, and paint.

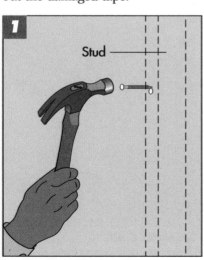

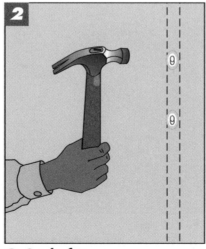

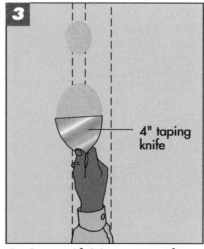

1. If nails have popped out, secure them with new fasteners.

If a nail is very loose, it may have missed the stud entirely; pull it out and drive a nail or screws into the stud. If it feels pretty firm, it either wasn't driven all the way or it barely caught the stud. Drive new ringshank nails or drywall screws just above and below the popped nail.

2. Set the fasteners.

If using nails, "dimple" the nails below the surface by tapping with a hammer. Take care not to break the paper. Drive screws slightly below the surface. Run a taping knife over the area to make sure that the fastener heads are recessed. Fill the dimples or screw holes with joint compound.

3. Cover with joint compound.

After the compound has dried, apply a second and perhaps third coat, until the hole is filled to the same level as the surrounding wall. Sand, prime, and paint.

PATCHING HOLES IN DRYWALL

Usually the space between studs is 14½ inches. If a hole or damaged area is fairly large, cut out a section that spans from stud to stud so the patch can be solidly attached to nailers fastened to the studs, as shown on page 273. Smaller holes can be patched without attaching to framing, but they will not be as strong.

Most drywall is ½ inch thick, but some walls have ⅜- or ⅝-inch-thick drywall. Purchase patching drywall to match your existing material.

If a wall is damaged due to a doorknob that knocks against it, install a stop at the bottom of the door to prevent further damage.

YOU'LL NEED...

TIME: 30 minutes of actual work, plus drying time.
SKILLS: Basic skills.
TOOLS: Taping knives, keyhole saw or drywall saw, hammer, drill, utility knife, sanding block or sponge, paintbrush.

EXPERTS' INSIGHT

OTHER PATCHING MATERIALS

Special drywall patching kits save time and hassle. Some kits use a screen that adheres to the front of the drywall; just apply joint compound over the screen. Other kits have clips that clasp a patch firmly to the surrounding drywall. You cut the patch, clip it, apply mesh tape, and cover with joint compound.

1. To repair a small hole, prepare the backing.
Cut a piece of pegboard that is slightly larger than the damaged area, but small enough to slip through the hole. Or use a piece of wood through which you have drilled two holes.

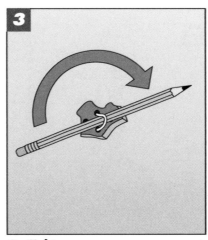

2. Insert the backing.
Tie a wire to the pegboard, smear joint compound on the inside perimeter of the pegboard, and slip the patch into the wall. When you pull back on the wire, the patch should cling to the back of the wall.

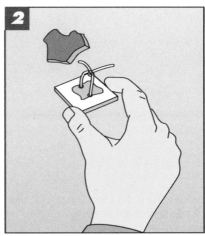

3. Tighten.
Tie the wire on the patch to a pencil or small stick, and twist it tight. After the patch dries, cut the wire off and use a taping knife to fill the recess with joint compound. (See page 270 for how to choose joint compound.)

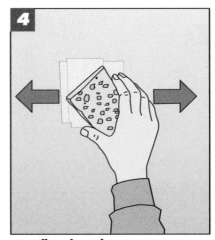

4. Fill and patch.
Allow the joint compound to dry. Apply two or three more coats, until the patch looks and feels level with the surrounding wall. Sand smooth or use a damp sponge to level the repair. Prime and paint.

1

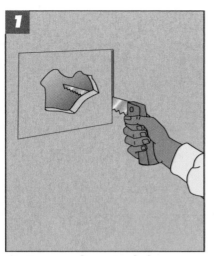

2

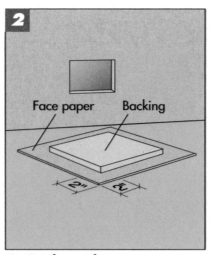

Face paper   Backing

3

1. For a medium-size hole, cut out a rectangle.

For holes up to 8 inches wide, mark a rectangle and cut it with a keyhole saw or a drywall saw.

2. Cut the patch.

Cut a drywall rectangle 2 inches larger than the hole on all sides. Turn the patch upside down and carefully use a utility knife to remove the 2-inch perimeter, but leave the face paper intact. Test to see that the patch fits comfortably into the hole.

3. Prepare for the patch.

Use a taping knife to spread a medium-thick bed of joint compound around the perimeter of the damaged area.

4

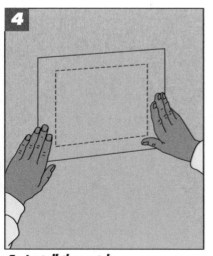

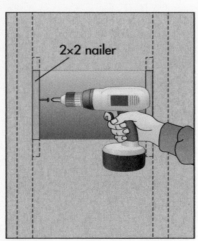

2×2 nailer

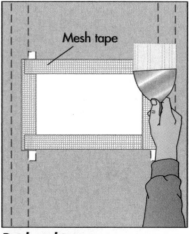

Mesh tape

4. Install the patch.

Insert the patch and smooth the face paper against the wall all around. (The face paper takes the place of drywall tape.) Blend the patch with the surrounding surface by feathering the edges with coats of joint compound. Sand or smooth with a damp sponge, then prime and paint.

To repair a large area, frame the sides.

For larger holes, cut a rectangle that spans from stud to stud. Cut 2×2 nailers slightly longer than the opening's height. Position the nailers as shown, and attach them by driving nails or screws.

Patch and tape.

Nail or screw the drywall patch into place. Apply fiberglass mesh tape to the perimeter, then cover it with three coats of joint compound. Allow each coat to dry and feather the edges to blend the patch with the wall. Sand it smooth or wipe it with a damp sponge. Prime and paint.

REPAIRING CRACKED PLASTER

*E*xamine plaster walls and ceilings before patching to make sure that repairs will last. Press hard with your hand on the surface all around any cracks. Here's what you may find:

■ If the plaster is solid and there are only a few hairline cracks, fill them with caulk or an aerosol crack sealer.

■ If the plaster is solid but there is a web of hairline cracks, the plaster itself is failing, perhaps because it was mixed incorrectly when installed. Usually the problem is cosmetic only, but could return after painting. Aerosol crack sealer may help, as may painting with latex semigloss paint, which remains flexible. Otherwise, either hire a plasterer or cover the surface with drywall.

■ If the area feels spongy, the plaster and perhaps the lath has come loose from the wall. Either remove all loose material and patch, or hire a plasterer. In extreme cases, or in the case of a loose ceiling, consider applying new drywall over the surface and taping it.

■ If a crack widens over time, the house is settling or you have a structural problem. You'll have to update repairs every so often. Seal the crack with flexible caulk.

The repairs shown here and on the next three pages are homeowner-friendly. For a new plaster surface that is rock-hard, you'll need to hire a plasterer.

YOU'LL NEED...
TIME: 1 hour of work, but allow for 2 overnight periods of drying.
SKILLS: Basic skills.
TOOLS: Hammer, chisel or old screwdriver, putty knife, taping knife, old toothbrush, sanding block, and a sponge.

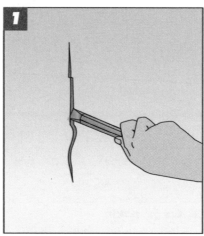

1. Enlarge the crack.
Widen a medium-size crack to at least ¼ inch with a chisel or old screwdriver, and blow out any loose plaster. Press on the area of the wall surrounding the crack. If any part is spongy, chip away the plaster until you come to solid material, then patch as shown on pages 276–277.

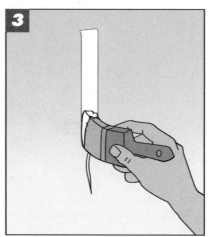

3. Seal the patch.
Seal patches with primer before painting or the patch may "bleed" through and change the color of the paint.

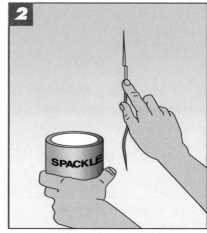

2. Fill with caulk or spackle.
Apply vinyl spackling compound, which retains some flexibility. Work it into the crack, and let it mound up a little. When it has dried, sand or sponge it smooth. Alternatively, fill the crack with latex/silicone caulk, which is more flexible but also more difficult to level with the surrounding wall.

EXPERTS' INSIGHT

PLASTER PATCHING MATERIALS

■ Dry-mix joint compound is strong, making it a good choice for wide cracks and holes.

■ Vinyl surfacing compound is soft and flexible. Use it for narrow cracks or holes.

■ Patching plaster or gauging plaster creates a genuine plaster surface, but it takes time to learn how to apply it correctly.

■ Latex/silicone caulk stays flexible and so can accommodate shifting cracks.

■ Aerosol crack seal is ideal for small cracks. Spray it just before priming.

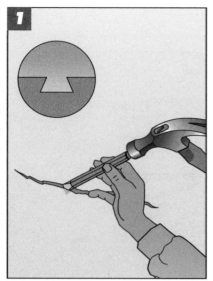

1. For a wide crack, use a chisel to "key" it.

Undercut wide cracks, making them broader at the bottom than the surface to lock in the filler material (see inset). Sometimes you can do this by scraping with a chisel or screwdriver; some people prefer to use an old-fashioned "church-key" type of can opener.

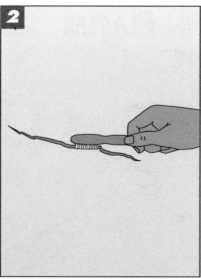

2. Remove loose material.

Clean the debris and crumbly material out of the crack with an old toothbrush or a wire brush. It helps to vacuum out the hole.

3. Wet the area.

Use a small brush to wet the crack before patching.

For a patch that is less likely to crack, apply fiberglass mesh tape over the crack. This will make the repaired area bulge a bit, so you will need to feather the compound out on each side (see page 277).

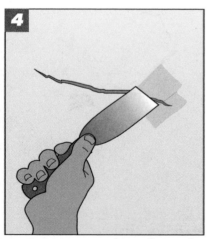

4. Force compound into the crack.

Pack joint compound, surfacing compound, or patching plaster into the crack with a putty knife or a wide-blade taping knife. First force the material into the crack, and then level it off.

5. Apply additional coats.

Let the compound harden, then level off the repair with a second and perhaps a third application. If you are using soft compound, mound the patch up a bit because it's easy to sand or sponge it down.

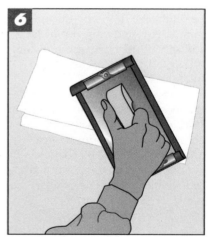

6. Smooth and seal.

Allow the patch to dry thoroughly, then either sand it smooth or rub it with a damp sponge. If you have not embedded mesh tape in the patch, spray the area with aerosol crack sealer. Seal it with primer, then paint it.

REPAIRING HOLES IN PLASTER

*B*efore you attack a big hole or bulge, find out what caused the plaster to fail. If the wall is water-stained or damp, solve the leak or plumbing problem and wait a month or two to make sure the area will stay dry.

In most cases, a hole in plaster is just the tip of the iceberg; the surrounding surface is likely loose and weak. Always cut back to sound plaster; you won't get a solid bond with crumbling edges. If most or all of a wall is loose and weak, consider removing all the plaster and installing drywall over the lath. You could also cover the plaster with drywall, but that will necessitate modifying your moldings to accommodate the thicker wall. See pages 140–145 for hanging and taping drywall. Usually you can remove the plaster only and leave the wood or metal lath in place. If the lath is rotted or badly rusted, replace it.

You may be able to fill a medium-size hole with dry-mix joint compound only, but make a stiff mix of the compound to ward off sags. Patching plaster is less likely to sag.

Once you have chipped away the loose plaster, carefully measure its thickness, which can vary considerably from area to area even on a single wall. The patching drywall may be thinner, but should not be thicker than the plaster. Usually, either ⅜- or ½-inch drywall will work.

YOU'LL NEED...

TIME: An hour of work and a day of drying time.
SKILLS: Basic skills.
TOOLS: Hammer, drill, masonry chisel or old screwdriver, utility knife, taping knife, sanding block, sponge, painting tools.

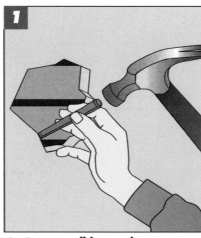

1. Remove all loose plaster.
Dig back with a masonry chisel, flat pry bar, or old screwdriver until you encounter solid plaster. Brush out any remaining debris.

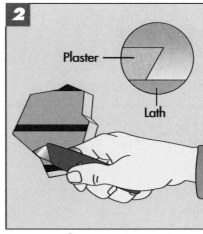

2. "Key" the opening.
Though not as important as with cracks, undercutting the edges makes a stronger repair. Scrape with a utility knife, chisel, screwdriver, or "church-key" type of can opener.

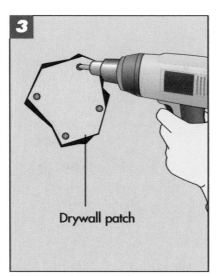

3. Cut and screw a drywall patch.
If there is wood lath behind the hole, cut a piece of drywall—the same thickness or thinner than the plaster—to roughly fit in the hole. Make sure it does not stick out past the plaster. Attach it to the lath with 1¼-inch drywall screws driven into the lath.

4. Fill the perimeter.
Blend a stiff batch of dry-mix joint compound, and use a taping knife to press it into the spaces between the patch and the wall. Then smooth the surface.

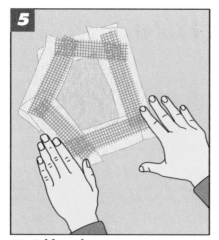

5. Add mesh tape.
While the compound is wet, cut pieces of fiberglass mesh tape and embed them in the compound. This will bond the compound with the surrounding wall and protect against cracks.

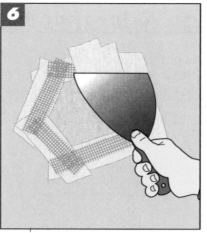

6. Smooth over the mesh.
Apply more joint compound and spread it over the mesh. The idea is to cover the mesh, but not build up the compound too thick. After it has dried, apply two more coats of ready-mix compound or surfacing compound.

7. Sand and finish.
Once the compound has dried, sand it smooth or rub lightly with a damp sponge to level the area. Apply primer and paint.

REPAIRING PANELING

If you scratch or mar paneling, you usually can make a cosmetic repair in a few minutes with paste wax or a crayonlike touch-up stick. Don't try to spot-sand and refinish your prefinished paneling; you risk doing more harm than good.

If a panel has suffered serious damage, you'll have to replace it entirely. Finding a match may be your biggest challenge.

If your paneling was glued directly to drywall, you may have to replace the drywall before reinstalling the paneling. If electrical wiring runs in the wall you're working on, shut off the power to the circuit before doing any cutting, sawing, or nailing.

YOU'LL NEED...

TIME: An hour of work per panel.
SKILLS: Basic skills.
TOOLS: Hammer, pry bar, pliers, taping knives, chisel, caulking gun, and nail set.

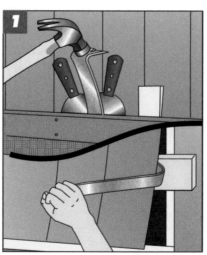

1. Remove the damaged panel.
Identify and mark the edges of the damaged panel. Pry off the baseboard and top molding by inserting a taping or putty knife, then a pry bar. Pull out the nails with pliers, then pull the panel off. Start at the bottom, where there's usually no adhesive. Pull out nails as they pop. Finish prying the panel away, working from the bottom to the top. Use a wood block to protect adjacent panels.

2. Install the new panel.
Remove all old adhesive with a scraper or chisel. Apply panel adhesive to studs with a caulking gun. Nail the panel loosely at the top and wedge it out, as shown, until the adhesive gets tacky. Press the panel into place, then use a wood block to tap it against the studs, as shown. Nail the edges with color-matched brads.

PREPARING INTERIOR SURFACES FOR PAINT

Paint works wonders for a room's appearance, but it can't perform miracles. Paint will not heal cracked walls, smooth rough textures, or fill any but the tiniest nail holes. In fact, paint applied to a wall that is not well prepared may peel, causing you major headaches later.

After you've cleared the room, but before you've opened the first paint can, give every surface careful scrutiny. Start with the walls, checking for cracks, runs, or ridges in the old paint. All of these can be treated easily with a scraper and sandpaper; then use a primer for bare spots. Use a paint remover to strip cracked or gloppy paint from woodwork. If the old paint is peeling, suspect moisture or poor preparation. Both problems require removing the old

paint and priming the surface. Of course, any moisture leaks should be immediately corrected at the source.

Mend superficial plaster or drywall blemishes with surfacing or joint compound. Bigger repairs (see pages 270–277) require more time, not only for patching, but also for curing and priming. (On textured walls, you may have trouble blending the patched area completely with its surroundings.)

You can paint over clean, sound wallpaper, but in most cases you're better off stripping it. If you decide to paint over wallpaper, paint a small test spot in an inconspicuous area and wait a few days. If the pattern bleeds through, apply stain-killing primer. If the paper begins to peel, strip all of the wallpaper.

After you've made repairs, give the ceiling, walls, and woodwork a thorough bath with household detergent, and rinse well. Prime exposed spots with a compatible primer. At this point, you've completed at least 50 percent of your painting project.

Use heavy-duty drop cloths that will stay in place to protect floors and rugs. If you step on a drip, you will likely track paint around the room, so cover a broad area.

YOU'LL NEED...

Time: 2 to 4 hours per room.
Skills: Basic skills.
Tools: Portable light, screwdriver, putty knife, sandpaper, sponge or mop.

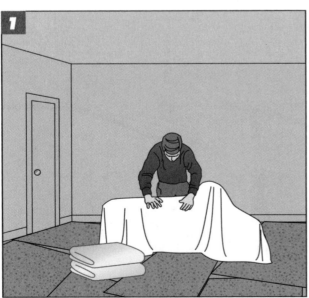

1. Clear and protect the room.
If practical, remove all furniture from the room. You may choose to group heavy items in the middle and protect them with drop cloths. Cover the floor carefully. Ideally, you should tape down a layer of heavy cardboard or plastic, and cover that with a heavy-duty drop cloth.

2. Provide lighting.
Set up strong lights so you can see what you're painting. Provide general lighting. Also, aim other lights at angles to highlight minor imperfections. If there is a ceiling light, disconnect it and let it hang (see page 280). Cover the globe to protect against spatters. Alternatively, disconnect the light entirely and replace it with a simple work light.

3. Remove coverplates.

It always saves time to remove obstacles rather than paint around them. Even if you plan to paint switch and receptacle plates, remove them and paint them separately.

4. Patch holes and cracks.

Regardless of the size, fill every hole and crack with vinyl surfacing compound. Allow it to dry, then sand it smooth. Prime all patches before painting.

5. Ensure the paint will stick.

Sand rough spots smooth, and sand any runs from previous paint jobs. To ensure that the new paint will stick, you have three options: (1) Sand all the walls and trim using 80- or 100-grit sandpaper on a drywall-type sanding pole; (2) apply liquid sander, which removes the sheen from glossy and semigloss paints; (3) paint the room with primer. If you will apply latex paint over existing solvent-thinned paint, perform at least two of these operations.

6. Clean the surfaces.

Wash the ceiling and walls with a sponge or mop, paying special attention to the tops of baseboards and moldings. Any dust will cling to your brush or roller and mar the paint job.

PAINTING CEILINGS

To succeed at painting a room, start at the top and work your way down. In other words, the ceiling comes first.

Unless the surface is brand new, you usually can get by with one coat of paint on a ceiling. Even stubborn stains will disappear if you spot-prime them first.

If you're planning a one-coat application, let the paint lap onto the walls. If you will apply two coats to the ceiling, cut in (trim up to the ceiling/wall line) with a trim brush. Otherwise, the paint will build up on the wall and leave a ridge.

Paint across the ceiling at the room's narrow dimension, especially if you're using a fast-drying paint. Otherwise, the paint may lose its wet edge.

A roller frame with an extension handle greatly speeds up the job, although you still need a trim brush to cut in the ceiling paint where it meets the walls. A doughnut-style roller makes quick work of painting the corner between a wall and the ceiling.

Rollers emit a fine spray of paint that settles over the room like dust. Cover furniture in the room, as well as the floor, carpeting, and woodwork. Canvas drop cloths work best because they absorb spills and are easy to walk on, but plastic drop cloths or newspapers will do the job too.

Buy ceiling paint—it is flatter than flat wall paint and hides imperfections very well. It is not scrubbable, but ceilings are not prone to handprints and smudges.

YOU'LL NEED...
TIME: 3 to 4 hours.
SKILLS: Basic painting skills.
TOOLS: Drop cloths, brushes, ladder, and a roller with an extension handle.

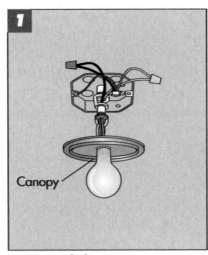
Canopy

1. Protect lights.
Usually you can remove a light fixture's canopy. Remove the canopy's mounting screws and allow the fixture to hang down, as long as it is not a heavy chandelier. Wrap the fixture in plastic, or cover the finish parts with masking tape.

2. Paint the corners.
Start a ceiling job by cutting in a strip along the walls, as shown. If you'll be applying only one coat, lap the paint onto the wall as well.

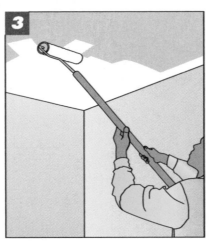

3. Roll and cross-roll.
Start rolling the paint with a series of diagonal swaths. Don't worry about spreading the paint evenly; just get it on the ceiling. Then even out the paint and fill in any open areas by cross-rolling.

4. Level the paint.
Continue working, spreading the paint from dry areas into the wet paint. Rollers slip on smooth surfaces, so check for skips. After you've finished a section, check to see whether you've created thick lap marks. If so, even them out by going over them lightly with a fairly dry roller.

PAINTING WALLS

Once the walls have been patched, perhaps primed, and cleaned thoroughly, the ceiling has been painted, and all of the switch and receptacle plates have been removed, you're ready to paint walls. Do all the edging first. This includes cutting in the ceiling and around moldings and trims. Once these details are done, it's payback time: You can paint the big, flat surfaces quickly.

A neat job requires concentration and a methodical approach. Take care to keep the edges wet to prevent lap marks. Keep the roller from slipping to the side and causing skid marks. Avoid the temptation to make a roller load last too long, or you will end up with places that are not fully covered.

When painting with semigloss or high-gloss finish, make the final brush strokes away from light sources, including windows. This way, the tiny ridges that a brush leaves won't be as noticeable.

Always give paint a brisk stirring before starting, even if the paint was just shaken at the store. As you work, stir the paint occasionally. Keep an eye on the paint in the roller tray. As long as you're filling the roller, the paint will remain properly blended. If you leave the tray for an hour or so, cover it with plastic wrap. When you're ready to get back to work, stir the paint lightly with a paint paddle. When left untouched, paint skins over.

YOU'LL NEED...
TIME: 5 to 6 hours for a 14×16-foot room.
SKILLS: Basic painting skills.
TOOLS: Drop cloths, ladder, brushes, specialty paint applicators for painting around trim, roller, extension handle.

1. Brush the corners.
Begin painting walls by cutting in the corners and around all of the woodwork. With practice, you can cut neat lines without the use of masking tape. If you will paint the trim later, lap the wall paint onto the trim slightly. Paint about 3 inches out from the edges.

2. Apply paint.
For large surfaces, load the roller and apply the paint in a large "M" shape. Start the roller going up, then pull it down.

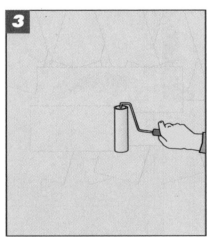

3. Even out the paint.
Level and fill in the M shapes by cross-rolling. You can work horizontally, as shown, or vertically. By working the paint this way, you get an even paint surface. Watch for roller skids.

4. Paint in planned sections.
Determine how much area a loaded roller can fully cover. Do not attempt to "stretch" the paint, or you will probably need to apply another coat. (You can see the coverage clearly only after the paint has dried.) Plan to work in sections that are similar in size.

PAINTING WOODWORK

Painting woodwork is hard work. Next to prepping, it's the most time-consuming painting job. If you master the tricks shown here, however, you'll minimize the tedium and speed your progress.

If at all possible, learn to paint freehand. With practice, anyone with a fairly steady hand and good brushes can master freehand techniques and save a tremendous amount of time compared to applying masking tape.

A coat of paint will probably emphasize rather than cover imperfections. Before you begin painting, patch holes with wood filler. Let the material dry overnight, then apply primer.

If you'll be using the same paint on the woodwork as on the walls, paint the woodwork as you come to it. Generally, however, you should use a higher gloss on woodwork. If you do, or if the woodwork will be another color, paint the walls first.

Windows and raised-panel doors are the toughest assignments because of the amount of cutting in and the fact that you can't use full brush strokes. If you can't paint freehand, cover the glass with masking tape or use a painter's shield. Some people find it efficient to paint windows somewhat sloppily and then scrape the excess afterwards. Use a razor blade scraping tool to clean off smeared paint.

YOU'LL NEED...
TIME: 1 to 2 hours for a standard window.
SKILLS: Moderate painting skills.
TOOLS: Sash brush, masking tape, painter's shield, putty knife, and a drop cloth.

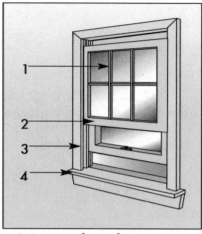

Painting a sash window.
Paint double-hung windows in the sequence shown, starting with the muntins, then working outward. Move the sashes several times while the paint is drying to make sure the sashes do not dry shut.

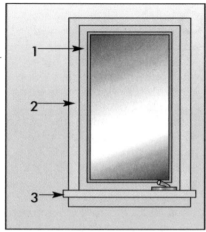

Casement window sequence.
Use the same sequence shown at left for casement windows. Keep the window slightly open until the paint is dry.

Mask window panes ...
Painter's masking tape protects windowpanes from paint. Peel off the tape immediately after you finish painting; if you wait until the paint is fully dry, you could crack it as you remove the tape.

Painter's shield

... or use a shield.
A painter's shield keeps paint off the glass, too. Keep a damp cloth handy to frequently clean the shield's edge as you work around the muntins.

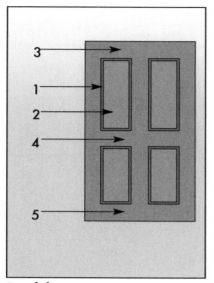

Panel door sequence.
Start painting panel doors at the molding edges. Then fill in the panels, the hinge stile, the rails, and the latch stile. To apply a gloss finish, use a cross-brush method: Apply paint on the door horizontally, then make vertical finishing strokes. Always finish a door once you've started it. If you don't, the lap marks may show.

Roll flush doors.
Flush doors are easier and quicker to paint. Either a brush or a roller will give good results. If you use a roller, be sure to roll the entire surface, because any brush marks will look very different.

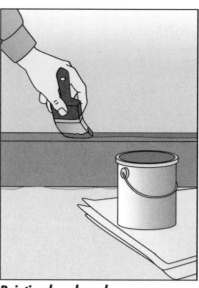

Painting baseboards.
Paint the top edge of a baseboard first. Next cut in along the floor, and then fill in between. Painter's masking tape helps if you don't have a steady hand.

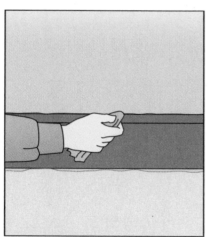

Clean as you go.
Have on hand a rag dampened with water or mineral spirits, depending on the type of paint. Clean up overlapping paint smudges as soon as they occur. If you don't, the paint will set up and be much tougher to remove.

Keep the floor clean.
A cloth wrapped around a putty knife works well to clean up paint drippings on hardwood and resilient flooring along baseboards.

Seal a stain.
If a woodwork stain bleeds through the paint, spray or brush on a stain-killing primer, let dry, then repaint.

INDEX

Adhesives
for carpentry jobs, 85
selecting, 111
tile, 217, 223, 231
Aluminum siding
repairing dented, 203
replacing end caps, 231
replacing section of, 201
Angle brackets, 158
Antiquing, 119
Ants, carpenter, 178, 236
Asbestos, 151
Asphalt shingles, 192
Augers, 62–63, 66

Backerboard
cutting, 228
installing, 229
types, 218
Backsplash, stainless–steel, 128
Ballcock, toilet, 58
Balusters, stairway, 155–156
Baseboards, replacing, 243
Basements
furring walls, 138–139
moisture damage, avoiding, 141
Bathrooms, tile flooring, 247–248
Bathtub. See Tubs
Beams, framing around, 136
Bifold doors, 172
Boiler. See Heating, radiant
Bolts, 85, 107
Bridging, floor, 148
Brushes, paint, 257–258
Bulbs
fluorescent tubes, 30–31
wattage, 29
Bus bar, 8–9

Cabinets
base, 126
wall, 125
Cable. See also Wires
choosing, 17
Greenfield, 17
Carpentry
hardware, 84–87
lumber, 103–109
tools, 71–76
Carpentry techniques
adhesives, 111

bolts, fastening with, 105–106
caulking, 111
cutting
inside and contour cuts, 97–98
using a miter box, 96
with circular saw, 94–96
drilling, 99–102
filling and finishing, 118–119
gluing and clamping, 110
holding and measuring in place, 90
joints, 112–113
marking techniques, 94
measuring and marking, 88–89
molding installation, 120–123
nailing, 103–104
removing nails and screws, 108–109
sanding, 116–117
screws, fastening with, 105–106
shaping and planing, 114–115
squaring, plumbing, and leveling, 91–93
Caulking
applying, 111
gun, 139
materials, 198
tile, 220, 240
Ceilings
installing electrical boxes in, 24
painting, 280
Cement board, 81
Chimneys
cleaning, 195
repairing, 195
Chisels, 99
Circuit breakers, 6, 8
Circuits
branch, 11
how they work, 6
load, 11, 12, 179
mapping, 12
plan, typical, 11
Circular saw, 94–96
Clamps and clamping, 110
Cleats, flooring, 148
Clogs. See Drains, unclogging

Code, building, electrical, 12, 18
Concrete
drilling into, 102
forms, 237–238
laying wood flooring over, 160
slabs, 237–238
Conductor, of electricity, 6, 17
Coping saw, 98
Cord, 16. See also Wires
Countertops
laminate, installing, 129–130
tile, 224
Crown molding, 122–123

Dead bolts, 175
Dimmer switch, 15
Diverters, 54
Doors
anatomy of, 168, 172
bifold, 172
dead bolts, 175
freeing a binding door, 168–169
installing, 176, 185–186
latches, lubricating, 171
prehung, 176
sliding, 172
squeaking hinges, 170
storm, 185–186
strike problems, 170
warped, 171
Drain cleaners, 62, 68
Drains, unclogging
drum traps, cleaning, 67
main, 68
plunging, 63
shower, 66
strainers, replacing sink, 65
toilets, 68
traps, dismantling, 64
tub, 67
with drain cleaners, 62
Drills and drilling
bit choices, 99
choosing, 74, 99
techniques, 99–102
Drip cap, 194
Drum trap, cleaning, 67
Drum–sanding techniques, 149

Drywall
finishing tips, 144
hanging, 142–143
laying out and cutting, 140–141
repairing, 270–273
taping, 144–145
DWV (drain–waste–vent). See Vents

Electric meter, 6
Electrical boxes
capacity, 18
choosing, 18
installation, 20
fixture/junction boxes, retrofit, 20
ganging, 18, 21
installing in finished space, 23–24
installing in unfinished space, 21–22
placement of, 21
securing, 22
size, 18
switch/receptacle, new installation, 19
switch/receptacle, retrofit, 19
wire connections in, 28
Electrical system. See also Cable; Circuits; Electrical boxes; Lighting; Receptacles; Switches
boxes, 18–24
circuit breakers, 6, 8
circuits, 6, 11–12
codes, 12, 18, 28
cords, 17
flow of electricity, 6
fluorescent fixtures, troubleshooting, 30–31
ground–fault circuit interrupter (GFCI) receptacles, 10, 16
grounding, 6, 8, 10, 28
incandescent fixtures, checking, 29
lighting, 22, 29
overview of, 6–7
plugs, 10, 28
polarization, 10
receptacles, 10, 16, 27, 32, 34–35
service panels, 8–9

shorts and faults, 19
switches, 15–16, 19, 28, 32–33
tools, 13–14
wire, 17, 25–28
Epoxy adhesive, 231
Expansion joints, 229, 238

Fasteners. *See* Hardware
Faucets
aerators, 54
base plate, sealing, 53
cartridge, 44, 46–47, 52
ceramic disk, 50–51
diaphragm, 44
diverters, 54
gasketed cartridge, 52
handles, 43–44
identifying stem, 42
leaks, 44, 53
pulling out handles and stems, 43
rotating ball, 48–49
seats, replacing and grinding, 45
washers, replacing, 43
Filling, 118
Finishing
antiquing, 119
stucco, 205
types of finishes, 119
Fireplace, cleaning and repairing, 195
Fixture/junction boxes, 20, 22
Flashing
inspecting, 191
repairing and replacing, 194
Float, toilet tank, 56–57, 68
Floor scraper, 154
Floors
anatomy, 147
leveling, 244
resilient tile, patching, 151–152
sagging, 148
sheet flooring, patching, 153–154
squeaks, 147–148, 157–158
tile, 224, 241–248
bathroom, 125
kitchen, 245–246
transitions, 244

wood
laying over concrete, 160
refinishing, 149–150
straightening boards, 160
tongue–and–groove, installing, 159–160
Fluorescent fixtures, troubleshooting, 30–31
Framing, walls, 131–139
Frozen pipes
fixing, 40–41
preventing, 39
Furring basement walls, 138–139
Fuses, 6, 9

GFCI. *See* Ground–fault circuit interrupter
Glaze, tile, 211
Glazing, window, 177–178
Gluing, 110
Greenfield, 17
Ground–fault circuit interrupter (GFCI), receptacles, 10, 16
Grounding, 6, 8, 10, 28
Grout
applying, 237–239
colored, 237
estimating needs, 223
grouting tools, 215
sealer, 221, 240
selecting, 219
Gutters
inspecting, 191
repairing and maintaining, 196–197

Handicap accessibility, designing for, 18–19
Handles, installing door, 174–175
Hardboard, 81
Hardware, carpentry, 84–87
Hardwoods, selecting, 80
Heat tape, 39
Heating, radiant, 208
Hinges, door, 169, 170, 171, 185
Hole saw, 228

Ice dams, 190
Insulation
fiber, incandescent fixture, 29
pipe, 39
window treatments, 167
wire, 6, 25–26

Joint compound, 270
Joints
dado, 113
expansion, 229, 238
half–lap, 113
types, 112–113
Junction box, 20, 22

Kickback, 94
Kitchens, 125–130
backsplash, stainless steel, 128
cabinets
base, 126
wall, 125
countertops, 129–130
tile flooring, 245–246

Laminate, countertop, 129–130
Latch, lubricating door, 171
Leaks
from faucet base plate, 53
from faucet handles, 44
in supply lines, 55
pipe, repairing, 40–41
roof, 191
Leveling, 91–93, 244
Lighting
incandescent fixtures, checking, 29
overhead light placement, 22
Linoleum, 153
Locks, door, 174–175
Lumber
board feet, determining, 77
dimensions, 77, 78
grades of wood, 77
hardwood, selecting, 80
inspecting, 77
sheet goods, selecting, 81–82
softwood, selecting, 79
types, 78

Marking, 88–89
Masking tape, 267

Masonry, drilling into, 102
Masonry nails, 104
Mastic, 111, 217
Measuring, 88–90
Metal
drilling through, 102
fastening with screws, 106
studs, 289–290
Miter box, 96
Mitering, 120, 122
Moisture, basement, 141
Moldings
alternative materials, 83
base, 121
buying, 120
crown, 122–123
cuttings, 98
installing, 120–123
selecting, 83
Mortar
bed installation, 218
mixing, 217, 230
spreading, 231

Nailer, power, 159
Nails
removing, 108–109
selecting, 84
setting in drywall, 142
sizes, 84
techniques, 103–104
tip shape, 84

O–ring, faucet, 44, 46, 48–49, 52

Pads, paint, 259
Paint and painting
brushes, 257–258
ceilings, 280
estimating needs, 253
exterior, choosing, 253–254
interior, choosing, 255–256
masonry, 269
preparing exterior surfaces, 264
preparing interior surfaces, 278–279
priming, 255
removing old exterior, 262–263
rollers, 259–262
siding, 266

trim, 267–268
vinyl siding, 204
walls, 281
wood, 119
woodwork, 282–283
Paneling, 277
Particleboard, 81
Pigtails, 28
Pilot holes, 85, 86, 105
Pipes
  framing around, 136
  frozen, 39, 40–41
  leaks, 40–41
Planing, 114–115, 169
Plaster walls
  repairing cracked,
    274–275
  repairing holes in,
    276–277
Plugs, 10
Plumbing, 114–116. *See also*
    Pipes
  clogged drains, opening,
    62–69
  faucet repair, 42–54
  frozen pipes
    fixing, 40–41
    preventing, 39
  leaks
    faucet, 44, 53
    pipe, 40–41
    supply line, 55
    toilet, 59
  old, 40
  replacement parts, 47, 49
  toilet repair, 56–59
  tools, 37–38
  tub and shower controls,
    60–61
Plywood, selecting, 81
Polarization, 10
Power tools, 74–76. *See also*
    specific applications
Priming, for paint, 255

Railings, stair, 156
Ramps, 8
Receptacle analyzer, 35
Receptacles
  choosing, 16
  GFCI, 10, 16
  grounded, 10, 16, 28
  polarized, 10
  replacing, 34
  switch/receptacle, 16, 32

terminal, fastening wire
  to, 27
testing, 34–35
Recessed lights, 22
Refinishing, wood floors,
    149–150
Resilient flooring, patching,
    151–152
Rod saw, 233
Rollers, paint, 259–261
Roofs
  asphalt shingle, 192
  flashing, 194
  gutters, 196–197
  inspecting, 190–191
  leaks, 191
  terminology, 188
  vents, 194
  wood shingle, 193
Roughing–in an opening,
    136

Sabersaw, 97–98
Safety
  asbestos, 151
  saw, 94
  tool, 76
  with metal, 136
Sanding
  techniques, 116–117
  tools, 75, 149
  wood floors, 149–150
Saws
  backsaw, 96
  circular, 94–96
  coping, 98
  hole, 228
  rod, 233
  saber, 97–98
  safety, 94
  types, 71–72, 74, 76
  wet, 232
Screening, window, 180–184
  buying, 183
  installing new, 183–184
  maintaining, 180
  repairing, 181
  replacing, 182
Screws
  fastening with, 105–106
  for drywall, 142
  removing, 108–109
  selecting, 85
Scribing, 114
Sealers
  choosing, 198

grout, 221, 240
tile, 221, 240
Seat grinder, 45
Seat washers, replacing, 43
Service panel, 6
  breaker box, 8
  fuse box, 9
  mapping circuits in, 12
Setting nailheads, 142
Shaping, 114–115
Sheet flooring, patching,
    153–154
Sheet goods, selecting,
    81–82
Shelves, brackets for, 86
Shims, 132, 148
Shingles
  asphalt, 192
  wood, 193
Showerheads, cleaning, 69
Showers
  controls, repairing, 60–61
  unclogging, 66
Siding
  aluminum, 201–203
  board, 199–200
  painting, 266
  stucco, 205–206
  vinyl, 204
  wood, 199–200
Sills, window, 179–180
Sinks. *See also* Faucets
  anatomy of, 63
  removing, 247
  strainer, replacing, 65
  traps, dismantling, 64
  unclogging, 62–66
Sliding doors, 173
Sockets, inspecting, 29
Softwoods, selecting, 79
Soldering, 27–28
Sprayers, sink, 54
Squaring, 91–92
Squeaks
  door hinge, 170
  floors, 147–148
  stairs, 157–158
Stainless–steel backsplash,
    128
Stains
  resilient tile, 152
  wood, 120
Stairs
  fixing, 155–156
  squeaks, 157–158
  tightening rails and
    balusters, 156

Starter, fluorescent
  fixture, 31
Stone, tile, 212
Storm door, 185–186
Storm windows
  buying, 183
  installing new, 183–184
  repairing, 181
Strainers, replacing sink, 65
Strike plate, door, 170
Stringers, stairs, 155
Stripping wire, 25–26
Stucco, 205–206
Studs
  measuring length, 133
  metal, 136–137
  wall framing, 131–135
Supply lines, leaks in, 55
Sweating. *See* Soldering
Sweep, door, 186
Switches
  dimmer, 15
  fixture–mounted, 33
  four–way, 15
  grounding, 28
  rocker, 15
  single and double, 15
  switch/receptacle, 16, 19,
    32
  testing and replacing,
    32–33
  three–way, 15, 32
Tape
  drywall, 144–145
  electrical, 27
  heat, 39
Thawing frozen pipes, 41
Tile, 208–251
  adhesives, 217, 230–231
  backerboard, 218,
    228–229
  caulk and sealers, 221,
    240
  cutting, 232
  floors, 241–248
    bathroom, 247–248
    kitchen, 245–246
  grout
    application, 237–239
    selection, 219
  laying out, 255–227
  materials, estimating
    needs, 223
  membrane use, 220
  mortar, 217, 218,
    230–231
  mosaic, 236

over tile, 248
project planning, 208–209
selecting correct, 210
setting, 234–236
setting beds, 218
site preparation, 224
size, 213
spacers, 216, 234
stone, 212
substrates, assessing, 222
tools, 237–240
trimming, 233
tub surround, 249–251
Toilets
anatomy of, 56
leaks, 59
removing, 247
repairing, 56–59
tank run–on, 57–59
unclogging, 68
Tongue-and-groove flooring, installing, 159–160
Tools. *See also* specific applications
carpentry, 71–76
drywall, 140, 143
electrical, 13–14
for furring basement walls, 138–139

hand, 71–73
plumbing, 37–38
power, 74–76
safety, 76
tiling, 214–215
Track lighting, installing, 36
Traps, 64, 67
Tubs
controls, repairing, 60–61
tile surround, 249–250
unclogging, 67

Underwriters Laboratories, 15

Veneer, wood, 115, 118
Vents, roof, 194
Vinyl flooring, patching, 153–154
Vinyl siding, 204
Voltage, 41

Waferboard, 81
Walls. *See also* Siding
building, 131–132
drywall, 140–145

furring basement, 138–139
installing electrical boxes in, 23
painting, 281
roughing–in an opening, 135–136
terminology, 189
tile, 215
Warps, door, 171
Washer, faucet, 43
Wet saw, 232
Window treatments, 167
Windowpanes, replacing, 177–178
Windows
casement, 166–167
cord, replacing sash, 163–164
double–hung, 162–164
freeing a sash, 162
mechanisms, 162, 163
rehabbing, 164
repairing, 162–167
screening, 180–184
buying, 183
installing new, 183–184
maintaining, 180
repairing, 181
replacing, 182

sill and saddle replacement, 179–180
sliding, 165
spring lift, adjusting, 162
windowpane replacement, 177–178
Wire connectors, 28
Wires. *See also* Electrical system
color, 17
connecting, 28
fastening to terminal, 27
gauge, 17
joining, 26
soldering, 27–28
stripping, 25–26
types, 17
Wood. *See also* Lumber
board siding, 199–200
grades of, 77
shingles, 193
Wood floors
laying over concrete, 160
refinishing, 149–150
straightening boards, 160
tongue-and-groove, installing, 159–160
Woodwork, painting, 282–283